ALSO BY JONATHAN W. JORDAN

Brothers Rivals Victors:
Eisenhower, Patton, Bradley, and the Partnership
That Drove the Allied Conquest in Europe

American Warlords:
How Roosevelt's High Command
Led America to Victory in World War II

Lone Star Navy:
Texas, the Fight for the Gulf of Mexico,
and the Shaping of the American West

To The People of Texas
(editor)

THE WAR QUEENS

Extraordinary Women who Ruled the Battlefield

❖   ❖   ❖

Jonathan W. Jordan
& Emily Anne Jordan

DIVERSION
BOOKS

Diversion Books
A division of Diversion Publishing Corp.
443 Park Avenue South, suite 1004
New York, NY 10016
www.diversionbooks.com

For more information, email info@diversionbooks.com

P. vii: THE QUEEN AND THE SOLDIER
Words and Music by SUZANNE VEGA
Copyright © 1985 WC MUSIC CORP. and WAIFERSONGS LTD.
All Rights on behalf of Itself and WAIFERSONGS LTD. Administered by WC MUSIC CORP.
All Rights Reserved
Used By Permission of ALFRED MUSIC

P. viii © Keystone Press / Alamy; P. 2 © FALKENSTEINFOTO / Alamy;
P. 130 © The History Emporium / Alamy; P. 228 © World History Archive / Alamy

Maps by Chris Erichsen

All other images in the public domain, except where noted.

Book design by Aubrey Khan, Neuwirth & Associates

First Diversion Books edition March 2020
Hardcover ISBN: 978-1-63576-719-3
eBook ISBN: 978-1-63576-718-6

Printed in The United States of America

1 3 5 7 9 10 8 6 4 2

Library of Congress cataloging-in-publication data is available on file.

CONTENTS

Introduction: Women Waging War   ix

Act I   The Mighty Arms of Atlas

ONE   "More Blood Than You Can Drink"   5

TWO   "My Women Have Become Men"   12

THREE   The Last Pharaoh   23

FOUR   A Thirst for Blood   50

ACT II   Women of a Certain Age

FIVE   Lion of the Caucasus   69

SIX   Year of the Tiger   83

SEVEN   Viper and Rose   96

ACT III   Empires and Rebels

EIGHT   Heart of a King   133

NINE   Baptized in Blood   167

TEN   *Philosophe* Warlord   192

ACT IV   Maps and Legends

ELEVEN   Red Durga   231

TWELVE   Babushka   256

THIRTEEN   Crossfire Hurricane   291

          Epilogue: The Final Argument of Queens   320

          Acknowledgments   325

          Bibliography   327

          Source Notes   335

          Index   349

          About the Authors   358

I've watched your palace up here on the hill,
And I've wondered, "Who's the woman for whom we all kill?"

—SUZANNE VEGA, "THE QUEEN AND THE SOLDIER"

INTRODUCTION

Women Waging War

FOR EIGHT MILLENNIA, men have won glory coaxing soldiers onto bloodstained fields to which only a few intrepid women have ventured. Fewer still left behind their stories of how and why they fought. Did they master rules laid down by their male counterparts? Does the mix of estrogen and testosterone matter when poured over a boiling battlefield? Is there an X-factor that makes women better suited to make life-or-death decisions on a mass scale?

Among the bones of the dead we unearth answers.

History's killer queens come in all colors, ages, personalities, and leadership styles. Elizabeth Tudor and Golda Meir were high-stakes gamblers who gazed into the fog of war with an unblinking, calculating eye. Angola's Queen Njinga, possessing limited resources but unmatched ferocity, shed (and occasionally drank) blood to build a stable kingdom in Africa's heart. The pious Queen Tamar embraced war as a natural part of life in the Caucasus, Caterina Sforza defended her children's legacy in Italy with cannon and scimitar, and Indira Gandhi launched a war to solve a refugee crisis.

In the pages that follow, we sidle up to each commandress-in-chief in an intimate way, watching them smash roadblocks thrown in their paths. In life, they saw themselves as problem-solvers, not trendsetters or role models for future women. Their job was to crack the ribs of a crisis and wrench a still-beating answer from its chest. If war was part of the solution, so be it.

The thresholds these women had to cross to enter the power game were daunting. For most of civilization's long history, ceding sovereignty to a woman was a nation's last resort, a necessary evil impelled only by a succession crisis or civil war. The sword was never handed to these women by benevolent, progressive-minded men; they wrested it from Arthur's stone. They fought for power, then fought to keep it, and when the battle trumpet sounded, they almost invariably faced a male foe. How they won, or lost, teaches valuable lessons as new leaders emerge from the political background and take their places on the front ranks.

❖   ❖   ❖

WAR ADDS A RADICAL DIMENSION to the political leadership game. Like blackjack, winning one battle is comparatively easy, but beating the house over time bucks heavy odds. For every Napoleon or Alexander the Great, the earth holds the bones of hundreds of kings who galloped to the sound of battle and returned on a fleeing horse or shield. Similarly, for every Elizabeth I or Catherine the Great, we find women who gambled everything and came up short. By studying the military campaigns of queens, we glean a clear-eyed look at why some lost and others won.

Some of history's most successful war queens are hardly household names, even though their military accomplishments rival those of King Frederick or Tsar Peter, both known to posterity as "the Great."

So why the lapse?

Humanity's reluctance to hand the reins to a woman is part of the answer, but the greater truth lies in the twisting path each woman's narrative took between her death and the twenty-first century. In some cases, the queen's war record was chronicled by the other side, such as the Vatican, the Romans, or the slave-trading Portuguese. In others, successor kings downplayed the accomplishments of their mothers or regents as a matter of garden-variety political pruning, rather than gut-level misogyny.

For other women, Fate simply placed them in a mist-bathed Avalon of gods, heroes, and monsters—an era when oral traditions ruled and written records would not stabilize their stories until a century or more after their deaths. For folkloric lions like Assyria's Semiramis, Japan's Empress Jingu, or the Viking shieldmaiden Lagertha, the line between fact and myth has become so faint that it is impossible to say exactly where one begins and the other ends. This class of *femmes fatales* will have to remain mythic heroines as we parse through the lives of the flesh-and-blood.

So let us take these extraordinary women and muster them into a platoon of leaders who walked through war's kiln and emerged from the other side, some burnished to greatness, others burned to cinders. All of them, legends.

THE MIGHTY ARMS OF ATLAS

❖   ❖   ❖

When the Himalayan peasant meets the he-bear in his pride,
He shouts to scare the monster, who will often turn aside.
But the she-bear thus accosted rends the peasant tooth and nail.
For the female of the species is more deadly than the male.

—Rudyard Kipling,
"The Female of the Species" (1911)

In an age of gods and god-kings, Eurasia's river valleys spawned empires that shaped the way neighboring kings lived, died, and ruled. Dynastic Egypt dominated its corner of Africa and the Levant. Babylonians, Persians, and Greeks conquered Mesopotamia. The Han dynasty held sway over East Asia, and Rome ruled Western Europe, North Africa, and a swath of the Middle East.

Warfare, like civilization, was finding its wobbly legs. Kings began employing professionals to manage military personnel, logistics, and tactics. Forward-thinking generals divided mobs into cohorts, myriads, and squadrons. Crude Stone Age tools evolved into bronze armor and the composite bow, while the chariot gave commanders devastating new options on the battlefield. Specialists like horse archers and engineers began carving their niches in a world where military might was the ultimate piece of the power game.

Because nature punishes the weak, imperial wolves like Egypt preyed on realms beyond their borders without bothering themselves over trivial matters like right or wrong, just or unjust. Dominance was the natural order of the world—a hierarchy of violence sanctified by Amen-Ra, or Ba'al, or Zeus, or . . . whomever the local hegemon claimed to follow. Lucky alphas were born into dynasties strong enough to run their affairs as they pleased, while less fortunate kings and queens (that is, nearly all of them) became sheep. Or, at best, porcupines.

Yet some of these porcupines brandished sharp quills. Israel's biblical judge Deborah mapped a battle plan that annihilated a chariot-mounted Canaanite army. The Trüng sisters of northern Vietnam conquered sixty towns in a two-year revolt against their Han overlords. Syria's Queen Zenobia built a buffer kingdom by playing two great empires against each other, and in Rome's marble twilight, Queen Mawiyya led an army of Arabs and Syrians that compelled Rome's emperor to sue for peace.

Poking through the detritus of war, we find the ancient war queens—forerunners of women who would lead nuclear states—struggling to find their voices in a world of seismic shifts and mass violence. They were smart, they were resourceful, and they were lucky.

They were also, as we shall see, prone to rage when provoked.

1

"MORE BLOOD THAN YOU CAN DRINK"

Tomyris of the Massagetae

"Listen to me and I will advise you for your good:
Give me back my son and get out of my country."
—QUEEN TOMYRIS TO CYRUS THE GREAT, 530 B.C.

THE MASSAGETAE, A ROUGH, RURAL FOLK, were little known to the glittering courts of the Persian Empire. Whenever King Cyrus the Great thought of them, which was not often, it was only as another target of conquest.

By 540 BC, Cyrus had forged the largest empire the world had seen. Overwhelming Medians, Babylonians, and kings of Asia Minor, he rode to greatness on the shoulders of his armies. His titles—Great King, King of Kings, King of the Four Corners of the World—reflected the grandeur and might of the vast Persian Empire.

That empire stretched from the Mediterranean in the west to the Indus River in the east, an area covering over two million square miles. To the northeast, the Great King's reach extended into foothills and plateaus as far as the Araxes River. And beyond that river, a nomadic people known as the Massagetae rode the west Asian steppes.[*]

---

[*] Writing a century after the death of Cyrus, Herodotus mentions the Araxes River several times in his *Histories* without fixing its location. Some modern sources, such as the *Encyclopaedia Iranica*, identify the Araxes as the modern Aras River west of the Caspian Sea, on Iran's northwestern border in the Caucasus region. Others claim it is the modern Jaxartes River, or Syr Darya, which flows into the Aral Sea east of the Caspian. Herodotus left few reliable clues, so the river's place on a modern map is uncertain.

❖ ❖ ❖

STRADDLING THE WORLDS of civilized and barbarian, the tough, weather-beaten Massagetae horsemen were known for their baggy trousers, peaked caps, and thick, colorful coats. Riding, fighting, and celebrating with the gusto of a people inured to hardship, the Massagetae embraced a life Cyrus and his worldly courtiers found primitive and brutish.

The Greek historian Herodotus, known as the "Father of History," described the Massagetae as an elusive tribe of herders and fishers who worshipped a sun god, ate meat and fish, and drank milk. Their weapons, armor, tack, and personal ornamentation were of bronze, often accented with gold.

Marital relationships within the tribe were more flexible than those of their urbane neighbors. "Every man has a wife," wrote Herodotus, "but all wives are used promiscuously . . . If a man wants a woman, all he does is hang up his quiver in front of her wagon and then enjoy her without misgiving."

Equally without misgiving was the Massagetae retirement party. When a tribesman became too old to hunt, fight, or hang up his quiver, his relatives would throw a banquet for him. Amid drinking, feasting, and storytelling, the guest of honor would be ceremonially killed. Meat sliced off his still-warm bones would be boiled and eaten by his family. "This," wrote Herodotus, "they consider to be the best sort of death."

A peacetime death, anyway. In wartime, the Massagetae were formidable fighters. Fast-riding horse archers and lancers softened up the enemy; behind the riders marched infantry, axes raised and spears lowered, as they closed in for the kill.

Over this mass of promiscuous, warlike riders stood Queen Tomyris, widow of the Massagetae king. Moderate and level-headed, she preferred a pragmatic approach to foreign policy. While in later centuries her descendants would run wild through Asia and Eastern Europe, toppling kings and slaughtering neighbors, Tomyris avoided conflicts in general—and with Persians in particular.

She had good reason to keep to her side of the Araxes River. The massive empire Cyrus had forged was running roughshod even over quiet nations that tried hard not to provoke him. As Tomyris watched him swallow one kingdom after another, she suspected it would be only a matter of time before the Great King turned his sword against her. She was in no hurry to initiate that contest.

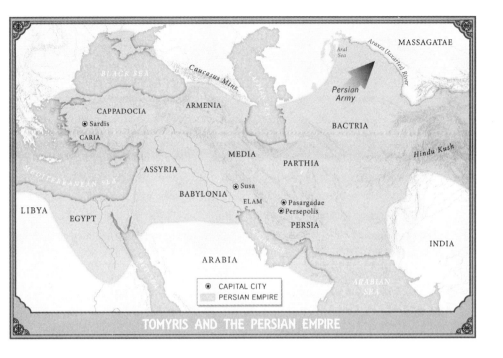

The Achaemenid Invasion

The season of swords arrived in 530 BC, when Cyrus turned his attention to his northeastern frontier. Buoyed by his reputation as a conqueror, the Great King first tried a soft approach with Tomyris: He would conquer the barbarian queen with soothing words and an enticing marriage proposal.

But Cyrus's charms didn't translate well into the Massagetae tongue. "The queen was well aware that he was wooing not herself but her dominions," says Herodotus. Seeing the royal proposal for what it was—a ploy for her lands—Tomyris declined to let Cyrus hang his quiver outside her wagon. He would have neither her bed nor her kingdom.

Not without a fight.

Unlucky in love, Cyrus girded his loins for war. He massed men, horses, weapons, and food on Persia's eastern frontier, then departed his capital with every reason to think the Massagetae would fall as easily as the ripe figs he had plucked from Bactria to the western sea. Lydians, Babylonians, Egyptians, even Indians had been swept aside by the Achaemenid army. Enemy generals had been beheaded, kings had prostrated themselves before the Great One. Now the Great One was about to swallow another nation and bring it into the empire.

Assembling his legions along the Massagetae border near the Araxes River, Cyrus sent forward military engineers with orders to build a bridge and ferry docks to transport his army over the river.

From the river's east bank, Massagetae cavalry scouts kept their queen advised of the Persian advance guard, major troop movements, and the progress of that ominous bridge. As Persian laborers sank support pylons and hammered spans, a nervous Tomyris steadied herself for a fight with the world's greatest power.

Before the arrows flew, Tomyris tried to dissuade Cyrus from crossing her border. "King of the Medes, I advise you to abandon this enterprise," read one message to Cyrus. "Rule your own people, and try to bear the sight of me ruling mine."

It was a reasonable diplomatic opening. But when it became clear Cyrus had no intention of abandoning his conquest, the queen's tone grew cold. Resigned to war, she offered Cyrus a fair fight in the open.

"If you are so bent upon trying your strength against the Massagetae," she wrote him, "give up the laborious task of building that bridge, and let my army withdraw three days' march from the river, and then come over yourself. Or, if you prefer it, retire the same distance yourselves, and let us meet you on your side of the river."

At first, Cyrus was unsure what to make of the queen's brash proposal. Stroking his beard as he mulled over his response, he summoned his military advisors and asked their opinions.

Almost to a man, his professionals advised him to let Tomyris cross into Persian lands, then fight on his side of the river. The queen's army couldn't operate in Persia for long, because her food and arrow supply could be easily severed from the rear by imperial cavalry once she crossed the Araxes. Should the Persian army defeat her in battle, as seemed likely, her fleeing men would be cut down by Persian riders as they tried to swim across the river. And in the unlikely event the Massagetae gained the upper hand in battle, Cyrus could simply pull back to familiar territory until reinforcements arrived, or until Tomyris and her isolated men went home.

Just when the matter seemed settled, a dissenting voice spoke. Croesus, the former king of Lydia, had been defeated by Cyrus years earlier. Cyrus had taken a liking to the feisty ex-king, and instead of beheading him, he took Croesus into his service as a court advisor.

Croesus argued that Tomyris had to be defeated on the east side of the Araxes. From a psychological standpoint, "it would surely be an intolerable disgrace for Cyrus, son of Cambyses, to give ground before a woman." Defeat in Persian territory, however unlikely, would also leave the eastern empire open to depredations by the Massagetae riders.

Whether afraid to be shamed by a woman, or wary of giving ground, Cyrus took the ex-king's advice. He sent a messenger back to Tomyris and arranged for her to withdraw from the river. She pulled back, as promised, and the Persian army crossed the Araxes unopposed. Cyrus and his army bivouacked in Massagetae territory as he planned his next move.

Acting on another of Croesus's suggestions, Cyrus set up a field camp in the style and splendor of an imperial court. He filled command and quartermaster tents with beautifully appointed banquet tables and stocked them with prodigious stores of sweet wine. He then marched off with the main body of his army, leaving his camp guarded only by a small, second-rate detachment.

The king's rich stores drew the Massagetae like a moth to fire. A third of Queen Tomyris's force, led by her son, Prince Spargapises, descended on the camp after scouts reported the movement of the main body. They attacked the encampment, slaughtered the guards, and ransacked the wine stores. Being unused to wine—their preferred intoxicant was a lightly fermented milk—the prince's soldiers promptly drank themselves into a stupor.

Cyrus timed his withdrawal carefully. When he calculated the Massagetae detachment would be attacking his richly baited trap, he wheeled his force and began a return march, ensuring that his army arrived when Spargapises and his men were asleep—or if awake, drunk, sick, or hung over.

It was an easy victory for the Persians. Cyrus's army slaughtered Massagetae soldiers and took many prisoners. Among those prisoners was Tomyris's son, Spargapises.

Sexual relationships might have been loose among the Massagetae, but family loyalty ran hot. A fiercely protective mother, Tomyris flew into a rage when she learned of her son's capture and the method of his humiliation. Unable to restrain pen or sword, she sent a final warning to Cyrus.

"Glutton as you are for blood, you have no cause to be proud of this day's work, which has no smack of soldierly courage," she chastised him.

Your weapon was the fruit of the vine . . . that is the poison you treacherously used to get my son into your clutches. Now listen to me and I will advise you for your good: Give me back my son and get out of my country with your forces intact, and be content with your triumph over a third part of the Massagetae. If you refuse, I swear by the sun our master to give you more blood than you can drink, for all your gluttony.

Shrugging off the venom of an unhinged mother, Cyrus pushed his army eastward until he met Tomyris and her main force.*

The battle, says Herodotus, "I judge to have been more violent than any other fought between foreign nations." The two armies tramped within range and loosed clouds of arrows until their quivers were empty. When the arrowstorm passed, surviving infantry closed in to decide the contest.

The fight was no tactical masterpiece, with elaborate flanking movements, choreographed feints, or exquisite positioning. It was a spit-and-blood struggle of unalloyed savagery. Sweating warriors hacked each other with battleaxe, spear, and sword. Neither side gave quarter; neither gave ground. Men were pierced and gutted, screamed, bled, and died, their bodies trampled into the mud. From opposing sides of the field, rulers fed their reserves into the bloodbath until the butcher's lullaby ended and one side was left standing.

The Massagetae.

Most of the Persian army was wiped out—the Latin writer Justin gives a fantastical figure of 200,000 Persians killed. Torn remnants of the empire's army streamed back over the Araxes River for the safety of Persia.

Tomyris had won.

❖　　❖　　❖

THERE ARE SEVERAL ACCOUNTS of Cyrus's fate. Many agree that the Great King died fighting Queen Tomyris, though they differ on what happened to his body. Some say Tomyris had his corpse crucified; according to others, it was brought back to Persia and buried at his capital, Pasargadae.

But the Father of History found the following version to be the most credible:

> *After the battle, Tomyris ordered a search to be made amongst the Persian dead for the body of Cyrus; and when it was found, she pushed his head into a skin which she had filled with human blood, and cried out as she committed this outrage: "Though I have conquered you and live, yet you have ruined me by treacherously taking my son. See now—I fulfill my threat: You have your fill of blood."*

---

* Tomyris would never see her son again. Filled with remorse and shame, Spargapises begged his captors to remove his bonds. As a courtesy to a prince, the Persians obliged him. Spargapises promptly killed himself, leaving Cyrus one less bargaining chip to play against a Massagetae mother's fury.

❖   ❖   ❖

THE PERSIAN EMPEROR—his head, at least —met an ignoble end at the hands of a furious warrior queen. But times change, and no enemy, no ally, is ever truly permanent. In two generations, a queen from modern Turkey would find herself serving Cyrus's grandson in one of history's greatest battles. Like Tomyris, this woman would impress Herodotus with her wise advice, strategic insight, and calculating ruthlessness.

2

"MY WOMEN HAVE BECOME MEN"

Artemisia of Caria

"If you do not rush into an engagement at sea, but hold the
fleet here waiting on shore, or if you attack the Peloponnese,
you will attain your objectives without trouble."
—Artemisia's advice to King Xerxes, 480 B.C.

Fifty years after Tomyris gave King Cyrus his fill of blood, another warrior queen found herself fighting alongside Cyrus's grandson. Of the royals fighting under the eagle banner of King Xerxes, writes Herodotus, "There is no reason for me to mention any of the other commanders, except for Artemisia. I consider her to be a particular object of admiration because she was a woman who played a part in the war against Greece."

Queen Artemisia's homeland of Caria, in what is now southwestern Turkey, fell under Persian rule about ten years before Cyrus met his messy end. The second-century Greek writer Polyaenus tells us that Artemisia was the daughter of King Lygdamis and an unnamed Cretan queen. The half-Greek princess of a half-Greek nation grew into a virago whom Herodotus praised for her energetic nature and "manly courage." After her father's death, her husband succeeded to the throne, only to pass it on to his widow, Artemisia. The new queen was more than ready for the challenge.

With no surviving coins, frescoes, or contemporary statues, Artemisia's face has receded too far into history's cave to see clearly. Born to a Cretan mother, she would have been disposed to an olive complexion, dark hair, a prominent nose, and deep, round eyes. But her father's Turkish bloodline, whether pure or alloyed, frustrates our efforts to see Artemisia as her servants saw her when she walked along Caria's sun-kissed coast.

She served the Persian emperor as a loyal vassal, and showed no aversion to doing the Great King's dirty work. When the Greek island of Cos refused to render him tributes of soil and water—standard tokens of submission—Xerxes ordered Artemisia to bring her neighbors to heel. She carried out her orders to the letter, bringing Cos, the island of Nisyros, and the Carian cities of Halicarnassus and Calynda under her personal rule, for the benefit of the Empire.

Having proved herself against the Adriatic Greeks, Xerxes kept Artemisia in mind for his next big feature. One in which other Greeks would be unwilling stars.

FOR NEARLY TWO DECADES, the Greek thorn pricked the side of Persian rulers. They stirred up revolts along Persia's Ionian coast, and in 492 BC a three hundred–ship fleet carrying a Persian invasion force was wrecked in a terrible storm off the north Greek coast. Two years later, Darius sent another army to subdue the Athenians, only to be repulsed at the Battle of Marathon. Thwarted by both Poseidon and Ares, Darius made plans for an even larger invasion, but he died in 486, before he could launch his arrow.

Six years later, his eldest son, Xerxes, prepared to realize his father's dream of crushing the Greeks. Assembling a massive army in Asia Minor—180,000 men strong—Xerxes marched his force to the Hellespont, that narrow strait dividing Europe from Asia. In a wonder of military engineering, his architects constructed two massive pontoon bridges from 674 boats, allowing his soldiers to walk dry-shod over the sea into Europe. Once across, the mass of armored men tramped toward the Greek heartland.*

To curious ravens circling overhead, the army column resembled an immense, bronze-scaled serpent slithering west—a mythical snake devouring everything in its path, stripping the land of whatever men could carry or oxen could pull.

---

* The size of the Persian invasion force is the subject of irreconcilable estimates. While Herodotus reckoned 1.8 million soldiers and a like number of support troops, modern sources argue that the Greek countryside was incapable of supporting more than one-tenth that number. One historian surmises that Herodotus, who had access to Persian archives, mistook a *chilead*, 1,000 men, for a *myriad*, 10,000 men, which would put the actual size of the Persian army at around 180,000. In view of the invasion's progress, this lower number seems a reasonable estimate.

Herodotus claims the Persian host gulped entire lakes dry, and the daily demands of nearly 200,000 hungry mouths were a constant source of worry to Xerxes and his generals.

With an army this large, Xerxes and his admirals knew that supply lines would determine the campaign's success or failure. They arranged for 3,000 merchant ships to shuttle between Asia Minor and Greece, their plump wooden holds bulging with food, messages, and reinforcements. To protect this vulnerable supply artery, Xerxes assembled a navy of 1,207 *triremes*: galley warships powered by three banks of oars, teeming with fighting men and tipped with bronze battering rams. These battleships glided along Greece's rocky coast in the spring of 480, shadowing the army that marched toward the Greek state of Attica and its capital city, Athens.

One squadron of these behemoths belonged to Queen Artemisia. Though half-Greek, her banner answered the Great King's call to arms, and her kingdom contributed soldiers and warships to the expedition. Her squadron fielded some of the most

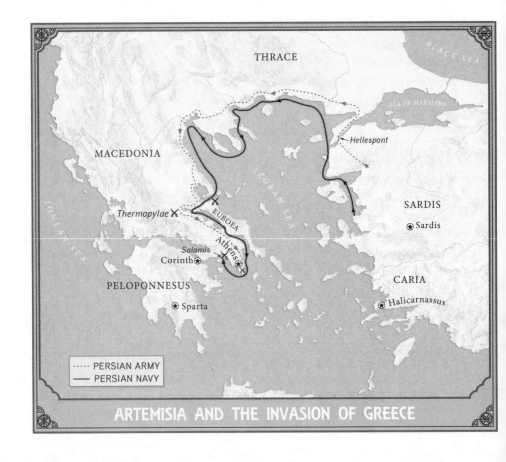

ARTEMISIA AND THE INVASION OF GREECE

aggressive, most agile fighting ships in the Persian navy, and on the journey to Athens, Artemisia won the Great King's favor through her charm and plain-spoken manner.

Xerxes Advances on Athens

On land, Xerxes proved unstoppable. He met no serious opposition on the march to northern Greece until a small force of Spartans, Thebans, and Corinthians managed to check the invaders briefly at a narrow choke point called Thermopylae. But once that bottleneck was cleared, the road to Athens lay open. Lumbering down the Greek peninsula like a cyclops on a rampage, Xerxes's army fell on the city and burned its acropolis to the ground.[*]

The Aegean Sea proved treacherous, however, for the waters were rough, rock-strewn, and guarded by a fearsome god the Greeks called Poseidon. Xerxes lost hundreds of ships in violent storms and in fighting off the coast near Thermopylae. In a fleet engagement near the island of Euboea, the Greek navy fought the Persians— including Artemisia and her Carian seamen—to a draw.

But the Persians could afford heavy losses, while the Greeks could not. The Greeks fielded a small fleet manned by lower-class sailors and drafted citizens, among them a young playwright from Eleusis named Aeschylus. These sons of Zeus came together in a colorful, quarrelling quilt of ships hailing from Sparta, Athens, Corinth, and other cities that had been at each other's throats for centuries.

As smoke drifted from the ashes of the Acropolis, remnants of the Greek army retreated west to the narrow Isthmus of Corinth. On that thin neck of land guarding the Peloponnese, Greek army commanders hoped to make another stand. At sea, their admirals beached their ships at a bay off Salamis Island, blocking a seaborne landing on the Peloponnese from the east. There they waited as vengeful winds filled Persian sails.

Persia may have been the world's greatest land power, but the King of Kings was uncomfortable fighting on water. Pausing at the port town of Phaleron in mid-September, he called a council of war to decide how to crush the Greek resistance. Sitting before a long table, Xerxes assembled his war chiefs in order of precedence: the King of Sidon, the King of Tyre, and so on, down to the lowest invitee.

At his signal, his chief military advisor, a general named Mardonius, asked the leaders for their opinions. To a man, they agreed the Persians should launch a

---

[*] Three decades later, Athenians built the famed Parthenon to replace the wooden temple that Xerxes and his men razed.

frontal attack against the Greek fleet in Salamis Bay. The Greeks fielded half their number of ships, and victory at sea would allow the Persian army to land behind the Greek lines on the isthmus. Once in the open country of the Peloponnese, the Persian army would destroy Sparta, Corinth, and any remaining Greeks who resisted.

The lone voice of dissent came from the woman in the tent. Artemisia, queen of a coastal kingdom, understood the political and military mindset of states surrounded by water. Being of Greek descent, she also had a window into the Grecian mind. When Mardonius asked Artemisia for her opinion, she turned to him and replied,

> *Tell the king from me, Mardonius, that this is his reply from one who showed herself neither the most cowardly nor the weakest in the naval encounters at Euboea . . . This is my advice to you: Spare your ships and do not fight a battle at sea. For their men are as superior to yours at sea as men are to women. Why need you run the risk of naval actions at all? Do you not hold Athens, the particular objective of your campaign, and do you not control the rest of Greece?*

Describing the picture from the Greek viewpoint, Artemisia predicted the collapse of the enemy coalition. Not from a single, dramatic battle, but from the asphyxiates of sinking morale, dwindling supplies, and that old Greek nemesis, disunity. In a clear, deliberate voice, she continued:

> *I shall explain how I think the enemy will fare. If you do not rush into an engagement at sea, but hold the fleet here waiting on shore, or if you attack the Peloponnese, master, you will attain your objectives without trouble. For the Greeks cannot put up resistance against you for long, but they will scatter their forces and run away, city by city. They have no supplies on this island, according to my information, nor do they consider it their home. If you send your army against the Peloponnese, it is not likely that any Peloponnesians in the Greek forces will be prepared to fight a naval battle in defense of Athens. If you bring on a naval battle right now, I am afraid that the fleet will be destroyed and involve the army as well in defeat.*

The rival kings smiled inwardly. Artemisia was advocating a cautious, unmanly approach, one the Great King would find repugnant. In rendering distasteful advice, the queen was destroying her reputation with Xerxes and would be ruined. The king had an unpredictable temper, and the headstrong queen might even find herself kneeling before an executioner.

But Xerxes was not irritated. He liked Artemisia. She was loyal, thoughtful, and unafraid to speak her mind. In council she had kept her head, and as a reward, she would keep her head.

He sided with the majority, however, for victory in Salamis Bay would put an end to the expensive, time-consuming war and allow him to get back to Persia. Xerxes sent about 30,000 men toward the Isthmus of Corinth to bottle up the Greeks on land, but he intended to fight the war's decisive battle at sea, off the eastern shore of Salamis Island.

Artemisia, begrudging but loyal, bowed to the emperor's wishes. She returned to her squadron and readied her ships for battle.*

The Battle of Salamis

Directing his staff to set up an observation post on Attica's western slope, across the narrow channel from Salamis Island, Xerxes reveled in the grandeur of unbridled military power. He and his aides were about to savor the destruction of the Greek fleet.

The Greeks, never good neighbors, had quarreled among themselves since before the invasion. As Artemisia predicted, most Peloponnese were loath to give their lives for Athens, while the Athenians were divided over naval and land strategy. With their warships beached on Salamis Island, admirals from Sparta and Corinth demanded a breakout to the open waters of the west. They ran into heated opposition from an Athenian admiral, a bulldog of a man named Themistocles, who urged the fragile coalition members to fight in the confines of the narrow Salamis Channel.

At the southern end of that same channel, Artemisia's sea captains barked orders to unstep masts and serve out boarding axes, shields, and polearms. Rowers took their places by their oars, archers gathered in forecastles, and blades were given a last grind on the sharpening wheel.

On the night of September 19, the queen, clad in armor, boarded her flagship. As oars dipped and swept to the mesmerizing cadence of voice and drum, Artemisia's warships took their station in the Persian line.

---

* While acclaimed as the "Father of History," specific anecdotes of Herodotus are subject to thoughtful criticism. Some appear to be based on records, others sound like educated guesses, and still others reflect local folklore. So it may be with his accounts of Artemisia, as some scholars have argued. In the absence of contravening evidence, we have accepted Herodotus's account as the best and most detailed available.

Egyptian
Squadron

BAY OF ELEUSIS

ATTICA

Throne of
Xerxes

S A L A M I S

GREEK SHIPS
PERSIAN SHIPS

BATTLE OF SALAMIS, 480 B.C.

While Persian galleys were forming up, a Greek slave privy to Athenian plans slipped past Xerxes's pickets and turned up in Attica. The slave, named Sicinnus, told his Persian interrogators that Greek unity had disintegrated, just as Artemisia had predicted. The Athenian contingent, he said, was preparing to flee to open water.[*]

To prevent an escape through the channel's western mouth, Xerxes sent his Egyptian squadron, two hundred triremes strong, around the island's far west side with orders to let no one slip out the back channel. As the blood-dipped sun began to set, Xerxes's main battle group rowed into the nearer east channel. They formed up opposite the Greek anchorage in three carefully choreographed lines.

Through the balmy September night, sweating Persian rowers kept their ships in close formation against the tide, heaving their oars at regular intervals and shaking

---

[*] The message, says Herodotus, was a ruse by Themistocles. Hearing what he wished to hear, Xerxes swallowed the story hook, line, and sinker.

off sleep's embrace. On pain of death, captains and officers kept a vigilant watch for the Greek breakout during the night. But as the moon rose and set, no ships appeared, no arrows flew.

Then, in the morning hours of September 20, as Helios towed the sun into the sky, a low murmur rose from the Salamis Channel. The baritone notes of the paean to Apollo, the mariner's hymn, drifted over the water as Greek galleys emerged from Paloukia Bay. Before bloodshot Persian eyes, the united Greeks formed up, Peloponnese to the right, Athenians on the left, the rest in the center.

Their oars began to splash.

Eight years later, Aeschylus recreated the scene from the Persian point of view in his drama *The Persae*:

> *An echoing shout of battle, like some triumph-song*
> *Went up from each Greek throat, and shrilly rang*
> *Reverberating from the island crags.*
> *Then fear gripped hold of us: our expectations*
> *Faded away. This sacred battle-hymn*
> *Did not betoken flight, but stubborn courage*
> *Impetuous for attack.*

As the impetuous Greeks advanced, a signal went up from the Persian command post: Charge the enemy and destroy him. Three lines of the Persian armada, which had been holding steady against slapping tides all night, lurched forward.

Artemisia's squadron advanced with its allies into the gradually narrowing channel. In response, the Greek fleet, slower and heavier, backed up in good order under the watchful eye of Themistocles.

The Greek retreat emboldened the Persian captains, and for a time none of them realized their colossal mistake. As the king's triremes pressed into the tightening narrows, their lines became crowded. Oars bumped, then tangled, then broke. Exhausted rowers, who had been up all night fighting the current, tried to haul in their oars and resume their rhythm, but confusion spread and the front line ground to a halt. Ships became snarled, and the second and third Persian ranks ran up against the first.

Without warning, the Greeks stopped backing. They charged.

Bronze-sheathed rams crashed into the sides of Persian hulls, splintering timbers with a roar. Seas poured in, men screamed, terrified sailors clung to flotsam. Arrows flew, warships capsized, and veteran Persian soldiers—most unable to swim even without armor—slipped beneath the waves as their last gasps bubbled to the surface.

Aeschylus bore witness to the carnage:

Crushed hulls lay upturned on the sea so thick
You could not see the water, choked with wrecks
And slaughtered men; while all the shores and reefs
Were strewn with corpses.

As the Persian line crumpled, a fast-moving Greek trireme yawed its ram toward Artemisia's ship. Caught at a vulnerable angle, the queen ordered her pilot to make a dash for the Attic shore.

If they were in open sea, Artemisia could have run up Greek colors and bluffed her way out. While the Greek high command had announced a huge bounty for her capture—10,000 drachmae—her ship had not yet been identified by enemy captains.

But they were not in open sea, and the Great King knew Artemisia's ship. Desertion, even to regroup, was a capital offense.

It may not have mattered anyway, for Artemisia was trapped. Jumbled Persian warships blocked her escape route, and there seemed no way out of certain destruction.

Then, as the enemy ship closed in on her, Artemisia did something that stopped her pursuers cold: She aimed her ship's ram at the flagship of one of her own allies, King Damasithymos of Calynda, and held on for dear life at the moment of impact. As her ram smashed into the Calyndian, she felt the violent grind of bronze on wood vibrate through her feet and legs. Timbers buckled, water rushed in, and the Calyndian ship went to the bay's bottom with all hands, including its king.

The captain of the Greek pursuer, seeing his quarry destroy a Persian, realized he had made a mistake. The ship he had been chasing was obviously Greek, not Persian, for there was no other reason she would attack the enemy. He heeled his ship around and rowed off in search of a new target.

Artemisia's maneuver did not escape the notice of the Great King's observers, either. From his throne ashore, Xerxes had watched his ships go down by the dozen in the Greek maelstrom. As he was sinking into despair, one of his staff, recognizing Artemisia's ship from a distance, assumed she had sunk a Greek foe and scurried to bring the king a rare bit of welcome news.

"Master, do you see how well Artemisia is fighting?" the aide asked. "She has sunk an enemy ship."

Xerxes, says Herodotus, replied with a mixture of admiration and despair: "My men have become women, and my women, men!"

As the occupants of the Calyndian flagship were either nonswimmers or encumbered with armor, Artemisia left no survivors to unmask her treachery. Word went round that on this day of disaster, Artemisia became the hero of the Persian navy.

By the time the sun reached its zenith, the Greeks had destroyed hundreds of warships and won one of history's most decisive battles. The battered Persian navy withdrew, and its stunned king called another council of war.

Persia's options, as Xerxes saw them, were to continue the war without his fleet, or to leave a puppet governor in Athens and bring his army home. General Mardonius urged Xerxes to ignore the recent setback and drive west against Corinth and Sparta. "It is not on things of wood that the issue hangs for us, but on men and horses," he assured his king.

The king was not so sure. His military experts had also assured him he would find an easy victory at sea, and the murky waters had swallowed that victory. So he dismissed all of his officers, save Artemisia. Having ignored her advice once, he was now ready to listen.

"Under the present circumstances, I believe that you should take the army back with you and leave Mardonius behind here," Artemisia told the king.

> *If he achieves what he says are his aims, and if his intentions go according to plan, the deed, master, is to your credit. But if things turn out contrary to Mardonius's plan, it will be no great loss, because you and the affairs of your house will survive . . . You, on the other hand, will be returning after burning Athens, the objective of your campaign.*

This time Xerxes took the queen's advice and returned home to Sardis. Thanking Artemisia, he gave her a set of Greek armor as a war trophy and sent her to Ephesus, where he did her the honor of placing some of his illegitimate sons in her care.*

Artemisia had served her commander well, and had come through a tight spot with both neck and reputation intact. Though she would always be a vassal queen,

---

* Like all good emperors, Xerxes acknowledged his vassals with the occasional thank you gift. In London's British Museum, a visitor can see a calcite jar taken from the legendary mausoleum of Halicarnassus, Artemisia's homeland. Inscribed "Xerxes Great King" in four languages, it dates from the time of Artemisia's rule. It is almost surely the king's present to his warrior queen.

Xerxes permitted her to rule her kingdom more or less independently. Sitting closer to the head of the command table than her colleagues had ever thought possible, Artemisia had become another chip at the ancient world's patronizing image of a queen at war.

THREE CENTURIES after Artemisia's clash at sea, another woman—a goddess, seductress, linguist, ruler, and intellect—held very different ideas about the relationship between client queen and emperor. She inherited a kingdom of fabulous wealth, she had charisma, and if she had her way, she would answer to no man.

3

THE LAST PHARAOH

Cleopatra of Egypt

"It was not easy to see how Cleopatra was inferior in intelligence to any one of the princes who took part in the expedition, she who for a long time had governed so large a kingdom by herself."
—PLUTARCH, *LIFE OF ANTONY*, C. 100 A.D.

MURDER CAME EASILY to the Ptolemy family. War, not so much.

Since settling in to rule Egyptian lands conquered by Alexander the Great, the Ptolemies kept their family tree neatly pruned with poison, the assassin's blade, and well-placed bribes to bodyguards. Ptolemaic pharaohs waded into war's reedy marshes from time to time—often against other Ptolemies—but battle was not one of the family's preferred tools. Egypt's immense wealth put a premium on peaceful and profitable relations with its Greek, Jewish, Asiatic, and Roman neighbors. Besides, as Virgil once remarked, "Blood is a big expense."

But the age of the Caesars was no ordinary time. Rome's long shadow stretched across the Mediterranean world, and in 55 BC the unruly republic elbowed its way into the land of pharaohs, pyramids, and gods.

And Cleopatra.

❖   ❖   ❖

CLEOPATRA THEA PHILOPATER, or "Father-loving Goddess," was raised in the court of her father, King Ptolemy XII, an effeminate fop derided as the "Flute

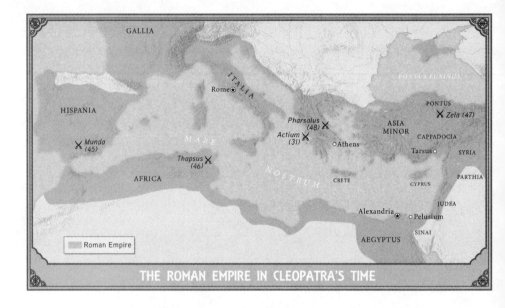

THE ROMAN EMPIRE IN CLEOPATRA'S TIME

Player." When Cleopatra's oldest sister, Berenice IV, drove their father into exile, the Flute Player offered colossal bribes to Pompey Magnus, Rome's preeminent general, to restore him to the throne. Pompey's legions deposed and executed Berenice, and to ensure the Flute Player repaid his debts, Pompey garrisoned Alexandria with 2,500 Roman legionnaires.

Four years later, the Flute Player died of a common illness—a death not fairly classified as "natural causes" to the Ptolemies. With Berenice out of the picture, in his will Ptolemy left his kingdom to his eighteen-year-old daughter, Cleopatra, and her twelve-year-old brother, Ptolemy. In keeping with Egyptian tradition, brother and sister ruled as the gods Osiris and Isis, and were joined on earth as husband and wife. Honoring their Greek heritage, they took the title *Theoi Neoi Philadelphoi*: "New Sibling-Loving Gods."

In time, the name would ring like a cruel joke.

The sibling-loving goddess was probably a typical shoot from her bamboo-like family tree. With a slightly hooked Macedonian nose, light bronze skin, full lips, and a sharp chin, Cleopatra's beauty, in Plutarch's words, "was not in itself so remarkable that none could be compared with her, or that no one could see her without being struck by it."

What *did* strike everyone was Cleopatra's intellect, wit, and charm. She had been raised by Alexandria's finest tutors in the academic center of the world. She mastered the arts of rhetoric and oratory at an early age. She recited long passages from

Homer, studied natural science, and read Greek plays from scrolls not far removed from their originals.

As a girl, Cleopatra discovered a gift for languages. Greek was her native tongue, but Plutarch claims she mastered eight others, including Hebrew, Arabic, and Parthian. She was also the only member of Egypt's royal family who took the trouble to learn Egyptian, the language of the people who worked her fields and carried her spears. Her fluency in Egypt's native tongue would prove invaluable when her family turned against her.*

For three years, Cleopatra and Ptolemy ruled as nominal equals. Ptolemy's advisors made decisions on the boy-king's behalf, but Cleopatra preferred to hold the reins in her own small, disciplined fingers.

Much of her crowded workday would have been devoted to managing price controls, tax levels, customs duties, food distribution, and other aspects of Egypt's tightly planned economy. She presided over religious ceremonies, convened judicial proceedings, and granted audiences to ministers, diplomats, bureaucrats, accountants, nobles, and other callers whose claims on her time even a goddess could not ignore.

The Alexandrian War

Given her clan's fondness for fratricide, patricide, sororicide, and other cides seldom seen in functional families, it is not surprising that Egypt's throne proved uncomfortably tight for two royal bottoms. Cleopatra, the older sister, grew too pushy for Ptolemy's liking as she reached her late teenage years. She approved coin designs bearing only her image—not her brother's, as was customary—and began dropping Ptolemy's name from official documents. None of this sat well with Ptolemy and his entourage.

Ptolemy's support centered on a palace clique led by his former tutor, a eunuch named Pothinus; his royal guard commander, General Achillas; and his rhetoric teacher, Theodotus. Thoroughly distrustful of the ambitious sister, the king's backers quietly lined up against Cleopatra and waited for her to slip.

In 49 BC a civil war raging in Rome triggered Cleopatra's first major political misstep. While Pompey the Great fought Julius Caesar for control of the Roman

---

* While Plutarch does not list Latin among Cleopatra's linguistic gifts, she probably learned that language, too. She may have traveled to Rome with her father during his exile from 58 to 55 BC, and if so, she would have lived in the Latin world's capital from ages eleven to fourteen, a time when children are adept at picking up new languages. In any event, Cleopatra would find ample reason to master Rome's native tongue.

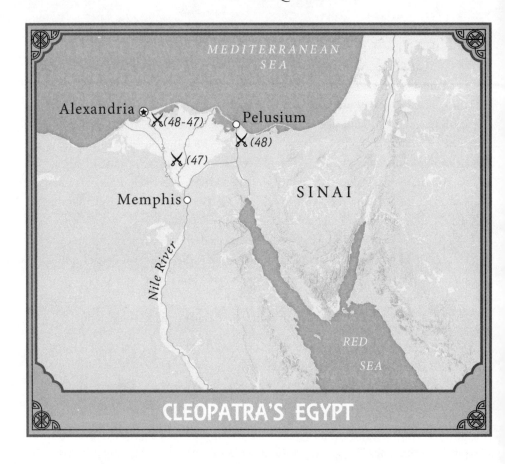

CLEOPATRA'S EGYPT

Republic, Pompey's son Gnaeus sailed to Alexandria with a polite but firm request for soldiers, grain, money, and a war fleet. As Pompey had been the Ptolemy family's patron in Rome, neither Cleopatra nor Ptolemy could decently refuse his request; they obliged him with ships filled with gold and grain.

Their decision didn't sit well with the Alexandrians, however. Egypt had been wracked by famine, and exporting grain to Pompey proved wildly unpopular among the urban crowd. With the dexterous hand of a political assassin, Ptolemy's ministers spread word around the city that Cleopatra, not her benevolent brother, had taken bread from starving Egyptians and shipped it to Rome. Demonstrators took to the streets and, emboldened by the outcry, Ptolemy's backers bribed the royal guards to move against their queen.

Cleopatra, who bankrolled a small army of spies, got wind of the palace coup and knew she was outnumbered. Gathering a few loyal retainers, she fled the capital before the blow fell and took refuge in the desert.

The world's richest refugee made her way east, using language skills and promises of wealth to recruit a mercenary army. In the deserts of the Sinai and southern Palestine, Cleopatra spent the winter and spring recruiting Jewish, Syrian, and Egyptian soldiers. As her retinue moved from one oasis to another, centurions drilled her recruits in desert camps, beating them into tactical formations and honing their skills with sword, spear, and shield.

By the summer of 48 BC, twenty-one-year-old Cleopatra commanded an army of twenty thousand fighting men. Enough, she calculated, to take back her kingdom. As Rome's civil war spilled into Greece, her army marched on Ptolemy's fortress at Pelusium, on the eastern corner of the Nile's delta. Strategically located between the sea and the desert, the red brick fortress commanded the eastern entrance to Egypt.

For the moment, Cleopatra's chief obstacle was neither Pelusium's brick walls nor its twenty-foot towers, but what lay behind them. Ptolemy's counselors had not been idle. Some twenty thousand legionnaires and mercenaries had enlisted in the king's service, and their army was led by the capable General Achillas. Time, moreover, was not Cleopatra's friend; unless she could fight her way past Achillas, her army would run out of food and water and wilt in the burning sands. Her royal ambitions—and probably her head—would be lopped off in short order.

In late August, as she weighed her next move, an unexpected visitor upended the plans of both Sibling-Loving Gods. A war galley carrying Pompey, his wife, and son Sextus dropped anchor off Pelusium with a message for King Ptolemy: Pompey the Great wished to meet the king of Egypt.

In Greece, Pompey's army had been soundly defeated by Julius Caesar at the Battle of Pharsalus, and word of the disaster had already reached the ears of Ptolemy's advisors. Caesar, Ptolemy knew, would not be far behind, and Ptolemy's viziers did some fast calculating to decide whom to support: Pompey, the family's longtime patron, or the newly ascendant Caesar.

The discussion wasn't a long one. Guided by the maxim, "Dead men don't bite," Ptolemy struck first and murdered Pompey as he came ashore. He had the dead Roman's head preserved—it would make a nice welcome gift for Caesar—and left the imperator's body to rot on Pelusium's beach.

Caesar followed, hot on Pompey's now-cold heels. Leading a squadron of twenty-three warships, he sailed to Alexandria with five thousand legionnaires. Gliding through the calm waters of the city's Great Harbor, Caesar's men stared in awe as they drifted past the legendary lighthouse, a 440-foot colossus that beckoned ships with its blazing, mirrored lamp. Conspicuous in his scarlet cloak, Caesar made his way through the crowds to the royal palace. He installed himself in its spacious guest quarters, then waited for King Ptolemy to return from Pelusium.

It was not only the fugitive Pompey that drew Caesar south. Egypt was a prime source of grain, which was a prime source of stability in uncertain times. In most years, the Nile's annual flood produced a surplus harvest that kept Roman bakers busy and Roman mobs quiet. Now that he was master of Rome, Caesar wanted no interruptions in the food chain.

He also had a legal matter to attend to. The Flute Player had named the City of Rome as executor of his will, and there was obviously a dispute among Ptolemy's heirs over the dead king's throne. As Rome's representative, Caesar would arbitrate the dispute. He summoned both warring siblings to Alexandria, where he would settle their quarrel.

Leaving his army under Achillas to block Cleopatra's return, Ptolemy scurried back to Alexandria. He presented the Roman general with Pompey's preserved head—the gift repelled the sentimentalist in Caesar—and Egypt's king and court played the role of well-mannered hosts.

While they fêted their distinguished guest, Ptolemy and his army kept Cleopatra well beyond Pelusium's walls. Behind the scenes, Ptolemy's courtiers stirred up anti-Roman feelings among the prickly Alexandrian populace, and soon ugly bands began milling about the royal quarter, demanding expulsion of the Roman barbarians. Caesar sensed an ugly, violent turn in Alexandria's mood.

As CAESAR STEWED in Alexandria's cauldron, Cleopatra remained locked out of her capital—and she could not afford to remain there for long. Everyone in Alexandria knew she had given aid to Pompey during his war against Caesar. And, it was rumored, she had given Pompey's handsome son more than just political support. Cleopatra could be certain Ptolemy's advisors were unraveling every compromising detail, true or not, and her chance to plead her case faded every day Caesar deliberated with her brother.

Ptolemy's army, however, was the immoveable roadblock. Cleopatra's force lacked the strength to fight past Achillas and his men, and if she asked her brother for safe conduct to Alexandria, as Caesar had commanded, she knew some regrettable accident would befall her on the way. The only question would be whether death would come quick and painless, or inconveniently slow.

Her life depended on finding another way in.

At the edge of the Sinai sands, Cleopatra, or one of her followers, hit on the idea of smuggling the queen into the capital. Seeing no other options, Cleopatra stowed aboard a tiny merchant boat that ferried her down the Delta's west fork to Alexandria.

Before the boat docked, Cleopatra folded her lithe frame into a large, nondescript sack, and a trusted servant, a Sicilian named Apollodorus, slung the sack over his shoulder. Casually traipsing into the palace, Apollodorus blended in with the hundreds of servants who kept the royal apartments running day after day. No one questioned the slave's business, or asked him where he was going.

He was going to Caesar's apartment.

Stepping out of the leather sack, adorned in gown and diadem, Cleopatra made one of history's most unforgettable entrances. Caesar, who appreciated good political theater, was intrigued by the *persona non grata* who had made a risky flank march through enemy lines. As the Greek historian Plutarch wrote, "This little trick of Cleopatra's, which showed her provocative impudence, is said to have been the first thing about her which captivated Caesar, and, as he grew to know her better, he was overcome by her charm."

Cleopatra worked her charm like a woman on a dagger's edge. She pleaded an eloquent case, and after hearing her side of the story, Caesar politely ordered the two siblings to make peace and rule as equals.

Cleopatra, with a sideways glance, resumed her place next to her brother. Ptolemy flew into an adolescent rage. He had paid for his kingdom with Pompey's head, and was furious with Caesar for siding with his sister. Plutarch claims the boy king ran into Alexandria's streets weeping bitter tears; that he tore the royal diadem from his forehead and threw it to the ground, wailing to one and all of his betrayal by an ungrateful sister and an uncouth Roman bully.

Ptolemy's lacrimal fit was no simple pubescent outburst. The presence of a Roman occupier—a Roman who had the gall to tell Alexandrians who their god-king would be—lit a tinder box under the citizenry. Anti-Roman riots, stoked by Pothinus, made it unsafe for Caesar's men to venture beyond the palace walls, and when General Achillas and his army returned from Pelusium, his troops laid siege to the palace complex. By autumn, Caesar found himself trapped in a bejeweled prison with four squabbling siblings: twenty-one-year-old Queen Cleopatra, her sixteen-year-old brother, King Ptolemy, their seventeen-year-old sister Arsinoe, and their twelve-year-old little brother, also named Ptolemy.

In the late fall, Arsinoe, as ambitious as her sister, escaped and rallied Alexandrian forces against Cleopatra and Caesar. The noose was tightening. With one less hostage to trade, Caesar sent messages by boat for help, fended off attacks, and waited for his chance to break out. Having no allies of her own, Cleopatra kept to Caesar's side, in the palace by day and in his bed at night.

Unlike Caesar, who dazzled Roman crowds with embellished reports of his exploits, Cleopatra left no surviving account of her role in Alexandria's palace defense. Though her experience in war could not compare to Caesar's, she had conversed, dined, and negotiated with generals for over a year. She recruited them, marched with them, paid them, and listened to them. She understood war at the political level, and she knew more than a little of the city's hidden nooks and crannies—including water sources and weak points Achillas was likely to attack. Because every battle is a child of topography, Cleopatra's insights likely contributed to the survival of Caesar and his men.

BY 47 BC, four months into the siege, the royal palace had become a theater of the surreal. Outside, howls of bloodthirsty mobs wafted through open windows on a harbor wind carrying the acrid smell of bonfires. Inside, Caesar and his generals fidgeted among Persian rugs, jewel-encrusted ivory chairs, and golden tableware with their Egyptian "hosts." The only friendly host was a strong-willed queen who was visibly pregnant with Caesar's child.

For now, Caesar could do little more than reinforce his lines to the Great Harbor and dispatch messenger ships demanding help. But time was running out, and winter forced him to take another calculated risk: Caesar sat down with Ptolemy and asked him to go outside the palace walls and persuade the Egyptian army to stand down. With tearful pledges of undying loyalty to Caesar, Ptolemy agreed, and Caesar released him.

What Cleopatra thought of Caesar's gambit is a mystery. Knowing her brother, she probably assumed Ptolemy would turn on Caesar as soon as he cleared Roman lines. On the other hand, if Ptolemy did defect, and if Caesar won, and if she survived the war—three very big *ifs*—Cleopatra would become sole ruler of Egypt. All she could do was wait for the gods to give her a signal.

Outside the palace, Ptolemy broke his word, assumed command of the Egyptian army, and renewed the assault. This turn of events would have been a fatal setback to Caesar and Cleopatra, but for a glint of hope that peeped over the winter horizon: Mithridates of Pergamon, an old ally of Caesar's, was marching from the east with a small but potent force.

In February, Mithridates captured Pelusium. Stung by the arrival of a second enemy, Ptolemy sent an advance column by barge up the Nile to fall on Mithridates before he and Caesar could join forces. Mithridates checked the Egyptian flying column, but was unable to push closer to Alexandria.

Seizing the opportunity, Caesar broke out of the palace and rushed his army toward Pelusium, leaving behind a small garrison to guard Cleopatra. He reached his ally's camp just ahead of Ptolemy, and in a two-day battle at the Nile, Caesar's professionals slaughtered the Egyptians. Ptolemy fled, and in the mass panic to escape, his overloaded royal barge capsized. Encumbered by ceremonial armor, the tantrum-throwing, Sibling-Loving God began his descent into the afterlife at the Nile's muddy bottom.

On Caesar's return, Cleopatra wined and dined the master of the Mediterranean. She showered him with gifts of immense value—handy, since Caesar had racked up crushing war debts back home—and tantalized the childless general with the prospect of a son and heir. Cleopatra's gratitude, her need for Rome's protection, and shared bonds of parenthood and wartime danger entwined her fortunes with Caesar's.

Before Caesar left Alexandria to return to Rome, he ensured that Cleopatra's hold over Egypt was unbreakable. He ordered three legions to remain in Alexandria as her home guard, then packed off her rebellious sister Arsinoe as one of his many war trophies. In chains, the princess would entertain the city's jeering crowds when Caesar held his triumphal procession down Rome's Via Sacra.

With Ptolemy dead, Cleopatra needed a figurehead to rule Egypt with her. Though incest was not common in Hellenistic culture, Alexandrian crowds shared the old Egyptian fondness for wedded siblings. As a sop to popular opinion, Caesar and Cleopatra placed the younger Ptolemy on the tandem throne. They figured the thirteen-year-old boy wouldn't dare cross his twenty-two-year-old big sister: a widow, expectant mother, war veteran, and mistress to the most powerful man in the world. Cleopatra married her brother in a proper Egyptian ceremony conforming to the old rites, then ignored him.*

With a free hand to run Egypt as she pleased, the heavily pregnant Cleopatra took a broom to the old government. First came the expected rounds of purges, confiscations, executions, and demotions of ministers whose loyalty during the war had been found wanting. Alexandrian priests, falling over themselves to prove their

---

* King Ptolemy XIV kept his nose out of state business and let his sister run the country as she saw fit. Discretion didn't save him, however, for Cleopatra had him murdered three years later to clear the way for her son. It isn't always good to be the king.

devotion to their beloved queen, double-checked temple inscriptions to ensure that they correctly and conspicuously emphasized Cleopatra's identity as the goddess Isis, whose word was divine law. Before long, every man, woman, and child in Alexandria knew who ruled Egypt.

The civil wars had been disastrous for the economy, but a bumper harvest and robust trade soon allowed Cleopatra to replenish the royal treasury. Grain, oil, glass, textiles, wine, and papyrus production reached prewar levels. Caravans from the east flowed into Egypt, their sacks bulging with goods sold in Alexandria's markets and shipped throughout the world. And everything brought into the city was subject to an import duty that, once the usual graft and bribery charges were deducted, ended up in Cleopatra's treasury.

Cleopatra's capital was, for the moment, a happy city that resumed its normal, bustling, rambunctious life. Priests proselytized, burglars burglarized, bureaucrats scrutinized, and the city's main thoroughfare, the Canopic Way, teemed with merchants, clerks, peasants, whores, teamsters, and ordinary folk who, when they thought about it, could not fail to be awestruck by the city's grandeur.

For a blissful moment, Cleopatra basked in the favor of the gods.

❖   ❖   ❖

ON JUNE 10, 47 BC, ten months after his arrival, Caesar left Egypt. On his way home, he put down a rebellion by the king of Pontus—adding another *vici* to his *veni* and *vidi*—and lingered in Rome long enough to clean up a mess left by his administratively challenged tribune Marc Antony. Marching to Spain, he crushed the last of the republican opposition at Munda and became the undisputed master of an empire stretching from the Atlantic Ocean to the Persian deserts.

The mutual attraction of Cleopatra's gold and Caesar's power was irresistible. With Cleopatra, Caesar had the money to build temples, pay his war debts, and spread wealth around Rome. And as long as Caesar held power, Cleopatra could rest easily.

By the next summer, Cleopatra had put her house in sufficient order to indulge herself an extended vacation to Rome. In the Mediterranean's wealth-obsessed capital, the richest woman in the world would see her lover again.

She arrived in Rome as a foreign queen, not Caesar's paramour, so protocol had to be observed. The conservative Roman crowd could be fickle and brutal, so she was careful not to overplay her personal relationship with the dictator. Keeping a low profile—by Cleopatra's standards, at least—she probably watched Caesar's triumphal processions that fall from a discreet distance. Atop a nearby roof, she would have been able to see trains of loot, exotic animals, soldiers, prisoners, more soldiers, more loot, and finally, Caesar himself, wind their way down Rome's streets to the Forum.

The Senate, tumbling over itself to curry favor with Caesar, had voted him an unprecedented four triumphs, one each for his victories over the Gauls, the Egyptians, Pontus, and the Numidians. The crowd-pleasing end to a triumphal parade was to cart the captured enemy leader through the streets in chains and lead him down a narrow stairway to the Tullianum, a small, dark cell where an executioner waited with a garrote.*

Cleopatra had reason to pay special attention to the parade dedicated to Caesar's Egyptian campaign. Wheeled carts ostensibly carrying captured war booty would have been stocked with Cleopatra's gifts to Caesar as proof of his military success. Had she a good vantage point, she also would have seen her sister Arsinoe, laden in chains, crying hysterically as her crude prison wagon rumbled past the jeering throng.†

She spent the winter of 45 BC in one of Caesar's elegant homes on the Tiber River's west side. She stayed close to Caesar, though not close enough to cause trouble with either his wife or the selectively moralistic Roman crowd. Caesar kept his personal and official intercourse with Cleopatra discreet—by Caesar's standards, at least—although he made an eyebrow-raising gesture by erecting a life-sized statue of the Egyptian queen in the temple dedicated to Venus, his family's patron goddess.

When Caesar sent Cleopatra home in the spring of 45 BC, he showered her with gifts and granted her the right to bestow his name on her son, now called Caesarion. She returned in the fall to see him off for his military campaign for the spring of 44 BC, when he would leave to subdue the Parthians in the east. That winter she became pregnant again, probably with Caesar's child. Life, for all its hazards, was a beautiful dream for the twenty-five-year-old queen.

---

* Caesar's Numidian triumph was really for his victory over Roman republicans at Thapsus. But a general was only entitled to a triumph for defeating a foreign army, not fellow Romans, and Caesar was not one to rub his former enemies' noses in defeat. So, he changed the identity of the vanquished republicans to Numidians and added their six-year-old ruler, King Juba II, to his procession.

† Arsinoe was, at least, spared a visit to the Tullianum; Caesar packed her off to Ephesus, in Greece, to live out her days at the Temple of Artemis.

The Republican War

Though Egypt had a long history of invading its neighbors, Cleopatra was content to follow Rome's lead in purely military matters. After all, kingdoms like Parthia, Pontus, and Rome produced much better fighting forces than the Ptolemies did. More rapacious than business-minded, those nations didn't mind converting wealth-producing peasants into wealth-consuming soldiers. Cleopatra did.

As quartermaster, armorer, and financier, Egypt had no equal. If, as Cicero quipped, the sinews of war are made of money, then Rome's wars required plenty of Egyptian sinews. Caesar's legionnaires would do the bloody work, while Cleopatra's merchants and builders became the arsenal of autocracy.

But the cornerstone of Cleopatra's foreign policy shattered in March of 44 BC, when a cabal of republicans set upon Caesar during a Senate meeting. Dagger blades plunged into the dictator's chest, neck, face, and legs twenty-three times. As red blooms opened across his toga, Caesar slumped to the slippery floor. The conspirators, their hands sticky with Caesar's blood, fled the theater, and an ominous quiet settled over Rome.

Marcus Antonius, Caesar's second-in-command, wrapped himself in a slave's tunic, retreated to his home and locked his doors. After he recovered from his shock, he rallied the city's mob and drove the conspirators from the city. Then he and Caesar's nephew, Gaius Octavius, gathered forces to avenge the great man's murder. Rome was plunged into another civil war.

Thoroughly shaken by her lover's assassination, Cleopatra fled by ship to Egypt, where she assessed Rome's badly torn web. Egypt remained Rome's ally, but what "Rome" meant was open to interpretation. Cleopatra had no strong ties to Antony, Octavian, or the conspirators, and aligning herself with the wrong faction could prove fatal. To survive the next act, she would have to pick the side that would remain standing when the swords were sheathed.

As Antony and Octavian hunted down the republicans, news from Greece told Cleopatra of a family problem that had cropped up in her absence from Alexandria. Her sister Arsinoe had assembled a coterie of Greek, Roman, Cypriot, and Egyptian backers at Ephesus. From the steps of the Temple of Artemis, Arsinoe declared herself queen of Egypt and announced that once she removed Cleopatra, she and their youngest brother, Ptolemy XIV, would rule Egypt as the latest pair of Sibling-Loving Gods.

To dissuade Arsinoe from moving back into the family palace, Cleopatra sent little brother into the next life and proclaimed her son, Caesarion, king of Egypt and

"Caesar, Father-loving, Mother-loving God." In temples, coins, and monuments, she had artisans portray her as queen and mother of Caesarion, reminding everyone who ruled Egypt.

That took care of family succession, but Arsinoe remained a long-term threat, and Rome's civil war was becoming hazardous to bystanders. Before the first courier ship rowed into Alexandria's harbor, Cleopatra knew every warring faction in Italy would call on her for financial and military assistance. The only questions were how much each would-be Caesar might demand, and whether aiding any of them would be a fatal mistake.

Loyal to the Caesarian side, Cleopatra first threw her support to Publius Cornelius Dolabella, an experienced naval commander and one of Caesar's favorites. Liberal with money but tightfisted with power, she told Dolabella her help would come at a price: Dolabella must promise that the Roman government would confirm her three-year-old son Caesarion as the rightful king of Egypt. Dolabella readily agreed, and Cleopatra sent him the three legions Caesar had left in Egypt, along with a fleet to carry the army against Gaius Cassius Longinus, one of Caesar's murderers.

As a reluctant Cleopatra stepped onto this new game board, disaster struck: A fleet of Cassius's warships captured Dolabella's navy. Caesar's Alexandrian legions defected to the republican side, and a forlorn Dolabella was soon back in Egypt begging for more assistance.

While Dolabella was making his pitch to the queen for a new fleet and army, a courier from the bloodthirsty Cassius arrived with a competing request for military aid—as a friend of Rome, of course. Repelled by the idea of throwing in with her lover's murderers, Cleopatra put off Cassius's emissary with excuse after excuse. Cassius eventually took her demurrer as a refusal and added the Egyptian queen to the list of Caesarians he would take care of in due course.

Unfortunately for Cleopatra, her naval commander on Cyprus defected and carried a second Egyptian fleet over to Cassius. With growing desperation, Cleopatra began building a third fleet for Dolabella, but it would never sail under his flag: Cassius caught up with him in Syria and destroyed his small army. The forlorn general sidestepped a slow, degrading death by ordering one of his own soldiers to kill him.

His appetite whetted, Cassius now set his sights on Egypt. Furious over Cleopatra's aid to his enemy, the conqueror of Syria prepared to march twelve veteran legions into Egypt. Horrified, Cleopatra scraped together a home defense and braced for the worst.

As Cassius was about to invade Egypt, Antony and Octavian landed in Greece and marched against a republican army under Marcus Junius Brutus, an ally of Cassius. Brutus sent word to Cassius, who dropped his plans to invade Egypt and ferried his army to Greece to meet the threat.

Seizing her chance to join forces with the Caesarians, Cleopatra readied another fleet. She weighed anchor from Alexandria with her navy, but a Mediterranean storm wrecked a portion of her fleet and forced a frustrated Cleopatra to return home.

In Greece, the gods smiled on Antony and Octavian, who destroyed the republicans at Philippi and divided the Roman world as their spoil. Antony took everything east of Italy, which included Greece, Egypt, and the Middle East, while Octavian took Italy and everything to the west. Egypt had a new Roman master.

Antony

Marcus Antonius had ridden to power on superheated winds of conquest, luck, and Caesar's patronage. Devilishly handsome, athletic and charismatic, at age forty-two Antony played as hard as he worked. He had fought under Pompey in Egypt, and under Caesar in Gaul, Italy, and Greece. He reveled in drinking, joking, and feasting much as in making love or war.

Noises from Antony's banquet halls and bedchambers have echoed through the ages. A protean man of protean times, Antony kept company with fools and sages, senators and sergeants, proper women and loose women—though he preferred the loose ones. The Jewish historian Josephus wrote that Antony "indulged himself in such pleasures as his power allowed him," and that power gave him plenty to indulge. His empire now included Egypt's ample resources, its fabulous wealth, and Cleopatra.

Antony intended to enjoy all three.

After Philippi, Antony marched his legions to Asia Minor. As with other eastern rulers, he summoned Cleopatra to set her straight on the East's new reality.

From her palace at Alexandria, Cleopatra knew she would be called to account for her failure to support the Caesarians during the recent civil war. But she had no intention of falling at Antony's feet and groveling for his forgiveness. She ignored his summons for six months as Antony busied himself reorganizing his kingdoms. Only after making clear that she would come on her own schedule did Cleopatra send word that she would meet him in Tarsus, in southwestern Turkey.

As a girl, Cleopatra had been raised amid the opulence of the Alexandrian court. Ornamental beauty, both physical and intellectual, was second nature to her. It was something she possessed and something every Roman despot desired. Watching triumphal parades snake down Rome's Via Sacra, she had witnessed the Italian love of pageantry, and she knew something of Antony's big Italian heart. He was an impulsive rogue who could be carried away with wine, beauty, or splendor.

She intended to carry him away with all three.

To the hypnotic thump of drums and the splash of oars, the line of Egyptian barges plodded up the Cydnus River toward Tarsus. From the lead barges billowed clouds of incense. Streams of flute and harp music mixed with dazzling imagery that wafted over grassy river banks and into the eyes, ears, and minds of wide-eyed villagers. Maidens clothed as sea nymphs adorned rigging and rudder, and Cleopatra's royal barge boasted a gilded stern and purple sails, while oars plated in silver undulated to the music.

In the guise of Venus, Cleopatra reclined on a divan under a canopy of gold lamé as young boys, costumed as cherubs, fanned their goddess. When her boat tied up to the harbor at Tarsus, attendants announced to the star-struck crowd that Venus had come "to revel with Bacchus for the good of Asia."

In the summer of 41 BC, Venus reveled on a scale that stunned Bacchus and his men. For the first banquet, her servants set up twelve rooms with richly upholstered couches. On table after table they heaped food on golden plates and filled gem-encrusted goblets with wine. Under a spiderweb of lights strung from tree branches, Antony and his guests gorged themselves until the early morning hours. When stomachs bloated and heads drooped, the rich tapestries, goblets, couches, and curtains were packed up and sent home with Antony and his tottering lieutenants as the merry queen's gifts.

Cleopatra's second banquet required Antony to wade calf-deep through rose petals into a banquet hall set in even greater splendor. Again, his stuffed, hung-over subordinates carted off the furnishings, this time with complimentary litter bearers and horses, whose silver-trimmed tack were gifts from Egypt's queen.

Lavish banquets followed, each more outlandish than those before, and the result was exactly what Cleopatra had planned. Within a few weeks Antony's heart and mind—the two rarely parted company—were hers.

Between cycles of indulgence and recovery, the two leaders found time to discuss practical matters of statecraft, the first being Cleopatra's conduct during the late unpleasantness. Cleopatra explained that she had not been culpable for the defection of Dolabella's legions or the loss of her fleet. She had done what she could, but events turned against her.

Accepting Cleopatra's alibi, Antony forgave her. He had his own reasons to accept Cleopatra as his ally, beyond his ever-present lust and greed. As his mentor

Caesar had once remarked, "There are two things that create, protect, and increase sovereignty—soldiers and money—and these two are dependent on each other. In case either were lacking, the other would be overthrown." Like Caesar, Antony had the soldiers. But Cleopatra had the money.

Cleopatra had her own reasons for supporting Antony. One was her troublesome younger sister, Arsinoe, who was noisily plotting a coup from Ephesus. With Caesar gone, Cleopatra needed to put Arsinoe in her place. A very quiet place.

Antony cut this particular Gordian knot in the old Roman manner. He sent an assassination squad to Ephesus, which hacked down Arsinoe on the temple's steps. Problem solved.

The second knot, Octavian, was not so easily sliced. Caesar's nephew had been named the great man's heir in his will, but his seat in the Senate would never be comfortable while Caesar's purported son, Caesarion, sat on a golden throne in Alexandria—especially when Antony, the "new Dionysus," sat next to him and Venus. The two conquerors had an uneasy chemistry, better suited to rivals than allies, and each could foresee things going badly for everyone should a quarrel arise between them.

In Antony's case, that trouble might easily begin with a woman. Or two.

But that was in the distant future. The present promised Antony and Cleopatra only bliss, and the next several months found the pair inseparable. They indulged their intellectual desires through the afternoon, and other desires from dusk until dawn. Shuttling between lectures at Alexandria's university and raucous drinking games in seedy taverns, the East's premier power couple basked in her wealth and his might.

Yet as the shouts, laughter, and clink of goblets echoed off palace walls, an old threat loomed on the eastern horizon. Parthia, which Caesar had intended to invade at the time of his assassination, had mustered formidable armies and was threatening Syria, Judea, and Asia Minor—regions whose trade revenues kept Cleopatra's treasury filled. Now pregnant by Antony, Cleopatra encouraged her Dionysus to draw his sword against the Parthians. A successful campaign would eliminate a threat to Egypt and raise his standing with the Roman public, which tended to forget leaders during long absences from the seat of government.

As spring broke in the year 40 BC, Cleopatra gave birth to twins: a baby girl named Cleopatra Selene, her "Moon," and Alexander Helios, her "Sun." The cries and laughter of the newborns mingled with the voice of six-year-old Caesarion and rang through palace hallways as wet nurses, tutors, and handmaids attended to them.

That same year, Antony sailed back to Rome to extend his peace treaty with Octavian to the year 33 BC. They sealed the pact with Antony's marriage to Octavian's sister Octavia, and Octavia fulfilled her matronly duties by giving Antony a daughter the following year.

Yet the pull of his Egyptian mistress never left Antony, and after a three-year absence, he left Italy to rejoin Cleopatra at the Syrian city of Antioch, where the twin aphrodisiacs of power and nostalgia brought their passion to new heights. So fervent had Antony's ardor for Cleopatra grown that he married her in the ancient city, and their faces began appearing together on Egyptian coins jingling in the purses of merchantmen throughout the Mediterranean world. It wasn't long before those coins turned up in Rome.

During their reign as Dionysus and Isis, Antony and Cleopatra lived in a dream-like procession of parties and banquets. They enjoyed absolute power and lived in a palace of besotted happiness where nothing could touch them. God and goddess, they had each other. Everything, it seemed, lay within their grasp.

But the snapping wolf of Parthia could not be held forever at arm's length, even if that arm belonged to the richest woman in the world. After gentle prodding by Cleopatra, in 37 BC Antony launched his long-awaited campaign to bring the Parthians to heel. He marched east with an army of 100,000 men, whose cost was underwritten by Cleopatra.

Fertile as the Nile valley, Cleopatra was pregnant with her fourth child when Antony left for his Parthian war. Hot and uncomfortable, yet willing to share some of the journey's hardships, she accompanied her husband east as far as the Euphrates River.

Seeing him off, the expecting queen waddled back to Egypt by way of Damascus and Jericho, where she settled trade and taxation questions in a heavy-handed manner with Judea's tetrarch Herod and other local strongmen. The economic and political deals she brokered garnered new revenues for the Egyptian treasury, and her mission was a spectacular success.

Antony's was a disaster. He marched through Armenia and made his way as far as Media, sending back word of his dramatic victories. Cleopatra knew better. Through her network of spies, servants, and diplomatic connections, she learned that Antony's army had gained no strategic objectives and lost its baggage train, its artillery, and a tenth of its soldiers.

Antony's battered army retreated from Media, harassed at every step by Parthian cavalry. Arrows, thirst, cold, desert heat, poisonous vegetation, and diseases cut huge swaths through his legions. Parched soldiers dropped like desert flies, their equipment left for nomadic scavengers, their bones left for the carrion eaters that roamed the wastelands.

Approaching the Syrian coast with an army of scarecrows, Antony sent his lover an urgent request for food, supplies, and winter clothing. With her usual efficiency, Cleopatra assembled a relief force and sailed through winter storms to save her husband. Supplies were hastily distributed among Antony's famished legions, and the couple returned to Alexandria to lick their wounds.

Another Civil War

While Antony recovered from his Parthian fiasco, Octavian baited a political trap. He sent his sister Octavia, Antony's Roman wife, to bring Antony 2,000 well-armed veterans, along with supplies, money, and food. When she reached Greece, Octavia bade Antony to let her come see him.

Octavian's gesture, well-publicized in Rome, tossed Antony onto the horns of a dilemma. The previous year Octavian had promised Antony 20,000 troops to fight the Parthians, and Antony had no intention of letting Octavian satisfy his debt at ten percent of the agreed price. But refusing Octavian's offer would have been seen as a slap in the face, potentially pitting himself against Caesar's heir and Rome itself.

Cleopatra didn't want Octavia anywhere near Antony. The sister of Antony's rival was likely prettier than Cleopatra—something no prudent wife could ignore with a man of Antony's tastes. At age thirty-five, Cleopatra was in late middle age by ancient standards. Her body had been stretched by five pregnancies, and she was no longer the lithe enchantress who stepped out of a peasant's sack to beguile Caesar.*

But she still had wealth. Immense wealth. And the world's best-educated woman was at her persuasive best when pleading her case in person. Cleopatra had been a close observer of human nature since childhood, and she knew the way to a man like Antony was not through his mind, or even through his loins. It was through his heart. So she wept, cajoled through intermediaries, and shut herself in her room, refusing to eat. She presented a pitiful sight that left her lover wounded.

Her performance, genuine or not, worked. She drew Antony's wayward heart from his Roman wife and carried it back to the bosom of his Isis. Antony declined to meet Octavia, pleading the needs of a second Parthian campaign he was preparing. As expected, Octavian spun the incident in a way calculated to to infuriate senators and nobles. Octavia—poor, rejected Octavia—had been cast aside, along with Octavian's generous offer to help a brother Roman. Wrapping himself in a toga

---

* During the winter of 44, as Rome's guest, Cleopatra became pregnant with her second child, but she miscarried shortly after Caesar's assassination.

of humiliation, Octavian drummed up local sentiment against the drunken whore-monger who had spurned his noble Roman wife and taken a barbarian harlot.

If humiliating Octavia displeased the Roman public, what Antony did next appalled even his supporters. In late 34, seated on thrones of gold and surrounded by courtiers and dignitaries in Alexandria's huge gymnasium, Antony and Cleopatra announced the distribution of new lands and titles to their children. First, they declared Caesarion, now thirteen years old, "King of Kings" and Cleopatra's official royal consort. Alexander Helios, also named King of Kings, was given the still-unconquered lands of Armenia, Media, and Parthia. Two-year-old Ptolemy Philadelphus received the Near Eastern kingdoms of Phoenicia, Syria, and Cilicia, while their daughter, Cleopatra Selene, received Cyrene. Cleopatra, Antony announced, would bear the ranking title "Queen of Kings," and he had Roman coins struck with his lover's likeness. For the first time in Rome's xenophobic history, a foreigner's face appeared on Roman currency.

The Donations of Alexandria, as they were known, ruptured the tense but work-able framework that held the fragile peace. In letters criss-crossing the Mediterra-nean, Antony and Octavian hurled insults and accusations at each other. Their letters were selectively published by friends in Rome, and nobles reluctantly began to choose sides—most professing their loyalty to the man in charge of Rome's vast western lands. When Antony's peace treaty with Octavian expired on the last day of 33 BC, neither man made a move to extend it. Instead, they drew swords.

OCTAVIAN DECLARED WAR against Cleopatra's Egypt, and the Senate voted to strip Antony of his consular titles, depriving him of legal authority to command troops. In response, Antony and Cleopatra set up a military base at Patras, a harbor town on Greece's Gulf of Corinth. They bivouacked the ragged remnants of the Parthian expedition, and supplemented their army with levies from Antony's client kingdoms. Cleopatra, whose shipyards were never idle, supplied a quarter of Antony's eight hundred ships, and she kept the army functioning with an immense payroll and steady stream of provisions to feed 75,000 legionnaires, 25,000 auxiliary troops, and 12,000 cavalry troopers.

Octavian, however, got the jump on Antony at sea. In March of 31 his naval commander, Marcus Agrippa, launched a lightning raid against Antony's squadron guarding the Peloponnese. Destroying the detachment, he ruptured Cleopatra's sup-ply lines running back to Egypt. As Agrippa's fleet captured one port after another along the Greek coast, Cleopatra's men were forced to unload their ships in harbors many miles from camp and haul food, money, weapons, and supplies by oxcart on a long, slow journey.

Supreme at sea, Agrippa's squadrons began ferrying troops from Italy to northwestern Greece. Soon Octavian and 80,000 well-fed legionnaires were fortifying a bridgehead on Greek soil. From there, they moved down the coast for a decisive battle.

Hoping Octavian would fight on unfavorable ground, Antony drew his forces into a defensive perimeter. He concentrated his five hundred warships inside the Gulf of Ambracia, a lake with a narrow opening to the sea. He set up catapults and missile-throwing artillery at the narrow point of the gulf's entrance, and consolidated his land forces at Actium, a little promontory on the south side of the gulf's mouth.

For weeks they sat facing each other, a shark and a tiger. Octavian controlled the sea, while Antony sat untouchable on land. But with the battlefield surrounded by water, time favored the shark. Antony's supplies dwindled as Agrippa's warships clamped a tight blockade on the Greek coast, and food stocks began running low.

Every cut in rations, every week of inactivity, every month of rain, heat, dysentery, and malaria bred disquiet among Antony's men. Morale plummeted, and Eastern princes began deserting, some coming over to Octavian, some merely fleeing a sinking ship. Antony had a minor king tortured to death for attempting to desert, but the degrading example did not dissuade everyone. In a shattering personal blow, Antony's close friend and ally, Gnaeus Domitius Ahenobarbus, reluctantly joined Octavian.

Antony kept up a show of confidence. A Roman historian recorded him telling his men, "You yourselves are the kind of soldiers that could win even without a good leader . . . and I am the kind of leader that could prevail even with poor soldiers." But Antony and Cleopatra were whistling past the necropolis. As weeks passed and their strength waned, the pair seemed oblivious to time's corrosive nature.

What was Cleopatra doing as the ground was rumbling beneath her feet?

Cleopatra was a political strategist, financier, and manager of generals, but no tactician. Any unease she felt would never impel a break with her lover. She trusted Antony to manage the campaign, and if they were flying too close to the sun, they would fly together. She was a gambler. She and Caesar had been in a far worse fix in Alexandria, and back then the old Caesarian luck held for them both. Perhaps it would hold for Antony, too.

Romans advising Antony saw a negotiated solution as the best way to get home with their heads attached. Octavian had declared war on Egypt, not Antony. There was no reason Antony should risk everything for one province—even a province as important as Egypt—much less a foreign woman. The wise move would be to sacrifice the queen to save the king.

The generals added a postscript: If Antony disregarded their advice and fought Octavian, he should at least send Cleopatra home. A woman in any military camp was an inherent distraction. It was unmanly and un-Romanly for a commander to give a woman a voice in military affairs, be she a mistress, wife, queen, even a goddess.

Cleopatra knew the price of a negotiated peace would be her head, and after all these years she was reluctant to part with it. Nor would she willingly surrender the dynasty she had built on wealth, intelligence, luck, perseverance, and fertility. Seeing in her lover a good-hearted man who lacked the resolution to resist his advisors, she wielded every weapon in her emotional arsenal to persuade Antony to stand with her.

In the end, he refused to send Cleopatra away. Antony had his flaws, but disloyalty was not one of them. Cleopatra had stood by him, bore his children, rescued him from the Parthians, made him a god. He trusted her judgment, and needed her ships, money, and supplies. They would defeat Octavian together.

The Battle of Actium

In late August, Antony held a war council and announced a new strategy: The army would move north, into the mountains of Thrace and Macedonia, where he would maneuver Octavian into a land battle. On open ground, Antony's army would crush Octavian's force before moving against Rome.

Strategically, Antony's plan made no sense. A land campaign in northern Greece wouldn't dent Octavian's base in Italy, and their undersupplied army would hemorrhage soldiers as it attempted a difficult march through the sparse Macedonian hills.

Cleopatra, probably among others, argued that a land battle was the wrong approach. Moving north would sacrifice Antony's powerful fleet, as well as the immense treasure she had shipped to Actium. In Octavian's hands, that treasure would buy yet another army, leaving Antony more outnumbered than ever.

Groping for the least of several evils, Antony reluctantly agreed with Cleopatra. He would have to fight Agrippa at sea. If the battle turned against him, he would sail back to Egypt and prepare for a second campaign with legions he had left in Cyrene, Egypt, and Syria.

Antony and Cleopatra put their faith in the heavy war galley, improved versions of the ships Artemisia commanded four centuries earlier. Antony's were larger than

Octavian's, and they packed a harder punch. In addition to their bronze rams, the largest in Antony's fleet were floating castles boasting towers several stories high and bristling with artillery, archers, and swordsmen.

Leaving the bulk of his army ashore, Antony embarked around 20,000 legionnaires, 2,000 archers, and 40,000 rowers in 180 large galleys. Lacking crews to man the rest of his fleet, he ordered eighty of Cleopatra's ships dragged ashore and had them burned to keep them out of Octavian's hands.

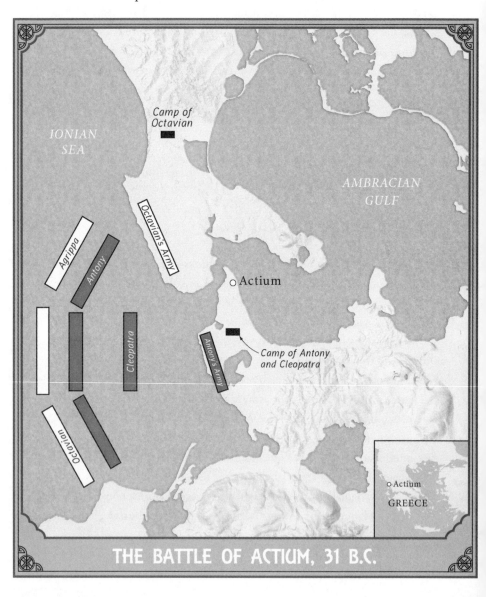

THE BATTLE OF ACTIUM, 31 B.C.

Just up the Greek coast, Octavian's fleet awaited orders to attack. Though his ships were smaller than Antony's, Octavian had more of them. Unlike Antony's galleys, which could be provisioned for a long cruise, Admiral Agrippa's fighting ships were light and maneuverable. They also carried more legionnaires, about 30,000 in all.

Antony kept his plans from his officers until shortly before the moment of launch. Several front-line captains, preparing for the final battle, were startled to receive orders to raise masts and mount sails. Galleys never used sails in battle, for sail and rigging got in the way of arrows and reduced maneuverability in a fight. Sails were for voyages too long for the stamina of rowers.

If Antony wanted masts and sails, it meant his goal was not to destroy the enemy. He was breaking for home.

As Antony's fleet weighed anchor, Agrippa moved his warships into a blocking position outside the gulf's narrow mouth. Octavian took station on the fleet's right, probably dressed in battle armor and an imperator's red cape. Agrippa took the left squadron, the flank most likely to encounter Antony.

Antony moved up on his fleet's right in a small, fast dispatch boat, which would allow him to dash among squadrons and issue commands as the battle shifted. His main squadron, around 120 ships, spread out opposite Agrippa. Cleopatra took her station with the reserve squadron in the rear. Her flagship, the ten-deck galley *Antonia*, carried the army's payroll and any other treasures her men could safely cram into the ship's hold.

From dawn until noon the fleets watched each other, neither side moving. To escape under sail, Antony knew he would have to time his attack to coincide with the afternoon breeze, then catch a puff of northerly wind. If the battle turned against him, his fighting ships would hold the escape hatch open long enough for Cleopatra and their remaining galleys to fly south to open waters. To Egypt.

As the sun reached its zenith, Antony launched his attack. Agrippa's ships showered the Antonians with artillery and arrows, then rammed or moved alongside to board and slay with swords at close range. Antony's outnumbered ships spread their line thin to keep from being outflanked to the north, but Agrippa's agile galleys converged on them like barracudas, and Antony's line crumpled.

While the battle raged, Cleopatra, watching from *Antonia*'s prow, ordered her squadron to weigh anchor and make for Egypt. Her galleys charged through the center, wind and oars propelling them fast enough to smash anything in their path. As Antony's soldiers on shore watched in disbelief, their leader followed Cleopatra in his small command boat, leading a few galleys that had managed to tear themselves loose from Agrippa's closing jaws.

Bereft of their leader, resistance among the Antonians collapsed, first at sea, then on land. As the mighty fleet of Antony and Cleopatra died off the coast of Greece, its general and queen fled over the silvery sea.

❖   ❖   ❖

THE SUN ROSE AND SET over the massive *Antonia* as she plodded back to Alexandria. Antony, who had come aboard, barely noticed. For days following the disaster at Actium, Cleopatra's Bacchus wallowed in depression. He sat in the bow of the flagship, staring into the horizon, seeing nothing, doing nothing as Cleopatra pleaded with him to eat, drink, and take heart.

Take heart? Why should he? His fleet was gone. His army was gone. His reputation was in tatters, and he could picture Octavian bribing his own legions to turn against him. He wouldn't blame them if they did.

With her lover submerged in self-pity, Cleopatra saw to Egypt's defenses. As soon as they dropped anchor in Alexandria, she lit into the palace and purged the capital of suspected traitors. She confiscated estates, seized temple treasures, and sent riders with letters to any kings of the East who might still support Antony. As insurance against another disaster, she also transported a squadron of galleys overland to the Gulf of Suez with secret orders to take her to India if Egypt were overrun.*

She also secretly opened negotiations with Octavian, in hopes of keeping the one thing most precious to her: her dynasty.

As a young woman, Cleopatra had risked her life to secure her claim to the Egyptian throne. Now she was prepared to give her life, if necessary, to preserve the legacy she had built. The one thing the Queen of Kings would never surrender was the dynastic birthright of Caesarion, Alexander Helios, Cleopatra Selene, and little Ptolemy. After that, nearly anything was negotiable.

Antony and Cleopatra agreed that Antony should go to Cyrene, pick up his legions there, and form them into the core of a new army. But when he learned that those legions had defected to Octavian, he slumped into another bout of melancholy. His friends stopped him from committing suicide, but Alexandria became Antony's black cave of depression. Nearly friendless, bereft of hope, he shut out the world, bidding only pity to crawl up beside him and keep him company.

---

* The Nabateans of the Sinai, never friends of the Ptolemies, set upon Cleopatra's laborers and burned her ships, cutting off this escape route.

As her world crumbled, Cleopatra flailed about for a solution. But events were spinning out of even a goddess's control. Her efforts to enlist Herod's Jews and Media's horsemen came to nothing. Antioch defected. Damascus defected. One by one, Antony's client kingdoms went over to Octavian, and the world grew eerily quiet. Cleopatra and her lover were truly alone.

The dark shadow that had followed them for so long finally took form in the early summer of 30 BC, when Octavian's massive army reached Pelusium, the place where Cleopatra's journey into legend had begun seventeen years earlier. Now, she knew, her journey was nearing its end.

FOLLOWING ACTIUM, Cleopatra and Octavian exchanged private letters in an attempt to settle their differences. Though Octavian had declared war against Egypt, both recognized that Octavian's real fight was with Antony, and Cleopatra hoped to broker a settlement between the Romans. Octavian informed Cleopatra that the price of peace was Antony's head.

Just as Antony had refused to betray Cleopatra in Greece, Cleopatra remained true to her crestfallen king. Besides, she had no reason to think Octavian would keep any promises he made to her. Negotiations broke down, and Octavian marched his army to Alexandria.

While Antony had nothing left to bargain with, save his own death, Cleopatra found one last card to play. Over the winter, she had a mausoleum built for herself. As Octavian's army approached, she ordered her servants to move gemstones, gold, inlaid furniture, rich tapestries, robes, spices, incense, pearls, and jewelry into the mausoleum and pile them atop an immense mound of pitch and kindling. If Octavian forced Cleopatra to die, her funeral pyre would be the most expensive blaze in history. And she knew Octavian, saddled with war debts, could not afford to let that happen.

Cleopatra barricaded herself in the mausoleum and had the massive doors fixed with iron bars and pins. Surrounded by a few loyal servants, knowing the end could not be long, she sent Antony a message that she was dead. He would be free to fight, flee, or take his own course without waiting for her.

Yet without Cleopatra, Antony had nothing to live for. He resolved to die by his own hand in the manner of great Roman imperators . . . which is to say, he ordered a slave to do the job for him.

Even that plan failed. His faithful servant instead killed himself, an example to which a resigned Antony paid tribute as he unfastened his breastplate. Unsheathing his gladius, Antony pressed the point under his rib cage and pulled the blade home, slicing through muscle and stomach in an upward motion. But he angled the cutting edge too low, and the blade missed his heart and lungs. Falling to his knees in agony, blood spreading over his legs, he begged his few remaining friends to end his suffering.

They too deserted him.

The outcry his botched suicide aroused brought Cleopatra to an opening in the mausoleum's upper section. Bursting into tears as her gore-smeared lover was carried to her tomb, Cleopatra called for her ladies to help her haul him to her window on construction ropes. As Plutarch wrote,

> *Never was there a more piteous sight. Smeared with blood and struggling with death he was drawn up, stretching out his hands to her even as he dangled in the air. For the task was not an easy one for women, and scarcely could Cleopatra, with clinging hands and strained face, pull up the rope, while those below called out encouragement to her and shared her agony.*

Cleopatra, bold political calculator, heir to a kingdom and founder of a dynasty, melted into grief. She smeared Antony's blood on herself, tore her clothes, and clawed her cheeks in anguish. She wept over her dying lover, who quietly asked her not to pity him. He had lived a full life, he said. He had only one request: a last drink of wine.

Cleopatra nodded, and one of her servants brought Antony a chalice to ease his way into the next life. He sipped, then whispered a farewell to his Venus. In the blood-stained arms of a goddess, Antony closed his eyes forever.

Octavian's emissaries negotiated with Cleopatra through the mausoleum's thick, barred door. As she listened to their entreaties, a few of Octavian's men managed to steal in through a window, climb down silently, and throw Cleopatra to the ground just as she drew a dagger to stab herself. They searched her carefully for vials of poison, assuring her that the benevolent imperator would treat her mercifully, even generously.

Cleopatra watched as her vast treasure was carted off to pay Octavian's war debts. She was held prisoner in her own mausoleum, and every item she could use to harm herself was confiscated by her guards. Dazed and defeated, she prepared her lover's body for the funeral pyre. As flames rose, she clawed at her face, shoulders, and breasts in the manner of a grieving Egyptian wife.

The wounds were more than just a show of mourning. Within days, infection set into the scratches, and she refused to eat, perhaps in hopes that infection—nature's poison—would carry her off. With Antony gone and her dynasty in ruins, she had nothing to live for. She had watched one Ptolemy paraded in chains down Rome's Via Sacra. There would not be another.

On the afternoon of August 10, Octavian broke the seal of a letter Cleopatra sent him through her guards. Her note asked one last favor from the new ruler of the Roman world: to be buried at Antony's side.

The letter jolted Octavian from his chair, and he sent aides flying to the mausoleum to find out what was going on. They burst inside to find a cold Cleopatra lying on a golden couch, clothed in her robes of office. Her motionless hands gripped the crook and flail of a pharaoh, and a royal diadem bound her hair. The thirty-nine-year-old queen was stone dead.

Kneeling at her side were two dying servants named Iras and Charmion. Through death's haze the two women hastened to join their mistress, the last pharaoh of Egypt, as she took wings and flew to her Dionysus.

"A fine deed this is, Charmion!" roared Octavian's furious aide at the swooning woman.

"It is indeed most fine, and benefitting the descendant of so many kings," croaked Charmion as she crumpled to the floor.[*]

CLEOPATRA'S DEATH struck down the last obstacle to Octavian's unification of the empire. But as the Caesars settled into an unprecedented era of wealth, power, and excess, subjugated men and women of the outlying provinces chafed against the iron collar of an arrogant city that taxed and commanded, offering nothing in return.

Less than a century later, one of these provinces—a dark, distant island known as Britannia—would take up arms against its Roman occupiers and unleash a torrent of blood under the ruthless command of a vengeful Celtic queen.

---

[*] How poison was smuggled into Cleopatra's chamber (and into her bloodstream) is a mystery that died with Iras and Charmion. Octavian claimed Cleopatra had an asp smuggled into her chamber, but as historian Stacy Schiff points out, early and contemporary biographers such as Strabo, Plutarch, even the overly dramatic Dio, probably didn't believe the snake story. An asp, or even a cobra, is hardly the tool for a quick, painless death. Nor is it reliable: A dry bite, a weak snake, or a victim's resistance to venom can weaken the poison's efficacy. As a Ptolemy, Cleopatra had an encyclopedic knowledge of poisons, and had once demonstrated a sample on a condemned prisoner for Antony's edification. Plutarch aptly concluded, "The truth of the matter no one knows."

4

A THIRST FOR BLOOD

Boudica of the Britons

"You will win this battle, or perish."
—Boudica, 62 A.D.

THE PAIN SPREAD EACH TIME the lash struck her bare back. She stifled her cries, for the sake of family if not her tribe, but instinctively jerked at the ropes binding her wrists as the serpentine leather strips licked her skin. Welts streaking over her ribs turned pink, then red, then crimson, then began dripping. Boudica, queen of the Iceni, had time barely enough to draw a haggard breath as the soldier raised his arm for the next blow.

The indignity of Boudica's flogging—her breasts laid bare, her back brutalized— was sharpened by the looks of the Roman Ninth Legion's soldiers. Some grinned smugly, some stared salaciously. Others seemed bored. To the men of the Ninth, the writhing, red-haired wretch was not a queen, nor even a plebian. It was an animal being taught a lesson in respect.

The lesson did not end with the scourge. The queen had two daughters, both too young to marry, and the cohort's commander decided to enlist Boudica's girls in his demonstration. His soldiers seized the daughters and raped them before the downcast eyes of the villagers.

With the ravaging of two Celtic princesses and the flogging of their mother, the commander decided the Iceni had been taught enough for one day. He formed up his men, mounted his horse, and marched his column off, leaving in his wake a violated mother to comfort her violated daughters.

❖   ❖   ❖

THE TORTURE CASUALLY INFLICTED on Queen Boudica was an unintended legacy of her husband Prasutagus, late king of the Iceni. The Iceni, a tribe in eastern Britain, descended from a Celtic wave that washed over northern Europe six centuries earlier. Tall and big-boned, with blond or reddish hair, the Iceni appear strong and wild in classical art. They wore deep-dyed clothing and adorned themselves with golden torcs—thick, rope-like necklaces that advertised their status in Celtic society. Isolated from the crowded Mediterranean cities, they reveled in a vivid world of color, darkness, blood, and wonder. A mystical land where trees, hares, and wolves were expressions of the gods.

The Celts were a brooding people who fought savagely in wartime but did not lack for manners. Their morals were preached by *druides*, who performed religious rites like human sacrifice. Julius Caesar once remarked that the entire race was "extremely devoted to superstitious rites"—big words coming from Rome's former high priest.

In battle, the high-spirited Celts charged into the thick of the fight, on foot or riding a light chariot. They were brave to a fault, and sometimes that bravery cost them. The temptation of glorious single combat, and their penchant for leaping from chariots into a bloody scrum, frequently threw away their advantages of mobility, mass, and shock power.

The Iceni first encountered Romans during Caesar's invasion of Britain in 54 BC, when his legions crossed the English Channel and pressed beyond the Tamesa (Thames) River. Caesar's army subjugated the Iceni and several other tribes.

"Subjugated," at least, is how Caesar chose to describe his conquests to the folks back home, knowing that few Romans were likely to swim over to Britannia to see for themselves how subjugated the tribes really were. The image of hairy, beastly barbarians prostrating themselves before a Roman imperator made wonderful copy, and declaring victory, Caesar returned to the Continent. For the better part of a century, the bewildered Celts must have wondered whether they would ever see these strange, short-haired foreigners again.

Their answer came in AD 43, when four legions splashed ashore under the jaded eyes of Emperor Claudius. Outdoing even the mighty Caesar, Claudius claimed that eleven barbarian kings submitted to Roman rule. And unlike Caesar, Claudius intended to make Roman rule mean something to the primitive Britons.

In AD 47, Publius Ostorius Scapula, a proconsul sent by Claudius, went on a warpath, putting down Iceni resistance with heavy-handed brutality. When the butchery ended, he designated the pliable chieftain Prasutagus as the rightful Iceni king. For Prasutagus, the price of kingship was fealty to Rome and to write Emperor Claudius into his will.

By AD 60, Rome's army of occupation was sitting on a rumbling volcano. The latest of Ostorius's successors, proconsul Gaius Suetonius Paulinus, and his financial procurator, Catus Decianus, became the focus of deep-seated Celtic resentment. "We gain nothing by submission except heavier burdens," Tacitus had the Celts murmuring to themselves. "Once each tribe had one king, now two are clamped on us—the legate to wreak his fury on our lives, the procurator on our property. We subjects are damned in either case."

The Iceni took Rome's treatment of their neighbors, the Trinovantes tribe, as a cautionary tale. Six years after building a fortified base in Trinovantian lands, Suetonius and his legions drove the inhabitants from their capital to make room for retired Roman veterans. Roman pensioners and their families were given lands in a town called Camulodunum (modern Colchester), and these interlopers became eastern Britain's new upper class. Adding insult to injury, the Romans erected a temple to the recently deified Claudius and forced local tribesmen to pay extravagant taxes to fund the temple's construction and upkeep.

FROM EARLY ACCOUNTS, archeological evidence, and what we know of other East Anglian tribes at the dawn of *anni domini*, we can piece together the story of how Queen Boudica fell under the Roman lash. Around AD 60, during the reign of Emperor Nero, King Prasutagus died. In his will, he left his kingdom to his two daughters, for whom his wife, Boudica, would rule as regent until the oldest was mature enough to marry and govern. To dissuade Rome from taking his kingdom after his death, Prasutagus left a portion of his lands and possessions to the emperor.

Yet to Rome, client kings were merely tenant overseers whose contracts lasted only until their deaths. After a king died, his domains might remain a client state under his heir. But if the dead king's domains were rich and easily governed, then Rome would annex them to the Empire and rule them directly through a proconsul like Suetonius.

The issue of gender was an added complication for the Romans. The Iceni, wrote Tacitus, "admit no distinction of sex in royal successions," and Prasutagus left only daughters as heirs and a wife to rule as regent. His tribesmen saw nothing wrong with his girls succeeding their father as ruler when they were old enough.

Rome did. To the Latins, a regnant queen was a preposterous basis for government. Roman wives might whisper suggestions from behind the throne, but none would dare sit upon it. A woman's place was tending the home fires and managing house servants—not interfering in public affairs. Foreign realms with female sovereigns were not entirely unknown to imperial Rome, but any such kingdom was, by the time of Nero, fair game for incorporation into the Empire.

To put Rome's stamp on the Iceni—and send a warning to other tribes—procurator Catus Decianus marched troops into the Iceni capital and seized treasures of noble families. An infantry detachment from the Ninth Legion robbed, raped, and pillaged its way through Iceni lands to ensure that natives would not so much as think of lifting a hand against Roman authority. To Decianus, the most efficient way to send this message was through a personal visit to the new Iceni queen, an impertinent, probably disloyal woman known as Boudica.[*]

Apart from her tawny hair and harsh voice, ancient sources tell us little of Boudica's appearance. She was probably around thirty or thirty-two years old when her husband died—old enough to rule as regent, yet young enough to have two unmarried daughters.

The flogging and rape of the Iceni royal family was merely a message, for the local commander did not behead Boudica or her daughters, as he would have if pure devastation were his objective. But to make the message count, he enslaved some of Boudica's relatives, stripped nobles of their lands, and levied crippling taxes, tributes, and high-interest "loans" on Iceni he judged wealthy enough to pay them.

The Iceni, restive for fifteen long years, could only be pushed so far. As a Renaissance writer remarked, "Tyranny often brings intolerable wickedness which provokes in its victims a thirst for revenge." Boudica's lips begged for a taste from those waters. When the Romans who brutalized her family marched off, she cradled her weeping daughters while her relatives salved her stripes.

Taking a deep drink from the cup of vengeance, she prepared to drench Britannia in blood.

---

[*] According to British historian Miranda Aldhouse-Green, Boudica may have led an anti-Roman faction among the Iceni. If so, Prasutagus, a Roman ally, may have believed that leaving his kingdom to Boudica would have been impolitic. We have no direct evidence of Boudica's political leanings before Prasutagus's death to tell us, but after his death, she made her feelings unmistakably clear.

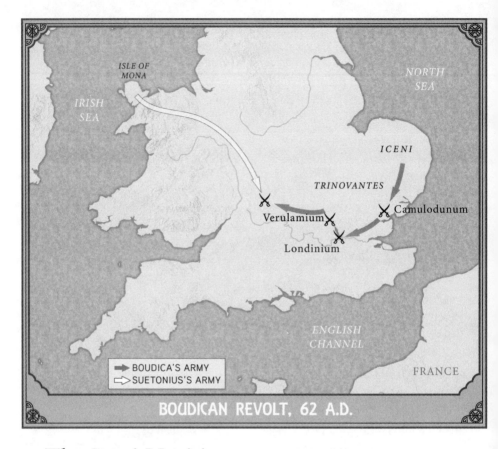

Map labels:
ISLE OF MONA
NORTH SEA
IRISH SEA
ICENI
TRINOVANTES
Verulamium
Camulodunum
Londinium
ENGLISH CHANNEL
FRANCE
➡ BOUDICA'S ARMY
⇨ SUETONIUS'S ARMY
BOUDICAN REVOLT, 62 A.D.

The Iceni Uprising

In the late winter of AD 61, Boudica's scars snaked her back like warpaint engorged with venom. That winter and early spring, she sent emissaries to tribes whose treasures had been stolen, or whose oak groves had been defiled, exhorting them to join her with men, horses, chariots, and weapons.

As she spoke to fighting men and their leaders, Boudica probably showed them her scars and assured them that the Romans were not invincible. With their help, the Britons would show the Romans no mercy. The Trinovantes, embittered by their eviction from Camulodunum, rallied to Boudica's cause, and the Iceni revolt pushed to the surface like belladonna through trodden soil.

The East Anglian countryside burst into flames that spring. As many as 120,000 rebels left their fields unsown and assembled with their families in groups. Many were armed; some were not. All were prepared to avenge the wrongs inflicted on them by the lash, the cross, and the sword.

Even at sixty, Suetonius, Rome's proconsul, was a man of rapid movement and decision. He had commanded legions in Africa and served as governor of Mauretania before the emperor dispatched him to Britannia as the island's ruler. Restless during peacetime, he looked forward to another chance to burnish his reputation as a military virtuoso.

The gods granted him that chance in the sixth year of Nero's reign. As Boudica's insurrection was bubbling to the surface, rebels had gathered off Britannia's west coast at the Island of Mona. The wild Welsh island had become a center of defiance, and Suetonius, leading the Twentieth Legion, prepared to mount a dramatic operation that would reaffirm Roman authority among the Celtic people—and enhance his standing with the Senate and people of Rome.

While Suetonius was marching to the end of the known world, Boudica, far to the east, eyed her first conquest. To a people bent on revenge, the Roman colony of Camulodunum was a plump, inviting target. The town's old walls, built by Celtic hands, had been razed to make room for civic buildings and farms. It was weakly held, for the retired veterans there had long since traded their swords for plowshares. As a crowning insult, the Romans had built a gaudy temple dedicated to the God-Emperor Claudius with funds extorted from the natives.

Skies grew ominous in Camulodunum as Boudica's horde began its slow and steady march. A statue of Victory in the village center inexplicably fell forward, turning her back to the townsfolk. Shrieks, probably from rebel fifth-columnists, were heard in the local assembly-house, and rumors of phantom settlements in ruins and the River Tamesa running red with blood shook veterans and their families.

When it became apparent that a mob was descending on Camulodunum, townsmen dispatched a swift messenger with a plea for help to Londinium, Britannia's financial center on the Tamesa River. But the procurator, the rapacious Catus Decianus, sent only a small, poorly equipped cohort of two hundred men to augment the local militia.

As Decianus was considering what other forces he could spare, Celtic infiltrators sabotaged last-minute attempts by the villagers to build ramparts and trenches. As Boudica's horde came into view, Roman veterans huddled with their families and braced for the coming blow.

❖   ❖   ❖

CASSIUS DIO describes Queen Boudica's eve-of-battle speech to her troops, some of whom presumably were close enough to hear her words. Writing in the early third century, Dio places a spear in her hand, which she jabs toward the sky. He covers her scarred back with a "tunic of diverse colors over which a thick mantle was fastened with a brooch" and rings her neck with a large golden necklace. Boudica lifted the fold of her dress, he says, from which a hare ran out "in an auspicious direction," prompting shouts of encouragement among her men. She then rendered prayers to the Celtic goddess Andraste, calling upon her, "as a woman speaking to a woman . . . I beg you for victory."

Dio flavors his account with a heavy dose of poetic license, but it is quite possible that Boudica resorted to a prophetic rabbit trick to encourage her men. The business of manufacturing omens is one of history's oldest professions, and at a minimum, she likely exhorted Iceni commanders, allies, and warriors to exact vengeance for their queen and families.

Eager for battle, Boudica's army fell on Camulodunum with the roar of a North Sea storm. Chariots broke through the brittle crust of militia, and Boudica's infantry, following close behind in the swirling dust, slaughtered the inhabitants within. Men, women, and children were butchered without distinction by frenzied swordsmen. Heads were taken, bodies were hung from crucifixes, and wooden homes were torched in a blaze hot enough to bake mud into pottery. Houses that did not collapse in the fire were methodically demolished, and an equestrian statue of Emperor Claudius was decapitated, its bronze head cast into the River Alde. Refusing to leave even the dead in peace, Celts tramped into the local necropolis and vandalized tombstones of soldiers and their families.

Survivors of the first wave huddled in the Temple of the God Claudius, fending off attack after attack, praying for deliverance. But the Roman god-head must have been busy elsewhere, for he did not intervene. After two days Boudica's warriors forced open the bronze doors and took the temple by storm. Terrified remnants of Camulodunum's colony were carved up on the spot or dragged out to be sacrificed.

The rape of the Iceni daughters had been answered by the rape of a Roman city.

Word of Camulodunum's fate, and the approach of Boudica's army, filled Londinium with dread. The lions had escaped the theater and were bounding with the numbers, and bloodlust, to tear the city apart. Catus Decianus, shipping off Londinium's records and treasury, frantically dispatched riders to find Suetonius and his army.

Suetonius was on the Welsh coast putting down the druid rebels at Mona, too far west to reach Londinium in time. A desperate Catus called up his reserve, the Ninth Legion in the north, and ordered them to check Boudica on the road from Camulodunum.

Roman intelligence was able to convey the destructiveness of Boudica's army, but evidently not its size. The Ninth Legion—probably around 3,000 legionnaires and a small detachment of cavalry and artillery—was dwarfed by Boudica's army, but the Romans did not know it.

They would. Soon.

On the march, a legion was normally preceded by native scouts or cavalry, to guard against ambush and pinpoint the enemy's location. The Ninth's commander, Petilius Cerialis, either underestimated rebel strength or was careless, and he paid for his mistake. The Ninth marched straight into a Celtic ambush, and its legion-naires died screaming. By the time the god Belenos pulled Britannia's sun down to the horizon, the white, expressionless heads of Roman soldiers adorned many a bentwood chariot.

Boudica's army advanced on Londinium like a wildfire. Decianus, whose avarice had thrown sparks onto the tinderbox, took passage across the Channel, never stopping until he reached the safety of Gaul. The fate of Britain would be decided by Queen Boudica and General Suetonius.

SUETONIUS AND HIS ARMY were encamped 250 miles west when news arrived of the massacre at Camulodunum. The veteran general ordered his men to break camp, then raced ahead of his infantry toward Londinium. Boudica, sated for the moment by the blood of Camulodunum, allowed her troops time to rest, loot, and pillage the countryside before moving on. Stealing a march on the queen, Suetonius and a small flying column breathlessly galloped into Londinium just ahead of Boudica's advance scouts.

Surveying the city's defenses, Suetonius concluded there was no use fighting there. The city of 30,000 was a burgeoning financial and administrative center, but Londinium had neither the walls nor entrenchments to survive a mass-wave assault. His army would arrive exhausted from a long march and would fight at the end of a long, tenuous supply line. Coldly working through the military calculus, Suetonius ordered all garrison troops to abandon Londinium and march with him west, back toward his main force.

Behind Suetonius snaked a column of terrified Londoners looking to the mighty Roman army for salvation. More remained behind—mostly those too old, young, or crippled to get away. As a dust cloud from the north announced the appearance of Boudica's army, the souls left behind could do nothing save pray to Jupiter for a miracle.

Jupiter, like Claudius before, refused to work miracles. Scorched coins, scorched roof titles, scorched pottery, and scorched timbers bear mute witness to the vengeance Boudica wreaked. Some fourteen feet below the modern streets of London, a black layer of debris is all that is left of the city Boudica and her men incinerated. Every inhabitant who could be found and dragged from hiding was butchered, and headless bodies littered Londinium's dirt streets by the time the Celtic army moved on.

Those killed in the initial assault were the lucky ones. Celtic armies rarely sold war prisoners; those they captured were crucified, hanged, burned alive, or had their throats and bellies slit open. Dio wrote,

> *Those who were taken captive by the Britons were subjected to every known outrage . . . They hung up naked the noblest and most distinguished women and then cut off their breasts and sewed them to their mouths, in order to make the victims appear to be eating them; afterwards they impaled the women on sharp skewers run lengthwise through the entire body . . .*

Death by torture, he writes, accompanied human sacrifice, feasts of thanksgiving, and other acts of "wanton behavior" dedicated to Andraste, their victory goddess.

With the taste of soot still on her tongue, the queen set her men on the road to Verulamium (near present-day St. Albans in Hertfordshire). Boudica's army stripped the countryside of cattle, horses, food, and anything of value as it lurched forward until it had Verulamium in its red-tinged sights.

As at Londinium, Verulamium was defended mostly by the reputation of the absent Roman army, and would suffer the same fate. Its few inhabitants were slaughtered, their homes burned, their city erased. The only difference from Londinium was that nearly all the town's residents, knowing what awaited them, had cleared out before the storm burst. When Boudica's chariots crashed into Verulamium, they entered a ghost town.

In driving on Verulamium and ignoring Suetonius, Boudica violated a cardinal military rule: Defeat the enemy first; take cities and plunder second. The character of her army—impulsive, impatient, brave and strong, but poorly suited to boredom or long campaigns—made it critical that she bring Suetonius to battle quickly. Whether overconfident, or simply unable to control the pulsating beast that was her army, Boudica let slip an opportunity to fall on Suetonius as he fell back.

Suetonius withdrew to the island's center to join up with his garrisons returning from Wales. He summoned the Second Legion to meet him in the Midlands, but its acting commander, Poenius Postumus, refused to move. Left in the lurch, Suetonius managed to pull cohorts from two other legions, plus some local auxiliaries, and patch together a force of around 15,000 men.

With a rough idea of the size of the queen's horde, Suetonius decided to use their numbers against them. He drew the Celts into a long, slow march, in which their food and water supplies would run low. Boudica's army, though large and vicious, was logistically undisciplined and encumbered with baggage, loot, slaves, and camp followers. Suetonius, by contrast, commanded a lean force used to marching eighteen miles a day. If he could find the right ground and prepare to withstand a shock assault, Suetonius and his men stood a reasonable chance of surviving.

He found that ground west of Londinium. Marching his men faster than Boudica's slow horde, he would have gained a four- or five-day lead on the Britons— enough time to secure the water supply, gather or burn all food in the area, and prepare defense works. As Boudica's army trudged west, Tacitus wrote, Suetonius took up a blocking position "in a defile with a wood behind him."*

The defile was well chosen. With thick woods at his back, Suetonius and his infantry needn't fear chariots bearing down on them from behind. Dense treelines on either side meant Boudica could not outflank him, and because the field narrowed as it reached the Roman line, Boudica's host would be pressed shoulder-to-shoulder as the Celts smashed into the Roman shield wall. With a narrow front, the Celts would be reduced to fighting a man-to-man infantry battle—a contest in which Rome had no equal.

Flushed with victory, Boudica's coalition had swollen to numbers beyond her ability to manage them. While she could influence the army's basic direction, the decision to fight Suetonius was probably not fully hers. Yet her strategy of bringing the Romans to battle quickly—if it was her decision—carried a logic of its own. Confidence begets victory, and the morale of Boudica's Celts was at an all-time high.

If Boudica's strategy was sound, her eye for terrain was imperfect. Giving battle on a narrow, wooded field meant her chariots could not swing wide and crash into the enemy's flanks. The longsword, so vicious in the hands of an Iceni warrior, needed space to swing and crush. Celtic *sturm und drang* couldn't be fully unleashed against an infantry shielded from the front and sides.

---

* In a detailed study of Roman and British logistics, and the availability of water at various march points, British historian Steve Kaye postulates that Suetonius fought at Mildenhall, about 70 miles west of London.

Yet how could she decline battle? The Second Legion might arrive at any moment, tilting the balance against her. Besides, on the other side of the field stood Governor Suetonius, commander of an oppressor that stole her lands, raped her children, and left her and the Iceni with deep scars. His obscene presence goaded Boudica into battle. Her blood was up, and Boudica, Queen of the Iceni, would fight a battle that would echo through the ages.

Boudica's Attack

She drew up her army at the far end of the clearing. Camp followers—families of warriors and the menagerie of sutlers, priests, slaves, wives, whores, and hangers-on that follow every army—formed a loose semicircle to the Celtic rear, behind the baggage train. The two sides, waiting for orders to kill, stared at each other across the long, green clearing. Each warrior eyed a man on the other side whom he might kill—or who might kill him. As they sized each other up, the contrast between the two forces could not have been more striking.

Most Celts brandishing sword or spear were farmers or cattlemen by trade. They had left their fields unsown that winter to answer Boudica's call, and they lacked training in large-unit tactics beyond what they learned from butchery on the march. The better-armed wielded a long Celtic sword and carried a shield, but wore no body armor and went into battle shirtless, typically shod in short boots tucked over loose-fitting trousers. Nobles who could afford horses moved about on light chariots—essentially two-wheeled wicker baskets from which they jabbed with thrusting spears or dismounted to fight on foot. They too disdained heavy breastplates and helmets. To the Celtic noble, such things were badges of rank, not articles of protection. Bravery was its own armor; courage was the Celtic key to victory.

The men marching with Suetonius had not worked on farms in years, if ever. They were professional soldiers whose weapons and tactics had been refined over a three-hundred-year march. The legionnaire carried a tall, rectangular shield, two javelins called *pila*, and a two-edged *gladius* for close-in killing. Unlike the Celtic broadsword, the Roman sword was a short, stabbing weapon that flashed from behind a shield to pierce the enemy's legs or abdomen. The idea was not to decapitate a foe with one dramatic swing, but to put him on the ground with a smash from the shield or a quick stab, where he could be finished off with a second thrust to the chest, neck, or head.

Discipline and training were the Roman keys to victory.

❖   ❖   ❖

NO ACCOUNT OF AN ANCIENT BATTLE would be complete without dramatic speeches delivered by the opposing generals. Boudica, says Tacitus, cantered before her troops in a war chariot, her daughters at her side, her claret hair cascading over a striped robe. "We British are used to women commanders in war," she tells her men. "I am fighting as an ordinary person for my lost freedom, my bruised body and my outraged daughters." Reminding her followers of the horrors of Roman rule, she ended with a challenge to the men of her ranks:

> *The Roman division which dared to fight is annihilated. The others cower in their camps, or watch for a chance to escape. They will never face even the din and roar of our thousands, much less the shock of our onslaught. Consider how many of you are fighting—and why! Then you will win this battle, or perish. That is what I, a woman, plan to do—let the men live in slavery if they will.*

On the other side of the clearing, Suetonius also pointed out the women in the Boudican army, though for a different reason. "In their ranks there are more women than fighting men," he sneered. The Britons would be easy prey. Their small, Roman force would cover itself in glory when the battle was done.

Boasting aside, Suetonius got down to business. He reminded his men, "Keep in close order. Throw your javelins, and then carry on: Use shield-bosses to fell them, swords to kill them. Do not think of plunder. When you have won, you will have everything."

Dio tells us that Suetonius added a warning that failure was not an option: "It would be better for us," he said,

> *to fall fighting bravely than to be captured and impaled, to look upon our own entrails cut from our bodies, to be spitted on red-hot skewers, to perish by being melted in boiling water—in a word, to suffer as though we had been thrown to lawless and impious wild beasts. Let us therefore conquer them or die here.*

Boudica had numbers, Suetonius had professionals. She was betting her life that valor, passion, and numbers would overcome the Roman murderers fighting so far from home.

Boudica then cast the die of Fate. It hung, for a moment, in the air.

In that blurred moment, a cacophony of druidic chants, trumpet blasts, and battle cries mingled and rose from the Celtic lines like a cloud of smoke. Swords flashing, spears raised, Boudica's warriors charged the Roman wall.

Steadied by years of harsh training, the Romans held their ground. As the Celts closed to within forty feet, legionnaires hurled their *pila* into the shrieking mass of men. Iron-tipped javelins pierced flesh and bone in the Celtic front ranks, taking out fighters and throwing successive waves into disorder as they stumbled over the bodies of the fallen. As blood-maddened tribesmen pressed forward, the field narrowed, and their outer files were squeezed toward the center, hampering the wide swing of their blades. Winded from their charge, they hacked and thrusted. But they could not cut a hole in the shield wall.

Awash in a din of whistles, screams, and bellowed orders, grim-faced legionnaires stepped forward in wedge formations, shields warding off blows and shoving Celts off balance. Gladius blades hacked and bit. Centurions kept their men in steady lines, relieving each rank with fresh soldiers at regular intervals. The day lengthened, and legionnaires cut into rows of muscular Britons like ugly, short-bladed scythes.

Boudica's men began falling back as the wall of blades and shields pressed forward. As they retreated, their rear ranks backed up against the wagons and camp followers. Fighters became mingled with noncombatants, and panic from children, old men, and women spread through their fighting lines.

"When you have won, you will have everything," Suetonius had promised. The Celtic host fractured, then split, and Roman cavalry armed with lances ran down men who had thrown down their weapons and were sprinting for their lives. They kept their discipline and spared no one; even the baggage animals were slaughtered. Milling, panicking, trying to buck their burdens, Boudica's horses died squealing, still harnessed to their wagons.

Celtic blood flowed through the field's furrows and left a metallic smell hanging in the air. By the time the grisly spectacle ended, Tacitus tells us, 80,000 Britons lay dead alongside 400 legionnaires. Most of Boudica's dead were probably cut down in the battle's pursuit phase, where an unsteady foot or tired legs meant death.*

One of those dead was Queen Boudica, though the brambles of time shroud the place and manner of her death. She might have fallen in battle, though Tacitus

---

* Tacitus takes these numbers "according to one report," implying that he was not altogether confident in them. Since long before Caesar, generals had a habit of exaggerating enemy dead in their dispatches home. But given the size of the Celtic army, and with easy pickings among women and children with the baggage train, a butcher's bill of 15,000 to 20,000 Celts is not difficult to imagine.

claims she took poison after her defeat, which was probably the version rustling through the Roman grapevine not long afterward.

Whether by sword or by poison, the horned god Cernunnos carried Boudica to the underworld as her remnants straggled back to their homes. As her daughters are never heard from again, it is possible the Iceni princesses, deflowered before their mother's eyes, shared their mother's fate.

The heartbeat of rebellion froze in the wooded defile. Dazed tribesmen and family members filtered home to unsown fields. By the time the uprising's corpse entered *rigor mortis*, the season had grown too late to begin planting crops. Thousands of Celtic families would be carried off by starvation before winter's solstice.

Driving the lesson home, Suetonius cut a fresh swath of destruction through East Britannia. He put farms to the torch, families to the sword, sacred groves to the ax, and confiscated gold in the provincial purse. The Iceni and Trinovantes paid dearly for their wellspring of blood, and would never rise again.

As a Caledonian leader grumbled a generation later, the Romans "create a desolation and call it peace." Suetonius bought peace, but at a horrendous economic, political, and military cost. The Ninth Legion had been torn to shreds, the countryside seethed in impotent rage, and the province's ability to pay taxes and make loans was crippled. Before long Emperor Nero replaced Suetonius with a more temperate governor from Gaul, who moved in fresh legions to keep the island pacified.

The question of dominion had, for a time, been settled. Boudica was dead, and Nero ruled the world from Britannia to Syria. Across Eurasia, a few plucky women rose in revolt, but it would take the fall of the Roman Empire, and the rise of new gods, to unleash the next great file of women war leaders.

ACT II

WOMEN OF A CERTAIN AGE

❖   ❖   ❖

When Nag the basking cobra hears the careless foot of man,
He will sometimes wriggle sideways and avoid it if he can.
But his mate makes no such motion where she camps beside the trail.
For the female of the species is more deadly than the male.

—Kipling

Four centuries after Boudica's death, the fall of the Roman Empire opened a power scramble from Spain to Judea. The eastern half of Rome's dominions broke away to form the Byzantine Empire, which would, in time, be toppled by Islamic caliphates spreading like ivy from India's frontier to the Atlantic Ocean. In Northern Europe, the imperial order shattered into a checkerboard of petty kingdoms with grand ambitions, while from the East Asia steppes horse archers of Genghis Khan thundered down to sweep aside potentates from China to Eastern Europe.

As in ancient days, during the Middle Ages men dominated the great game. Whether Saxon or Norman, Liao or Ming, Muslim or Christian, the establishment was a men's club where the rule of primogeniture was almost inviolate. A woman's place could be in the throne room, or even beside the throne, but never *on* the throne.

Unable to shatter the glass portcullis, the brightest medieval queens tended to work behind the tapestry, often as diplomatic agents of their husbands, or regents for boy-kings. Dynamos like Eleanor of Aquitaine, Brunhilda of Austrasia, and Anne of Kiev changed history as ambassadors, advisors, alliance pawns, and, most importantly, vessels for the production of male babies. Anything but rulers.

Yet from the cesspool of the Dark Ages, a few women clawed their way past their male competitors. Succession laws grudgingly conceded exceptions as far-sighted fathers, or the untimely death of a male heir, forced kingdoms to entrust their fortunes to the weaker sex. In the right circumstances, a girl could find herself ruling in her own name, consolidating regional power—even leading a conquest—if she played her cards right.

Several played their hands deftly. In northern China, Empress Chengtian of the Liao Dynasty carved broad exceptions to the rule that men lead in battle and at the peace table. In northern India, Razia al-Din, one of those rare female sultans, rode an elephant at the head of her army. To the west, Countess Matilda of Canossa ruled much of northern Italy as she battled Germany's Emperor Henry IV. Another Matilda, of English descent, crossed the Channel to claim the throne of Westminster. Spain's Queen Urraca fought her ex-husband for control of León, Castile, and Toledo, then battled her half-sister for the throne of Spanish Galicia. In the fourteenth century, Queen Margaret of Denmark, derided as "King Pantsless" by her enemies, used an army to forge a Scandinavian union. And during the fifteenth-century Wars of the Roses, Queen Margaret d'Anjou, Shakespeare's "tiger's heart wrapped in a woman's hide," rallied the Lancaster faction when her husband, King Henry VI, went mad.

In an age where absolute power was less than absolute, warrior queens learned to manage a class of headstrong, self-serving nobility. England's Wars of the Roses and Mongolia's succession wars, both taking place around the same time, underscored the need for a reigning queen to hold the confidence of nobles and generals whose fighting qualities she could not equal. Unable to lead in battle by example, she learned to rely on intelligence and force of will. Herding fractious aristocrats was a challenge for any royal; getting them to take orders from a woman was all but impossible.

Yet it could be done. In the rugged Caucasus Mountains, a land uneasy with change, one woman threaded the golden needle to rule a feudal kingdom in her own name. Balancing old religion with new realities, she paid homage to ancient traditions while breaking virgin ground. She was intelligent, she was pious, she loved to sew, and she was burdened with one of history's most annoying ex-husbands.

She also knew how to inspire soldiers, by walking barefoot among her troops before battle.

5

LION OF THE CAUCASUS

Tamar of Georgia

"Though indeed she be a woman, still as sovereign
she is begotten of God. She knows how to rule."
—POET SHOTA RUSTAVELI, C. 1200

As NIGHT FELL, THE QUEEN PICKED HER WAY among her encamped soldiers. Ten thousand fires punctured the darkness, warming the cool air wafting among bedrolls, wagons, horses, and soldiers who knelt before their queen.

In the amber glow of the flames, she gazed at the faces, young and old, their eyes locked on her. The moment of battle was drawing near, and some of those faces watching her would close their eyes forever come the morrow. They belonged to sons and husbands who would soon be sleeping in the arms of the Blessed Savior.

Beyond the horizon's veil lay many more faces. Faces of men, she knew, who would be turned away by the Blessed Savior. Followers of the Crescent, sleeping peacefully in their tents, knowing nothing of the storm about to crash upon them. As with Joshua, with Gideon, with Constantine and Charlemagne, the Lord was about to decide the fate of His people with a bolt of lightning—a bolt He had placed in the hands of a woman.

Tamar, King of Kings, Queen of Queens, ruler of Caucasia's Georgian kingdom, had assembled an army of 80,000 soldiers, the largest Georgian force ever fielded. But the Sultan of Rum and his allies boasted twice as many conscripts. He had vowed to sweep Christianity from the Caucasus and consign Queen Tamar to his personal harem, where he would do to her body what his men would do to her lands. And the queen's scouts had warned her that the sultan had enough men to keep both vows.

Surrounded by war banners, holy relics, and icons of saints, Tamar gave encouraging speeches to clusters of men, imploring them fight for their God, their country, their homes, their queen. Then she slipped off her shoes and walked, an unshod penitent, in the direction of the great Vardzia monastery. There she would prostrate herself before the Icon of Vardzia and await the divine verdict.

As she left to take her station, rough-hewn, bearded soldiers lifted spears and raised their voices to the sky.

"*To our King!*" they roared.

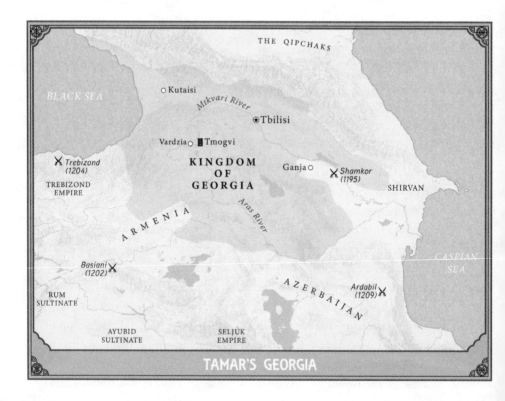

TAMAR'S GEORGIA

❖   ❖   ❖

THE WOMAN WHO DEFIED THE SULTAN began her walk in 1178, when her father, King Giorgi III, appointed the eighteen-year-old as his co-ruler of the Kingdom of Georgia.

Tamar's home between the Black and Caspian Seas lay on a fault line between three treacherous frontiers. Georgia's northern border faced the unstable kingdom of Ossetia, the freebooting Qipchak Turks, and the Kievan Rus. To the south lay the battlefield nations of Azerbaijan, Armenia, and petty Muslim emirates allied with powerful sultans. And to the west lay the tottering Byzantine Empire, brutal and poorly led, but still powerful enough to menace its neighbors.

Though his daughter was the fruit of the House of Bagration, a dynasty that had ruled Georgia for nearly two centuries, King Giorgi knew the transition from father to daughter would be fraught with danger. When his older brother, King Davit V, was murdered (on Giorgi's orders, it was whispered), Giorgi assumed the regency to protect his brother's son, then usurped the throne. He watered down privileges of Georgia's *aznaurni*, or nobility, and when a baronial faction rose to restore his nephew, Giorgi brutally crushed the revolt. He had his nephew castrated for good measure, eliminating the threat of a competing heir, and infuriated the nobles by replacing senior ministers, giving loyalty and merit primacy over birth.

Ruling a coterie of barons who would gladly open his throat, Giorgi nervously pondered the state of the kingdom after his death, when Tamar would be most vulnerable. To forestall a coup, he declared his daughter a sovereign and co-ruler during his lifetime. At his palace in Tbilisi, Georgia's capital city, he placed on her head a golden crown glittering with rubies and emeralds. Draped in fringed purple robes with gold embellishments, Tamar sat at the right hand of the father as their joint reign commenced.

Fawning medieval chroniclers were struck by Tamar's piety, beauty, and humility. An early biography extols her dark eyes, rosy cheeks, and pleasant, cheerful voice. A contemporary described her as "fortunate and God-fearing, beautiful and good-natured . . . a lover of churches, monks, and nuns; she gave alms to beggars and helped those looking for justice."

Georgian chronicles, such as the thirteenth-century "Histories and Eulogies of Kings" and Shota Rustaveli's epic poem "The Knight in the Panther's Skin," described a deeply pious woman who "was fond of praying like a nun, both praying and reading the vespers psalms before going to sleep."

"Blessed be the Lord, who hath not given us as prey," declares one of those psalms. Tamar would need the spiritual succor of the psalmist's verses—and the aid of a large army—because life was about to become far more difficult.

❖   ❖   ❖

TAMAR'S FATHER DIED in 1184, leaving a throne surrounded by the *aznaurni* and ambitious men from the Orthodox Church. To the old guard, Tamar was nothing more than an inspiring figurehead, and she would spend the first few years of her reign fighting attempts to shut her into a cramped political box.

Though the Bagration family was a venerated institution in Georgia—it claimed descent from the Bible's King Solomon—the Orthodox Church cast a far longer shadow. Brought to Georgia a thousand years earlier by the apostles Andrew and Simon the Zealot, in Tamar's day the Orthodox faith was led by a bearded patriarch who ruled much like a Roman Catholic pope. Mikel IV, the current patriarch, was an opportunistic, seasoned politician with a keen eye for royal weakness.

The feudal *aznaurni* elbowed their way into the power vacuum created by Giorgi's death. Enlisting the support of the Church and Tamar's influential aunt, Rusudan, the nobles first demanded that Tamar hold a second coronation ceremony to confirm her legitimacy. Tamar reluctantly agreed—there was precedent for the demand—and she was crowned by a senior bishop, while two barons presented her with her regalia of office: a sword, scepter, and wooden cross.

The emboldened nobles then demanded that she strip the royal chancellor, appointed by her father, of his titles and power. Tamar knew she lacked the political or military support to defy the lords, so she reluctantly relieved the minister of his office. A rook was sacrificed to save the queen.

Their confidence growing, the nobles ordered Tamar to take a husband. They argued that the nation needed a military leader, and the idea of a woman riding into battle was preposterous. On this last point there was general agreement, and various factions presented candidates for the queen's hand. The council of lords eventually made Tamar's choice for her: the son of the Duke of Kiev.

Yuri Andreevich Bogoliubski was a small-time warlord whose prowess had been honed fighting relatives in southern Russia. Ejected from his lands by a hostile uncle, Yuri had taken refuge among the Qipchaks, a Turkic tribe that eked out a living raiding settlements in the northern Caucasus. Queen Tamar's marriage to Yuri, the nobles hoped, would forge an alliance with Kiev that would secure Georgia's borders to the north, enabling the kingdom to concentrate its southern defenses against Muslim Turks and Byzantine Christians.

When Tamar balked at marrying a stranger from a strange land, her Aunt Rusudan, Patriarch Mikel, and a Georgian noble sent messengers to Yuri with a marriage offer and began wedding preparations. The marriage contract and ceremony were rushed through before the bride could mount an effective protest, and Yuri was crowned king, or *mepe*, of Georgia. Because Tamar descended from the great Bagrationi line of kings, the council of nobles was careful to ensure that a foreigner's title would not outrank that of a full-blooded Georgian queen. It bestowed upon Tamar the rank *Mepeta-Mepe, Dedopalta-Dedopali*, or "King of Kings, Queen of Queens."*

It was a grand title, and on parchment, Georgia's power was vested in Tamar. But for now, real power rested with the *aznaurni*. Confident to the point of arrogance, the barons, led by an ambitious lord named Qutlu Arslan, made their most audacious demand of all: They called for the establishment of a House of Lords that would pass all laws and appoint all ministers. Arslan worked behind the scenes for his appointment as commander of the queen's armies, positioning himself as a contender to fill the throne should anything happen to the queen.

If Arslan and the nobles had their way, Tamar's role would be to give royal approval to decrees passed by the nobility. She would serve as Georgia's beautiful, charming, and utterly harmless figurehead.

In time, however, the pendulum began to swing toward Tamar. Two years into her rule, Patriarch Mikel died, removing one obstacle to power. "Nobody was sorry for him, neither great, nor small, because everybody despised him," wrote Tamar's chronicler. Mikel's brother, Tevdore, acceded to the ecclesiastical throne, but Tamar sensed it would be some time before the younger brother felt secure enough to interfere in court politics.

Tamar used the transition of Church leadership to begin some ministerial housekeeping. As her early biographer observed, "She began to sharpen her double-edged sword to eliminate the sources of evil, and called a council in order to define and establish the order of all the great and general councils." She bestowed lavish gifts on bishops and abbots to keep them quiescent, then swept away noble appointments that had proved troublesome. She commissioned a new army commander, a new finance minister, and a new internal affairs minister. Loyalists now held the key royal posts.

---

* Tamar, "King of Kings, Queen of Queens," incorporated a masculine title, but made no effort to cloud her femininity in either image or dress. She is uniformly depicted as a beautiful Caucasian woman.

Tamar completed her sweep by arresting Qutlu Arslan and holding him in Tbilisi's imposing Narikala Castle. When rebel lords threatened to attack the palace if Arslan were not released, Tamar sent two loyal women to negotiate with the rebels while she quietly prepared her real response. Assembling a royal army outside Tbilisi, she marched her forces to the capital and prepared to strike if the nobles refused to stand down.

After a short but tense standoff, Tamar reached a settlement with the nobles that did not require her to shed blood. She instructed her envoys to offer pardons to all rebels except Arslan, then waited for the coalition to splinter. Rebel lords grew uneasy as they wondered who among them would be the first to break ranks. Then, when they learned the size of Tamar's army, they recalculated the odds, abandoned the uprising, and begged the queen's forgiveness.

"What would she do with the rebels?" Every Georgian noble nervously pondered this question. Tamar's grandfather had been ruthless in stamping out embers of rebellion, gouging eyes, castrating, and executing those who rose against him. But Tamar opted for a lighter touch. She pardoned the rebels, other than Arslan, whom she merely ejected from public life.*

"The snare is broken, and we are escaped," rejoiced the psalmist in a passage Tamar read many times. She would have seen the Lord's guiding hand in her deliverance from the *aznaurni*. And from His anointed patriarch.

But there was one snare she still had not broken. Having rid herself of threats from the nobility and the Church, Tamar prepared to lance another of the kingdom's inflamed boils: her degenerate husband.

FOR NEARLY THREE YEARS, Yuri had served as his wife's military commander, successfully leading her men against Muslims in Armenia. He managed the battles, and the queen accompanied her armies to the farthest church or monastery, inspiring the soldiers with speeches and victory prayers.

The division of responsibilities suited Tamar. She was a hardy ascetic who enjoyed life on the road, and she used the campaigns as opportunities to visit friendly vassals, tour churches and cities, and take the pulse of her kingdom. As monarch, she

---

* Georgian justice was humane by medieval standards. Long-term prison sentences were nonexistent, so in lieu of beheading a serious criminal, the felon would often be blinded and released to his village, no longer posing a threat his neighbors.

could make strategic decisions, such as allocation of tax revenues or production, to ensure the army was well provisioned. Though as a woman she could never make tactical decisions, sharing with her men the rigors of campaign life gave her a sense of what armies needed to survive in the field.

When Yuri was away on campaign, the arrangement worked passably well. Georgian armies marched unimpeded through lands once roamed by Scythians, Parthians, and Massagetae, and the royal consort was hailed as a conqueror. Coins were struck bearing the inscription, "God magnify the king and queen."

Tamar might have wondered whether God had much to do with the "king" part, for despite their limited military successes, the two made a terrible personal match. Tamar had grown up in the Church, and the Orthodox faith was deeply embedded in her soul. She attended liturgies, prayed daily, and sewed clothing to distribute to Tbilisi's poor.

Yuri also claimed the Orthodox faith, but in practice he worshipped wine, sex, and sadism—approximately in that order. King of a land famous for sweet wine, he often became drunk and left a wake of poorly concealed mistresses. "The Russian when drunk showed his Scythian habits . . . utterly debauched and utterly depraved, he even went in for sodomitic behavior," a disgusted contemporary wrote. "He subjected honorable men to beating and to torture by tearing off their members."

Tamar had never loved Yuri, and it is unclear whether the marriage, forced upon her by the *aznaurni*, had even been consummated. When Yuri's debauchery progressed from merely boorish to homicidal, she sent a deputation of monks to talk sense into him. The Russian shrugged off their warning and continued tormenting the Tbilisi court.

After three long years of embarrassments, Tamar finally demanded an annulment from the Church. The bishops, who despised Yuri as much as the nobles did, quickly granted her request. Tamar's courtiers hastily packed Yuri off to Constantinople with a cache of gold and best wishes for his future pursuits, so long as those pursuits did not involve Georgia.

With the nobles in line, the old patriarch dead, and her ex-husband in Constantinople, Tamar was finally free to chart a new course—and choose a new husband, should she wish.

For a time, she did not wish. Princes from surrounding kingdoms traveled to Tbilisi for her hand, but having been burned in one marriage, she resisted their entreaties. "God is my witness, that I never wished to get married, neither in the past, nor now, so I would ask you to release me of that necessity," she told a group of nobles.

But her Aunt Rusudan and the nobles persisted. Tamar grudgingly reconsidered what had become a distasteful prospect, and she imposed her own conditions for any new marriage: Love would be a requirement.

Once Tamar had a voice in her marriage selection, it did not take her long to fall in love. Davit Soslan, prince of Ossetia, was a distant relative of Tamar and arrived in Tbilisi with solid credentials. "Of medium size, nicely built, broad-shouldered and handsome," an early Georgian manuscript describes him, Davit was an excellent horseman with fine military talents. Tamar and Davit wed in 1189, a year after Tamar's annulment.

Tamar's second marriage became one of those rare political unions to find success in court, on the battlefield, and in the royal apartments. Within two years, the royal couple conceived their first child, and in the year 1192 Tamar gave birth to a prince, the future King Giorgi IV. A year later, she delivered the kingdom a princess, named Rusudan after her meddling aunt.

Yuri's Revolt

Tamar's early years of marriage to Davit were happy ones, but a storm swept her kingdom in the form of her wayward ex-husband. Though her father would have blinded or disemboweled a ruffian like Yuri Bogoliubski for his conduct at court, Tamar, who opposed the death penalty, never sought his life.

She may have regretted her leniency.

Yuri had grown restless in his second bachelorhood, and in 1191 he and the Sultan of Erzurum—a western kingdom dominated by Georgia—raised an army to invade Georgia and reclaim Yuri's "lost" throne. Marching with his supporters up the Black Sea coast, Yuri suddenly appeared at the royal palace of Kutaisi in northwest Georgia. Recalling Yuri's penchant for violence, local nobles promptly crowned him king.

Shocked by Yuri's reappearance at the head of an army, Tamar resorted to the same tactic she had used with rebellious nobles a dozen years before: She sent negotiators to buy time while she hastily concentrated her forces. She dispatched Patriarch Tevdore and a local bishop to talk sense into the noblemen supporting Yuri, but this time the ploy didn't work. The rebels took the risky move of dividing their army and attacked from two sides. Sending one wing under Yuri into eastern Georgia to divert loyalist attention, the main rebel force moved south, burning towns and marching on the mountain fortress of Tmogvi, a castle high atop a craggy promontory in Georgia's mountains.

Informants kept Tamar apprised of her ex-husband's moves, and in response she, too, split her forces. She sent her high constable and the largest part of her army south to meet the main rebel force, while her current husband led a smaller army against her ex.

At the River Mtkvari, the main armies clashed. Opposing forces unleashed a barrage of arrows to soften each other's infantry, then spent the day hacking, stabbing, and gouging each other. The rebels broke first and withdrew, and in a second battle Tamar's forces decisively defeated them, leaving her the unquestioned mistress of the Georgia heartland.

Learning of the defeat of their southern wing, Yuri's coalition of Qipchaks, rebel Georgians, and petty nobles splintered. Tamar's forces hunted down rebel commanders, and when they opened their net, up came Yuri Bogoliubski, whose comrades betrayed him to win leniency from the queen.

Still reluctant to take his head, Tamar shipped Yuri back to Constantinople, this time empty-handed. She stripped rebel barons of their lands—after all, rising against the queen should never be a risk-free proposition—but she permitted them to keep their heads, bowels, eyes, and genitals, for which they were presumably grateful.

The rebellion of 1191 was not Yuri's last effort to amend his divorce decree. To Tamar's dismay, two years later Yuri turned up again, fighting at the head of an Azerbaijani army. Fortunately for Tamar, Yuri had been careless, and one of her dukes managed to capture him. While Yuri again kept his head, a supremely annoyed Tamar declined to send him back to Constantinople for another cycle of rinse and repeat. She had him imprisoned in a monastery at Tbilisi, held in a small cell where he plagued no one except his guards and the local monks.

Having at long last set her royal house in order, Tamar could turn her eyes to enemies beyond her borders.

The Battle of Shamkor

As a kingdom nestled among Muslim sultanates and the embers of a dying Byzantine Empire, Georgia had a tense relationship with its neighbors in the best of times— and Tamar's were not the best of times. Splayed across Asia Minor stretched Byzantium's Trebizond Kingdom, the Sultanate of Rum, the Ayubid Sultanate, Armenia, and Azerbaijan. To the east, squeezed along the Caspian coast, lay Caucasian Albania and Shirvan, a Georgian ally.

Tamar's relations with her neighbors were a function of power. Large Muslim kingdoms like the Ayubs of Egypt or the Seljuk Turks had to be handled with kid gloves. No good could come from poking those sleeping bears, so she used diplomacy, not force, when dealing with those potentates.

Religious differences did not necessarily mean enmity. Some Muslim rulers, she found, were men with whom she could do business, just as Christian merchants did a brisk trade with their Persian and Arab counterparts. With one sultan she negotiated safe passage for Georgian pilgrims to the Holy Cross monastery in Jerusalem. To another Muslim ruler she promised, "In the name of the Father, Son, and Holy Ghost to be friend of your friends, enemy of your enemies, as long as I am alive, to have the best intentions, never to attack your towns, states, or fortresses."

But smaller kingdoms, whether Muslim or Christian, could be pushed around with impunity, and on the birth of her son Giorgi, Tamar allowed the proud father to indulge in the traditional show of force that marked the birth of a Georgian prince. Davit raised a small army, and Tamar bade her wolves to ravage. Marching southeast to Azerbaijan, Davit's army captured an old Albanian capital. He then led a raid west, into Erzurum, a tributary that paid protection money to the Sultan of Rum.

Tamar's men returned from Erzurum with women and children, horses and livestock, coins and goods, and the queen expected the raid to intimidate surrounding rulers. But Davit had been just a bit too successful, and Tamar misread the diplomatic picture. Caucasian pashas and mullahs petitioned Baghdad's Caliph al-Nasir to teach the Georgians a lesson, and the caliph obliged them by ordering all Muslim rulers to wage jihad on Georgia.

The *atabag* of Azerbaijan, an ambitious murderer named Nusrat al-Din Abu Bakr, stepped up with a coalition army. Assembling 60,000 men, he invaded the Georgian protectorate of Shirvan and drove out its shah, who then fled to Tbilisi and begged Tamar for help. The queen was careful not to back the conquest of Azerbaijan—a move that would surely draw in more Muslim armies—but she quietly told the shah that she and Davit would do what they could to recover his kingdom.

In the spring of 1195, a Georgian army of about 30,000 men was ready to march against the Muslim tide. Tamar joined her army near the southern border and remained with Davit and the troops for several days, praying, displaying religious relics, hardening them to the task ahead.

"My brothers, let not your hearts tremble for fear that there are so many of them, while you are few, for God is with us," she emoted. "With the help of the Holy Mother of God, storm their country and assault the enemy with the power of the invincible Cross."

Having spoken to her men, Tamar walked the rocky ground, barefoot as a proper penitent, to the church of the Mother of God in Metekhi. Falling prostrate before the holy icon, the queen shed tears and prayed fervently to the Virgin for the safety of her husband and men.

Davit's force drove down the Araxes River and caught up with Abu Bakr's army on the first of June at the Azerbaijan city of Shamkor. Davit and his vanguard fought their way inside the city gates, while his main army swung wide to hit the enemy's flanks and rear.

The defenders fought hard, but timely reinforcements turned the tide for the Georgians. "The arrows were drunk with blood, and the swords devoured the flesh of their enemies," one chronicler wrote. After a terrific struggle, Davit's men slaughtered or captured most of the city's defenders.

Abu Bakr and the remnants of his army fled east. Davit pursued him, capturing the minor province of Ganja, where the citizens hailed him as their new emir. Tributes poured in from neighboring princes, and Davit forcibly converted mosques into churches. "In the place of muezzins they rang bells, and in the place of the voices of mullahs, the voices of priests were heard," wrote Tamar's biographer.

Though not decisive, the Battle of Shamkor was a tremendous victory for Tamar's Georgians. Davit carted off some 12,000 prisoners, 2,000 horses, 7,000 mules, and 15,000 camels, as well as gold and fine linens. Slaves and livestock crowded Tbilisi's outskirts, and the market for captives became so glutted that for a time slaves could be bought in town for the price of a wooden measure of flour.

After the victory at Shamkor, Tamar kept a close watch on her borders. She assigned great families to protect sections of Georgia's frontiers, and when border guards heard rumors of approaching Turks, they immediately reported back to Tbilisi. Tamar would then decide whether to muster troops, which she would place under command of one of a few trusted generals. "She did not allow her army to stay idle," her biographer wrote, with Georgian understatement.

The Battle of Basiani

While Tamar was guarding her frontiers, the ambitious Sultan of Rum, Rukn ad-Din Suleimanshah II, was building a would-be empire to the southwest. Overthrowing his brother and seizing the throne, Suleimanshah prepared to drive his armies into the neighboring Trebizond kingdom, an old Byzantine remnant that formed a buffer between his domain and Tamar's. In 1201, the sultan's army captured a king who was paying Tamar protection money, nobly called "tribute."

Georgia and Rum had been on good terms for many years. They exchanged gifts occasionally and maintained embassies in each other's capitals. But when Suleiman-shah broke with Georgia, he did not want diplomatic niceties to dilute his message. He sent a herald to Tbilisi with a written demand that left little room for specula-tion: Tamar must rescind all tribute taken from Muslim kingdoms and convert to Islam—or face the consequences.

"You have ordered the Georgians to take up the sword for the destruction of Muslims. It is a sword that was granted by God to the great Prophet Mohammed, the chief of his people," came the voice of the envoy as he read Suleimanshah's words. "Now I am sending all my army in order to destroy all the men of your country; only those will survive, who will come to meet me, bow to my yashmak, trample down the cross which is your hope, and adopt Mohammed!"

Not a promising preamble, but Tamar listened as the messenger read the sultan's terms. If she renounced Christianity, he would take her as one of his wives. If she refused, he would destroy her people and add her to his harem.

The envoy's words and arrogant tone prompted a noble to knock him senseless, and a livid Tamar warned him, "If you were not an envoy it would be proper to cut first your tongue then remove your head for your impudence." But she didn't cut his tongue or remove his head. She sent the man back to the sultan, unharmed, with her expected reply.

With the ambassador's departure, Tamar summoned the crown council. A con-temporary writer wrote that she "took counsel with them, not like a helpless person, or a woman, and [she] did not neglect the dictates of reason." Supreme faith in her soldiers enveloped her like Christ's shroud, and she ordered a general mobilization of troops.

The nobles answered her call, and soon Tamar and her allies had mustered an army of about 80,000 men, the largest Georgian force ever assembled. She sent her troops in the direction of the main Seljuk army, around 150,000 strong, and encamped in the Basiani valley, an Armenian border region.

The two sides, each beseeching the god of Abraham for victory, were comparably equipped. Georgia's elite cavalry was similar in fighting style and weapons to the Seljuk horsemen, and both armies relied heavily on mounted archers. Both fielded detachments of Frankish and Qipchak mercenary knights, and the infantry fought with the traditional sword, spear, and shield.

While Georgian troops concentrated at their staging ground near the mountain-ous redoubt of Vardzia Monastery, Tamar appeared before her armies, again unshod but clothed in garments rich in religious symbolism. She rallied her men with an inspiring speech invoking God's blessing, at the end of which they hailed her as their king. She then withdrew to a monastery to pray and sing hymns of supplication as her troops moved rapidly through Basiani.

The lightning advance of the Georgian army caught the Seljuk commanders by surprise. When Davit's vanguard fell upon them, many Turks were still in their tents. "The battle began, cruel and fierce, of which the like took place perhaps only in ancient times," wrote Tamar's chronicler.

The Seljuks threw up a makeshift defense and fended off the first Georgian assaults. Davit followed his frontal attack with two flanking cavalry assaults in a classic pincer movement. The sultan's banner fell and the Turkish lines broke. Many Seljuks were slaughtered in the battle's pursuit phase, and Tamar's army seized an immense haul of treasure, prisoners, and elite captives who could be ransomed in due course.

Tamar's signature victory had secured her kingdom, and with it, Georgia became the dominant power in the Caucasus. But problems with other Orthodox kingdoms continued to absorb her attention. In 1203, her large donation to Georgian monasteries in Antioch and Mount Athos was seized by Byzantium's emperor. Enraged, Tamar began making plans to overrun the Kingdom of Trebizond, the empire's puppet on the Black Sea coast.

The following year, as French, Venetian, and Germanic troops of the Fourth Crusade busied themselves sacking Constantinople, Tamar sent an army under command of two nephews to capture Trebizond's capital. Her nephews established a pro-Georgian state, and with the backing of Tamar's armies they expanded their new kingdom into a small regional empire, giving Tamar an ally, trading partner, and influence over a stretch of the Black Sea coast.

Battles between Georgian and Turkish forces erupted for several more years. In 1209, the Emir of Ardabil slaughtered 12,000 Armenian Christians and enslaved many more. In reprisal, Tamar ordered a surprise attack on the Muslim holy day of Eid the following year. Her Georgians destroyed the city of Ardabil, slaughtered a reciprocal 12,000 Muslims, and took slaves, cattle, and plunder.

In the years that followed, Tamar occasionally sent armies to raid Persia or put down mountain rebellions. One of her generals, learning of the murder of Georgian guards of the city of Miana, had the local governor and his children skinned and hung from a minaret as a warning to those who opposed Tamar's might. With a mixture of terror and diplomacy, Tamar set Georgia's security on a solid long-term footing.

BY THE CLOSE of her twenty-fourth year as queen, Tamar had surpassed the achievements of her forefathers. But time is a relentless horseman, and in 1207 her beloved Davit died. He was followed in death by Tamar's trusted vizier, and then by her senior general. Growing lonely as she reached fifty, the aging queen looked back wistfully at long-ago days when generals and ministers drank from a horn of conquest she had filled.

With little to feed her mind's flame, Tamar slowly withdrew from the cares of government. She crowned her teenage son, Giorgi Lasha, as her co-ruler, just as her father had crowned her nearly thirty years before. In her last year, she ruthlessly put down a Chechen rebellion, but more often she left questions of strategy to an emerging class of younger leaders.

When she succumbed to illness in early 1213 at age fifty-two, Tamar ruled the largest swath of land Georgia would ever claim as its own. Portions of Armenia and Azerbaijan were vassalages, and Georgia dominated the surrounding Arab and Seljuk principalities. Her capital city, Tbilisi, thrived on commerce, religious architecture, science, and literature such as the country had never seen before—and would never see again. The wealth generated from her wars, and the trade relations they strengthened, gave rise to a popular reminiscence of Georgia's golden age: "Peasants were like nobles, nobles were like princes, and princes were like kings."

But another Georgian adage went to the heart of the kingdom's success: "We know a lion by its claws, and Tamar by her deeds; who wants to know her, let him see the towns, fortresses, and regions, which once belonged to the sultans and were taken by her; the frontiers, which she doubled in size compared to those she received on ascending the throne."

TAMAR WAS HARDLY THE LAST WOMAN to expand the bounds of an old, unstable dynasty. On the far side of Asia, two centuries into the future, a woman with a deep appreciation of history dreamed of restoring the glories of a once-great empire. Unlike Tamar, she personally led troops in battle, riding with bow and quiver to smite enemies and claim their lands for her united people.

A woman with a passion for feather-topped hats.

6

YEAR OF THE TIGER

Manduhai of the Mongols

*Queen Manduhai the Wise, recalling the vengeance
of the former khans, set out on campaign.*

*She set in motion her foot soldiers and oxen-troops, and
after three days and nights she set out with her cavalry.*

*Queen Manduhai the Wise, putting on her quiver
elegantly, and composing her disordered hair,*

Put Dayan Khan in a box and set out.

—*ALTAN TOBČHI*, VERSE 101, 1651

THE RAGGED FELT TENT didn't look like a fulcrum of history. Lashed onto a stout wooden cart, the weatherbeaten shrine tottered uneasily as short-legged horses drew their load along the steppe's rutted dirt roads. But to the rural tribespeople trailing behind, the tent was a channeling point for the First Great Queen, the goddess who animated the windswept land they called home.

Against this backdrop, a twenty-three-year-old Mongolian widow named Manduhai stood in the bright red robes of a *khatun*, or Mongol queen, before a gathering of clan leaders. Her short stature was offset by a peculiarly Mongolian symbol of authority: an impressively tall, green felt hat crowned with bright peacock feathers. In a loud, high voice, she prayed to the First Great Queen for guidance on the tribe's choice for its next leader.

Though she chanted to a spirit in the sky, Manduhai's real audience was the collection of nobles hanging intently on every word. Her speech to the First Queen was Manduhai's way of announcing a decision that would affect her people for the next three hundred years.

❖ ❖ ❖

TWO AND A HALF CENTURIES EARLIER, Genghis Khan cut a swath of destruction across Eurasia from the Pacific Ocean to Central Europe. The conqueror's sons served their father as the empire's spear points, leading armies deep into the Caucasus and Russia. But Genghis entrusted his wives and daughters with the far more delicate task of governing the empire's heartland: China, Siberia, Mongolia, Central Asia, and the lucrative Silk Road trade routes.

Since those long-ago days of butchery and mirth, the Mongol Empire had fractured into semi-independent khanates run by estranged kinsmen. As alcoholism, palace intrigue, megalomania, and violent purges claimed his descendants, the laws Genghis had carefully laid down to preserve family peace had been casually tossed aside. In ten generations, Mongol rulers had been swallowed by the cultures they conquered, intermarrying and adopting customs of the people they subjugated. Ethnic Mongols were left hanging onto the empire's old core: modern Mongolia and eastern Siberia.

Even the label *Mongol* was deceptive, for the steppe herders had been little more than a fractious confederation of Asiatic tribes. By the mid-1400s, the northern Mongols were split into eastern and western clans. The eastern Borijin, from which Genghis Khan hailed, claimed the Mongolian Plateau north of the great Gobi Desert. Being blood descendants of the empire's founder, the Borijin leader traditionally carried the title "Great Khan of the Mongol Empire," and theoretically ruled all tribes of the plateau as far west as the Altai Mountains of Siberia.

But the Borijin ruler was a great khan in name only. By the fifteenth century the empire had atrophied to the point that rival tribes no longer dreaded the Borijin. While eastern and central clans still swore fealty to the Borijin leader, western warlords ran their lands independently, and many of their rulers saw themselves as the real Mongol power behind an impotent, distant throne.

West of the Borijin dwelt the Oirats, an interbred hodge-podge of Central Asians, Siberians, and Mongols. Although the Oirats had once served Genghis Khan as loyal allies, his later successors treated them like conquered slaves. Rival foreign powers loosened the ties binding Oirats to the Great Khan, and by

Manduhai's time, the Oirats had accepted a *taishi,* or chief of the Turkic Mongol tribes, as their unofficial sovereign.

In 1452, an evil *taishi* launched a power play to decapitate the Borijin leadership. Luring their nobles to a feast, his assassins murdered all but a handful. The few who escaped his knives and poison were cowed into submission, and the *taishi* installed a pliable survivor as his puppet ruler.

One of the few surviving Borijin males outside the *taishi's* control—unborn at the time of the purge—was his baby grandson, the offspring of his daughter and a minor Borijin noble who had descended from Genghis Khan. When the *taishi* learned of his grandchild's birth, he knew a male child with the blood of Genghis Khan might pose a threat someday, and he dispatched a squad to eliminate the threat. He told the platoon captain to find the mother's *ger,* or tent, and see whether the newborn was a boy or a girl. "If it is a girl, comb her hair," the warlord told his captain. "If it is a boy, comb his throat."

Like Moses, the baby escaped death through the help of a woman, the *taishi's* Borijin grandmother. Concealing the baby's male parts from a very superficial search, the old woman managed to pass off the child as a girl until she could smuggle him to safety.

The murderous *taishi* fell two years later, the victim of a revenge killing, and a Turkic warlord named Beg-Arslan took his place. Beg-Arslan replaced the old Borijin puppet khan with a noble named Manduul. To strengthen his dynastic ties, Beg-Arslan forced Manduul to marry his daughter, a famously ugly woman whose name meant "Big Nose" in Mongolian.

In a society in which beauty was defined by round faces and tiny features, Big Nose's western looks offered nothing to arouse Manduul's passions, and in 1464, an attractive Choros girl named Manduhai caught the khan's eye. Her name, Manduhai, meant "rising" or "ascending," and the name seemed prophetic when Manduul took her as his junior wife.

But Manduhai's prospects were limited: While she conceived a daughter with the king, she did not bear him a son. With no heirs and in poor health, Manduul Khan groomed his nephew for the role of khan. The boy, Bayan Mongke, was the newborn who had escaped the *taishi's* assassin squad during the Borijin purge years earlier. Raised in hiding by nomadic herders, Bayan, now a teenager, was the only other lineal male descendant of Genghis Khan.

For a time, Bayan was the son Manduul longed for. The king adorned his nephew in silk robes and a golden belt, bestowing on him the title of *jinong,* or "Golden Prince." Bayan Khan, it was thought, might one day resurrect the empire of his

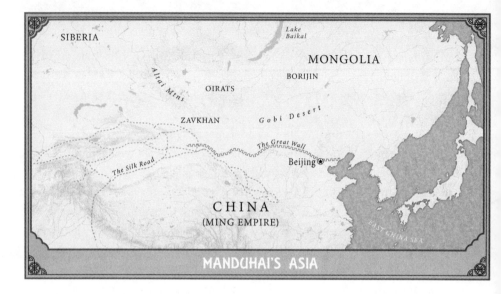

MANDUHAI'S ASIA

famous forefather, and Manduul pinned on Bayan his hopes for Mongolia's next generation.

But the Golden Prince was also a threat to men who coveted Manduul's title. A warrior chief named Ismayil, Beg-Arslan's protégé and a warlord in his own right, spread rumors through agents that the *jinong* was having an affair with Manduul's senior wife. After letting his whispering campaign take root, Ismayil, a frequent visitor to the Borijin court, secretly told Bayan his uncle suspected the seduction and was about to have him killed. Shocked, Bayan fled the royal camp and galloped to the edge of the Gobi Desert.

The khan took Bayan's flight as an admission of guilt, and Manduul asked Ismayil to send a cavalry party to track down the fugitive prince. When the riders reached Bayan's camp, the nineteen-year-old *jinong* fled deeper into the wilderness, abandoning his wife and newborn son. Alone in the desert, he chanced upon a band of highwaymen who, eyeing the lone rider's luxurious clothes, killed him, stripped him of his robes and belt, and left his corpse to rot in the wilderness.

About the time of Bayan's exile, Manduul Khan died, leaving no male heirs.* His throne became an invitation to mischief by gods and men. Meanwhile, Manduhai's marriage had elevated her to the lofty rank of *khatun*, though the title carried no power independent of her now-dead husband. Unless she found a legitimate basis

---

* The circumstances of Manduul's death have been lost, but with so many competing factions looking to take the throne, murder is not an implausible explanation.

for ruling in her own name and secured the support of the army, she would become a royal pawn, pushed around a chessboard of tent beds and grass oases as would-be khans jockeyed for position.

STANDING BEFORE THE FIRST QUEEN'S SHRINE, Manduhai saw a treacherous road stretching before her people. To the west, the Oirats were restive. To the south, the *taishi* of the Silk Road oases grew wealthy and powerful, while the Ming Chinese controlled trade along the road's eastern terminus. Both the *taishi* and Ming emperor would gladly hack off pieces of the Mongolian rump state if they sniffed out weakness, and a widowed woman was just the sort of weakness that might tempt them to act.

Preserving the old Mongol Empire meant finding a new khan, which meant finding a husband. Two candidates were natural suitors for the widowed queen. The first was the ranking Borijin general, a nobleman named Une-Bolod. Charismatic and well-connected, Une-Bolod held an impressive battle record. He commanded the support of the Mongolian army and had served as the Borijin family's unofficial leader after the Oirat purges sixteen years before.

Une-Bolod's only weakness was his bloodline. He was born to a cadet branch of the Borijin, but he was not a lineal descendant of Genghis Khan. That posed a problem, since Manduhai, too, carried none of the founder's blood in her veins. To marry Une-Bolod would dilute the Borijin title of "Great Khan" by abandoning the royal lineage. Her people were looking for familiar guidance, and Une-Bolod's line was not of the right family.

Her second option was riskier. Ismayil, *taishi* of the Oirats, had taken power in the west and ruled independently of his nominal liege, Beg-Arslan. Seeing in Manduhai a path to becoming a legitimate khan, Ismayil tempted her with the prospect of a safe, secluded, and luxurious oasis home.

Choosing Ismayil meant a life of jeweled goblets and sweet wine as the *taishi*'s consort. But it would also mean turning her back on her people and losing her place as a Mongol leader. As one supporter warned her, "You will divide yourself from the people, and you will lose your honored and respected title of *khatun*."

The warning weighed heavily on Manduhai's heart.

Her final option was to surrender the empire. China's Ming dynasty had driven the Mongols out two centuries earlier, and its current ruler, Emperor Chenghua, was determined to end the Mongol threat once and for all. To the logical minds of Chinese mandarins, a political marriage was preferable to a long and expensive war. The wealth of the Mongols—even a *taishi*'s treasury—was nothing compared to the opulence of the Ming court. If Manduhai accepted Chinese overtures, she could look forward to a life of ease and luxury as a barbarian oddity in a glittering world of Ming splendor—but her country would become a vassal of China. Manduhai would be handing over her legacy and forfeiting any chance of restoring the old empire.

Each choice carried the alluring promise of a secure, comfortable life, a life unimaginable to a girl raised in the hardships of the steppes. But each demanded a supreme sacrifice: the forfeit of her right to rule what was left of Genghis Khan's great empire. Whatever her title or social status, Manduhai would never hold real power if she chose the Borijin general, the Oirat *taishi*, or the Chinese emperor as her suitor.

So, she chanted before the shrine of *Eshi Khatun*, the First Queen. As the wind blew and the grass swayed, she performed the ritual of *tsatal*, throwing fermented mare's milk into the air as an offering while praying for wisdom and insight.

As Manduhai's words hung in the air, a young, emaciated boy pressed through the crowd. He wobbled up to the queen in large, stiff boots, and Manduhai reached out to him.

WHAT MANDUHAI KNEW, and the nobles did not, was that this sickly child crawling from the shadows would become the symbol her people needed. Batu Mongke, the abandoned son of the dead prince Bayan, had clung to life under the care of an old peasant woman. The harsh climate of the Mongol steppes—where dust storms could suffocate an unwatched toddler, and freezing temperatures could turn wet diapers into death traps—placed a premium on child care and nutrition, and young Batu lacked these basic necessities in his first few years. His back was hunched and his skeletal legs could barely support his gaunt frame.

When Manduhai had learned of the boy's survival, she secretly arranged to move the frail child to the safety of a rural foster family before his rivals could make short work of him. As the sole surviving male lineal descendent of Genghis Khan, Batu became the banner Manduhai needed to install herself as regent and assume power over the eastern Mongols.

In the magical days when the empire was young, the process of choosing a new khan involved spiritualistic rituals, long prayers, and election by a conclave of leaders. The ways of the old khan had been cast aside by Manduhai's time, and Manduhai was not about to put the matter to a vote. It was vital for the new khan to be inaugurated in a manner likely to be accepted by her people, but she would not risk an election that could be rigged to give a rival claim to the title.

She turned to religion. If properly invoked, rites sanctioned by the old gods were a well-worn path to legitimacy, or at least popular acceptance. In years long past, when Genghis Khan wished to take up a cause his people might be reluctant to support, he ostentatiously made a pilgrimage up to a sacred mountain and prayed to the Eternal Blue Sky until he could report to his people that he had secured divine blessing.

Following the founder's example, Manduhai set her gaze toward the ancestors. Her ceremony before the First Queen began with a declaration of her unwillingness to wed Une-Bolod because he was a descendent of the great khan. She asked the She-God to punish her if she ever chose him as her husband.

Knowing her rejection of a popular Borijin general would unnerve her followers, Manduhai quickly followed her rejection of Une-Bolod with a second vow, sealed with a loyalty oath sworn by Mongol soldiers before battle: If she ever deserted her people, or brought them any harm, she asked the goddess to tear "my shoulders from my thighs."

As the weight of her violent promise sank in, Batu Mongke toddled forward and stood beside the *khatun*. His triple-soled boots did little to hide his age—he was only five years old—and his frail frame made him look even younger. But Manduhai presented the urchin to the goddess of the sky and announced, "I wish to make your descendant Great Khan even though he is still a young boy."

Manduhai assured her audience that the gods concurred. She gave Batu the imperial title of Dayan Khan, meaning, "Khan of the Whole," a name conjuring an aura of unity and solidarity. As regent, she would rule the Mongols during Dayan's minority, and when he came of age, Manduhai would marry him. They would reign together as khan and *khatun*.

It was 1470—the Year of the Tiger.

The Conquest of Zavkhan

Rituals and prayers threw a veneer of legitimacy over Dayan Khan's title, but the realist in Manduhai knew that without the backing of an army, her protégé's claim—and his life—meant little. Enemies stirred on every frontier, and Manduhai had precious little time to marshal her forces if she were to defend her throne, unite the Mongols, and expand the empire.

She began by shoring up the allegiance of her rejected suitor, Une-Bolod. Under a succession order worked out behind closed tent flaps, Une-Bolod would stand next in line to the throne if Dayan Khan unexpectedly died. Also, if Manduhai died during Dayan's youth, Une-Bolod would step in as regent and govern until the boy could rule for himself.

In pledging her support to Une-Bolod in the event of Dayan Khan's death, Manduhai trusted Une-Bolod not to hasten that day. But she was a shrewd judge of character, and her faith in Une-Bolod was rewarded: He served his *khatun* loyally and brought with him the support of the eastern and central clans.

Across the Gobi Desert, far to the south, opposition was building. To the southwest, restless Turco-Mongolian tribes led by Ismayil and Beg-Arslan grew in power. To the southeast, the Ming Chinese saw in the ascendant widow and her helpless khan an opportunity to expand the empire.

The most effective arrow in Manduhai's quiver, economic negotiations, could not be loosed, since Mongolia had little to offer merchant nations like China besides good horse flesh. That left her with the military option. The prowess of her riders, and her position north of the Gobi Desert, conferred strong advantages to a woman short on advantages. To guarantee her rule, and the safety of the young khan, Manduhai would have to prove herself on the battlefield.

From pages of the *Altan Tobchi*, the secret chronicles of the Mongol rulers, Manduhai emerges as a talented amateur strategist who could visualize economic, political, geographic, and military variables and combine them into a workable plan. She executed that strategy in three phases. The first was to pacify the western tribes on the Mongolian Plateau. Next, she would make peace with Ming China to the south, hopefully without forcing a treaty through violence. Finally, she would neutralize the armies of Ismayil and Beg-Arslan from the southwest, take control of key points on the Silk Road, and use the lucrative trade and customs revenues to strengthen her kingdom.

To bring the western tribes into her fold, Manduhai chose Zavkhan, a province west of the Khangai Mountains, as the backdrop for her first campaign. It was an astute choice. Zavkhan had pastures and water to sustain a large cavalry-based army, and because it lay north of the Silk Road oases, control of the region would give her a ligature on the world's biggest economic artery.

Whether her warriors would give their all for an untested *khatun* was an open question, and Manduhai knew her first campaign had to be a success. Though she lacked the expertise to drill soldiers or execute the tactics, she consulted her generals and gave a great deal of thought to logistics and leadership. Before deploying her cavalry, she sent caravans of ox carts laden with food, arrows, and supplies to waypoints along her march route, then followed her teamsters and quartermasters with foot infantry.

"Queen Manduhai the Wise, recalling the vengeance of the former khans, set out on campaign," wrote the *Altan Tobchi*'s chronicler. "She set in motion her foot soldiers and oxen-troops, and after three days and nights she set out with her cavalry."

Battle leadership was another concern, for as every soldier knew, women had no place in the combat ranks. Flowing hair could become tangled in a quiver, and her tall, feather-topped *bogta,* would fly off during a cavalry charge. If nothing else, the image of a woman on a horse was not a natural morale-builder for the average Mongol horse archer. Manduhai knew she needed a man to help lead her army—even if the man was too young to bend a bow—so she took little Dayan Khan with her as a living war banner. She had him shoulder a symbolic bow and quiver, and had a harness strapped onto his horse's back to keep him from toppling off his saddle during the long ride.

Braiding her hair, Manduhai replaced her *bogta* with a warrior's iron helmet and shouldered her own bow and quiver. Together, the middle-aged widow and her malformed child fell into column and rode off to war.

Manduhai's Zavkhan campaign played out in a series of punishing skirmishes, rather than epic battles. Clashes took place with hundreds, perhaps thousands of men, not the 10,000-man *tumens* of the glory days of Genghis Khan. But as she moved west, steadily gaining ground, Manduhai's reputation among the Oirats rose.

The *Altan Tobchi* described one skirmish in which Manduhai galloped through a cloud of dust and arrows. As she jerked in the saddle suddenly, her helmet slipped from her head, presenting a perfect target for her foes.

An enemy warrior cried out, "The queen has no helmet!" But instead of driving his spear tip at the *khatun*'s bare head, he bellowed, "Bring another!" When no man came forth to offer his helmet, the Oirat removed his own, galloped up to Manduhai, and offered it to the woman riding with the enemy.

The chivalrous gesture, if it happened the way the chronicler claims, bought no favors from Manduhai. Her blood was up, and she charged back into battle. According to royal records, Manduhai and her bodyguards pushed through a thick cloud of Oirats "and annihilated them."

The brief war between Manduhai's eastern Mongols and the Zavkhan Oirats ended in victory for the queen. Summoning the defeated clan leaders, she announced new symbolic laws that left no doubt about who was in charge. Tall, plumed headdresses of the nobility would henceforth be limited to feathered crests no higher than two finger lengths. Oirats must sit on their knees in the presence of the khans. They could not refer to any *ger* as an *ordon,* or palace, and they were forbidden from using knives when eating meat.*

---

* This last proscription is not entirely clear from surviving Mongol records. It is possible that the cutlery rule was simply a confiscation of all knives as a precaution against assassination until Manduhai and Dayan Khan had safely moved on.

Manduhai's conquest of Zavkhan told steppe tribesmen that the energetic young *khatun* had the blessing of the First Great Queen. She sent emissaries to demand submission from other Oirat tribes, and one by one, clans that sat out the Zavkhan war pledged their loyalty to Manduhai. By the end of her campaign, Mongols and Oirats of the Mongolian Plateau stood joined under the Borijin banner.

Confronting Beg-Arslan

Manduhai's steady consolidation of power in the north unnerved Ming rulers, who for two centuries had been raised on bedtime stories of Mongol savagery. But full-scale invasion was more than the insular Chinese could stomach. The Gobi Desert was a far more forbidding obstacle than even the Great Wall, and cost-conscious mandarins shied away from funding a military expedition so far from home.

Striking with treasure rather than steel, Chinese officials clamped an embargo on Manduhai's kingdom. Luxury items like cloth, incense, medicines, and tea would be cut off until the Mongol queen accepted Ming demands for annexation. Denying Manduhai goods that made life on the steppes palatable would compel her to submit to what spears and crossbows could not.

But commerce is a two-way trail, and Manduhai retaliated with an embargo of her own. Because Mongolia was China's chief source of horses, the trade war produced a major shortage of cavalry mounts for the Chinese army. As China's herds dwindled, Ming purchasing agents scoured East Asia to find sources of horseflesh. Prices rose, and black-market profiteers grew rich. Before long, an average horse went for the unthinkable price of a bolt of high-quality silk, eight bolts of coarse silk, and currency equal to two more bolts of silk. An excellent horse fetched 130 *chin* of tea, a small fortune.

Groaning under the trade war's unintended consequences, the Mings hoped to persuade the obstinate woman to submit to Chinese rule. But Manduhai stood her ground. She would fight the commercial war until Beijing backed down.

Victory in Zavkhan did not shield Manduhai from her southwestern rivals, Ismayil and Beg-Arslan. While the Gobi Desert formed a defensive belt against invading armies, the southwestern warlords were well placed to cut off Mongolia's trade by posting troops at critical points along the Silk Road. Like the Ming, the *taishis* could wage a devastating war against Manduhai's kingdom without laying a single arrow across a bow.

Yet Manduhai knew she was not their only target. The aggressive Beg-Arslan also had been pecking away at Chinese security through border raids and short-term incursions. Friendly merchants and clan leaders kept Manduhai informed of Beg-Arslan's provocations, and she calculated that it was only a matter of time before the Mings declared war. With luck, the Chinese might destroy her Turkic rivals—or at least, drain enough blood so that her army could gallop in for the kill. Time was, for the moment, on her side.

Riding the storm out was not a risk-free proposition, however. If the Chinese army failed, Beg-Arslan's star would seem ascendant to wavering tribes, which would flock to his banner. Should that happen, it would only be a matter of time before Beg-Arslan rode north of the Gobi to claim Dayan Khan's throne for himself.

Manduhai's strategic gamble paid off. Just as she had hoped, the border raids stung the Ming emperor into a military response. In February 1472, Chinese general Wang Yue assembled an army of 40,000 soldiers. Wang struck the Turkic base camp, then ambushed Beg-Arslan's main force, scattering his horsemen. The old warlord was forced to retreat north.

The Chinese victory had bought Manduhai a temporary reprieve, but Wang Yue had not eliminated Beg-Arslan as a threat to Manduhai's kingdom. Just the opposite: By pushing the warlord's disordered armies north, the buffer between the *khatun* and her rival thinned. The Ming emperor, having given Beg-Arslan a black eye, then shifted to a defensive strategy. Pulling back his expeditionary force, he strengthened the Great Wall on his northern border, signaling that China would no longer operate north of the wall unless forced.

To Manduhai, China's defensive pivot was an ominous sign. It meant that Beijing intended to keep out of Mongol affairs as long as the Mongols left them alone. And without the Chinese, it would fall to Manduhai's armies to keep Beg-Arslan and Ismayil in check. The war she had been trying to avoid now lurked just beyond the horizon.

While fighting between Beg-Arslan and the Chinese flared along her southern border, Manduhai had not sat on her laurels. She formed alliances with independent clans that might join her against Beg-Arslan, the strongest of which was a cluster of tribes known as the Three Guards. The clans had once sworn fealty to the Ming Court, but in the past few decades their loyalty waned as the tides of the war shifted. After Manduhai's victory at Zavkhan, she skillfully won over the Three Guards and prepared for another war.

She planned to hit Beg-Arslan and Ismayil separately, before they could join forces. Around 1479, her armies were ready to take the offensive. She fastened her helmet and mounted her war horse once again, this time accompanied by an older, stronger, and more capable Dayan Khan.*

The combined armies of the Three Guards and Manduhai's Mongols invaded Beg-Arslan's domain and established a forward base south of the Mongolian Plateau. Under Manduhai's tutelage, Dayan Khan, now a teenager, took charge of the campaign's next phase. Learning from scouts that the enemy was thinly spread, they launched a surprise attack against Beg-Arslan's headquarters.

Seeing the enemy army bearing down on him in overwhelming numbers, Beg-Arslan lost his nerve and abandoned his camp. Switching helmets with one of his lieutenants to throw off pursuers, he galloped away with a small band of retainers.

He did not get far. The imposter was caught, and in return for his life he gave up Beg-Arslan's hiding place. Dayan's men "caught up with Beg-Arslan, seized him, and killed him," laconically records the *Altan Tobchi*. "It is said that salt grew at the place he was killed."

With his tribe outnumbered, Ismayil, too, went into hiding. Around 1484, Manduhai ordered local warlords to track down the fugitive *taishi*. A clan chief set out with 250 horse archers to find the man who had once been suitor to the queen. The bowmen found him in an isolated camp and shot him dead.

❖   ❖   ❖

BY THE TIME OF ISMAYIL'S DEATH, Dayan Khan's apprenticeship had come to an end. For the next three decades, Manduhai and Dayan ruled their realm as husband and wife, governing a kingdom stretching from Siberia's Lake Baikal to the edge of Korea's Yellow River. With the death of the Ming emperor in 1487, a new and mutually productive chapter opened in Sino-Mongolian relations. Trade flourished, and a revitalized Mongol kingdom entered a new period of stability.

There were still dangers, as there always would be, and revolts flared from time to time. When Manduhai was forty years old and eight months pregnant with twins, she saddled up and led troops into battle. Exhausted from her exertions, she fell from her horse as one battle raged. Her bodyguards jumped from their horses and formed a human shield around their queen until she could be helped back onto her mount.

Manduhai and Dayan remained inseparable, and their marriage produced eight

---

* Mongol chronicles do not specify whether Manduhai managed to buy off Ismayil at the critical moment, or whether Ismayil was occupied with his own troubles when Manduhai launched her campaign against Beg-Arslan. In any event, he remained out of the picture while Manduhai went after his ally.

children, including three sets of twins. Consolidating their power, the royal couple reorganized the tribes by killing or deposing stubborn leaders and putting their own sons and daughters on the vacant thrones, just as Genghis Khan had done 250 years before. They abolished the rank of *taishi* and decreed that all Mongols were brothers, whether Oirat or Borijin, Ossetian or Three Guards, Choros or Tumed. Like the Mongols of old, all would bow to one Great Khan.

Manduhai was blessed to grow old in a world she had brought back to a lost time of pride and prosperity. The Earth Mother reclaimed her in 1509, when she was around sixty years old. Rising from a humble *ger*, she had ably united and led her nation for three and a half decades, leaving behind a resurrected dynasty that would rule Mongolia until its conquest by China's Manchu in the early seventeenth century. Later generations of Mongols would revere her as "Manduhai the Wise."

HALFWAY AROUND THE WORLD, another remarkable woman died the same year Manduhai's narrative ended. Like the Mongol queen, this woman would mount a horse while pregnant and lead soldiers in battle. But the scene of her drama was unimaginable to a girl raised on the Mongolian steppes. A galaxy from the world of tents and ponies and grasslands, she grew up in a palace, surrounded by the gilt and intrigues of the Italian Renaissance.

7

VIPER AND ROSE

Countess Caterina Sforza

*"She wore a dress of satin with a train of two arms-lengths,
a black velvet hat in the French fashion, a man's belt and a purse
full of gold ducats, a curved falchion at her side; and among the soldiers and the cavaliers she was much feared, because when
she had a weapon in her hand, she was fierce and cruel."*
—BARTOLOMEO CERRETANI, C. 1500

THE CROWD WATCHED IN SILENCE as the bedraggled countess stepped toward
the drawbridge. Her husband's butchered corpse lay in a pauper's grave, and she was
surrounded by menacing armed guards. Her six children were prisoners of her enemies, and her captors had threatened her with death by spear, death by starvation,
and an eternity of damnation at the hands of a vengeful god.

Her life, and the lives of her children, hung on a desperate promise she had made
to her husband's assassins: If her captors would permit her to return to her fortress,
she would order the garrison to surrender.

Failure to follow her instructions to the letter, the men assured her, would mean
a violent death for her children, one by one.

The tear-streaked widow walked, as if in a waking nightmare, to the moat's edge.
The curtain of spears parted, and she stepped onto the drawbridge. With measured
steps, she reached the castle's yawning entrance, then turned to the crowd.

Glaring at the men holding her children hostage, she raised her hands to the heavens, then curled her fists into two obscene gestures and disappeared into the castle.

❖   ❖   ❖

CATERINA SFORZA RIARIO lived in a world of beauty and filth, of piety and depravity. A land where the scent of jasmine mixed with the stench of sewage, where priests moonlighted as assassins, where cardinals and popes indulged carnal desires when not leading holy sacraments. She mingled with painters like Leonardo da Vinci and Sandro Botticelli, negotiated with Niccolò Machiavelli, and fought papal armies while Michelangelo chipped *Pietà* from a block of marble. Bride at ten, widow at twenty-five, botanist, warrior, cosmetologist, rape victim, general, tyrant, mother, and penitent, Caterina Sforza lived the most interesting life of any woman of the Italian Renaissance.

She was born to a family of soldiers, *condottieri* who amassed fortunes leading mercenary armies for popes, kings, and petty nobles who claimed fifteenth-century Italy as their own. Her grandfather conquered Milan and built it into northern Italy's economic and cultural powerhouse. Her father, Duke Galeazzo Sforza, was a man of contrasts. Ruthless—even cruel—in battle, he was both a soldier and patron of the arts, slaughtering enemies while commissioning artworks and funding ornate theaters and palaces.

As the illegitimate daughter of the Duke of Milan, young Caterina enjoyed every advantage education and wealth could confer. Raised in the splendors of the Sforza castle at Porta Giovia, she was schooled alongside the duke's other children, no distinction being made among male or female, legitimate or bastard. Tutors drilled her in poetry, Latin, chivalric romances, history, and religion, and in her idle hours she pored over some of the thousand books lining the walls of the great ducal library.

The Sforza parents stressed the importance of hunting, combat, and leadership. As a girl, Caterina learned to wield a sword and shield, and the family's horses, falcons, dogs, and hunting weapons kept her happily occupied whenever she could get into open country. Spurring mounts at breakneck speeds in pursuit of boar, stag, or rabbit, the little hoyden learned to banish fear and focus her mind on duty to family, whatever that duty might demand.

As it turned out, duty demanded her virginity. In 1471, the pope died and a new pontiff, Pope Sixtus IV, took the throne of St. Peter. The following year, when Caterina was about ten, the pope's hard-drinking, womanizing nephew, thirty-year-old Girolamo Riario, paid the Sforza family a visit over Christmas. By the cold winter fireplace, Riario and the Sforza father negotiated a business deal that would change Caterina's life.

Milan's people accepted Duke Galeazzo as their leader, but his title was clouded by the Holy Roman Emperor's refusal to confer a formal dukedom on the Sforza patriarch. Pope Sixtus wished to consolidate his power over the small city-states of Romagna, north of Rome, and he was looking to buy the Sforza-owned city of Imola to bestow on his nephew Girolamo. If Duke Galeazzo would sell Imola to the Papal States, the pope promised to use his influence to sway the Holy Roman Emperor to confirm Galeazzo's title as Duke of Milan. To seal the bargain, Galeazzo offered his eleven-year-old niece, Costanza Fogliani, as Girolamo's bride.

Among Italian nobility, marriages were commonly arranged while bride and groom were still sexually immature. Though the marriage contract remained legally binding, it was customary for newlyweds to remain with their families until they were old enough to bear children, generally around age fourteen. Unwilling to wait, Girolamo insisted on taking the eleven-year-old girl to bed with him immediately, a condition the girl's appalled mother refused. With the business deal breaking down, a desperate Galeazzo offered to substitute his ten-year-old daughter Caterina. Girolamo accepted, and the two were married three weeks later.

Caterina left no record of the physical or emotional trauma of intercourse at age ten, and exhibited no aversion to sex later in life. She idolized her father, trusted his judgment, and believed family duty came before every other consideration. By taking this gruff old man to bed, young Caterina played her part in forging a crucial link between the House of Sforza and the Holy See. That was enough for her.

The marriage sealed, the Sforza family avatar—a serpent eating a child—joined the rose of the Riario clan. But a week after the wedding night, a satiated Girolamo returned to the more refined pleasures of his mistresses in Rome. He would not see his child bride for three more years.[*]

As she awaited the return of her husband, Caterina grew into a young woman. Her skinny child's frame bloomed into a slender waist, a lithe, sensuous neck, and long, strong legs. Tresses of reddish-blonde hair fell over the nape of a neck set off by smooth, white skin and enchanting green eyes. With access to the best cosmetics and finest clothing in Europe, Catarina blended conviviality, energy, beauty, and sophistication into an intoxicating brew that mesmerized men.

In 1476, three years after her wedding, Caterina lost her beloved father to a nest of rivals, who stabbed him to death before an altar as he celebrated the Feast of St. Stephen. As his blood pooled on the chapel floor, Caterina's stepmother, Bona de

---

[*] The viper, or *biscione*, was originally the symbol of the Visconti family that ruled Milan before the Sforza conquest. The Sforzas combined it with the image of a human, possibly a baby, being swallowed as a warning to their enemies. A cleaned-up though recognizable version of the grisly image can be seen today in the grill badge of cars made by Milanese manufacturer Alfa Romeo.

Savoy, sprang into action. She immediately declared herself regent for her six-year-old son and summoned loyalist troops to her aid. Drawbridges were raised, allies were assured that the assassins acted alone, and troops were stationed at critical junctions throughout Milan. The killers were hunted down and slaughtered without pity.

Her father's bloody denouement taught Caterina a lesson she would inscribe on her soul: When the father falls, the mother must take command. At her husband's side, a wife should be supportive, fertile, practical, domestic. But if there are no men left to draw the sword, then the woman must—without hesitation.

Courting the Papacy

At age thirteen, Caterina found herself riding the road to Rome with a retinue of Sforza soldiers, servants, and relatives. Traveling south from Milan, she stopped at her new domain, the city of Imola in the Romagna region, about two hundred miles northeast of Rome. Wrapped in a gold dress embedded with nearly a thousand small pearls, she dazzled locals with a choreographed display of Sforza wealth and power. Pearl ropes loosely circled her neck, and a black, gem-studded silk cape hung from her shoulders.

She spent two weeks greeting noble and commoner, and her enthusiastic subjects fêted her with banquet after banquet. She then made her way to Rome, where her party was greeted at the city gates by 6,000 horsemen of the papal army.

Weighed down like a servant sent to advertise the wealth of the Sforza clan, Caterina walked slowly through the doors of Saint Peter's Basilica wearing a gold brocade mantle and long crimson skirt. Heavy gemstone necklaces pressed into the nape of her neck, and her long, slim fingers reflected light off rubies and emeralds. Before the assembled cardinals and courtiers, the glittering bride knelt before His Holiness and kissed the pontiff's slippered feet.

After her formal introduction to the Vicar of Christ, Caterina was presented to the College of Cardinals, kissing hands, kissing rings, smiling broadly, and paying compliments to the wise old men who favored her with their blessed presence. Completing the rounds of curtseying and kissing, Caterina Sforza Riario took her place as the guest of honor at a wedding feast thrown in over-the-top, theatrical Roman style. Before the night was over, the sophisticated, beautiful girl from Milan had won the hearts of the papal crowd.

As Caterina's star waxed, her husband's waned. The Medici family of Florence refused to loan the Vatican the 40,000 ducats the pope needed to buy Imola from Caterina's father. Miffed, Pope Sixtus took out the loan from a rival banking family, which ignited a blood feud among the two banking houses. To put the Medici family in its place, in 1478 Girolamo Riario hired assassins to kill their patriarch, Lorenzo de Medici. The killers would strike in a spectacularly Florentine setting: the sacrament of communion at the great Cathedral of Santa Maria del Fiore.

The plot failed miserably. Though his brother fell with nineteen dagger blows, Lorenzo escaped and fled to his stronghold. Most of the hired killers—including the archbishop of Pisa and the priest who led the communion ceremony—were rounded up and promptly hanged. Their bodies were left to rot from the ropes they strangled on, and the scene was recorded on a wall fresco by a thirty-three-year-old Florentine painter named Botticelli.*

The clumsy assassination attempt was a bitter public humiliation for Girolamo and for the pope, who had more than a vague knowledge of the plot. It also proved deeply embarrassing to Caterina, who admired Lorenzo and cherished close ties of friendship to the Medici family. Realizing that her husband was an unstable vessel for her ambitions, she began paying closer attention to the murky world of Italian politics.

In August 1479, the countess fulfilled an important obligation by giving birth to a male child. The arrival of Ottaviano Riario, grand-nephew of the pope, was celebrated by Rome's ecumenical elite. Foremost among the Vatican's faction heads was Ottaviano's godfather, a clever cardinal from Spain named Roderigo Borgia.

Through patronage and simony, Cardinal Borgia had amassed a fortune, and he intended one day to offer part of his riches as a "tithe" to well-placed cardinals in exchange for the throne of St. Peter. A man of epic sexual appetites even by the debauched standards of fifteenth-century Rome, Cardinal Borgia rolled into one charismatic figure wealth, intelligence, and an eloquence that led an unending stream of swooning women—casual liaisons and beloved mistresses—into, across, and eventually out of his most sanctified bed.

Cardinal Borgia was a man with the ambition and means to seize the papacy at the right moment. Caterina would learn to keep a watchful eye on him as papal politics took their inevitable twists and turns.

---

* Executions were popular art subjects during the Italian Renaissance. In a year, another of Girolamo's assassins, Bernardi di Bandino Baroncelli, would be hunted down, dragged back to Florence in chains, and similarly strung up. His dangling body would be sketched by a twenty-six-year-old Tuscan artist named Leonardo da Vinci.

The Seizure of Castel Sant'Angelo

The year after Ottaviano's birth, Pope Sixtus expanded Girolamo's holdings to include Forli, a city ten miles south of Imola with a population of 10,000 souls. Forli's military center was Rocca di Ravaldino, a walled, moated castle with four round towers anchored by a forty-five-foot-tall keep.

For fifty years, Forli had been the dominion of the Ordelaffi family, which had burned itself out in rounds of fratricide that killed off the family's senior members. Pope Sixtus invalidated all remaining Ordelaffi claims upon Forli, and faithfully carried out God's divine will by bestowing the city and its castle on his nephew Girolamo.

Wary of assassins and deeply suspicious by nature, Girolamo postponed his inaugural visit to his new domain. It was not until the following spring that he and a pregnant Caterina entered Forli in a procession led by acolytes waving palm fronds, a gesture reminiscent of Christ's entry into Jerusalem. Unlike the donkey-riding Jesus, however, Girolamo and Caterina rode in a carriage drawn by fine horses, and Jerusalem's fishermen and beggars were replaced by a parade of gold-brocaded knights, blaring trumpets, crucifixes, reliquaries, and opulent baggage wagons.

As in Rome, Caterina charmed crowds that gathered to greet the new rulers. She touched the hands of townspeople and promised her jeweled overdress as a gift to the men who took charge of her mount. After a day and night of celebrations, she and Girolamo stood at their palace balcony before a cheering crowd and tossed coins to the throng below. A mock battle that afternoon commenced a month of festivities honoring the new count and his fertile wife.

It was a fine start. But over the next four years, Girolamo sank into a bog of isolation, paranoia, and cruelty. He provoked war with a neighboring family and had its captured patriarch tortured for a month before ending his misery by beheading him. He was quick to order secret assassinations, but timid when called to open battle. When Pope Sixtus fell ill, the dying pontiff handed Girolamo control over government functions, and by 1484 the nephew was acting as a virtual pope. As Girolamo's power grew, his despotism and violence stoked a fire of revenge among his rivals.

The death of Pope Sixtus on August 12, 1484, unleashed a long-expected wave of anarchy and violence. In the absence of a living moral authority figure, Romans traditionally spent each papal interregnum looting, burning, and beating until a new Holy Father took the throne to remind them of the wages of sin. The purge of 1484 was particularly virulent, and much of the larceny and destruction was aimed at Riario palaces in Rome.

When mob rule broke out, Girolamo happened to be in the countryside, waging another of his vendettas. Hearing that her husband's exiled enemies were streaming back into the city, Caterina, now seven months pregnant, knew it would only be a matter of days before those enemies intimidated the College of Cardinals into electing a foe of the Riario clan to the papacy. Retribution was certain to follow.

No, she concluded. If there were any intimidating, it would be by her. Sweating under a riding cloak and carrying the weight of an unborn baby, Caterina mounted her horse and led a flying column to Rome's Castel Sant'Angelo, the Tiber River fortress that commands the road to Saint Peter's Basilica. Two days after the pope's death, she reached Rome and galloped up the ramp into the fortress mouth.

Showing no signs of fear, Caterina dismissed the senior officers—including the head castellan, appointed by her husband—and made military and political decisions on her own authority. She ordered the castle's bronze cannons trained on all access roads to the Vatican, barring the way to the papal conclave that would elect the new pope. As her sergeants glowered from the castle's ramparts, the twenty-one-year-old pregnant noblewoman dominated Rome.

While her husband sat encamped outside the city, raging impotently at his enemies, Caterina had executed a brilliant tactical move. Her guns on the castle's ramparts backed her demand that the cardinals confirm Riario family titles and lands bestowed by the previous pope. When, from the street below, the ecclesiasts demanded that she turn over the fortress to God's anointed representatives, she yelled back that Pope Sixtus had made her husband commander of the castle, and she would turn it over only to him. If anyone disagreed, her cannon would allow the offender to discuss the matter with his Father-Who-Art-In-Heaven at infinite length.

Caterina's defiant response put the cardinals in a bind, for Sant'Angelo's guns cut off their access to the Sistine Chapel, the site of the papal election. If they dared cross the Tiber Bridge and move toward the chapel, she might gun them down. There would be no new pope—and no end to Rome's mob violence—until Caterina permitted the cardinals to cross the Tiber.

Five days later, the cardinals bought off Girolamo with a payment of 8,000 ducats, indemnity for his destroyed property, confirmation of his titles to Forli and Imola, and his continued captaincy of the papal armies. With his honor and financial interests satisfied, Girolamo agreed to call off his wife.

Caterina distrusted men of the cloth, and she stubbornly remained behind Sant'Angelo's massive walls for several more days. Believing her husband was making a dreadful mistake by trusting the Vatican's emissaries, she smuggled in 150 additional soldiers and prepared for a long siege.

But the August heat permeated the castle, and the countess fell ill. With her husband having given up and with a baby to carry to term, she reluctantly concluded that family interests required her to give the Vatican back to the cardinals. She signed agreements protecting her husband's interests and led her men out of the fortress.

Caterina drew crowds wherever she went, but her exit from Castel Sant'Angelo was striking even for her. No longer the demure beauty who once graced the gates of Milan and Forli, she left Rome's greatest fortress as a battle captain. Her blend of beauty, intelligence, willpower, and courage called out to the Roman people, who

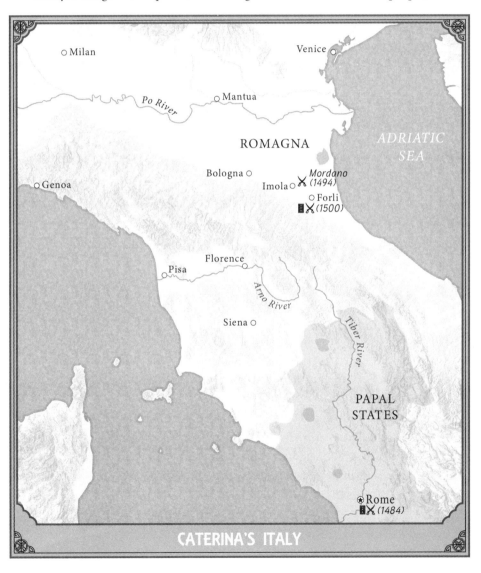

craned their heads for a glimpse at the virago from the north. In a brown silk dress with a long train, her locks topped by a black velvet cap, the countess calmly rode her horse over the wooden drawbridge, an escort of lance-wielding soldiers at her side.

From her bulging hips swung a long, sharp sword on a soldier's belt.

"She Will Fight You to the Death"

The girl who had been deflowered at ten was but a faded shadow of another time. In her place stood a cunning, iron-willed woman in her prime, and for four years that woman played the roles of diplomat, counselor, negotiator, and public face of the Riario family. When Roman nobles came to visit, she served as hostess, chatting amiably over banquets. When bubonic plague hit Forli in 1486, she ignored the hazards and appeared in the town's poorest neighborhoods, handing out food and medicines she concocted from her own recipes. When Girolamo grumbled over slights, she blunted his impulse to violence, and when he fell ill, she laid contingency plans against invasion or assassination.

Caterina could be as ruthless as the situation demanded. When a commander of doubtful loyalty refused to obey her order to leave the fortress of Ravaldino, she secretly bribed a well-known enemy of hers to work his way into the castle and assassinate the castellan. The officer's body was thrown down a well, and Caterina, "pregnant up to her throat" with her sixth child, rode over the drawbridge to install the keeper's replacement.

Despite his wife's efforts to run their dominions wisely, Girolamo alienated townsfolk with heavy taxes, unnecessary cruelty, and standoffishness. Terrified of assassins, Girolamo kept to his palace, venturing out only under heavy bodyguard.

The optic of a fearful, insecure ruler undermined the count's already-dismal reputation. When he tried to please Forli crowds by publicly pardoning several conspirators, even his clemency backfired: The pardoned men withdrew to the shadows to plan fresh attempts on his life.

The situation in Rome made that life even more precarious. Despite the concessions Caterina had won at the castle in Rome, the new pope, Innocent VIII, was no friend of the Riarios. Without the patronage of a sitting pope, the Riarios had to rely on their own lands to produce income. Money became tight, and Caterina had to pawn gems and pearls to help pay public officials.

Like many married couples, Caterina and Girolamo began arguing over family finances, and the stress of assassination attempts and debt flared into bitter arguments. "You don't know how awful things are between my husband and me," a despondent Caterina confided to Milan's ambassador one day. "The way he treats me is so bad that I envy those who have died by him."

Seeking relief from the pressure cooker of government, Caterina wrung from Girolamo permission to visit her family in Milan, where the Medici court's cultural bonfire, a Florentine artist named Leonardo da Vinci, was painting figures in bright, sensual colors. It was a delightful respite for Caterina, but as soon as she returned to Forlì, the demands of state resumed their incessant baying.*

As Girolamo dissipated physically and mentally, Caterina kept an eye on their circling enemies. A neighboring duke began inciting uprisings on their borders, and in 1487 the former ruling family of Forlì, the Ordelaffi clan, attempted a coup while the count and his wife were away in Imola.

Though she had given birth to her sixth child only a month earlier, Caterina again mounted her horse and galloped to the scene. Her soldiers apprehended a number of Ordelaffi conspirators, and after personally questioning two prisoners, she concluded that one was innocent and sent him back to his family. The other she sent to the gallows. On her orders, six more were brought to the town square and beheaded. She had the corpses quartered as a warning to would-be rebels.

By 1488, Girolamo Riario's luck had finally run out. The count had been hounding two petty nobles, Ludovico and Checco Orsi, over debts they owed him, so the Orsi family decided to square accounts by murdering Girolamo.

Co-opting two of Girolamo's bodyguards, the Orsi brothers approached the palace as supplicants seeking an audience to resolve Checco's debts. When Girolamo greeted Checco, Checco drew his dagger and drove it into Girolamo's chest. The count staggered back, and other Orsis broke into the room, threw Girolamo to the floor, and stabbed him until he was a bloody heap of meat, organs, and bones. To announce Girolamo's early retirement, the assassins casually heaved his body out the castle window onto Forlì's square below.

Meanwhile, Caterina and her children were having lunch in the *tinello*, a breakfast room near the palace tower. Hearing the commotion inside the palace and in the square, below the window from which the count's body had been tossed, she scooped up her children and ran to a strong room in the tower. She and her servants bolted the door to buy time as she thrashed around for her next move.

From the commotion within the palace, Caterina knew the stronghold was a lost

---

* In 2002, art historian Magdalena Soest produced a photoanalysis comparison of da Vinci's famous *Mona Lisa* and a portrait thought to be of Caterina Sforza by contemporary Lorenzo di Credi to support her claim that *Mona Lisa* is based, at least in part, on di Credi's portrait of Caterina.

cause, and she and her children would soon be captured. But she hadn't forgotten the leverage a fortress offered. Spotting a servant in the crowd below her tower window, she barked an order to run to the fortress of Ravaldino. There he must tell the captain never to surrender the fort under any circumstances. *Under any circumstances,* she emphasized. All troops loyal to her were to gather at Ravaldino, and they must never surrender the castle.

Under any circumstances.

The retainer dashed off, and moments later the door broke open. Caterina, surrounded by six trembling children and frightened servants, was taken prisoner by men whose best move would be to kill her.

The assassins herded the family into the Orsi palace and sent messengers to rally anti-Riario friends. But the town lay under the guns of the fortress. The next day a standoff hardened between Riario loyalists, who held Ravaldino; the Orsis, who controlled the town; and a startled Pope Innocent, whose emissaries galloped to Forli and persuaded the town council to place the city under the protection of the Church.

Recognizing too late that they could never be safe as long as Ravaldino was in Riario hands, the Orsis tore Caterina from her children and marched her to the castle. She burst into tears at the moat's edge.

Her castellan appeared above the ramparts and asked what his lady wanted.

"Give the fortress to these men, so they will free me and my children!" Caterina blurted out between sobs.

The keeper respectfully shook his head. Duty required him to surrender the castle only to Girolamo's heir, her son Ottaviano. The castle, he declared, would remain in Riario hands.

Caterina wailed louder. She and her children would be slaughtered upon their return, she pleaded. He must give up the fortress, for the sake of her children's lives.

Her flood of tears was no use. Unmoved, the stone-faced captain repeated his orders. In a loud, clear voice, he said that Caterina hailed from the mighty Sforza family of Milan, and the Riarios were allied to the great houses of northern Italy and Rome—names not lost on Caterina's captors or city onlookers. Under the circumstances, the captain said he must do his duty.

To the Orsis, the exchange between Caterina and the captain seemed vaguely scripted. Townspeople who gathered to watch heard the names of Sforza, Medici, Bentivoglio—powerful families with large armies—and listened intently as a loyal soldier invoked the name of Ottaviano, Forli's rightful heir.

Getting nowhere with either hostage or castellan, the Orsis cut off the colloquy and marched their prisoner away.

They seethed on the road back to their palace. In the palazzo, one of the men who betrayed Girolamo snarled at the countess, "You could turn over those castles if you wanted to, but you don't want to, do you?" Aiming the tip of his spear at Caterina's breastbone, he added, "I could just run this spear from one side of you to another and you would fall at my feet, dead!"

The weeping widow of an hour earlier turned to ice. "Don't you try to frighten me," she spat, venom flowing from her lips. "You can hurt me, but you can't scare me, because I am the daughter of a man who knew no fear. Do what you want. You have killed my lord, and you can certainly kill me. After all, I'm just a woman!"

The conspirators stared at her blankly.

I'm just a woman, she had said.

Yes, they could kill her. But murdering a widow in cold blood—still less her children—was not part of the plan. Killing her family might bring down fire and steel from the Medicis or the Sforzas, either of whom would be happy to add Imola and Forli to their holdings while avenging a family wrong. Unsure how to respond to her defiance, the killers sent Caterina back to her children and mulled over their next move.

The next day, the Orsis tried to break her with a different threat. They sent a priest into her locked room to lecture her on the fiery tortures awaiting her in hell if she didn't surrender her castle to the Orsis, in obedience to God's holy will.

The prospect of eternal damnation left a deeper impression on Caterina than the threat of Orsi blades. Emotionally exhausted, her resistance reaching its breaking point, Caterina banged on her cell door and demanded to have the priest thrown out.

The next day a local bishop, nervously eyeing a heated reaction from Milan and Florence, ordered the Orsis to move Caterina and her children to the tower of San Pietro, a neutral spot under the bishop's control. San Pietro proved far less secure than the Orsi palazzo, and soon one of Caterina's servants managed to talk his way into her room. As sympathetic guards strayed from the door, Caterina and her servant exchanged a few hushed words. Then the servant left.

The next morning, Ravaldino's castellan sent the bishop an offer of compromise: He would surrender the fortress on two conditions. First, the countess must pay back wages she owed him. Second, she must write him a letter of recommendation, explaining to future employers that he was a good soldier who had not betrayed the Riarios, but surrendered the castle on express orders of his mistress. Caterina, he said, would have to come alone to the castle and sign the documents in the presence of a notary and witnesses.

Smelling a trap, the Orsis protested. But the pope had put the bishop in charge of Forli, and the bishop would have the final say. The bishop's heart was moved by the beautiful, frail widow. Besides, he pointed out, the contessa's children would remain as hostages to her good behavior. So the bishop and his entourage led Caterina, under Orsi guard, to Ravaldino's walls for a second time.

Caterina called to the captain from beyond the moat. She promised, before the eyes of the town, to pay him and write his letter of reference. But he must surrender the fortress to the Orsis.

The captain again shook his head. An oral promise would not do. The countess must sign the legal documents before a notary, and she must sign them within the castle walls, to prove that she was acting of her own free will and not under duress. For his own protection, he would permit Caterina to bring one servant, no more.

Desperate to end the standoff, the bishop sent Caterina to the drawbridge, giving her a strict three-hour time limit to complete her business and return.

Accompanied by a strapping manservant, Caterina slowly walked through the forest of lances and crossed the wooden bridge. She stopped before the castle's massive doors. Her heart racing, she turned to her captors and shot them an obscene gesture known as *fare quattro fichi*: a fist with the thumb curled between fore and middle fingers.

Then she walked through the gate, and the drawbridge clanked shut.

After milling about for three hours, the Orsis grew nervous and the bishop grew confused. The time limit expired with no sound from the countess, the captain, or anyone inside. Rumors of armed columns marching from Milan and Bologna began wafting through the crowd, and townspeople looked at the bishop, then at the Orsis, wondering what they would do next.

Finally, the bishop called out to the castle. Then he called again.

No one answered.

Eventually, the keeper's helmeted head appeared over the battlements. He had captured the countess, he announced, and would only surrender her in exchange for several senior Orsi hostages. There would be no capitulation.

He disappeared.

Frightened and furious, the Orsis sent for Caterina's children, whom they hustled to the moat's edge. They had the countess's children, they screamed, and would slaughter them before the castle walls if the captain and Caterina did not surrender at once.

The Orsis were betting all their ducats on the turn of one, devastating card: Caterina's love for her children. They knew that a mother's tenderness, her innate urge of self-sacrifice, must overcome all other considerations. Protection of her offspring was womankind's oldest rule and highest law.

But Caterina played by a different set of rules. She calculated that surrender would mean death for herself, for Ottaviano, and for any other family member who might one day take revenge against the Orsis—probably from an undisclosed illness after a meal, but perhaps from an accidental fall, an accidental stabbing, or an accidental encounter with a heavy, blunt object.

Niccolò Machiavelli and other chroniclers of the day recounted a version of what Caterina did next. According to Machiavelli, Caterina appeared on the ramparts and looked down with scorn on the men holding knives to her children's throats.

"She threatened them with death and every kind of torture in revenge for the murder of her husband," Machiavelli wrote.

Stunned, the Orsis repeated that if Caterina did not surrender, her children would die on the grass before their mother's eyes.

"Do it, then, you fools!" she shouted back, face flushed. "I am already pregnant by another child by Count Riario!"

Hiking up her dress, she exposed her groin to her enemies. Pointing between her legs, she added with contempt, "I have the means to make more!"*

The Orsis looked at each other, dumbfounded. As they caucused over what to do next, soldiers began appearing on Ravaldino's walls in strength, and a flurry of activity rippled along its embrasures. The Orsis at the moat saw cannon barrels traverse and elevate, their artillerists checking angles and squinting toward Forlì. She was aiming her heavy bombards at the town.

Grasping the stakes Caterina played for, the Orsis sheathed their daggers. The bishop's soldiers seized the children and hustled them back into papal protection, and the Orsis scurried back to their family palace in Forlì.

Within their palazzo, eighty-year-old Andrea Orsi, the ailing family patriarch, was furious to learn that his sons' coup attempt had backfired. "She will fight you to the death," he spat from his sickbed. "All of you—even me, old and sick as I am—will have to bear the punishment for your lack of foresight!"

The bishop dispatched a rider to Rome to beg for soldiers to maintain order, but Pope Innocent, waiting to see which side would gain the upper hand, remained

---

* Other witnesses claimed she did not come to the battlements—or was not permitted to do so by the castellan, for fear that she might lose her nerve. It seems unlikely a woman of Caterina's mettle would have given way to fear, knowing that her best chance for saving her children came from holding the fortress until help arrived. Yet neither she nor the castellan probably wanted to take any chances.

motionless. Caterina did not. From her castle walls she fired artillery salvos at the homes of her enemies, and before long the town's leading merchants and artisans began defecting to Caterina's side.

Five days later, an 800-man battalion from Bologna appeared on the horizon and bivouacked outside Forli's gates, its troops smiling at the pleasant thought of sacking, pillaging, and raping everything in sight when the city fell. Behind the Bolognese marched a 12,000-man army sent by Caterina's brother, the current Duke of Milan. Merchants in Forli began hiding valuables, and parents looked for places to hide daughters and sons when the troops were unleashed. They demanded that their city elders do something.

With her allies camped before the city gates, Caterina offered the townspeople a path to redemption by ordering them to drive out the Orsi conspirators. "My people of Forli," she announced in a proclamation spread by arrows launched into the city, "Put to death my enemies! I promise that if you deliver them to me, I will take you as my dearest brothers. Quickly then, fear nothing!"

Before any town vigilantes worked up their courage, the conspirators fled Forli, leaving behind old, sick Andrea Orsi, as well as their wives and children.

Caterina emerged from her fortress, the unquestioned mistress of Forli.*

RESUMING HER PLACE in Forli, Caterina's first order of business was to rid her lands of the Milanese army. The relieving army had served its purpose—ejecting the Orsi faction—but Forli's residents, who had looted the Riario palace during the uprising, now dreaded the wrath of soldiers hungry for plunder, sex, and wine.

Milanese soldiers had spent their days in camp mentally assessing the city's value, planning their day's schedule of pillage and rape, and running through mental checklists of the usual peasant hiding places: freshly dug holes, crawl spaces, mattresses, swallowed gems, and the like. They were therefore deeply hurt when Caterina met with Milanese commanders and ordered them to leave Forli.

When the officers protested that they had marched an awful long way and were entitled to a fair sacking, Caterina politely replied that her family jewels, her

---

* Fortresses, being immobile, are notoriously bad military investments in wartime, especially when a besieging army can be resupplied. But Caterina used Ravaldino to buy time, a job for which castles are well suited. "In our days, fortresses have not profited any ruler except the Countess of Forli, after her husband Count Girolamo was killed," Machiavelli mused in *The Prince*. "Her castle did enable her to escape popular attack, to wait for aid that was coming from Milan, and to regain her position."

furniture, and her clothing had been looted after Girolamo's death. These treasures now lay scattered about the city, and she was going to recover them. She had no wish to see her family gems—*Sforza* family gems—ride off with soldiers in knapsacks and saddlebags.

She assuaged the fury of the officers with wine and reassuring words of eternal friendship. The disappointed host marched off, and as dust clouds from their columns drifted away, relieved townspeople hailed the countess as "The Savior of Forli."

The Savior of Forli then turned her attention to cutting out the cancer still lodged in the town's breast. That would require particular expertise, so she sent for a misshapen, hulking giant named Matteo Babone and hired him as the city's bailiff and chief executioner.

Caterina kept Babone fully employed for a time, starting with the conspirator who threw Girolamo's body out the palace window. She ordered him thrown from the same window, a rope around his neck.

Like many top-level professionals, Babone liked to add a dash of theater to his work. After shoving the noosed man from the window, Babone swung him back and forth like a pendulum as he kicked and thrashed in the air. The crowd jeering below his jerking feet loved it. Before the man expired, Babone played to the locals by dropping him amongst the Forlivesi, who proved their loyalty to the countess by tearing the helpless man to pieces.

Next came the young man who had butchered Girolamo's body. Caterina had pardoned him for crimes before, but this outrage was unpardonable. He, too, went out the count's window. As he swung from the noose like a piñata, eyes and tongue bulging as blood welled in his head, the crowd pulled him down, slit his throat, then dug out his intestines, genitals, and heart.

A third conspirator, who had sensibly urged the Orsis to murder the Riario wife and children, went to a more conventional gallows. His stretched body was casually jabbed with lances and spades for the amusement of bored soldiers.

The next morning, Babone's deputies yanked the aged Andrea Orsi from his hiding spot in a local convent. Babone marched him, a noose around his neck, to his family home, where a crowd of soldiers and builders waited with construction tools. The old man was forced to watch as the Orsi palazzo was demolished, its timbers and plaster set afire.

As smoke from his family home filled his nostrils, Andrea bitterly cursed his sons for being fools. They should have known Caterina would take revenge; they should have slaughtered her the moment they had her. Now, as he had foretold, his blood would pay the price of their stupidity.

His executioners led him to a platform, where he was given a moment to say prayers for his soul. The old man trembled as Babone pushed him down onto a flat wooden board lying on the street, to which he was tied with his head hanging off the board's back end. The board was affixed, feet first, to the back of a horse, and Babone spurred the mount into a canter around the town square.

The old man held up his head to keep it from banging on the square's cobblestones, but it was only a matter of time before his neck muscles tired and the back of his skull began bouncing along the pavement. He left a smear of gore on the city square as he died. The rust brown trail served as a chilling reminder to Forlì's citizens of the penalty for betraying their mistress.

The mistress also indulged a bit of psychological terror. One conspirator brought before her begged, "Glorious Madonna, be merciful with a miserable sinner."

Looking at him coldly, Caterina replied, "Let vengeance rule, not pity. I shall let the dogs tear you to pieces." Then she sent the man back to his cell. Dreading daily the howls of dogs that never came for him, he eventually escaped and fled, never to set foot in Forlì again.

Finally, the countess summoned the Orsi wives, sisters, daughters, and children, who were led trembling through the iron gates of Ravaldino. They stood shaking before her as she calmly told them they were free to go, to live in Forlì, or to depart to the homes of relatives as they saw fit. They were innocent, she said, and there would be no retribution against the innocent.

Caterina closed the episode by summoning the heads of every family in Forlì. Soldiers sorted them into groups of twenty-five and herded them before the countess, who sat on a throne behind a table with a Bible opened to *John* 1:1: "In the beginning was the Word, and the Word was with God, and the Word was God."

The Word, in this case, was read from a parchment by a lieutenant, enjoining every family to loyal behavior, and submitting each to the punishment of their temporal lord, Caterina, should they fail. Each father, called forward by name, placed one hand on the Bible and pledged his family's undying allegiance to Ottaviano, Count of Forlì, and to his regent, the Countess Caterina Sforza di Riario.

With these assurances, Caterina's vendetta ebbed, though blood still oozed as enemies were belatedly captured. In all, she ordered a dozen or so executions and announced a reward for the capture of the chief conspirators: a thousand ducats alive, five hundred, dead. She also left the parts of the executed decorating public walls as a reminder to wayward minds of the price of rebellion.

Entre Le Roi

For five pleasant years, Caterina ruled as regent for Ottaviano. She could be ruthless, and the stench of death lingered in the memories of her subjects long after the rains washed Orsi blood from Forli's square. But she governed her lands fairly, kept taxes reasonable, and tried to ensure there would be few legitimate complaints to alienate her people.

Her personal life was, for a time, a happy one. She couldn't marry, for a new man, no matter how loving, would pose an inherent threat to the succession of her son. But a year after Girolamo's death, she fell head over heels for a former stable boy named Giacomo Feo, the younger brother of her chief castellan, about eight years her junior.

Though he lacked noble blood, Caterina gave in to her emotional and physical desires, and the twenty-year-old Giacomo worshipped his mistress with the blind passion of youth. Overlooking his political immaturity, she knighted her lover and deferred to him on matters of state. As a sign of her absolute trust, she even promoted Giacomo to keeper of her most precious possession, the fortress of Ravaldino.

Before long she bore him a son. Rumors swirled that she secretly wed him, and jealous courtiers watched as a lowly stable boy ascended to become the real power of Imola and Forli.

As her lover's authority grew, Caterina found more time to indulge personal interests. Long a student of botany and home remedies, she spent hours collecting plants and herbal recipes for ailments ranging from impotence to bubonic plague. As a woman whose beauty was both her status symbol and a tool of power, she experimented with cosmetics recipes for every imaginable need, from lotions to keep breasts soft to creams for reducing skin blemishes. Like many Renaissance men, she kept detailed notes of her discoveries, filing her findings away with voluminous personal papers.

As Caterina withdrew from power politics, the world outside Forli changed. King Ferdinand and Queen Isabella of Spain completed their conquest of Granada. An Italian explorer named Columbus set foot on an island far across the ocean. Pope Innocent VIII died, and Cardinal Roderigo Borgia took the throne of St. Peter under the name Alexander VI. France's King Charles VIII came of age and signed a peace treaty with Henry VII of England, freeing Charles to turn east in search of new conquests.

Family and political intrigues began pulling apart the web of alliances that had kept the peace in Italy. In the far south, the Duke of Calabria and the King of Naples prepared to go to war with Caterina's uncle, Milan's Duke Ludovico Sforza. As the

Neapolitans marched north to Milan, Pope Alexander granted them free passage through the Papal States, which nominally included Caterina's lands. To counter the central Italians, Duke Ludovico invited France's King Charles to march his army over the Alps and stake his claim to the Kingdom of Naples.

Forli and Imola stood in the path of two rolling boulders, Naples and Milan. That put Caterina in an uncomfortable spot. Milan had marched to her aid when her husband was murdered, and Milan was Caterina's family home. Yet her lands fell under papal jurisdiction, and the pope was actively supporting Naples. If she crossed Pope Alexander, there would be hell to pay—a temporal one definitely, and perhaps a spiritual one, too. So she played for time, desperately hoping the situation would resolve itself in some way that did not turn her lands into Italy's next battlefield.

As French and Neapolitan armies converged on her lands, Caterina sent word to farmers and merchants to move inside city walls for protection. She reinforced her three largest fortresses and prepared to withstand the largest war Italy had seen in decades.

Diplomatic pressure on Caterina intensified as the armies approached. Pope Alexander offered her a 16,000-ducat payment for her support and agreed to add a small territory to her dominions, pitting funds against family. For a woman habitually in financial straits, Alexander's bribe tipped the balance. Turning her back on Milan, she threw her support to Naples.

By accepting the pope's bribe, Caterina avoided the fire. But the frying pan proved uncomfortably warm. In October a combined French-Milanese army besieged her fortress of Mordano, near Imola. Though her soldiers defended their walls valiantly, after a day of cannon bombardment the attackers breached the walls and overwhelmed the defenders. Razing buildings, slaughtering prisoners, raping women, and carrying off everything of value, the French-led army gathered its strength to move against Forli.

While Mordano shuddered under French guns, Caterina wrote to the Neapolitan court, begging for help. But her letters were greeted by silence, and not one spearman was sent to her aid. Feeling furious and betrayed, Caterina told her people that her alliance with the Vatican, Naples, Calabria, and Florence had failed its primary object: to protect Forli and Imola from French depredations. Her allies had forsaken them, and now Forli was in peril. In response she announced that Forli had changed sides; she would now permit French and Milanese troops unmolested passage through her lands.

Free of Caterina's resistance, King Charles moved rapidly through Tuscany. He took Florence without a fight, then marched down the Via Emilia toward Rome. He defeated a Neapolitan coalition at Fornovo and was crowned King of Naples. He returned to France the way he came, leaving Italy in much the same condition it had been before his invasion.

Except that Forli and its contessa had earned the undying wrath of Pope Alexander VI.

Exit the Stable Boy

Forli's court mandarins, so often at each other's throats, all agreed on one weed that needed pulling: Giacomo Feo.

Having descended from no great house, Feo lacked allies and had no allegiance to anyone but himself. He also showed little talent for governing. But Caterina had fallen under her lover's spell. Her infatuation for the younger man blinded her to the realpolitik of central Italy, and her famous willpower all but dissolved around him. The Florentine ambassador complained to his master, "The countess will bury her children, her allies, and all her belongings, she will sell her soul to the devil, she will give her state to the Turk, before she gives up Giacomo Feo."

In the summer of 1495, a small group of loyalists resolved to rid Forli of the low-born usurper. After Caterina, her children, Feo, and a small bodyguard had spent a merry day hunting and picnicking, a few smiling court retainers stepped into the column ambling home. Working their way into the column's midst, they casually cut off Feo and his horse from Caterina's main party while making small talk.

While one conspirator chatted with Feo, another crept behind him and drove a dagger into his back. He fell from his horse, and the conspirators leapt on him. Blades flashed, then plunged, then rose again as blood spurted from Feo's flesh. Fearing for her life, Caterina leapt from her carriage, jumped on a mount, and galloped off to Ravaldino to rally her troops. Ottaviano and his younger brother Cesare ran to the house of a local nobleman, and the twenty-four-year-old Feo, now a bloody, lifeless mess, lay in a ditch.

The assassins were certain that Caterina would realize the damage her lover had posed to her reputation and lands. When she reflected on her own best interests, she would show mercy to her subjects. Perhaps even honor them for their awful but necessary service.

They did not understand that Caterina, having finally tasted true love, had felt every dagger's bite as if the blades had been plunged into her own breast.

Her justice flew swiftly. The chief assassin, Giovanni Ghetti, was run down by two vigilantes in a cemetery. His head was cloven with a blow that split his skull from crown to teeth. His home was torched, and his wife and most of his children were thrown down one of Ravaldino's wells to die together. When Ghetti's five-year-old son was discovered hiding a few days later, his throat was promptly slashed.

Blind with rage, Caterina bathed her grief in blood. She ordered families known to be hostile to Feo exiled, imprisoned, or hanged in the public square. She had an entire neighborhood destroyed, and her henchmen rounded up and tortured any-one remotely connected with the conspirators.

When the second chief conspirator was caught, he was seared with hot irons and coals until he revealed every name connected with the plot. Caterina's deputies then dragged him by his feet behind a horse over the city's paving stones and side-walk sewage, just as Andrea Orsi had been dragged to his death years earlier. But his ordeal was shorter, and somehow the conspirator survived. So Caterina's sol-diers sliced his face open, then clubbed, stabbed, and dismembered him as he lay gasping for breath.

Severed heads of other conspirators decorated the municipal bell tower for over a year after Feo's assassination. When the slaughter ended, a local chronicler listed thirty-eight dead and a small host of survivors who had been tortured, thrown into dungeons, or driven into exile. At one point, Caterina even placed Ottaviano, the rightful count, under house arrest until she was satisfied that he had nothing to do with Feo's murder.

In the wake of what Pope Alexander called "unheard-of bloodthirstiness commit-ted to satisfy her passions," Caterina moved from benevolent ruler to pariah. Her people learned to fear her, and other Italian princes saw her as weak and unstable.

A year after Feo's death, the hole in Caterina's heart was patched—though never filled—by a handsome Florentine businessman named Giovanni di' Medici. Unlike the brute Riario, or the immature Feo, Giovanni was an educated gentleman who could appreciate Caterina's wit, curiosity, and mental energy. When she experi-mented with herbs and roots, Giovanni helped her find rare ingredients and took an interest in her progress. Dance, literature, and discussions of commerce filled their evenings.

They spent their nights in the privacy of Caterina's quarters at the fortress of Ravaldino, and in the summer of 1497, the countess became pregnant with Giovan-ni's child, a boy also named Giovanni. In September, she married her lover in a secret ceremony.

It was the second time she had found love, and for a second time, love was ripped from her. Shortly after the marriage, the older Giovanni died of fever. He was her first husband lost to natural causes.

Daughter of Iniquity

The next world is eternal. That is what the Church taught, and Caterina believed it with all her heart. But the temporal world changes, and in 1498 it was changing faster than usual. France had a new king, Louis XII, and Pope Alexander quickly cemented an alliance with him by sending his son, Cesare Borgia, to Paris with a papal bull permitting Louis to divorce his current wife so he could marry a better one.

There would be strings attached, of course: The pope planned to bring Caterina's restive Romagna provinces under his son's personal rule, and he wanted Louis to loan Cesare enough soldiers and artillery to invade them. An obliging Louis bestowed the title "Duke of Valentinois" upon Cesare, and the pact was sealed with yet another political marriage, this one between Cesare and the sister of King John of Navarre.

Before tasking Cesare to invade Romagna, Alexander first tried to win Caterina's holdings through a marriage proposal for her son. He offered his sixteen-year-old daughter, Lucrezia Borgia, to Caterina's son Ottaviano. Recognizing the pope's play to wrest control of Imola and Forlì from her children, Caterina declined his offer in characteristically blunt terms.

The pope took serious personal offense, and the next year he issued a bull denouncing the countess as Forlì's "daughter of iniquity." He declared Cesare's right to rule over Forlì and Imola, and ordered his son to take them by force.

Realizing her mistake, Caterina belatedly tried to patch things up with the pontiff. But Alexander was through trying to win over the headstrong woman. She had turned against him during the first French invasion, and now His Holiness would let Cesare's armies do what God had not yet gotten around to.

With the ground rumbling beneath her feet, Caterina wrote to Milan for help. Unfortunately, Milan's duke, her uncle Ludovico the Moor, was up to his gorget preparing to fend off French and Venetian armies and could spare nothing for his niece. Caterina made military alliance overtures toward Florence, but those talks—negotiated for the Medicis by Niccolò Machiavelli—went nowhere.

On November 1, 1499, the pontiff penned a handwritten note declaring an end to Riario rule. The papal army under Cesare broke camp and began marching north. Caterina summoned the men of Forlì's governing council and made them swear oaths of loyalty to Ottaviano, then ordered all buildings within a quarter mile around the town burned, starting with her own farmhouse. She cut down parks within a mile of the fort to provide her artillery with a good field of fire, and stationed lookouts in the palace's bell tower. All townspeople within "three artillery shots" of the city were ordered to harvest their grain, store three months' rations within the city walls, and remove any portable goods. If Cesare Borgia and his men wished to eat, at least they would not dine on Forlì's food.

Laying up stores of weapons, food, and medicine, Caterina drilled her men-at-arms, purchased small arms from Florence, and stockpiled gunpowder and cannon shot. Just beyond the fortress walls, she built *rivellini*—triangular redoubts mounting three cannons apiece—which would defend the curtain walls from enemies with scaling ladders or siege engines. She also recruited soldiers and built barracks to house 800 men inside the castle, sparing Forlì's residents the unpopular burden of quartering troops.

As a final precaution, she sent her children to Florence to live with her Medici in-laws. If Ravaldino fell, the rightful count could carry on the struggle from Tuscany. "If I have to lose," she wrote her uncle, "I want to lose like a man."

But she was not ready to lose—not yet. Having outlasted enemies twice before, she understood the value of a well-positioned fortress. Ravaldino had been home, inner sanctum, and source of security for eleven years. She knew every inch of the castle, knew the men of its garrison, and had spent years thinking about how to defend it.

While Cesare prepared for a war of swords, his father launched a war of words. Pope Alexander claimed that Caterina had tried to poison him with a letter that she had buried with a plague victim.*

Because Caterina was an outlaw in the eyes of the Holy See, smaller states, taking the hint, made no move to assist her. Only the Florentines continued to aid Caterina, quietly selling her weapons and using their diplomatic connections to protect Forlì from the rising power of the Borgia pope.

Cesare Borgia, captain-general of the Papal Armies, led a force of 12,000 men north from Rome to Imola. His army's core of 2,000 Spanish soldiers and 2,000 Frenchmen was augmented by hired companies of German swordsmen, Swiss pikemen, and Flemish crossbowmen.

The force was large enough to intimidate Imola's town fathers, who quickly surrendered. The city's fortress, Rocca Sforzesca, held out for another two weeks, but it was clear that resistance was hopeless. The castle surrendered on honorable terms, and Cesare prepared to move against Forlì.

As Cesare's army approached, the Forlivesi began to waver. Caterina had ruled them wisely in peacetime, but the bloodbath after Giacomo Feo's assassination left

---

* Neither Pope Alexander nor Caterina ever produced reliable evidence to indict or exonerate her from the charge of attempted poisoning.

them with a lingering fear of what she would do under stress of battle. She had turned Ravaldino's guns on the city once before, and she might do it again. And if she should lose a pitched battle, the rape and pillage by papal soldiers would destroy Forli's future for generations to come.

So, the city's leading citizens sent her a delegation to respectfully suggest that Forli's mistress leave town. Perhaps, they offered, she could return when Alexander had died and a new, friendlier pope had taken his place.

Caterina refused. Running, even as a tactical retreat, was not in her nature. Audacity had protected her, and audacity would keep her.

But she could not control the city from behind Ravaldino's walls, and on December 14 two retainers, both of whom owed their success to the countess, betrayed their mistress. They sent a delegation to Cesare Borgia and surrendered the City of Forli.

Caterina stood alone.

The Battle of Ravaldino

Optimism, sometimes to the point of terminal delusion, is a standard requirement of battlefield leadership. Caterina refused to believe Ravaldino would ever fall. Leading her men from the high ground, on December 26, 1499, she mounted the ramparts in a flowing dress topped by a custom-made breastplate. The steel shell, like Caterina, was a blend of feminine form and military-grade steel. Forged in Milan, the cuirass was etched with an intricate floral pattern and the figure of Saint Catherine of Alexandria, Caterina's patron saint.

Below her ramparts stretched the might of the papal armies. In addition to his 12,000 men, Cesare fielded a formidable artillery park. With seventeen mobile guns, he could concentrate fire on defenders at critical points and inflict limited damage on the castle's walls. His largest siege gun, a bronze monster named Tiverina, boasted a nine-foot barrel, firing stone or iron balls a foot in diameter. Given enough time, Tiverina could bring down the stoutest of Ravaldino's walls.

As conversant on artillery as any of her generals, Caterina was well aware of the hazards Tiverina and her sharp-nosed sisters posed. But she also appreciated the value of time in siege operations. Cesare could not maintain his position indefinitely. His polyglot army was built around mercenaries who killed for pay, not religion, fealty, or kin. The longer his soldiers remained in the field, shivering in tents, eating fetid rations, and dropping from dysentery, the more expensive and unreliable his army became.

Cesare's French troops were the least reliable of all, for they considered themselves agents of King Louis, not the pope. Prone to outbursts of chivalry, many French officers openly admired the beautiful contessa who bravely defended her lands. As long as Caterina's rose-and-serpent standard flew over Ravaldino's tall keep, she held out hope that her Sforza uncle, or perhaps Florentine allies, would come marching over the hills to her rescue.

Cesare pretended not to notice these risks. Wearing an exquisitely tailored silver and black cloak over his armor, the handsome prince cantered on a white horse to the moat's edge and dismounted. He doffed his black beret and made a courtly bow to the woman scowling from the wall. Caterina, striking in her breastplate and sword belt, returned Cesare's bow with a gracious nod.

Cesare knew how attractive women found him. He was one of the first Renaissance men to reject fashionably bright clothes in favor of solid black, which set off his fair skin and brown hair. That day his fine figure was accented by the formidable army assembled behind him, and he intended to use looks and words to purchase victory on the cheap.

From the moat's edge, he showered a treasure chest of bejeweled words on Forli's countess. He told Caterina that if she, a wise, beautiful, and prudent mother, would merely bestow Ravaldino on the Vicar of Christ, the Holy Father would reward her generosity with lands, castles, and perhaps even a fine home in the Eternal City suitable to her station.

Listening to the prince pontificate on Alexander's generosity, Caterina knew that the Holy Father's reward would likely be to turn a blind eye as she was poisoned. At best, he might give her a decent funeral in St. Peter's. Her face inscrutable, she thanked Cesare for his gallant and flattering eloquence but stood firm. Cesare, she said, had overlooked her most important quality: She was fearless. She was the daughter of a conqueror, heiress to the indomitable will of a Sforza soldier. Born to a noble house, she would never bow to a lesser family—especially not one known for its deceit and impiety.

"All of Italy knows the worth of the Borgia word," she yelled from the battlements, her voice rising. "The bad faith of the father has removed any credit from the son."

"Surrender, Madonna," Cesare pressed.

"Signor duke," her biographer has her reply, "Fortune helps the intrepid and abandons cowards. I am the daughter of a man who did not know fear. I am resolved to follow the course until death."

Giving Cesare a formal salute, she turned and walked down the bastion stairs, disappearing from view.

Stumped by the woman's impudence, unsure what to do next, Cesare returned to his lines, thought for a few minutes, then decided to try again. He trotted to the moat a second time and had his trumpeter blow "parlay."

More amused than contemptuous, Caterina spoke to her gatekeeper, and a moment later the drawbridge clanked down. She walked toward the end of the wooden planking and the two commanders spoke, their words inaudible to soldiers watching them from the walls and siege lines.

After a few moments, Caterina gestured for the prince to follow her. As he stepped onto the drawbridge, it lurched upward with a loud clatter. Cat-like, Cesare jumped back in time to avoid being scooped into the castle's mouth, cursing and screaming to all within earshot that he would give a thousand ducats to the man who brought him Caterina's dead body.

Caterina, reappearing on the wall's ridge, screamed back that she would give five thousand ducats to the man who brought her Cesare's corpse.

The two screaming generals were done talking. It was time for war.

The next day Cesare ordered his sappers to begin digging a tunnel under the moat and into the castle's deep walls. But the December soil was hard as granite, and soldiers broke their tools and backs trying to carve the frozen earth. Unable to tunnel, Cesare ordered his smaller cannon to disperse and fire one-pound iron shot at the stone bastion.

Cannonading began in earnest on December 28. Massed fire from Cesare's bombards demolished the upper reaches of one of the castle's defense towers and smashed Caterina's personal quarters. Concerned, but not overly so, Caterina moved her belongings into the fort's forty-five-foot-tall keep—a castle within a castle—and ordered her guns to concentrate their fire on the enemy artillery.

Her shots struck home. Caterina's guns killed many of Cesare's artillery specialists, including his highly valued French artillery commander. Caterina's chief artillerist, Bartolomeo Bolognesi, laid down such accurate fire on papal forces that Cesare offered a thousand ducats for Bolognesi's corpse, and another two thousand for him alive.

The siege dragged on another week. While Caterina hunkered down behind her walls, sympathy for her plight grew abroad. In early January, a group of forty pilgrims came down the north road, wearing cloaks of poor travelers. They petitioned Cesare for safe passage through the war zone as they made their way to Rome. Cesare naturally granted the request. As the penitents walked through the lines, chanting their hymns, they passed near Ravaldino's entrance. Without warning, the castle drawbridge dropped, and the pilgrims broke into a dash for the fort's open mouth.

The drawbridge snapped shut, and the travelers doffed their vestments, taking their places on the ramparts alongside Caterina's other defenders.

Cesare had been outfoxed again.

He was frustrated, angry, worried. The longer his army was stalled by a woman, the weaker the House of Borgia looked to its enemies. His army was restive, his French allies seemed to admire the virago on the walls, and Cesare could not feed and pay his mercenaries indefinitely. He had to end the siege, and soon.

Getting down to business with his field commanders, Cesare spent two days moving his cannon opposite what his experts said was the castle's weakest section, the south wall. But his deployment was interrupted temporarily by the Feast of the Three Kings, a religious festival his soldiers celebrated by pillaging Forlì's inhabitants, raping local girls, and coupling with town prostitutes.

When Cesare's soldiers resumed their places a few days later, they began pounding Ravaldino with round after round of iron shot. Balls slammed into stone like giant chisels, knocking chunks out of the wall with every hit. By night—muffled by the sounds of drums and pipes, the music of dancing and celebration—Caterina's men quietly patched the holes with sandbags, stones, and dirt. While the repairs were haphazard and improvised, they were good enough to stop onrushing infantry. For the moment.

But the battle for Ravaldino was a turtle against a wolf, and given enough time the wolf will find a way to crack the carapace and sink his fangs into flesh. The turtle can do nothing but wait for the wolf to tire and move on.

This wolf would not move on.

Over the next two weeks, the weight of cannon shot began to tell. The defenders diligently patched broken sections of wall, but large chunks of stone fell into the moat, creating a kind of rough causeway. It wasn't long before the hole in the castle wall was wide enough, and the debris in the moat thick enough, to allow Cesare's men to sally over the moat and tie log rafts to the rubble. Cesare now had an entrance and a rude but effective bridge.

On January 12, three weeks into the siege, he boasted to his lieutenants, "Today is Sunday. By Tuesday, Lady Caterina will be in my hands."

Brimming with confidence, he brushed off warnings from his field officers that she would simply retreat to her inner keep and fend them off longer. The handsome prince offered a 300-ducat bet against any man that by Tuesday he would have the countess in chains.

Knowing where the attack would come, Caterina ordered her cannon massed in front of the wall's gaping hole. She had her guns loaded with bags of one-inch iron and stone balls, and when the pope's warriors came, she would cut them down before they could debouch from the wall's narrow opening.

Just after the noon meal on Tuesday, Cesare's troops were in position for the charge. He ordered his men forward. Pikes lowered, they sprinted across the moat's rubble and pitched headlong through the wall's opening, into the mouths of Caterina's waiting guns. To death, to fire and smoke . . .

To silence.

Caterina's gunners had deserted their posts. Not a gun boomed. A thin but growing thread of Swiss, German, French, and Spanish troops began filing into Ravaldino's courtyard and lining up against the remaining defenders.

The countess had no time to rage over the treachery of her gunners. She ordered loyalists to form a line in front of the keep. Sword in hand, she led a detachment in a furious counterattack, lunging, stabbing, and slashing from the front ranks. For nearly two hours she fought, and an admiring Venetian mercenary wrote afterward that she "wounded many men" in the melee.

But her defenders tired, and Cesare's men kept streaming in. To buy some time for another attack, Caterina ordered a squad to fight a delaying action while others piled a wall of ammunition, furniture, boxes, straw, and anything else that would burn. Her men fired the combustibles, and a wall of flame and smoke flew up, blocking the enemy.

When French soldiers pulled apart burning flammables and beat down the flames, Caterina's men charged through the smoke, pikes and swords pointed in all directions. They slaughtered French, they slaughtered Spaniards, they slaughtered Swiss and Germans. But they were badly outnumbered, and the battle for the courtyard was hopeless. With their backs to the keep, Caterina's men began laying down their arms as their perimeter shrank.

Having no interest in being captured, chained, tortured, or quietly murdered, Caterina ordered her remaining defenders to follow her into the keep for a final stand. Loyalists, entangled with the advancing enemy, fought with swords and knives to protect the escape route as men poured through the keep's arch.

Then the door slammed shut.

At age thirty-seven, Caterina's world had shrunk to a single, stubborn tower.

The keep was formidable and well-provisioned, but Cesare, like Octavian with Cleopatra, finally had his enemy boxed in. Riding through soot and moans of the dying, Cesare had his trumpeter blow "parlay" again. As Caterina stood behind the keep's walls, he implored her to end the bloodshed.

Spattered in dirt and blood, Caterina yelled back that if Cesare really was moved by human suffering, he would not have allowed his soldiers to murder, rape, and loot innocent villagers of Forli. She would never surrender.

But a burly arm shot forward and wrapped around the countess from behind. As she struggled, a French voice announced, "Madame, you are a prisoner of my lord, the Constable of Dijon."

Observers on the outside were astounded that Caterina had been taken alive, and they never quite figured out who betrayed her. In his book *On the Art of War*, Machiavelli, an admirer of Cesare, concluded, "The poor defenses of the fortress and the little wisdom of those defending it shamed the great undertaking of the countess."

The Florentine also blamed Caterina for failing to keep the loyalty of her subjects. "The best possible fortress is not to be hated by the people," he wrote in *The Prince*. "Although you may hold the fortress, yet they will not save you if the people hate you, for there will never be wanting foreigners to assist a people who have taken arms against you."

Prisoner of the Borgias

The Battle of Ravaldino was not quite over when a dispute flared over the castle's great prize. The French soldier who captured Caterina refused to release the countess until he was paid his 10,000-ducat reward. When Cesare ordered the man repaid with 2,000 ducats instead, the enraged soldier drew his dagger and put his blade to Caterina's throat. It was a "dead or alive" offer, he reminded Cesare. Unless Cesare rendered unto him that which was his, he said, he would take the lesser reward for the countess's corpse, which he would deliver on the spot.

As the prince and the soldier haggled over Caterina's life, the French commander, a captain named Yves d'Allegre, stormed into the keep. D'Allegre bellowed that Caterina was a prisoner of King Louis XII, not the pope and not the pope's son. Smitten by the disheveled beauty, d'Allegre informed Cesare that under French law, no captured woman could be tortured, killed, or imprisoned. The countess, he said, would remain in protective custody of the French.

It took some time to sort out legal title to the prisoner, and it wasn't until after midnight that she was led out of her keep. She walked past seven hundred men lying dead on the fortress battlements, in its courtyards, its barracks, and its inner towers. Caterina's sanctuary had become a soot-filled charnel house, and the sulfuric smell of burned gunpowder, blood, and smoke mingled into a diabolical odor she would remember to the end of her days.

Under heavy guard, she was led to a local Forli palace, where Cesare waited for Caterina's children, chained goslings to come waddling behind the feast goose. To his shock, he learned that Caterina had again outflanked him by sending her children—the lord and heirs to Forli and Imola—to the safety of Florence. Her children were technically Florentine citizens through her marriage to Giovanni di' Medici, so Cesare had no legal right to require the Medici to give up the children. And as long as Ottaviano and his brothers were beyond his grasp, his claim to Caterina's domains would remain clouded.

Thwarted again, Cesare ordered his men to bring the captive to his quarters. If he could not take her hereditary claims, or break her spirit, he would at least enjoy the body so many men had fantasized about. He spent a night of pent-up vengeance raping Caterina, smirking to his retinue the next morning, "She defended her fortress better than her virtue."

Cesare attacked that virtue again and again over the next nine days. He shared meals with her by day and took her to his bed by night, delighting in the subjugation of so famous a woman.

Yet the reputation of his prisoner grew as word spread of her valor on the battlements. "Although this woman is an enemy of the Venetian state," wrote one Venice citizen, "she truly deserves infinite praise and immortal memory among the famous and worthy Roman captains." A French biographer of King Louis wrote, "Under her feminine body she had a masculine courage; she had no fear of danger; no matter how close it approached, she never backed down."

The plaudits meant nothing to the Borgia clan. Caterina was taken to Rome and held in a comfortable Vatican palace until an ill-planned escape attempt failed. Pope Alexander used the attempt as an excuse to settle a longstanding grudge, and ordered the countess thrown into the dreaded dungeon below Castel Sant'Angelo—a fortress she once commanded in the violent wake of a pope's death.

To the Borgias, the dark, muggy cells of Sant'Angelo would make a perfect setting for the second act of their Forli drama. As her final public humiliation, Alexander planned an exquisitely produced show trial. The charge: attempting to poison His Holiness.

As scripted, the countess, wearing the white robe of a penitent, a heavy rope hung around her neck, would kneel before the pontiff and confess crimes attested by two torture-wracked "accomplices." The pope, sitting on a golden throne under a fresco of the Archangel Michael, would pronounce both verdict and sentence upon Forli's daughter of iniquity. The trial of Caterina Sforza Riario would make a lovely spectacle for the voyeuristic Roman mob.

Again, Caterina outmaneuvered the Borgias. When the master of ceremonies came to her cell to discuss the upcoming trial, Caterina calmly outlined her public defense: After being taken prisoner in an honorable battle, the son of the Holy Father had raped her nightly in his bedroom. Alexander's holy warriors had similarly violated young, faithful Catholic girls of Forlì during a religious holiday. Cesare's men demolished churches, defiled holy altars, stole the property of innocents, and slaughtered the guiltless. "If I could write of it, I would shock the world," she declared.

Caterina's recitation of Cesare's crimes was so extensive, so vivid, so specific, that Alexander thought better of giving her a public platform. He quietly let the trial project drop.

Papal agents tried bribing Caterina with promises of money, homes, and—most enticing of all—freedom from the fetid air of Sant'Angelo's dungeon. They permitted letters from Ottaviano and other children to reach her, pleading with their mother to give up her claims. The children needed a free mother, they said. If she were not at liberty to send money to Florence, they could not sustain their luxurious lifestyles. Surely Madonna Caterina didn't wish to see her children reduced to poverty.

When letters from spoiled children failed to work, her captors took a different tack. They dragged her out of her cell and led her to a gallows, where they told her she would be executed that day. But first, they had something to show her. As she stood below the scaffold, her two alleged accomplices were led up the stairs and died on the rope. The jailers left the bodies dangling as they escorted Caterina back to her cell. When they shoved her inside, her guards told her the two men's deaths had bought the woman a little more time. Just a little.

Bowed under a barrage of carrots and sticks, Caterina refused to break. She calculated, probably correctly, that once she gave in, the Borgias would have no reason to let her live. She might fall ill to a mysterious ailment during dinner, lose her balance over a deep well, or find herself run through with the blade of an unknown bandit.

The pope knew this. He could have allowed Cesare to poison Caterina's food and deal directly with the weak-willed Ottaviano. That was the obvious answer. But he had another angle to consider, an angle that stayed his hand. Through her last marriage, Caterina was a citizen of Florence and member of the powerful Medici and Sforza families, which kept a close eye on the whereabouts of their famous daughter. Caterina also had admirers in the French army, such as Captain d'Allegre, who had demanded guarantees of her safety before turning her over to the Borgias. The once-dangerous hoyden had become a figure of sympathy, even martyrdom, by the growing anti-Borgia coalition.

In the spring of 1501, the French army, marching toward Naples, camped near Rome. Hearing of Caterina's plight, a furious d'Allegre rode to the Vatican palace and demanded to see the pope. He informed Alexander that his treatment of the contessa violated the agreement the French army had made with Cesare. Every indignity he and his son inflicted on his woman prisoner was an affront to the honor of King Louis.

Alexander protested that he, who had been nearly poisoned by the countess, was the real victim. D'Allegre dismissed Alexander's charade. If the pope did not release the countess immediately, his soldiers would storm Sant'Angelo and liberate her themselves.

The pope was not prepared to fight a military siege, especially one laid by the King of France. He reluctantly agreed to release Caterina, on one condition: She must sign away her claims to Imola and Forli. D'Allegre walked to the castle and pleaded with Caterina—for her life, for the good of her children—to resign her regency of lands she had plainly lost. It was the moment Caterina had resisted for months with every fiber of her soul. Yet the psychological horrors of dungeon, rape, and near-death had ground down the spirit that had commanded battlements three times. Her son was old enough to take what belonged to him, if he were worthy of it, and there comes a bittersweet season when a mother must step aside and let her children take flight to wherever they will go.

With a heavy heart, Caterina agreed. Her one condition was that she would sign the documents outside the castle, among the safety of the French soldiers.

FROM ROME, a newly freed Caterina made her way to Florence, eluding one of the pope's well-known assassins as she traveled north. She spent time as a guest of the Medici family and was loaned a nice villa in the town of Castello. A far cry from the last two castles she had defended, her borrowed villa boasted cheerful courtyards to stroll through, intelligent horses to ride, and art to admire, including an enchanting living room piece by an old acquaintance named Botticelli called *The Birth of Venus.*

Never one to let mind or body remain idle, Caterina made up for time lost in the dungeon. She resumed her lifelong interests in botany, alchemy, and beauty aids, and

---

* Caterina's attributes, and possibly her likeness, turn up in two of Botticelli's paintings: the famous *Primavera*, in which she is said to appear as one of the Three Graces, and a portrait in the Lindenau Museum in Thuringia, Germany.

wrote extensive notes on preserving a woman's looks into her later years. Redder lips, whiter teeth, golden hair, and fair skin were but a few of the topics her 454 herbal and mineral prescriptions addressed. She compiled her remedies in a manuscript entitled "*Experimenti*," which made its way into the Florentine state archives.

When she left Rome, Caterina Sforza Riario de Medici parted with war like two old spouses agreeably leaving a failed marriage. In middle age, her battles moved from castles to courtrooms. Commanding a team of lawyers with the fire of her days defending ramparts, she waged a successful custody battle for her youngest son, overcoming claims that, having been to prison, she was an unfit mother.

Pope Alexander VI died in August 1503, but the change of popes brought Caterina no closer to reclaiming the lands she had first laid eyes on as a teenage bride to a debauched pope's nephew. Her lance was broken, and she would never rule Forli again.

Older and wiser, she preferred to let her son take up reins or sword as he saw fit. To her disappointment, he took up neither. Ottaviano lacked the fire of a true Sforza. In time, he settled for a cardinal's hat, in exchange for waiving all claims to lands his mother once defended with her life.

CATERINA DIED on May 28, 1509, surrounded by priests, retainers, and Medici relatives. Her worldly vanities—those she could not cast into the bonfire—were distributed according to her will.

Not yet fifty when she passed away, Caterina planted one seed she would not see flower: Her eleven-year-old son Giovanni, fathered by her Medici husband, had inherited the spirit of his warrior mother. Like her, he was headstrong and fearless. In time, Giovanni would find himself leading a company of soldiers into battle, and would, like his great-grandfather, prove his worth as a *condottiere* in the service of Europe's warring kings.

Through Giovanni, Caterina's grandson would grow to become Cosimo de Medici, the first Grand Duke of Tuscany and Florence's greatest ruler. Blessed with the dominating will of his grandmother, Cosimo would lead Florence into its golden age of power and influence, about the same time an orphaned girl was preparing to set her island nation on a path to empire.

ACT III

EMPIRES AND REBELS

❖   ❖   ❖

But the Woman that God gave him, every fibre of her frame
Proves her launched for one sole issue, armed and engined for the same;
And to serve that single issue, lest the generations fail,
The female of the species must be deadlier than the male.

—KIPLING

As smoke from Caterina's guns wafted over Romagna's rolling hills, rising houses of Europe lifted women to new heights. The old warrior king who waded into battle with his band of brothers, splattered in blood, broadsword singing, gave way to a new breed of sovereigns who commanded from council chambers. Hovering over maps in palaces miles from the sounds of battle, they fought their wars with gold, parchment, and quill.

In this evolving world, primogeniture, custom, and religious strictures fell before a recognition that intelligence, not brawn, might guide royal succession. In ancient and medieval times, women had ruled in the name of husbands or sons. But soon after the deaths of Manduhai and Caterina, a new class of women parted the curtain and took the scepter in their own hands.

Not everywhere, of course. Because the leadership of Confucian China, the Tokugawa shogunate, and Islamic caliphates were men-only clubs, feminine power-brokers from the Renaissance to the French Revolution tended to be European. Isabella of Castile ruled Spain as an equal partner with her husband during the Reconquista. Queen Anne, sovereign of a new union known as "Great Britain," shared power with Parliament during her wars against the Sun King and Spanish crown. Maria Theresa, Archduchess of Austria, joined Russia's Empress Elizabeth to fight Frederick the Great in the heyday of powdered wigs and linear infantry tactics.

Unlike medieval rulers, whose agrarian economies put a premium on territorial conquest, women of the sixteenth through eighteenth centuries came of age when imperial might turned on trade, and trade often turned on maritime power. Advances in navigation and shipbuilding opened the New World and Pacific Islands to European exploitation as Columbus, Magellan, da Gama, Cabot, and their brethren touched off an imperial race for silver, spice, and slaves not seen since Rome ejected Carthage from *mare nostrum*.

Imperial ambitions beget instability, and instability is war's tinder. Great nations are most successful when they jealously guard what they possess, but are not too envious of what other great powers own. Emerging kingdoms from 1500 to 1800, reluctant to abide by this maxim, fell into wars with distressing regularity under both kings and queens.

By the end of the eighteenth century, the great powers had tacitly divided the globe into spheres of influence—a practice continued through the decades by

Napoleon and Alexander, Victoria and Bismarck, the Kaiser and King Edward, and Truman and Stalin. The imperial pretentions of old echo today in modern strategic hotspots like Eastern Europe, the Pacific Rim, and the Crimean.

Like their royal brothers, warrior queens after the Renaissance faced three daunting hurdles: The first was to defend (or take) the throne from challengers, which at times included other women. Second, they had to strengthen the national economy by dominating commerce, either through land conquests or command of the seas. Third, their increasingly interconnected world required them to form alliances with other powers to check rising enemies.

This was a tall order for any sovereign, but a lucky few female monarchs succeeded. Three of these legends ruled thriving kingdoms in Europe and Africa, and they now bask in history's glow.

The first, improbably enough, was an illegitimate orphan whose father killed her mother.

8

HEART OF A KING

Elizabeth I of England

"I am come amongst you, being resolved, in the midst and heat of battle, to live and die amongst you all; to lay down for my God, and for my kingdom, and my people, my honour and my blood."
—ELIZABETH ON THE EVE OF THE ARMADA INVASION, 1588

SHE WAS A BASTARD in the eyes of the law, a disinherited orphan whose mother had been executed on her father's order. At twenty-one, she had spent weeks locked in London's dreaded Tower, interrogated by agents of her half-sister, a heresy-hunting queen known in later years as "Bloody Mary."

But four years after her arrest, as church bells tolled and the November wind whipped, smiling lords in coats and plumes galloped from afar to pay their respects to the woman standing placidly beneath an oak tree. She knew for whom those bells tolled, and why men had ridden all the way from London to see her.

Dismounting from their tall saddles, the men bowed low to the woman they called "Your Majesty." Elizabeth Tudor's sister Mary was dead, and no one else held a better claim to England's throne. She was King Henry's daughter, and she had the red hair and iron will to prove it. With all the crown's dangers, for all the poisons and daggers and arrows lurking behind tapestries unseen, her time had finally come.

The time of Elizabeth, Queen of England, Wales, and Ireland.

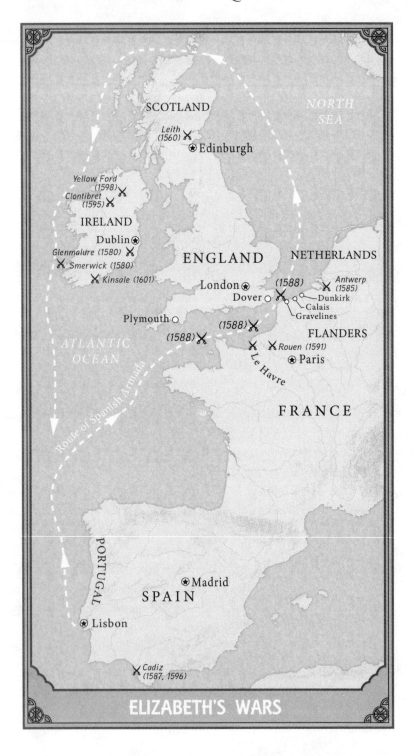

SCOTLAND

Leith ✕
(1560)
⊛ Edinburgh

NORTH
SEA

Yellow Ford
(1598) ✕
Clontibret ✕
(1595)

IRELAND

Dublin ⊛

Glenmalure (1580) ✕

✕ *Smerwick (1580)*

✕ *Kinsale (1601)*

ENGLAND

NETHERLANDS

London ⊛
Dover ○

(1588) ✕

○○ Dunkirk
Calais
Gravelines

Antwerp
(1585) ✕

Plymouth ○

(1588) ✕

(1588) ✕

FLANDERS

✕ ✕ *Rouen (1591)*

⊛ Paris

ATLANTIC
OCEAN

Le Havre

FRANCE

Route of Spanish Armada

PORTUGAL

⊛ Madrid

SPAIN

⊛ Lisbon

✕ *Cadiz*
(1587, 1596)

ELIZABETH'S WARS

❖   ❖   ❖

HER FAMILY CAME OF AGE in fratricide and blood. Her grandfather won a Lancastrian victory in the Wars of the Roses and seized the throne as King Henry VII. His son, Henry VIII, went through six wives, tore England from the Catholic faith, and plunged his realm into a costly war with France.

The younger Henry's first wife, a Spanish princess named Catherine of Aragon, gave him a daughter, named Mary. But Catherine's womb produced no son to inherit the throne, and tiring of Catherine, Henry fell for a reform-minded beauty named Anne Boleyn. When the pope refused to annul Henry's marriage to Catherine, Henry declared himself free of papal authority and married Anne, who gave him a second daughter, named Elizabeth.

Anne, like Catherine, did not produce a son. Itching to find a new wife, Henry charged Anne with treason and had her beheaded. He then married Jane Seymour, who died after giving birth to his only son. Three wives later, Henry died, and his crown went to ten-year-old Edward Tudor.

Edward lacked his father's robust constitution and died as a teenager. Mary, the older of the Tudor girls, inherited the throne in the summer of 1553. The next year she married Crown Prince Philip of Spain, who would become Spain's king upon his father's death. Under solemn wedding vows, Mary joined the English and Spanish royal families in a formidable alliance.

Mary, a Catholic, remained deeply suspicious of Elizabeth's religious beliefs, and when ecumenical tensions in the countryside flared into rebellion, she had her half-sister imprisoned in the Tower of London. For the next few weeks the young princess lived in daily dread of assassination or, following in the footsteps of her mother, a date with the headsman.

Despite stringent interrogation of Elizabeth's servants, Mary's investigators could find no credible evidence of Elizabeth's heresy or treason. Mary grudgingly allowed the princess to keep her head, but the psychological scars throbbed long after. Elizabeth knew her every move was being watched, every conversation overheard. Sensing just how precarious life was for a Tudor royal, she would play her cards close to her corset for the rest of her life.

In November 1558, Mary fell ill without an heir. Under Henry's will, Elizabeth stood next in line to the throne. As Queen Mary lay dying, royal courtiers, like hounds on the hare's scent, rode north to pledge their loyalty to the next Tudor queen.

Headstrong like her father, Elizabeth unleashed on Whitehall Palace an insatiable intellect and vigorous physical energy. She put in long hours each day studying matters of crown business, diligently riding a magic carpet of paperwork that consumed much of a sovereign's day. Fluent in Latin, Italian, French, Welsh, and Spanish, she read the New Testament in Greek and was conversant on virtually any subject, from crops and sex to theology and economics. In court, in council, or around the banquet table, she used her sharp sense of humor to put diplomats and courtiers at ease—or set them on edge.

Lustful of life, Elizabeth played as hard as she worked. She loved horseback rides, hunting, and shooting crossbows at targets in the courtyard. She laughed heartily and delighted in swapping court gossip with her ladies of the bedchamber.

And did she ever love to dance. Returning from palace balls, foreign ambassadors would write to their masters of the queen's spirited galliards and vigorous leaps through five, six, even seven numbers that left her dance partners gasping for breath.

Reveling in the vanity of a woman who reigned supreme, she wore heavy makeup that gave her complexion a smooth, white appearance. Each of her four coronation robes was made of twenty-three yards of gold and silver lamé trimmed with ermine and gold lace. She kept a wardrobe of 3,000 gowns, and frowned at pious Protestant preachers who thundered from pulpits against vainglorious vestments.

Despite her prodigious talents, the English—commonfolk and nobles alike—could be stubbornly old-fashioned, and many were reluctant to follow a woman. Men led armies, men led churches, and the turbulent years of Bloody Mary's rule convinced a sizeable number that men, not women, should lead kingdoms. "It is more than a monster in nature that a woman should reign and bear empire over man," Scottish firebrand John Knox groused the year of Elizabeth's accession. Knox's polemics reflected the views of many.

Sensitive to these prejudices, Elizabeth often referred to herself in public speeches as a prince, not a queen. She dotted royal pronouncements with references to her masculine forbears, and often alluded to her larger-than-life father. "Although I may not be a lion," she reminded courtiers, "I am a lion's cub, and inherit many of his qualities."

One quality she did *not* inherit was Henry's penchant for jumping from one marital bed to the next. The choice of husband was especially tricky in an age where mixed-faith kingdoms were divided, on the surface at least, into Catholic and Protestant camps. Spain and France were Catholic. The Habsburg Empire was Catholic. The Low Countries were Protestant (though nominally ruled by Spain's Catholic king), and Scotland was Protestant (though nominally ruled by France's Catholic queen). England was Protestant under Henry, but reverted to the Old Religion under Bloody Mary. Now, under Elizabeth, it was Protestant again. More or less.

While religion served as shorthand for a hodgepodge of strategic, political, and social affiliations, it was still a potent force in European kingdoms, where international policy was personal. Marrying a Catholic king would alienate Protestant nations like Scotland, just as marrying a Protestant would risk reprisals from Catholic powers like Spain. Elizabeth prudently postponed the question of marriage, never turning down a royal suitor—yet never giving her hand, either.

French in Scotland

A court observer likened the new queen and her kingdom to "a bone thrown between two dogs." The first dog, Spain, controlled the Low Countries, the Americas, and much of the Mediterranean. Ships bulging with silver from the New World enabled His Most Catholic Majesty to field a huge professional army, giving this dog long, sharp incisors.

The second dog, France, controlled Scotland through its crown prince, Francis, and his beautiful wife, Mary Stuart, Queen of Scots. As a great-granddaughter of King Henry VII, Mary of Scotland also held a solid claim to the English crown. Should Elizabeth's foot slip, France, with a waiting heir and large army, might be tempted to remove Elizabeth and set her Catholic cousin on Westminster's throne.

Appreciating the vulnerability of her kingdom, Elizabeth took up home defense as her government's first priority. Despite an inherited crown debt of £300,000, she sent agents to banking houses in Antwerp and borrowed enough money to buy fresh stocks of arms and armor. Soon 16,000 bow staves, 6,000 pike heads, 420,000 gunpowder charges, 18,000 metal corslets, and 33,000 assorted firearms made their way into the Tower's vast armory.

She would blood these new weapons on England's northern border.

Eight months into Elizabeth's reign, the death of France's King Henri II in a jousting accident elevated his son Francis to the throne. That made sixteen-year-old Mary queen of both Scotland and France. Supported by her mother's powerful family, the House of Guise, Mary began thinking of acquiring a third crown, and tipped her hand with a rash choice of heraldry: a coat of arms featuring the three rampant lions of England, Wales, and Ireland.

During Mary's reign, Scotland, that bleak and beautiful country to England's north, writhed in the throes of a power struggle between the Catholic crown and Protestant nobility swept up in a wave of religious reformation. If Mary defeated the Protestant lairds, France would gain a base in the British Isles. The French could raid, even invade, northern England, a threat Elizabeth could not permit.

Seeking to roll back French influence without triggering open warfare, Elizabeth launched a covert war against Mary and her French backers. She began by subsidizing Protestant Scotch rebels with stockpiled French currency, which allowed her to meddle in Scottish affairs while denying English involvement. When money alone failed, she sent a fleet of warships to blockade the Firth of Forth, the aquatic highway linking Edinburgh with the North Sea. Wearing a fig leaf of deniability, she forbade her fleet to fly English colors; it would sail north as a "private enterprise."

The Edinburgh blockade failed to drive off the Frenchmen, and in late 1559 Elizabeth took the drastic step of sending 4,000 English soldiers to Berwick, a town on the English side of the border. She told her privy council she intended to launch a lightning attack against nearby Leith, the main French base near Edinburgh, to drive the French army off the British Isles.

On Christmas Day Elizabeth ordered the attack. Then she began having second thoughts. English sons killing French sons was a dangerous escalation between two unfriendly kingdoms. No longer a "British-only" quarrel, an attack on the French garrison might drag England into full-blown war with France. She ultimately concluded that the risk was too great, and abruptly canceled the invasion.

Elizabeth's *volte-face* threw her military advisors into fits. They served at Her Majesty's bidding, but they needed consistency from their liege to chart England's foreign policy. Her commanders and councilors read into the queen's reversal a dangerous hesitation, characteristic of the female sex, to force events by violent means when necessary.

They might not have seen into Her Majesty's mind as clearly as they thought. Elizabeth was not opposed to violence when she thought it necessary. But her feelings toward war with Scotland—or any war, for that matter—were tempered by two fears.

The first was the economic legacy of her father's conflicts, which had nearly ruined England during her childhood. Wars in the age of pike and cannon were not cheap affairs. Her father's campaigns in France had gained the port of Boulogne and a slice of the French coast near Calais, but they hatched a financial dragon that cast a dark shadow over the realm. War debts forced Henry to borrow £1 million from Flemish moneylenders, sell church lands, debase England's pound by diluting coins with lesser metals, and raise taxes to their highest rates in two hundred years. Debasement of crown currency alone set off a wave of inflation that cut landowner wealth in half within five years and shook the people's faith in their economy.[*]

---

[*] One of Henry's few decisive victories was actually won by his first wife, Queen Catherine of Aragon. In 1513, while Henry was away fighting the French in Normandy, Catherine assembled an army and defeated Scotland's King James IV at the Battle of Flodden. She shipped a torn, bloody portion of the dead Scottish king's surcoat to her husband as a war trophy.

Her second fear was the effect of a foreign war on her grip on power, for generals rise to prominence in wartime—and armies can make kings. As a princess, Elizabeth had no training in martial affairs. She hadn't drilled with a sword as a child, and had never taken part in raiding expeditions or long marches. She therefore could not pretend to give more than the most rudimentary guidance to her generals. Even if she could offer practical advice, the idea of her riding among encamped soldiers on a white horse, wearing a steel breastplate, was preposterous to any sensible Englishman. In wartime, the disability imposed by her gender left England's fate in the hands of men on horseback with direct access to raw power—not the queen whose banner they fought under.

A long war, Elizabeth concluded, was something to avoid whenever possible. She would not cry havoc and let the dogs slip in Scotland that winter.

By spring, however, the strategic landscape had changed. In France, an uprising against the Guise faction shook the confidence of the ruling clique. With Paris embroiled in domestic unrest, Elizabeth calculated that the French king could not afford to send reinforcements to Scotland and escalate a war. Reversing herself a second time, she ordered her army of 7,200 foot and horse soldiers to drive the French out of Leith.

Her local commander botched the assault and lost five hundred men. Elizabeth had no choice but to send reinforcements and ordered her navy to clamp a blockade on Leith from the sea. The blockade proved more effective. Before long, famished French defenders were scrounging for shellfish on the beach, and in July 1560 King Francis agreed to quit Scotland. His soldiers embarked in transports, French fortifications were razed, and, with Queen Mary's French support gone, the Scottish center of power passed to a council of Protestant nobles.

The north was finally secure.

The Huguenot Debacle

The expulsion of the French from Scotland was Elizabeth's first major military victory. It gave England a spell of peace, and forced King Francis to recognize Elizabeth as England's rightful ruler. French negotiators assured Elizabeth that King Francis's wife, Mary of Scotland, would renounce her claims to the English throne, and they signed a treaty waiving Mary's right to succeed Elizabeth. Things seemed to be moving in Elizabeth's direction.*

---

* Queen Mary, who was not part of the conversation, felt differently and refused to ratify the treaty. Her obstinacy, as we shall see, caused no end of trouble with her royal cousin.

But five months later, sixteen-year-old King Francis unexpectedly died of an ear infection. His death shifted power from the Guise clan to an anti-Protestant clique led by Catherine de Medici, mother of the new king, ten-year-old Charles XI. French Protestants, calling themselves Huguenots, soon launched a struggle to up-end Catholic dominance. Sensing an opening to destabilize England's ancient foe, Elizabeth's privy council urged her to aid the Huguenots in bringing down the Parisian Catholics.

Elizabeth's heart was with the Huguenots, but she was no religious zealot. While she officially outlawed the Latin Mass at home, she preferred to downplay Protestant orthodoxy and simply leave and let live. To Elizabeth, England's interests lay in unsettling her enemies, not championing this dogma or that.

Yet the voices of her counselors rang loudly in her ears: She should strike the French while they were in disarray.

As in Scotland, Elizabeth dipped a toe in the dark waters of revolt. In the summer of 1562, she sent a squadron of warships to blockade the French coast under the dubious claim that they were hunting pirates. Before long, English volunteers and English gold began turning up in the Huguenot stronghold of Rouen. Elizabeth's invisible hand in the French revolt grew more visible with each passing day.

The Huguenots couldn't take Paris, even with smuggled gold and English mercenaries, and a reluctant Elizabeth openly joined the fray with royal troops. But her tactics backfired when Medici propagandists publicized English interference in a French quarrel. The odious presence of Englishmen enraged both Catholic and mainstream Protestant French, all of whom were repulsed by the thought of English knights flying the three lions banner over their soil. After a short struggle, Catholic forces defeated the Huguenots, and in March 1563 the two war-weary sides agreed to a truce.

Two months later, the French turned their cannons against the English and drove them off the Continent.

The Huguenot debacle was a bitter pill for Elizabeth, who learned the hard way that most Frenchmen were French first, Catholic or Protestant second. Adding injury to insult, her surviving troops carried the plague into her capital, unleashing an epidemic that killed 20,000 Londoners. The Spanish ambassador, Bishop Alvaro de Quadra, gleefully reported to King Philip that English commoners were losing confidence in the woman who led them. "God help England and send it a king," the people grumbled, according to the bishop's reports.*

---

* While defeat and plague excited Bishop de Quadra's hopes for the queen's overthrow, Elizabeth had the last laugh. De Quadra became one of the thousands killed by the plague introduced to London by her defeated troops.

Back in Whitehall, long-faced exchequer accountants bent over their ledgers and tallied the cost of Elizabeth's foreign adventures. In four short years, she had managed to rack up a bill of nearly £750,000—an oppressive debt, even for a sovereign.

Alarmed at the rate war debts were piling up, Elizabeth scoured her budgets for new ways to economize. She laid up most of the Royal Navy and slashed garrison strengths in Dublin and Berwick. She authorized ministers to take out new loans in Antwerp and sold more Crown lands to raise money. She pinched pennies to save on household upkeep, servants, gifts, and clothes, and refused to send further aid to French Protestants.

War's economic shock waves were not confined to the royal treasury. Conflict with France had a ripple effect on English export markets, especially wool. English investors, watching in dismay, saw textile profits plunge and were forced to comb the Levant, Southern Europe, and North Africa to find new markets to sell their wares. Elizabeth's wars, like those of her father, were becoming a national drain.

Pirates on the Spanish Main

For most of the 1560s, Elizabeth focused on economic stability and strategic independence, not power plays in foreign lands. She had learned her lesson when her soldiers were driven off the Continent, and for a time she had no stomach for war.

Yet she couldn't turn a blind eye to the Catholic-Protestant struggle. Once France was united under Medici leadership, or the rebellious Low Countries were pacified by Spain, either of those great powers would be free to turn their arms against England. Peace on the Continent, she reasoned, was not in England's interest, so she quietly loaned money to Dutch and French agitators to keep the pot bubbling.

Piracy, in the form of privateers, was another unofficial tool of Elizabeth's covert wars. Her father had granted ship captains royal commissions to prey on French and Scottish vessels. In return for a license to commit what was otherwise piracy, the Crown received a share of the spoils.

The practice of licensing privateers became so popular—and so lucrative for investors—that it had continued long after Henry's land wars ended. By Elizabeth's time, metallurgists had perfected a revolutionary method of producing cheap but effective cannons, enabling ship owners to arm their vessels at low cost. Soon, gentleman captains like Francis Drake and John Hawkins were preying on Spanish shipping in the Caribbean Sea and eastern Atlantic.

To Elizabeth, privateers offered three advantages over a royal fleet. First, they were deniable. They flew no royal colors, and Elizabeth could truthfully swear that sea dogs like Drake and Hawkins were beyond her control once they left English ports. Second, the financial risk of the expeditions was borne by private investors, not the Crown, which reaped profits but lost nothing if a ship sank in a storm. Finally, privateer expeditions incubated a class of independent, energetic naval leaders who would become one of the kingdom's greatest assets if a larger war broke out with Spain or France.

There was one risk Elizabeth could not avoid: While privateers flew private colors, they were manned by Englishmen, and Elizabeth's game of galleons threatened to turn a cold war with Spain into a hot one. In September 1568, Captain John Hawkins and his squadron were caught off the Mexican coast by a Spanish war fleet. Cornered at the Spanish coastal fort of San Juan de Ulloa, Hawkins shot his way out, but only two of his nine ships escaped, leaving Spain with a fine catch of English prisoners.

The battle in the heart of the Spanish Main outraged Spain's public, which cried out for war. Two months later, Elizabeth's customs officials added fuel to smoldering tinder by detaining a squadron of Spanish ships driven by storm into an English port. Their holds, it turned out, were filled with the payroll of Spain's army in the Netherlands, the princely sum of £85,000. Elizabeth ordered the ships detained while she mulled over whether to keep the money. In retaliation, the Spanish commander in Brussels seized English goods in Dutch ports. Elizabeth then froze Spanish assets in England, including the army payroll that started the round of sanctions.

A sudden pro-Catholic rising in the north of England, intended to place Mary of Scotland on the English throne, forced Elizabeth to send an army of 20,000 to put down the rebellion. The rising's collapse dashed Mary's hopes of taking Elizabeth's kingdom. Protestant lairds drove Mary out of Edinburgh and replaced her with her infant son, King James VI. Mary fled to northern England, seeking refuge.

Elizabeth took no chances with her high-born cousin. In 1569 she had Mary escorted to central England and held at Tutbury Castle as her honored guest and unofficial prisoner. Watched carefully by her hosts and surrounded by polite but firm guards, a frustrated Mary had little choice but to bide her time. She strolled the castle grounds, held court with a small band of servants, and embroidered colorful cloth scenes as she waited for Elizabeth to make a fatal error.

In Whitehall, Elizabeth and her ministers fretted over what Mary might be weaving besides cloth pictures. Unsure what to do with a queen who was too famous to eliminate, too dangerous to liberate, they too waited, watching for Mary to slip.

"The World is Not Enough"

The rift between England and the Catholic kingdoms widened in February 1570 when Pope Pius V issued a papal bull declaring the English queen a heretic. "The pretended Queen of England, the serpent of wickedness," as the pope denounced her, was unfit to govern her Christian subjects. Pius absolved any Catholic of sin, including murder, committed while overthrowing the English serpent.

Like the French Protestants, the great majority of English Catholics remained loyal to their state and sovereign. The great majority considered themselves English first and Catholic second, and they would have resisted any invasion of their homeland—even by fellow Catholics.

But *majority* is not the same thing as *everybody*. It took only one lucky fanatic to kill a queen, and with the scratch of a pope's venomous pen, Elizabeth now had to consider every Catholic subject a potential traitor.

Storm clouds thickened in late 1571 with rumors of conspiracies to assassinate Elizabeth, land Spanish troops in England, and put Queen Mary on the throne. Nothing came of the plots, but there was enough circumstantial evidence to persuade Elizabeth that King Philip of Spain was actively working to topple her.

She was right. Elizabeth's years of proxy wars, funding rebels in the Spanish Netherlands and prosecuting an undeclared war at sea had convinced Philip that England would be an implacable foe as long as its crown rested on a Protestant head. With an imprisoned Catholic queen next in line of succession, Philip's best option was to foreshorten Elizabeth's reign.

AS AN ISLAND, England looked to the Royal Navy as its first line of defense. Working from an inherited fleet of thirty-nine ships, Elizabeth and her ministers charted a slow but steady course that balanced the kingdom's economy against its defense needs. She kept the navy on a moderate but steady budget throughout the 1560s, neither launching crash building programs in times of danger, nor slashing her naval budget when waters were tranquil. Taking this middle way, she ensured that England kept an adequate peacetime defense.

To subsidize the upkeep of shipyards, in 1566 Elizabeth approved England's first national lottery, with a £5,000 first prize to be paid in available cash, gold, tapestries, and "good linen cloth." As an added incentive, a ticket bought its holder immunity from arrest for misdemeanors. Ticket sales came to a respectable £20,000.

When Spanish threats grew too sharp to ignore, Elizabeth spurred the pace of ship-building. In 1570, her Navy Board launched the heavy galleon *Foresight*, and followed up the aptly named warship with four more in 1573: *Dreadnought, Swiftsure, Achates,* and *Handmaid.* Her Majesty's Government also entered into a series of long-term contracts to moor, caulk, and refit ships on a regular basis until a projected end date of 1597—an extraordinary level of advance planning for the sixteenth century.

Unlike the hulks of King Henry's day, Elizabeth's fleet was built around a fast, light, "race-built" hull. These newer ship models placed less emphasis on musket-armed soldiers, archery towers, and small deck-sweeping guns. Instead, they concentrated their firepower in big, smashing cannons capable of sending thirty-pound iron balls through enemy timbers and rigging.

Elizabeth would need guns and ships, and plenty else, for as she reached her late forties, her throne was beset by enemies foreign and domestic. In 1579, an Italio-Spanish army commanded by an Irish rebel landed in western Ireland at the instigation of Pope Gregory XIII. The rising was put down with the usual massacres, but tensions simmered on both islands.

Her clouds darkened when a French-born nobleman managed to overthrow Scotland's pro-English regent and shift Scottish power to King James VI, the fifteen-year-old son of the imprisoned Mary. As with Ireland, Elizabeth would have to keep a careful watch on Scotland.

Worst of all, in 1580 the King of Portugal died without an heir. King Philip of Spain seized the opportunity to invade Portugal, taking Lisbon's throne for himself and uniting the Portuguese and Spanish empires.

Philip's conquest of Portugal was a body blow to Elizabeth. From West Africa to the East Indies, the Spanish king now controlled a network of foreign trading posts and colonies spanning the globe. He fielded the world's largest merchant fleet, and his navy, commanded by the formidable Marquis de Santa Cruz, seemed invincible. "Even Christ is no longer safe in Paradise," impious Spanish sailors boasted, "for the marquis might go there to bring him back and crucify him all over again."

Philip's royal motto, *Non Sufficit Orbis*—"The World is Not Enough"—seemed deadly serious.

As the walls closed in, anxiety sketched its lines across Elizabeth's face. Her red hair receded, her cheeks grew hollow, and the smile of her youth tightened into a frown as she wrestled with the demands of state. Only her eyes—large and round under high, arched brows—retained the impish joy of the young woman from the palace dance floor.

The queen's first priority was to secure England's border with Scotland. In the spring of 1581, she ordered soldiers to concentrate in northern England to restore the Protestant regent to power. Then, to the dismay of her ministers, she changed her mind and canceled the operation—just as she had reversed herself at Leith two decades earlier.

Elizabeth's reversal was no flight of feminine fickleness, as some of her shaken advisers assumed. Under Mary's son, James, Scotland was susceptible to Catholic and French influence. But the Scots were not active enemies of England, and James had every reason to hope he might succeed the childless queen on Westminster's coronation chair. Sensing that fresh military action might drive an enraged Scotland into French arms, Elizabeth dangled before James the lucrative prospect of being named her successor. Her condition: Scotland must remain a friend of England during her lifetime.

To the west, in Ireland, Elizabeth saw only a military solution. A second Catholic force sent by Pope Gregory was defeated near Limerick, but the incursion required Elizabeth to deploy another 6,500 soldiers. In the process, her Whitehall ministers spent another £300,000, a severe drain on what was becoming a cash-strapped kingdom.

Parrying blows in Ireland, Elizabeth took the offensive at sea. Spain's treasure ships, she knew, were the empire's jugular vein. If Philip pointed a dagger at her throne, she would aim a cannon at his economy. She called for her sea dogs.

In September 1580, Captain Francis Drake stunned the world when he arrived safely at the English port city of Plymouth after a three-year circumnavigation of the globe. His squadron's plunder was officially reported at £307,000—roughly Elizabeth's entire annual income—but the real value of the haul was probably more than twice what his books reflected. Drake's sensationalized reports of weakly held Spanish settlements, fat merchant ships laden with tobacco and silver, and lands ripe for the taking spurred a seafaring industry built on legalized piracy, and Elizabeth's government obliged by issuing more letters of marque.

As in the past, Elizabeth admitted no official connection to Drake or his fellow privateers and disclaimed all responsibility for their depredations. But the woman who raked in immense profits was hardly discreet about her unofficial support. On Drake's return, she publicly knighted him, prompting shaken heads and appalled looks from embarrassed foreign ministers. Ignoring the diplomatic community, she even docked Drake's flagship, the *Golden Hind*, at Deptford and made it a tourist attraction. Plausible deniability was becoming less plausible every month.

❖   ❖   ❖

ELIZABETH CONTINUED TO FRET over war's economic burden. A quarter of
the Crown's revenues came from customs duties, much of which were paid by Spanish merchants entering English ports. Those revenues would vanish the moment war
was declared by either England or Spain. Lord Burghley, a level-headed Protestant
and the queen's closest advisor, argued that a new war would set in motion an economic crisis, and perhaps even ignite rebellion in the English countryside. Do not
provoke the Catholic monarchs, Burghley counseled.

Elizabeth tried to follow Burghley's advice, but she found herself pulled into an
undertow of blood as events on the Continent struck at her safety. By 1584, she
could no longer ignore mounting evidence that King Philip had embarked upon a
two-pronged strategy to incite Elizabeth's Catholic subjects to assassinate their
queen and set Mary, Queen of Scots, on England's throne.

Elizabeth's response to Madrid's threat required her to look to an unlikely war
theater: the Netherlands.

The bulk of Spain's veteran army was tied down in the rebellious Dutch provinces, and Elizabeth made that distraction the cornerstone of her survival strategy.
Whenever Spain began to gain the upper hand, Elizabeth would stir the pot with a
fresh military operation to support the Dutch Protestant rebels, just as she had supported French Protestant rebels years before.

She would learn that the sinews of proxy wars, like those of national wars, are
immense commitments of money and men. In August 1585, she agreed to send
4,400 English infantry and horse soldiers to Holland. The following month, Dutch
rebels suffered a setback when they lost the great port of Antwerp to Spanish troops.
By now Elizabeth had gone too far to turn back, and she reluctantly committed
more men and money to propping up a cause that was losing momentum.

For a time, King Philip chose to overlook English provocations. He was fighting
Turks in the eastern Mediterranean, Portuguese rebels in the Azores, Dutch rebels
in the Low Countries, and pirates at sea. At the moment, he had no wish to open a
new war with Elizabeth.

But in 1586, Drake's privateers looted and burned Santo Domingo and Cartagena, two pillars of his New World empire. Humiliated by the blow to Spanish
prestige, the sallow-faced Philip concluded that he could not swat at English
wasps forever. As his international strategist, Don Juan de Zuniga, aptly put it, "To
fight a purely defensive war is to court a huge and permanent expense, because we
have to defend the Indies, Spain, and the convoys traveling between them." Siding

with Madrid's hawks, Philip opened the year 1586 with a plan to destroy the heretic queen.

He would launch the Enterprise of England.

Queen of Scots

To soften England for the kill, Philip clamped a boycott on English goods. France, Flanders, and Hamburg joined the embargo, isolating England from the rich Continental trade while Philip pushed his next phase: Elizabeth's overthrow.

In Paris, Don Bernardino Mendoza, Spain's former ambassador to England, coordinated plots with Catholic expatriates to assassinate Elizabeth and replace her with the imprisoned Queen Mary. While the embargo set in and conspiracies took root, Philip turned to the military side of his strategy, an operation painstakingly worked out by his generals, admirals, and political advisors.

The operation's first phase would be a diversionary landing in Ireland. Once Elizabeth's forces were drawn west, Philip's war fleet would race from Spain to Flanders. From there it would cover a massive troop landing in southeastern England by a veteran army led by the formidable Duke of Parma. Brushing aside poorly trained defenders, Parma's army would march on London, depose Elizabeth—assuming she was still alive—and ride with Mary in triumph to Westminster.

In the summer of 1586, the Enterprise of England took a dark and unexpected turn. A plot to kill Elizabeth collapsed when a young zealot named Anthony Babington and a handful of conspirators were detected by Elizabeth's spies. Decrypted correspondence between Babington and Mary implicated the captive queen in a plot to assassinate Elizabeth. The English collaborators were rounded up and interrogated. And after a quick trial in which guilt was never in doubt, the would-be regicides were sentenced to death.

Elizabeth, normally a lenient person, exploded with rage when she learned of the plot. In a heated tirade in the council room, she told her ministers she wanted to send a message to all would-be assassins: There would be no nice, easy, lopped-off-head sort of punishment this time. She ordered her councilors to arrange an execution method more painful and more terrifying than the lawful means of dispatching rebels: hanging almost to the point of asphyxiation, then disemboweling, emasculating, and quartering the condemned while alive and, ideally, still conscious.

When her advisors demurred, the queen's face flushed. She insisted that there *must* be some more horrific means of death, and demanded that the smart men sitting around the table put their intelligent minds to finding one. Elizabeth eventually calmed down when her councilors assured her that the law's prescribed method, if followed to the letter, would be sufficiently gruesome to send a vivid message to the masses.

It was.

THE VIVISECTION OF BABINGTON and his confederates forced Elizabeth to deal with her second most dangerous opponent, and make one of the most difficult decisions of her life.

For nineteen years, her advisors had urged her to try and execute Queen Mary. Lord Burghley, Sir Francis Walsingham, and many trusted members of council and Parliament reasoned that the queen's life would never be safe while Mary remained a rallying figure for Catholic conspirators. And for years, Elizabeth refused to take the life of a fellow royal.

The Babington Plot finally moved Elizabeth to act, though not without a show of tearful indecision, some of which was genuine. A few months after the Babington plotters were arrested, Elizabeth finally agreed to put Mary put on trial. The court found Mary guilty of treason and conspiracy to murder the queen and sentenced her to death. Ministers prepared Mary's death warrant and brought it to Whitehall for Elizabeth's signature.

Elizabeth wrung her hands over the sentence. With a stroke of her quill, she would be putting to death her cousin, one of God's anointed sovereigns—a woman whose blood, like hers, was royal. Morality aside, Mary's execution would also inflame the Catholic world and potentially infuriate Mary's estranged Catholic son, Scotland's King James VI, a monarch Elizabeth could not afford to alienate.

Groping for another way out, she privately asked whether Mary might be quietly poisoned in her apartment, rather than openly executed. The official word could be that Mary had died of natural causes.

Elizabeth's ministers were appalled at the queen's suggestion that they assassinate a royal for the crime of conspiring to assassinate a royal. Convenient as poisoning might have been, Elizabeth's suggestion went nowhere, and the queen put off the agonizing decision week after week through January of 1587.

Then, on the first of February, a frowning Elizabeth took a pen in her long, thin fingers and signed Mary's death warrant. Seven days later, kneeling on a low wooden platform at Fotheringhay Castle, the forty-four-year-old former queen of France and Scotland was sent into the next life with three clumsy blows of an axe.

Anxious English eyes now turned toward Edinburgh. The two nations had fought for hundreds of years over far less provocation than the beheading of a queen. Fortunately for Elizabeth, King James's ambition outweighed his loyalty to his dead mother's memory. He knew he might be crowned king of England on Elizabeth's death, provided he didn't stir up ill feelings in Westminster. Besides, Mary's execution was an accomplished fact; going to war would not put her head back on her shoulders. James made a pro forma protest, but took no steps to avenge his mother's death. He sat out the coming war. Through careful diplomacy rather than military conquest, England's northern flank had finally become secure.

"A Weak, Feeble Woman"

If Mary's execution deprived King Philip of one *casus belli*—to set Mary on the English throne—it animated him with a fresh one: revenge. Catholic Europe exploded over Mary's beheading, and Philip grew more determined than ever to rid the world of the Tudor heretic.

But revenge would have to wait. The previous spring, a squadron of warships under Sir Francis Drake had fallen upon Spain's sleeping fleet like a wildcat. In a lightning raid on the Spanish naval base at Cadiz, Drake had destroyed thirty-seven galleons and burned an entire merchant fleet to the waterline. He also captured *San Felipe*, an immense silver ship, netting Elizabeth's treasury a tidy £40,000 profit.*

Drake's exquisitely timed raid sent Spanish merchants into a panic and compelled a frustrated King Philip to spend the year 1587 rebuilding his naval forces. He signed a treaty with the pope that granted Philip the right to nominate whomever he wished to succeed Elizabeth, and ordered General Parma to build a fleet of invasion barges to ferry his army from Flanders across the English Channel. He then instructed his admiralty to plan a dash from Lisbon to the Flemish coast, where his battle fleet would escort Parma's barge flotilla to the English beaches.

If Philip's plans went as expected, Elizabeth would follow her cousin to the block. The Tudor dynasty would die with her, and Spain would helm the destiny of the British Isles.

Elizabeth and her ministers spent a frantic winter and spring of 1588 building, crewing, and upgrading the war fleet. She bought the armed galleon *Ark Raleigh*

---

* According to Lord Burghley, the queen, worried about provoking Spain, had tried to cancel Drake's brilliant attack on Cadiz. Fortunately for Elizabeth, the messenger ship was turned back due to adverse winds and never reached Drake's fleet.

from Sir Walter, renaming it *Ark Royal*, and added nine smaller warships to her battle line. To manage her sea defenses, she appointed Lord Charles Howard of Effingham to the posts of Lieutenant General, Lord High Admiral, and Commander of the Fleet. Howard would command one of her fleet's wings, while Drake, based in Plymouth, would command the other.

On land, preparations to meet the invader were far less impressive. Coastal defenses erected by Henry VIII had fallen into disrepair, and the Crown lacked the time and money to rebuild them. Unable to throw back the invaders on the beaches, Elizabeth and her ministers prepared for a war of depth and maneuver. Militias served out pikes and muskets, bridges were prepared for demolition, and signal stations were manned along England's southern coast.

Having flirted with war for so long, Elizabeth now found herself desperate to avoid it. In the spring of 1588, she sent a delegation to the Netherlands to seek a truce with Parma. A cease-fire with Philip's field commander, she hoped, might expand into a *modus vivendi* in which England and Spain could live in peace. To keep the process going, she even refused to allow Drake to leave Plymouth while talks dragged on.

A flustered Drake countered that England's best defense was an offensive against the Spanish coast, just as it had been the year before, when he devastated Cadiz. Parma, Drake reasoned, wouldn't dare move his slow, fat troop transports unless Spain's battle fleet supported him. "With fifty sail of shipping," he wrote the queen's privy council, "we shall do more good upon their own coast, than a great many more will do here at home." Sir Francis followed his letter with a personal appeal to the queen: "The advantage of time and place in all martial actions is half a victory; which being lost is irrecoverable."

Elizabeth's eleventh-hour peace feelers came to naught. Parma had no interest in delaying the invasion, and he prolonged talks only so he could complete his preparations—a *ruse de guerre* Elizabeth's advisors saw with perfect clarity. "For the love of Jesus Christ, Madam," an exasperated Admiral Howard wrote Elizabeth, "awake thoroughly and see the villainous treasons around you, against Your Majesty and your realm, and draw your forces round about you like a mighty prince."

Elizabeth couldn't argue with their logic. With a heavy heart, she set down the olive branch and took up the mace. The time for talk had passed, and the dogs of war were straining at their leash.

❖   ❖   ❖

BY THE SUMMER of 1588, England's untested defenses were as ready as Elizabeth could make them. To defend England on land, her generals deployed four armies. One army of 20,000 men would shadow the Spanish fleet as it moved along the English coast, ready to pounce on the landing force. A second force, which would grow to almost 35,000 men, would guard west London and the queen. The main army, under the Earl of Leicester, would screen the Thames River estuary, a natural landing site for any invader, and a fourth, smaller army would defend the north in the unlikely event of a landing there.

The picture at sea was more complex. Faced with two enemy fleets—Santa Cruz's battle fleet in Lisbon, and Parma's invasion flotilla on the Belgic coast—the queen stationed Admiral Howard's squadron on England's southeastern coast, near Dover, to hold off Parma's force. Drake would command the larger battle fleet at Plymouth, in England's southwest, closer to the route she expected the Spanish to take. If and when her two wings converged on the enemy, Admiral Howard would assume command of the combined fleet.

Elizabeth's "Navy Royall" consisted of thirty-eight warships, of which only nineteen carried twenty or more guns. Her government hired another sixteen armed merchant ships to reinforce the line of battle, while privateer, supply, coastal, and messenger vessels brought Elizabeth's total to 208 ships. In all, her first-line fleet mounted 770 heavy cannons commanded by 555 skilled naval gunners.

While Elizabeth's privateer war over the past two decades had pushed the nations to war, it also bore unexpected fruit. She refused to entrust her generals with the land war in the Netherlands and bombarded local commanders with advice, criticisms, and unrealistic demands. But at sea she had little actual power. Drake, Hawkins, Raleigh, and the rest were beyond the queen's reach from the moment they weighed anchor, and Elizabeth learned, grudgingly, to trust the judgment of her naval captains. The Spanish Main had become a training ground for commanders who could make critical decisions without waiting for orders from London.

Those captains intended to wage a sea battle very different from the orthodox tactics handed down since the days of Artemisia and Cleopatra. Instead of fighting man-to-man—closing with the enemy, throwing boarding hooks over the side, and feeding soldiers into the slaughter—the English would stand off a healthy distance and smash Spanish rigging and hulls with long-range guns until the enemy struck his colors. Or sank.

Naval victory required two elements, wind and guns, and for the moment, Elizabeth had only one of these on her side. The Atlantic's winds often blew foul and did not favor the Royal Navy that summer. By June 23, Howard had weighed anchor for Lisbon three times, only to turn back as southerly breezes forced him home.

And far to the south, the winds that pressed Elizabeth's ships against their berths filled the sails of the Spanish Armada.

King Philip's *Gran Armada* was the most formidable killing machine in the world. Combining the terror of a sea kraken with the firepower of an army, his 129 warships groaned under the weight of 2,485 cannons. The 20,000 soldiers who embarked on those galleons had trained until they were as sharp as the pikes they wielded. On cue, they would board the English ships and fight to the death with musket and sword.

Admiral Alonso Pérez de Guzmán, Duke of Medina Sidonia, commanded Spain's main battle fleet. To him fell the daunting task of running along the English Channel from Lisbon, finding Parma's barge fleet on the Flemish coast, and protecting the soldiers as their fat, low barges waddled across the Channel. A capable administrator and unimaginative man, Admiral Medina Sidonia was chosen to command the Armada for one reason: He would obey Madrid's orders to the letter, even when the gods of battle urged a different course.

❖   ❖   ❖

TO THE HERD-LIKE THUNDER of feet on decks and the clanking of anchor chains, in July 1588 the galleon *San Martin de Portugal*, flagship of Admiral Medina Sidonia, weighed anchor and led the Armada to England's southern coast.

The forest of masts and sails was first spotted at Lizard Point, on Britain's southwestern tip, and a warning beacon lit up on July 20, sending flames and smoke into the summer sky. In slow succession, pyres flared in a line across southern England, spreading the dreaded word: The Spanish were coming.*

As church bells called farmers, smithies, and merchants to arms, Queen Elizabeth remained outwardly calm. Confident, even. "It is a comfort to see how great magnanimity Her Majesty shows, who is not a whit dismayed," wrote Lord Burghley's son, Robert Cecil.

---

* Dates are given here in "Old Style," in contrast to the "New Style" calendar introduced by Pope Gregory XIII in 1582. For a century, England refused to buy into the papal dating system. English records, using the calendar introduced by Julius Caesar after he met Cleopatra, ran approximately ten days behind Gregorian dating.

But the queen's advisors were alarmed at what seemed her dangerously cavalier attitude to the leviathan plowing straight for London. They spent their days spreading meager defense resources along the coast and deflecting pleas from generals for gunpowder, pikes, beer, barley, and gold.

Appalled that the queen's ministers were pinching pennies with the enemy at the gates, Elizabeth's spymaster Walsingham bemoaned "so great a danger hanging over the realm so lightly regarded and so carelessly provided for. Would to God the enemy were no more careful to assail than we to defend." Admiral Howard, put out over the government's chronic parsimony, added, "For the love of God let Her Majesty care not now for charges."

Howard asked permission to sail to Spain and hit the Spanish off their own coast, but Elizabeth, worried that the Armada might slip past him, overruled her admiral and ordered him to keep his squadron close to home. With the enemy in sight, Howard and Drake weighed anchor on July 20. Lookouts high in the crosstrees squinted into the western horizon, looking for a telltale forest of sail that would signal their chance to tear into the Spanish lion.

Fate offered that opportunity the next day, when Drake and Howard intercepted the Spanish battle fleet. Medina Sidonia ordered his ships into a *lunula*, or crescent-shaped battle formation, the horns of which stretched nearly six miles across. Sails emblazoned with the red cross of Spain rippled in the wind as the fleet plowed ahead, white plumes feathering over painted bows. Guns ran out of their portals, sand was spread across decks to soak blood, and heavy nets were raised over decks to protect the crews from falling yards, spars, and tackle blocks when the iron flew.

Keeping their distance, the English galleons opened fire with their heavy guns. Orange flashes knifed from bronze mouths as thunder boomed over the waves. At each gun carriage, thick, sulfuric smoke stung eyes as sweating sailors sponged hot barrels and rammed home powder and shot. Gun captains squinted over sights and barked orders as men ran out the long barrel. With the next roar from the dragon's mouth, the murderous work began again.

Across Spanish decks, iron shot crashed into rails, sending wooden splinters flying like daggers into flesh. Arms and legs were torn off by round balls, sails were shredded, and masts and yards crashed onto dead and dying men. Spain's Biscayan squadron, hammered by Drake's *Revenge* and her sisters, fled to the fleet's protective center, and during the battle, the vice-flagship, *San Juan de Portugal*, was pummeled by three hundred iron rounds.

More was to come in succeeding days. Howard's *Ark Royal* and Drake's *Revenge* followed the Armada as it pushed toward Flanders. Off the Isle of Wight four days later, Drake's guns perforated the 768-ton *Santa Ana* so badly her captain ran her aground to keep her from sinking.

With any other fighting fleet, the bites Drake and Howard tore from the Spanish hide would have ended the invasion. But the Armada was no ordinary fleet. It was a floating city six miles wide, and the loss of a few large galleons would hardly slow it down—or blunt its fangs. Medina Sidonia followed the king's orders and pressed on for Gravelines, the nearest Flemish port. He was now only fifteen miles from Dunkirk, General Parma's embarkation point.

The English struck again in the first hours of July 28. They attacked the anchored Spanish fleet with fireships, stripped-down warships filled with pitch, kindling, and loaded cannons that they set afire and sailed into the Spanish host. The floating bombs did little direct damage, but the combination of night blazes, spontaneously firing cannon, and danger that the hellburners might be packed with explosives spread terror through Spanish crews. Ships unfurled their courses and ran blindly into each other in the night, snapping yardarms and tangling rigging. In the confusion, the Spanish fleet scattered.

Unprepared for his success, Admiral Howard did nothing to complete the Armada's destruction that night. By daybreak, the Armada was spread over several miles, but Admiral Medina Sidonia quickly reformed his squadrons near the small port of Gravelines before the English could pick off his isolated ships.

While Howard busied himself with a meaningless Neapolitan prize, Drake drove his squadron within cannon range of the enemy and blasted away. Hundreds of Spanish crewmen died in the iron hailstorm—a Levantine was seen with her portholes draining blood—and the galleon *Maria Juan* went to the bottom, taking 188 men with her. Corpses were heaved overboard and wounded were carried belowdecks for their appointments with surgeons, ligatures, and bone saws. In a day's bloody work, Medina Sidonia lost 1,800 men and five capital ships.

With his sailors verging on panic, Medina Sidonia decided to make a run for it. A timely change of winds blew his ships out of the lion's mouth, but his retreat up England's east coast left the Spanish war fleet hopelessly scattered. The English drove after the Spaniards in hot pursuit, bow waves flashing as they chased their quarry.

Drake and Howard had exhausted nearly all their powder and shot, so there was little they could do if they caught up with Medina Sidonia. But the Spanish admiral didn't know that, and he drove the remnants of his fleet north, intent on rounding Scotland and sailing down past Ireland. Raging storms off Scotland and Ireland cost him another forty-four warships and a third of his battle survivors before the bedraggled flotsam of the *Gran Armada* limped into Lisbon.

❖   ❖   ❖

For a time, no one on terra firma appreciated the battle's outcome. As far as Elizabeth knew, Medina Sidonia might be circling back for another try. Even if the battle fleet were defeated, the Duke of Parma might still hazard an unescorted jump across the Channel with 16,000 veteran soldiers of his landing force.

Anxious to participate in a more direct way, Elizabeth believed the queen's presence at the coastal encampments would rally her men-at-arms. She proposed touring the front lines—the English southern coast—but an alarmed Earl of Leicester, her senior general, diverted her to Tilbury, a hamlet on the Thames estuary. There, said Leicester, his men would welcome the reassuring presence of their monarch.

To field officers, the commander-in-chief is never a welcome sight on the front lines, and neither Leicester nor his lieutenants wished to shoulder the heavy burden of protecting the queen in a potential combat theater. Compounding the risk to Her Majesty was the ever-present threat of traitors, who might take the pope's edicts as divine license to commit regicide.

But the needs of the kingdom came first. Cautioned against exposing herself to heavily armed men, some of whom might be tempted to run her through, Elizabeth smiled pleasantly and thanked her advisors.

Then, as usual, she did what she thought best.

Ever since her ride to claim the crown thirty years before, Elizabeth had made a point of being visible to her subjects. Now that her subjects were defending the island they called home, she felt it was her duty to join them. Descending the Privy Stairs at Whitehall in a drenching rain, she stepped onto a royal barge that carried her down the Thames. She disembarked a few hours later near the army's camp at Tilbury, and that night she slept in a borrowed manor home, a guard of 2,000 foot soldiers silently watching over her.

In the morning, she emerged to show her fighting men what a warrior queen looked like.

For longer than mankind's memory runs, commanders have moved soldiers with oratory and drama. Alexander at the Hydaspes, Caesar's red cloak, Spartacus killing his horse, Cortez burning his ships: They used words, dress, symbols, and theatrical acts to steady nerves and knees before the moment of decision. Channeling the power of pageantry, Elizabeth appeared before her men in the guise of a medieval Athena. Wearing a white velvet gown beneath a shimmering silver breastplate, she held a marshal's baton as she rode a white gelding through Tilbury's encampments.

Gaping at the sight of their armored queen, Leicester's men dipped their guidons and pikes in salute. Knees bent, and soldiers gathered around her as she sat on her horse near an old windmill, surrounded by military attendants.

Those within earshot heard Elizabeth render one of the greatest speeches in the English language.

"My loving people," she began, her voice clear as a starling's song,

> *We have been persuaded by some that are careful of our safety, to take heed how we commit ourselves to armed multitudes, for fear of treachery; but I assure you I do not desire to live to distrust my faithful and loving people.*
>
> *Let tyrants fear. I have always so behaved myself that, under God, I have placed my chiefest strength and safeguard in the loyal hearts and goodwill of my subjects; and therefore I am come amongst you, as you see, at this time, not for my recreation and disport, but being resolved, in the midst and heat of the battle, to live and die amongst you all; to lay down for my God, and for my kingdom, and my people, my honour and my blood, even in the dust.* *
>
> *I know I have the body of a weak, feeble woman; but I have the heart and stomach of a king, and of a king of England too, and think foul scorn that Parma or Spain, or any prince of Europe, should dare to invade the borders of my realm; to which rather than any dishonour shall grow by me, I myself will take up arms, I myself will be your general, judge, and rewarder of every one of your virtues in the field.*
>
> *I know already, for your forwardness you have deserved rewards and crowns; and We do assure you on a word of a prince, they shall be duly paid. In the meantime, my lieutenant general shall be in my stead, than whom never prince commanded a more noble or worthy subject; not doubting but by your obedience to my general, by your concord in the camp, and your valour in the field, we shall shortly have a famous victory over these enemies of my God, of my kingdom, and of my people.* †

---

* In "plac[ing] my chiefest strength and safeguard in the loyal hearts and goodwill of my subjects," Elizabeth echoed the words of Machiavelli, originally written to criticize Caterina Sforza. Machiavelli, who wrote of the countess's defense of her castle in Forli, was a popular subject of intellectual discussion in Elizabethan England.

† There are at least three versions of Elizabeth's Tilbury speech. The version presented here was taken down sometime after 1623, although the writer, Dr. Leonel Sharp, was Leicester's chaplain and heard it straight from Elizabeth's lips. Other versions, by William Leigh (1612), and one inscribed in St. Faith's Church, Gaywood (probably early 1600s), have been found. Sharp's version is the most famous, though no contemporaneous copy survives.

Her words thrilled the hardened men who heard them, whether from her lips or in words retold over campfires and in tents that night. Leicester later declared that the queen's oration "so inflamed the hearts of her good subjects, as I think the weakest among them is able to match the proudest Spaniard that dares land in England."

But the men in camp would have no chance to match the proudest Spaniards, for the North Sea did their work for them. Winds and shoals off Scotland inflicted far more damage to the Armada than even Drake and Howard dared to hope for, and the invasion died before it touched a grain of English soil.

As soon as it became clear that the Duke of Parma would not be marching on Whitehall Palace anytime soon, Elizabeth returned to London. Just as her field commanders had feared, she mothballed warships, discharged militia, and sent men back to their farms to reap the autumn harvest. Though she had assured the men at Tilbury they would be justly repaid, "on the word of a prince," few received a penny's compensation.

Parsimony aside, Elizabeth's reputation soared with the Armada's defeat. Even her enemies paid her grudging tribute: "She is only a woman, only mistress of half an island, and yet she makes herself feared by Spain, by France, by the Empire, by all!" waxed an admiring Pope Sixtus. France's King Henri III claimed her victory over the Armada "would compare with the great feats of the most illustrious men of past times." The Venetian ambassador wrote that Elizabeth had never "lost her presence of mind for a single moment, nor neglected aught that was necessary for the occasion. Her acuteness in resolving the action, her courage in carrying it out, show her high-spirited desire of glory and her resolve to save her country and herself." As storms buffeted the kingdom, that resolve and courage had been enough.

Spain, Redux

In a fairytale world of Athenas on white horses and commoners waving pikes, Elizabeth's speech at Tilbury would have been the benediction to a victorious war, the commencement of a glorious age of English culture, discovery, and prosperity.

But England was no fairytale kingdom, and to an empire the size of Spain, even the defeat of the *Gran Armada* was but a major setback. King Philip had been hoisted on a watery petard, but General Parma still ruled the Low Countries. Moreover, Philip and his admirals absorbed the hard lessons of 1588 and learned from them. They began building new ships along the English lines—race-built hulls mounting heavy guns—and before long they completed a dozen seagoing monsters known throughout Europe as the "Twelve Apostles."

To kill the Spanish phoenix before it could rise from the ashes, Elizabeth authorized another privateer attack against Spain's fleet in the spring of 1589. But the Fates were indifferent to her enterprise, and the raid broke down under the weight of divided command, divided motives, bad weather, and bad luck. The Spanish fleet was left largely unmolested, and an English flotilla was ambushed off the Azores by a squadron of "Apostles." In a follow-up raid, Drake's old flagship *Revenge* was captured, and the myth of English invincibility was broken.

As Elizabeth's fortunes waned at sea, they collapsed on land. In the summer after the failed raid, King Henri III of France was assassinated by a rival Catholic faction. His cousin, a Huguenot from the House of Bourbon, took the throne as King Henri IV, and France found itself embroiled in a civil war between Henri's Protestant supporters and the Catholic League.

The English people were war-weary, the Crown's finances were exhausted, and Elizabeth had no desire to send men of Kent, York, and Wales to die for a French king. But the thought of a pro-Spanish France was the stuff of nightmares to Elizabeth and her ministers. With few options, in the summer of 1591 she sent an army of 4,000 men to capture Catholic-held Rouen.

From Whitehall, she and her council watched the lunge at Rouen fall apart under ham-handed management in both France and London. Though the expedition was led by her current court favorite—Robert Devereux, Earl of Essex and stepson of her beloved Earl of Leicester—Elizabeth told Essex she wanted the campaign wrapped up *quickly* and *cheaply*, and she refused to foot the bill for army operations beyond October. When King Henri dragged out the campaign, the queen stopped paying her own soldiers, forcing Essex to meet the army's massive expenses from his own pocket or face a mutiny.*

As much as she liked him, Elizabeth found Essex's actions during the Rouen crusade troubling. Essex had knighted two dozen men for battlefield valor, normally a king's prerogative, and the charismatic earl developed a budding friendship with King Henri that Elizabeth found disconcerting. Essex, for his part, was furious with Elizabeth's government for cutting off funding for his expedition. When Henri took his French army to face Parma, Elizabeth recalled an embittered, financially broken Essex to London.

---

* Essex, like Leicester, was a handsome, headstrong man whom Elizabeth doted upon. Although Leicester's death in 1588 left Essex deeply indebted, Elizabeth transferred Leicester's court offices to Essex. She also gave Essex his stepfather's sweet wines monopoly, imbuing him with considerable income to service his massive debts.

IN 1596, the aging queen ordered another sea raid against Cadiz, this time under the joint command of Essex and old Admiral Howard. On June 21, the dashing earl led the assault in person. His men landed in boats and forced open the gates, whereupon the stunned city fathers surrendered Cadiz with surprisingly little bloodshed.

Little bloodshed . . . but prodigious arson. Retreating Spanish soldiers set fire to the merchant fleet to keep it out of English hands. Rampaging English soldiers, following suit, ignored orders to spare churches and tried to burn everything the Spaniards hadn't torched. "If any man had a desire to see Hell itself, it was then more lively figured," wrote Raleigh. Essex and Howard had won the greatest land battle of the Anglo-Spanish war, but much of the spoils lay in ruins.

Hubris got the better of Essex. He persuaded Admiral Howard to let him garrison the city, in violation of the queen's express orders. When the booty that survived the fire was collected, his troops began agitating to return home, where they could enjoy their newfound wealth without being shot at. Men grumbled and morale sank as the Spanish gathered their forces for the inevitable counterattack.

Essex's position became untenable, as Elizabeth knew it would, and in August he and Howard meekly embarked their men on transport ships and returned to England. Essex sent his Dutch soldiers back to Holland and transferred a thousand men to Ireland to keep order. The rest, discharged for want of pay, walked home.

When the haughty general returned to the English court, Elizabeth was furious. For all his glorious swordplay, Essex had fulfilled neither of the queen's strategic objectives: naval supremacy and economic gain. The main Spanish battle fleet had been left unmolested, and rumors swirled that the merchant fleet the Spaniards had burned was worth £3.5 million, ten times Elizabeth's annual income. Adding insult to injury, Essex had knighted another sixty commoners for heroism, a prerogative Elizabeth had already told him belonged to the queen.

Embarrassed but not hobbled, King Philip prepared a retaliatory strike. By October 1596, he had built another fleet to invade Ireland. The news threw Elizabeth and her ministers into another costly round of militia drafts, coastal fortification programs, and ship refitting. But the weather proved inauspicious for Spanish sailing, and four days after Philip's fleet left port, an October gale destroyed a quarter of his ships. Nearly 3,000 men drowned in the squall, and the survivors limped home.

The following spring found the queen and her ministers planning their now-standard tactic: a preemptive strike while the enemy's ships lay in port. Elizabeth again appointed Essex as her expedition's commander.

This time, Elizabeth was unsure whether she picked the right commander. National rulers tend to see war as a means to political ends—ends usually brought home through diplomacy and negotiation. The sword stiffens the quill, but does not supplant it. Kings need the flexibility to heel the dogs of war when the time is right, and for political and economic reasons, Elizabeth wanted to keep her wars limited and her generals under her control.

Romantics like Essex saw war as a substitute for diplomacy, not a supplement. They envisioned themselves dictating peace terms from horseback in the enemy's capital. Essex tended to think in expansive terms that required England to inflict deeper and deeper wounds on Spain. Elizabeth, thought Essex, could not simply parry Spain's blows; she had to riposte if her kingdom were to survive. He felt his queen had been blind to an obvious strategic conclusion: Unless England took the war to Spain, England would never be safe.

Although Elizabeth and Essex differed sharply on grand strategy, the queen had little choice in her commander. Admiral Howard, her most experienced leader, was too old for long seagoing campaigns. Essex, for all his emotional baggage, was her most successful general and was absolutely loyal to her. So, with pursed lips and furrowed brow, she promoted Essex to the ranks of Lieutenant General, Admiral, and Master of Ordnance, and ordered him to sail against Spain.

In August 1597 Essex, ignoring the queen's wishes, proposed a dash for the Azores. There he hoped to catch the Spanish treasure fleet returning from the New World. Elizabeth would have none of it. She reminded Essex that the fleet's primary mission was to protect the coast by destroying the Spanish navy. "You vex me too much, with small regard for what I bid," she complained to him, warning him not to let his ambitions "make you [so] bold to heap more errors on our mercy."

Doing exactly what Elizabeth told him not to do, once out of port the earl shaped course for the Azores. Learning through friendly sources that Essex and the English fleet were out hunting in the Atlantic, King Philip ordered his navy to capture the English port of Falmouth, which he would use as a launching pad for a full-blown invasion of England later.

Spy reports of the planned Spanish attack at Falmouth stunned Elizabeth, who had confidently expected Essex to sink the enemy fleet—or at least keep it bottled up in port. When Essex finally straggled home after a fruitless search for doubloons, his men were too exhausted to sail. Southerly winds kept his fleet in port, helpless to assist Falmouth. England lay naked to invasion.

As in the year of the Armada, the weather came to Elizabeth's rescue. When Philip's fleet sailed past the Lizard, England's southwestern tip, a fierce gale scattered his warships. Assuming that Essex was regrouping his ships at Plymouth, the king's admirals decided to turn back. Elizabeth was spared a Cadiz in reverse.

She resolved to punish Essex for his insubordination, but the handsome earl was a master at pulling his queen's heartstrings. On his return to London, he wrote Her Majesty a plaintive letter defending his actions and declaring his undying affection for her. Taking no chances, he took to his bed, feigning illness, and awaited Her Majesty's response.

For all his pig-headedness, Essex knew how to appraise his queen. More than a little soft-hearted to the stepson of a man she had secretly loved, Elizabeth forgave him. Treating him like a wayward but good-hearted son, the sixty-year-old monarch took him back into her confidence. She promoted him to Master-General of Ord-nance, and let him return to his seat on the Privy Council.

Emotion is a dangerous indulgence for a ruler. When treated generously, most subjects will respond with loyalty, even affection. But for a few, goodwill cannot be banked. Seeing only what lies immediately before them, these subjects take what they might, whenever the opportunity presents itself; past kindness enters into nei-ther heart nor mind.

Elizabeth, a seasoned ruler, still had not fully learned the darker side of generosity.

In April 1598, Elizabeth's ambassadors informed her that France and Spain had signed a peace treaty, ratcheting down tensions between the two great Catholic ri-vals. The shock of Franco-Spanish détente set the stage for a showdown between Elizabeth's two closest advisors over how to respond to the specter of a Catholic-dominated Western Europe.

True to form, Essex argued that the realm's safety lay in a large military budget, a "council of war" to make all military decisions for the queen, and an aggressive for-eign policy. A renewed war, either at sea or in the Low Countries, would keep Spain off balance, so it could not mount another major invasion.

Old Lord Burghley, who had never liked Essex, counseled peace with Spain. Burghley contended that peace terms would be more favorable now than a year or two hence, when Spain redeployed troops no longer needed to guard its French frontier on the Pyrenees. He turned up the temperature in council chambers by implying that Essex was a warmonger and adventurer.

After listening to both sides, Elizabeth agreed with Burghley. So long as there was no realistic threat of invasion, it would be folly to finance a new war abroad. As for

Essex's "council of war" idea, the queen wanted no prophylactic between herself and her generals. She was commander-in-chief of royal forces, and she would act like one.

Essex loved his queen, but saw her gender as an impediment to military efficiency. A king on the battlefield could see problems and rectify them immediately. A woman playing cards at Kenilworth or Greenwich, or any other palace in England, could not.

During his campaigns in Holland and France, Essex had lived among ragged soldiers who ate rancid food due to the penury and maladministration of far-off London. Civilian ministers—whom Essex considered a corrupt, self-interested lot—were temperamentally ill-suited to make the swift decisions needed in war. If the queen took the advice of her bureaucrats, as she usually did, disaster would befall the realm. She needed a military man making military decisions.

Since the burning of Cadiz, Essex's position in court had fallen. But he had been the queen's favorite for so long that he felt he could speak his mind to her whenever he pleased. One day at Whitehall he nearly crossed the line that separates impertinence from treason. During a heated council meeting in the summer of 1598, the thirty-four-year-old earl argued bitterly with his queen over an appointment she was considering in Ireland. Arguments became shouts, then barbs. An indignant Elizabeth rose from her chair and stood over Essex. He turned his back on her, and she boxed his ear, telling him to go be hanged.

Essex instinctively put his hand on his sword pommel, as if to draw it on the queen. A visibly shocked Admiral Howard stepped between them and talked Essex to his senses. Essex, as shocked at himself as everyone else was, stormed out of the council room to sulk at his residence.

The outburst should have ended his career, possibly even his life. But fortunately for Essex, the following month the venerable Lord Burghley died. Feeling deeply the loss of her senior minister, and in need of capable men to advise her, Elizabeth took Essex back.

But without Lord Burghley, the Privy Council lacked a voice loud enough to rein in the queen's swashbuckler.

The Emerald Isle

As the curtain began to fall on the Tudor century, Elizabeth found a project to occupy her high-maintenance general: She sent him to Ireland.

The emerald isle had long been the kingdom's bleeding ulcer. Beyond the Pale, that brittle shell around Dublin controlled by the Crown, Irish lords ruled from

Connaught to Cork. Most were virulently anti-English, and none more so than the fearsome Hugh O'Neill, Earl of Tyrone.

Elizabeth's hold on Ireland was slipping by 1599, and as the threat from Spain receded, her government began shifting its thin resources to subdue rebel warlords, who were thickest in the northern region of Ulster. Her father had been ruthless with the smattering of Irish nobles who opposed him, and as King Henry's daughter, Elizabeth would not allow brigand warlords and barefoot peasants to flout her authority. Disdaining negotiations, she was prepared to spend lavishly on armies, manacles, gallows, and rope until every Irishman bent his knee to the Crown.

To enforce her law, the queen assembled an army of 17,000 foot and horse soldiers, a colossal commitment for a woman who prided herself on thrift. Wages alone would run almost £290,000 annually, and expenditures for firearms, gunpowder, and other tools of war piled burden upon burden on the quivering shoulders of her finance ministers.

Essex, who had been absent from court since the day the queen boxed his ear, was recalled to Whitehall Palace in the midst of a heated debate over who should lead the Irish expedition. As the ministers went through their short list of candidates, Essex lambasted each man as perfectly incompetent or ill-suited for the task.

When the ministers reached the end of the list, Elizabeth turned to Essex and asked if he would take the job. Having eliminated everyone else from contention, Essex could hardly refuse. He packed his bags and crossed the Irish Sea to Dublin.

Though he loved chasing glory wherever glory could be chased, Essex chafed at the thought of living in a rude Irish backwater. He had grown used to the pleasures and intrigues of London and wanted to be in the room where the Crown's decisions were made. To keep his absence as short as possible, he planned a three-pronged, lightning attack against Ulster for the summer of 1599.

In June he and his regiments moved steadily through central Ireland's green fields. But the country swallowed up what had seemed so great an army when it left England. Unable to bring Lord Tyrone to battle, after weeks of encampments, marching, and counter-marching, he returned to Dublin to ponder how to extricate himself from a bloody, expensive stalemate.

He wrote to London for reinforcements, but as with Leicester's Dutch war, Elizabeth chastised him for spending too much on the summer operation—£336,000, more than she had spent in Ireland during the previous four years. "If you compare the time that is run on and the excessive charges that is spent, with the effect of anything wrought on this voyage," she lectured him, "[we] can little pleasure ourselves hitherto with anything that hath been effected."

Essex was more concerned with his personal standing in court than with what "hath been effected." Elizabeth was forcing him to fight a war he could not win. A war, he feared, that would leave his reputation in ruins. He brooded over conspiracies against him by jealous rivals in London, and dark thoughts of an invasion of Wales—perhaps even a palace coup—took form in his troubled mind.

On Elizabeth's direct order, at the end of August a reluctant Essex resumed his march north. But his army, whittled down by disease, garrison detachment, and desertion was a shadow of the host that had left England in the sunny spring. Outnumbered and unable to breach or flank Irish defenses, he asked Tyrone for a parlay on September 7. The warlord agreed to meet Essex at the River Lagan in County Down.

The two opposing commanders, a red-haired Englishman and a black-haired Irishman, trotted their horses to a ford in the middle of the river and spoke. Out of earshot of their retainers, they agreed to a truce, but neither man documented their agreement, and Essex was curiously vague about what England was getting for its investment in lives and gold.

Learning of the truce several days later, a dumbfounded Elizabeth refused to ratify it. She insisted that Essex renew the offensive and wrote him bluntly, "We absolutely command you to continue and perform that resolution." It was as peremptory an order as she ever gave.

Terrified that his position at home was slipping beyond salvation, Essex again defied Elizabeth and sailed back to England with a few trusted companions. Galloping hard across Wales and England, he burst into the queen's bed chamber at Nonsuch Palace in the early morning hours of September 28 as Elizabeth was getting dressed for the day.

Standing over the sixty-six-year-old woman in his mud-spattered riding clothes, an almost incoherent Essex launched into a rambling defense of his actions and wildly accused her ministers of plotting against her.

Shaken by the abrupt arrival of a wild-eyed, gesticulating man wearing a sword, Elizabeth concealed her alarm and listened to him calmly. Because Essex was covered in mud, and she was in the middle of her morning makeup-and-dress routine, she nonchalantly suggested they should freshen up a bit and meet later that day to discuss matters in detail. Essex, relaxing visibly, agreed and went back to his mansion on London's Strand.

As soon as he left, Elizabeth ordered his arrest.

The next day Essex was brought before the Privy Council and interrogated for five hours by Elizabeth's ministers, who found him guilty of dereliction of duty.

Placed under house arrest, Essex was tried before the Star Chamber and stripped of his public offices. Saddened but resolute, Elizabeth canceled the lucrative monopoly on sweet wines she had given him upon Leicester's death, cutting off a prime source of income for the disgraced nobleman. Bankrupt and depressed, Essex attempted an ill-designed coup in late 1600. For his troubles, he lost his head.

❖   ❖   ❖

ELIZABETH'S REJECTION OF AN IRISH PEACE committed England to a war of attrition. During the next two years, her government would spend over £800,000 on military operations there, bringing the cost of her Irish wars to nearly £2 million. Forced loans from nobles, higher customs duties, sales of monopolies, increased fines, and mandatory "gifts" from wealthy merchants deepened war's economic burden on her people—the very people whom Elizabeth, as a young queen, had wished to protect from the rapacious mouth of war.

But she was an old queen now, and the dogs of war were baying to be fed. She reluctantly sold Crown lands and put some of her jewelry up for auction to pay the piper. She permitted her finance ministers to debase English currency, a blow to the realm's economic health, as she knew from her father's experience. Elizabeth's ministers eventually hectored her into a treaty with Lord Tyrone that pardoned the rebel leader and suspended, for a time, the ghastly drain of blood and treasure.*

As she lay on her deathbed in 1603, at sixty-nine years of age, Queen Elizabeth had come full circle. The daughter who had labored to undo the effects of her father's wars had mortgaged the realm to finance new wars in Scotland, Spain, France, the Low Countries, the New World, and Ireland. For all the expense, for all the red-spattered butcher's bills her subjects paid, she added not an inch of new territory to her kingdom.

But the red-haired orphan had preserved her legacy against the world's most formidable powers. Under her leadership, England and Wales had turned back a mighty fleet, fended off assassins, defied the pope, and won the grudging respect of the queen's mortal enemies. With the realm secure, she also fostered the enlightenment of Shakespeare, Marlowe, and Bacon in a time celebrated for centuries to

---

* The treaty between England and the Irish lords was negotiated just before Elizabeth's death on March 24, 1603. Her successor, James VI of Scotland—King James I of England—immediately shut down English military involvement in the Low Countries and negotiated a peace treaty with Spain in August 1604, ending Queen Elizabeth's long wars on the Continent.

come as the "Elizabethan Era." And she set England on the path to become the world's greatest empire.

OTHER MARITIME EMPIRES had a head start on England, of course. Four decades after Elizabeth threw back the Spanish Armada, Portugal, one of the world's oldest trading empires, found itself at war with an African queen who was as agile on the battlefield as Elizabeth was at the council table. The woman from the Angolan highlands fought more skirmishes, waged more campaigns, conducted more retreats, and killed more men in battle than any other warrior queen in history. And her geopolitical instincts were, in their own way, every bit as sharp as Elizabeth's.

ABOVE: Queen Tomyris pays her respects to the head of the Persian Empire in this classical painting by Flemish artist Peter Paul Rubens, c. 1623. In a pitched battle, her Massagetae warriors defeated the world's greatest empire.

BELOW: Turning the Tide: The battle between Greeks and Persians at Salamis is depicted in this 1868 painting by German artist Wilhelm von Kaulbach. Artemisia, Queen of Caria, provided brilliant military advice to the Persian leader. When he followed her lead, he did well. When he didn't, disaster struck.

ABOVE LEFT: Grand Entrance: Cleopatra smuggles herself past assassins and soldiers into Caesar's apartment in this 1866 painting by French artist and sculptor Jean-Léon Gérôme. Her audacious entrance launched a sixteen-year alliance with Rome that changed history.

ABOVE RIGHT: A first-century Roman marble bust of Cleopatra's Bacchus, located in the Vatican Museums. Marcus Antonius, a protégé of Julius Caesar, led soldiers assembled, supplied, and paid for by Cleopatra.

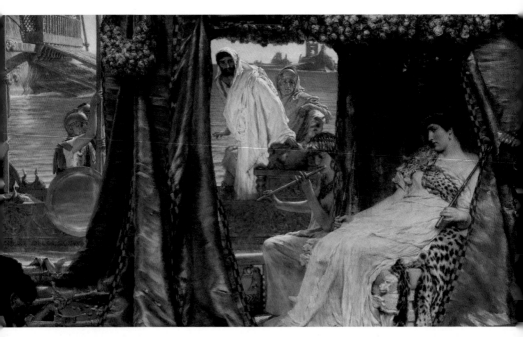

The Meeting of Antony and Cleopatra, 41 BC by Dutch-British painter Sir Lawrence Alma-Tadema, 1885. The ancient world's original power couple fused personal and political attraction into a force that dominated half of Rome's territories for a dozen years.

Photograph by Paul Walter

Cry Havoc: *Boudicea and Her Daughters*. A bronze statue of the Celtic queen, constructed between 1856 and 1883 by English sculptor Thomas Thornycroft, glares today over the city she once burned to the ground.

Boudica's desperate appeal to avenge the mistreatment of her people by the Romans is portrayed in this neoclassical engraving from Ebenezer Cobham Brewer's *Character Sketches of Romance, Fiction and the Drama* (1892).

Magdalena Paluchowska/Alamy

A fresco at the Vardzia cave monastery on Erusheti Mountain, c. 1185, pays tribute to Queen Tamar. Tamar would secure Georgia's borders, expand its holdings, and reign over Georgia's golden age of prosperity and culture.

Queen Manduhai fought a Chinese emperor and Turkic rivals to rebuild the old Mongol empire of Genghis Khan. In this modern reconstruction, she wears the tall, feather-topped hat of a Mongol noblewoman.

ABOVE LEFT: Mona Lisa with a Sword: This oil portrait, thought to be of Caterina Sforza, was painted by Italian Renaissance artist Lorenzo di Credi, c. 1482. Caterina's beauty was matched by her ability with a sword or cannon.

ABOVE RIGHT: The Rock of Forli. Caterina took refuge against assassins and the Pope's army at Rocca di Ravaldino, her moated fortress. She knew every inch of the castle and was prepared to defend it with her life.

Rome's River Fortress: In 1484, Caterina commanded Rome's Castel Sant'Angelo, seen in this mid-nineteenth-century photograph, mounting cannon and dominating Rome during a papal succession crisis. Years later, she would be imprisoned in the castle's dungeon by the Borgia pope, Alexander VI.

Regina Triumphant: An anonymous painting tribute to Elizabeth I's victory over the Spanish Armada. Besides her signature victory, Elizabeth waged wars in Scotland, France, the Netherlands, Spain, Ireland, and on the seas to defend her kingdom.

ABOVE LEFT: Elizabeth Tudor's coronation portrait, painted c. 1600 by an unknown artist. Elizabeth I took the throne of England, Wales, and Ireland in a time of great religious and territorial upheaval. Assassins lurked, and many did not expect her to survive long.

ABOVE RIGHT: Elizabeth's implacable foe, Spain's King Philip II, is portrayed in this c. 1550 painting by Italian artist Titian. Philip would be on the giving and receiving end of naval attacks in a war with Elizabeth that would outlive them both.

ELIZABETH'S NAVY BATTLES
THE SPANISH ARMADA

English and Spaniards close in for the kill in this c. 1623 painting by Dutch artist Cornelius Claesz van Wieringen. Elizabeth's intelligent management of technology, procurement, and command leadership gave England the edge in the epic battle.

ABOVE: In this seventeenth-century sketch based on an eyewitness account, Njinga is shown seated on one of her servants as she negotiates with the Portuguese governor of Angola, Correia de Sousa, who pointedly failed to offer her a chair.

BELOW: Njinga leading a war party, from the "Araldi" manuscript of the Italian Capuchin missionary Giovanni Cavazzi da Montecuccolo, who joined the queen's court in 1662. Njinga prided herself in leading from the front, and trained with bow, axe, and musket. Leading mass armies and shock troops, she was feared by Portuguese colonizers and their allies.

Victorian-era portrait of Queen Njinga, who survived bloody purges to become queen of a war-ravaged kingdom in Angola.

Grand Duke Peter (later Peter III) and Grand Duchess Catherine (later Catherine the Great) during their unhappy union, in a portrait by German painter Anna Rosina de Gasc, 1756. Catherine's husband was cruel, sickly, immature, and extremely unpopular among the Russian elite.

Russian general Alexander Suvorov storms the Turkish fort of Ochakov in this dramatic 1853 painting by Polish artist January Suchodolski. Catherine deftly managed her generals, including Suvorov, in two wars against the Ottoman Empire. With her command center far from the battle lines, she gave her commanders wide discretion.

ABOVE LEFT: "For a man's work, you needed a man's outfit." In 1762, Catherine took matters into her own hands and led a palace coup against her abusive husband, donning the dark green uniform of the elite Preobrazhensky Regiment. Her triumph was commemorated in this painting by Danish artist Vigilius Eriksen the same year.

ABOVE RIGHT: The lioness in winter. In 1794, Russian painter Vladimir Borovikovsky portrayed Catherine in her later years, accompanied by her beloved Italian greyhound, Zemira. Before she died, Catherine expanded her empire's borders, expanded trade with the West, and made Russia the dominant empire in Eastern Europe.

ABOVE:
Indira confers with General Sam Manek-shaw, India's chief military strategist. They formed a brilliant partnership: Indira set the political objectives, while Sam planned the war's operations and tactics.

RIGHT:
Indira Gandhi, shown seated in this 1979 photograph, launched a war to solve a humanitarian crisis sparked by Pakistan's repressive leaders. *(Keystone Press/Alamy)*

Mother and Sons: Golda Meir reviews Israeli troops on the Golan Heights. The Israeli prime minister took the deaths of her countrymen personally, but was prepared to do what was necessary to ensure Israel's survival. *(AFP/Getty Images)*

Golda surveys fighting on the Sinai Peninsula with General Ariel Sharon during the 1973 Yom Kippur War. Golda knew almost nothing about military formations and tactics. But she was a brilliant strategist, and senior commanders came to her for military advice. *(World History Archive/Alamy)*

Boudica Redux: Thatcher on a British Challenger tank, 1986. After the Falklands War, her reputation—and the standing of the British Empire—soared.

Modern War Queens: Margaret Thatcher visits Indira Gandhi in India. The two women—a conservative follower of Churchill, and an anticolonial socialist—led their democracies in war. Thatcher particularly admired Gandhi, a fellow alumna of Oxford's Somerville College.

9

BAPTIZED IN BLOOD

Queen Njinga of Ndongo-Matamba

"I never feared facing a group of 25 armed
soldiers, except if they had muskets."
—Njinga, 1657

Twenty years after Elizabeth's death, a Mbundu woman in south-western Africa became the talk of the Catholic world. General, diplomat, slave trader, fashionista, and hands-on warrior, Queen Njinga of Ndongo and Matamba elicited equal parts admiration and revulsion from missionaries, cannibals, kings, and two empires vying for control of Africa's coast.

In the late sixteenth century, when West Africa was the hub of the Atlantic slave trade, Portugal was one of the trade's biggest players. Lisbon dominated trading ports from China to Brazil, and its Brazilian sugar plantations drove the empire's agricultural engine. And those plantations required slaves. Lots of them.

To fill the cane fields, Portuguese explorers, envoys, and conquistadores established trade relations with the Kongo kingdom on Africa's southwestern coast. Kongolese war parties would raid neighboring villages and take prisoners, or they would simply buy slaves—locally called "pieces"—from discount middlemen in Africa's interior. They would march the unfortunates to Portuguese markets near the coast, then sell their human chattel to white merchants who would ship them to Brazil. As the demand for "pieces" grew, Portuguese agents began moving south in search of larger sources.

Around the time that Spain's King Philip was squaring off against Elizabeth's sea dogs, the Portuguese quietly established a thriving trade center at the mouth of the broad Kwanza River. In two generations, this outpost would shatter the lives of thousands who claimed the Kingdom of Ndongo as their home.

❖   ❖   ❖

NDONGO STRETCHED nearly a hundred miles down Africa's Atlantic coast, from Luanda in the north to the Longa River in the south. Thrusting some two hundred miles east into Africa's heart, Ndongo lands ran an ecological gamut from semi-arid coastal scrubland—domain of the *imbondiero*, or baobab tree—to cool plateaus, tropical river valleys, and savannahs.

Ndongo's semi-divine king, or *ngola*, was elected from one of several qualifying families by a clique of nobles. The *ngola* ruled his lands, called "Angola" by the Europeans, from his capital at Kabasa in Ndongo's central highlands, and he administered the kingdom through local nobles called *sobas*.

The Mbundu who lived there were a traditional people who worshipped nature and communed with their dead ancestors. A class of clerics called *ngangas* healed the sick, guarded ancestral bones, coaxed rain from the sky, performed human sacrifices, and functioned as the *ngola*'s diplomatic corps. *Ngangas* were the spiritual lubricant that kept Mbundu villagers content, and the system held together reasonably well when not subjected to extreme stress.

But extreme stress showed up in 1575, when Portuguese conquistadores, merchants, and settlers built a mission on the coast called São Paulo de Luanda. Lisbon followed up by sending an army to Africa's interior with instructions to subjugate "Angola." Setting out from the coast, the conquistadores razed villages, carried off livestock, and took prisoners for the Brazilian cane fields. The accompanying slaughter was prodigious. Soldiers cut the noses off the bodies of Mbundu men and women to verify death counts, and after one battle the army had to assign twenty porters to carry all the severed noses back to the local presidio.

To the Portuguese, severed black noses, stolen cattle, and slaves all served a greater good. Especially the slaves. The commoditization of humans, wrote one conquistador,

is not only useful for commerce, but still more for the service of God and the good of their souls. For with this trade, they avoid having so many slaughter-houses for human flesh, and they are instructed in the faith of our Lord Jesus Christ and, baptized and catechized, they sail for Brazil or other places

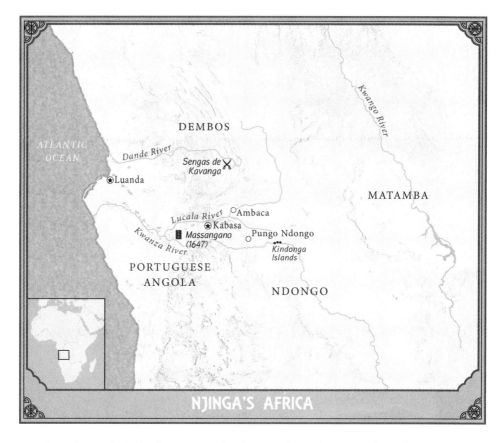

NJINGA'S AFRICA

where the Catholic faith is practiced. They are thus taken away from their heathen ways and are redeemed to live lives which serve God and are good for commerce.

By 1600, the conquistadores had redeemed thousands of lives for God and commerce. Governors, missionaries, and generals became the ruling class of Ndongo's coastal lands, and Jesuit missionaries converted much of the Mbundu elite. The extension of Christianity into Mbundu society was a blow to the ruling *ngola*, whose divinity could now be questioned, to *nganga* priests, whom Jesuits condemned as Devil-communing sorcerers, and to the political stability of the native kingdom.

❖   ❖   ❖

SIX YEARS BEFORE the Spanish Armada weighed anchor, a Mbundu baby struggled to enter the world. An umbilical cord wrapped itself like a tree root around her neck, and *nganga* oracles predicted that she would not live a normal life, assuming she even survived infancy.

But she survived, and her father, thinking of that umbilical cord, named his daughter Njinga, after the Kimbundu tree root *kujinga*, meaning to "twist, turn, or wrap."

Njinga.

Njinga's father was a king, but war was her raging stepmother. Before her first birthday, her *ngola* grandfather fled his capital ahead of marching conquistadores. He died when Njinga was ten, setting off a wave of power struggles and political backdealing until her father was elected *ngola*. As a child, Njinga learned to fight with the battle axe, the Mbundu weapon of choice, and like other warriors, she mastered martial dancing, where nimble steps taught unshielded men how to dodge arrows and outmaneuver their opponents.

For a quarter century Njinga grew up in a kingdom buffeted by slavery, nomadic war bands, and Christian missionaries. In 1617, when Njinga was a thirty-five-year-old mother, her father was betrayed by his men and murdered. Supporters of Njinga's brother, Mbande, promptly declared him the new *ngola*, but his position was insecure. Moving quickly, he orchestrated the murder of any relatives who might advance rival claims, leading a purge of senior courtiers, nobles, and various family members.

Njinga escaped death, but not without cost. She had grown up as the sparkle in her father's eye, the family favorite who had demonstrated mental and physical superiority to her brother. She also had a newborn son, fathered by one of her concubines, who could grow into another potential rival. Mbande had Njinga's baby killed. He then sterilized his three sisters to ensure that no offshoots of the family baobab would threaten his line of succession. According to a missionary to whom Njinga related her ordeal, *ngangas* mixed herbs and oils and placed them, "while boiling, onto the bellies of his sisters, so that, from the shock, fear & pain, they should forever be unable to give birth."

Njinga never recorded her feelings over the death of her baby and her sterilization. Neither could she forgive her brother. She moved with her concubines and supporters inland to the neighboring kingdom of Matamba, where she settled in for the next nine years.

Njinga's exile in Matamba hardened her independence. As a woman of royal blood, she kept an assortment of concubines, male and female. She also refused to take a chief husband, preferring to share sexual intimacy with whomever she wanted, whenever she wanted.

She did not take criticism lightly from her inferiors, and could be cruel when crossed. When a courtier once criticized her for taking so many lovers—she brought shame onto her father's court, the man said—Njinga addressed the man's complaint by having his son brought in and murdered before his father's eyes. Then she had him executed.

As Njinga lived in exile in Matamba, to the west the Portuguese pried away her brother's lands. Four years into Mbande's rule, the Ndongo kingdom had shrunk to half its former size as the border of Portuguese Angola pushed east behind a curtain of steel and gunpowder. Mbande was nearly captured when Portuguese raiders charged into his capital of Kabasa, and influential *sobas*, sniffing a Portuguese victory, began pledging fealty to King Philip III.[*]

Mbande's only wise move had been to form an alliance with two Imbangala clans. The Imbangalas, or "Jagas," as the Portuguese called them, were loose-knit bands of mercenary warriors who fought for the highest bidder. Violent in the extreme and prone to cult rituals like cannibalism and child sacrifice, the Imbangalas formed a fearsome corps of auxiliaries for any army looking to dominate the Kongo-Ndongo-Matamba region.

IN OCTOBER 1621, a fresh breeze blew into Angola with the arrival of a new Portuguese governor. João Correia de Sousa set foot on Luanda with a more circumspect approach than his predecessors. He took the long view of colonization, and saw slaughter and conquest as inefficient tools of wealth building. The *raison d'être* of the colony was economic: It produced slaves. War disrupted the slave trade and cost money. Therefore, war was bad for business.

Governor de Sousa believed limited negotiations with Mbande might produce better long-term results than the old raid-and-conquest method. To negotiate a permanent peace with Mbande, he invited the king to send a delegation to Luanda, and Mbande dispatched messengers to Matamba to retrieve his sister. With her brother's summons, Njinga began her rise to power.

---

[*] King Philip III of Portugal held a second day job as King Philip IV of Spain. His grandfather, Elizabeth's old foe Philip II, had usurped the Portuguese throne in 1581.

Ana de Sousa, Regent Queen

In 1622, Njinga marched down Luanda's central boulevard at the head of a parade of brightly colored retainers, bodyguards, slaves, and ambassadors. The governor welcomed her with a Portuguese honor guard, and soldiers escorted the princess into the town square, where she was greeted by the city's leading citizens. Artillery and musket volleys boomed in salute, and musicians played songs from Mbundu and European instruments.

To Njinga, style mattered. Rejecting the drab European garb worn by Portuguese settlers, she set society tongues wagging with her vibrant Ndongo style. Strolling about Luanda's streets mingling with the city's upper class, she flashed her brand of elaborate cloth wraps, heavily jeweled bracelets and anklets, and colorful feathers radiating from her hair.

But the warm welcome was for public consumption only. When Njinga arrived at the government house to open negotiations over trade and border recognition, de Sousa's men gave her a not-so-subtle message. Stepping into the meeting room, Njinga found the standard welcome for native guests: a seat for the governor only. Tribal emissaries sat on the floor at the feet of the governor, who negotiated from the comfort of a velvet-covered chair. The seating arrangements left no doubt as to who was the master, and who was the supplicant.

Njinga was ready for the old colonial ploy. When the governor's aide gestured to an empty space on the carpeted floor, Njinga motioned to one of her female attendants. The woman walked to the spot selected for her princess, then dropped to her knees and elbows as Njinga settled herself onto the woman's back. Through the long hours the two leaders negotiated, Njinga's "chair" never moved.

Escorting the princess from the parlor when their work was done, Governor de Sousa turned and noticed Njinga's attendant, still crouched on the floor. When he pointed out the servant, and Njinga blithely told him the woman was a gift. An envoy of the *ngola*, she said, need never sit in the same chair twice; she had many other chairs like this one.

The Lady of Angola charmed de Sousa during her stay in Luanda, and on behalf of her brother she made several important concessions: a military alliance, peace, and the return of runaway slaves.

The one demand she refused was an annual tribute of slaves to the Portuguese king. *Ngola* Mbande, she observed, had not been conquered, and a tribute was only proper from a conquered people. "He who is born free," she told de Sousa in her high-pitched voice, "should maintain himself in freedom, and not submit to others . . . [B]y paying tribute, her king . . . would become slave instead of free."

Failing to look beyond short-term economics, the Portuguese insisted on their tribute. The market was booming, and slavery was a prime source of colonial wealth. When it became clear that both sides were at an impasse, Njinga played one last card: She agreed to be baptized into the Catholic faith.

The governor and his Jesuits, welcoming Njinga into Christ's flock, modified their tribute demand. In an elaborate ceremony in Luanda's main church, Njinga took the sacrament of baptism in the presence of Governor de Sousa, who stood as her godfather. For her Christian name, she took Ana de Sousa, honoring both the governor and a Portuguese noblewoman who stood godmother to her.

By the time she returned to Kabasa to report to her brother, Njinga had won over the Portuguese governor. Though de Sousa would take a hard line with her brother on occasion, he privately told Njinga that he wished to stay, informally, on friendly relations with Njinga's own territory of Matamba. Reflecting on her visit years later, she told a Capuchin missionary she had felt a sense of "profound happiness and an extraordinary peace" during her time in Luanda.

Her brother would never know that peace. A novice at power plays, Mbande made the mistake of naming Njinga as regent for his son upon his death, giving Njinga every reason to hasten that day. As he grew dependent on her for political advice, Njinga pushed her fragile brother to his psychological breaking point. She berated, needled, and discredited him behind his back, and hectored him into awkward, hard-line stances with the Portuguese. He was no *ngola*, she told him. He was not even a real man. If he could not rule with strength and confidence, he should find himself a farm in the forest and till his garden.

Mbande took his sister's abuse meekly, reducing him further in the eyes of his followers. He sank into a deep, dark melancholy. Longing for tranquility, he turned to traditional healers, but the *ngangas* could not help their king. In the spring of 1624 Ngola Mbande, King of Ndongo, swallowed poison. One Portuguese chronicler commented that Njinga "helped him to die," while others concluded that he took the elixir of his own volition, to quell the black dog tearing at his heart.

Whether suicide or fratricide, Mbande's death opened a power vacuum into which Njinga nimbly hopped, assembling enough electors to confirm her as regent for Mbande's seven-year-old son and heir.

❖   ❖   ❖

THOUGH MBANDE HAD NAMED NJINGA protector of her nephew, her first order of business was to squelch any claims her nephew might make to his father's throne. This was easier said than done, because before dying, Mbande had the good sense to send his boy to live with an Imbangala warlord named Kasa, who promised to protect him.

In September 1625, Njinga approached Kasa with a message: She was rapturously in love with him. As regent, she said, she needed a husband, and she underscored her missives with extravagant gifts.

Kasa was dubious at first. It could be a trick to get at Mbande's son. Besides, Njinga was older than he was, and as an Imbangala chief he could have his pick of much younger women. He wasn't certain he wanted even her, and for a time he put her off. But Njinga continued to plead for his affections, and eventually Kasa relented.

The happy couple set a wedding date, with nuptials to be held in Matamba, near one of Njinga's camps. The little nephew, delighted to be included in the family celebration, accompanied Kasa to take part in the family rites.

He did not play the part he expected. The ceremony came to a screeching halt when Njinga had the boy seized and killed him on the spot, tossing his body into the Kwanza River. In a flash, her men and women drew weapons and set upon stunned relatives and guests, slaughtering any who might come back later seeking revenge. Surrounded by still-warm bodies and crimson pools, Njinga roared that she had avenged the murder of her baby son.

Njinga's red wedding sent invitees scampering into the forest, unsure which guest list their names were on. But in the end, most remained loyal to the new queen. It was common for a new *ngola* to kill his rivals, including family members, and many saw Njinga as the better ruler. Other claimants to the title would only create problems for everyone, so the boy had to go.

Ndongo's new queen soon turned to implementing the informal understandings she had reached with Governor João Correia de Sousa. She dictated a letter to the new governor, Fernão de Sousa, in which she promised to reopen slave markets her brother had closed. Her people would trade "pieces" for manufactured goods like muskets and cloth, and she offered to let Jesuit priests work in Ndongo under liberal conditions. In return for these concessions, the Portuguese must remove one of their forts and free some captured serfs and *sobas* to return to their villages.

The new governor privately believed the bloody campaigns of his predecessors had been bad policy decisions. But those campaigns had weakened Ndongo, and he was not about to let the new queen rebuild her old state into a future threat. Bypassing Njinga, Governor de Sousa sent emissaries to meet with local leaders and established Portuguese-controlled slave markets. He forced all *sobas* in Portuguese territory to pay regular tributes and bow down in the dirt to colonial officials in a ceremonial act of submission.

The new policies told the Mbundu what kind of government they could expect. Voting with their feet, *sobas* and villagers packed their belongings and migrated east, seeking safety in Njinga's domains. Falling in with the stream of refugees were scores of *kimbares*, Mbundu warriors who had been pressed into Portuguese service.

Njinga welcomed the new blood into the ranks of her growing army. She began forcing *sobas* sitting on the fence to fall into line, and she sent agents into the countryside urging pro-Portuguese *sobas* to join their countrymen.

Her propaganda campaign produced results. A frustrated de Sousa reported to the royal council in Madrid that Njinga was promising villagers "she would give them land where they could till and live." The Mbundu, he conceded, were "better off being masters of their native land than our captives."

The migration cost the Portuguese crown a small fortune. A year later, de Sousa sheepishly reported that he could not collect the tribute called for in his budget because "of the war and the uprising of Dona Ana [Njinga] and because many of the *sobas* of His Majesty have gone over to her side."

To arrest the colony's slide, de Sousa recruited a Portuguese-friendly alternative to the headstrong queen. He published a proclamation decreeing that Hari a Kiluanje, a Catholic *soba* from a rival lineage, would henceforth be Ndongo's new *ngola*. Declaring Queen Njinga a usurper, the governor assembled an army to find and kill her.˙

Retreat From Kindonga

The army Njinga commanded inherited Mbundu traditions dating back centuries. Levies made up the bulk of her force, though Njinga commanded a core of professional warriors who answered directly to her. She also oversaw a rudimentary staff that coordinated movement, food supplies, and operations of provincial troops.

As with the Celts of Britain, Mbundu military campaigns were loosely organized community events, which did not always work well in a long season of war. "The people go to battle in great numbers and in great disorder; no one remains behind,"

---

* Hari a Kiluanje had an axe to grind with Njinga—a literal one—because in 1625 she had beheaded one of his relatives who had refused to accept her election as *ngola*.

wrote a Portuguese observer. "So it happens that they all arrive at a certain place with the whole army and there consume all their provisions. Then, with nothing left to eat, and just when the need of the expedition is at its height, the army breaks up and, forced by hunger, they return to their own country."

Though disorganized and unwieldy, in battle Mbundu armies packed a punch. They deployed masses of archers armed with short bows and poison-tipped arrows. Arranged in three divisions—a center and two wings—warriors advanced under a cloud of arrows until they could fight hand-to-hand with light axes. The first rank, lined with toughened soldiers, would break the enemy's line and force opposing infantry to flee. Musketeers, usually few in number, were deployed either in the center or on the wings to cut down enemy foot soldiers as they advanced.

Mbundu infantry carried no shields, for the axe-fighters relied upon their superior agility for protection. "All their defense consists of *sanguar*, which is to leap from one side to another with a thousand twists and such agility that they can dodge arrows and spears," wrote a Jesuit. Njinga, who excelled in this defensive art, often led troops in these dance drills.

Njinga launched her first campaign against Hari a Kiluanje's domain, which had recently been reinforced with Portuguese soldiers and *kimbares* in Portuguese service. The queen's army suffered heavy casualties, but her men overwhelmed the enemy. The *kimbares* they captured were executed or kept as slaves.

In retaliation, Governor de Sousa assembled an army near Luanda under Captain Bento Banha Cardoso. On the other side of the frontier, Njinga concentrated her forces around the Kindonga Islands, on a wide stretch of the steep-banked Kwanza River. From her riverine redoubt, she dictated a letter to de Sousa asking him to abandon Hari and accept her as Ndongo's rightful rule, signing her letters, "Ana, Queen of Dongo."

Governor de Sousa had no interest in letting an energetic, independent queen control his prime source of slaves. He had also heard enough stories from Hari's faction about her duplicity to think twice before trusting Njinga's honeyed words.

Captain Cardoso, who had been assigned to hunt her down, was even less willing to negotiate. Preparing for a campaign to hunt down the queen, he ended one reply letter to Njinga with the warning, "God protect you if he can."

To the tattoo of drums and de Sousa's harangues, Cardoso's troops marched out of Luanda on February 6, 1626. The men with muskets, thundered the governor, were fighting "in the service of God, the king, and the good of the Kingdom." Accompanying Cardoso's conquistadores were two Jesuit priests, who had solemnly pronounced the war "necessary and just." Down the road they tramped, and the forest swallowed them up.

Cardoso's line marched east to Pungo Ndongo, a formation of grassy monoliths near the Kindonga Islands on the Kwanza River. From there, Cardoso harried local *sobas* and forced them to supply his army with food.

Word of Cardoso's advance alarmed Njinga. Though her people detested the Portuguese, Ndongo was a decentralized kingdom in which no *soba*'s loyalty could be taken for granted—especially when his village faced the wrath of conquistadores. Even the *soba* of her mother's birthplace, one of Njinga's most reliable supporters, began wavering in the face of Portuguese guns.

Njinga fortified her islands for the coming blow. She built a system of guardhouses, bells, and signal stations to sound the first warning, and ordered her men to dig protective trenchworks on the perimeter. Laborers carved well-concealed caves as ambush points, and she spread soldiers armed with bows and arquebuses in forward positions as pickets. She also stocked the islands with enough cattle, provisions, and medical supplies to hold out against a long siege.

As she often did, Njinga turned to diplomacy. "Nothing is accomplished by force and to do so would bring both me and [the Portuguese soldiers] harm because everything can be done peacefully and without force," she wrote Cardoso. But the general had no interest in negotiations, and his first blow fell in the last week of May. Portuguese troops crossed the river in canoes, fishing boats, and barges, converging on Mapolo Island, Njinga's strongest redoubt.*

The queen's troops hit back with a shower of poison-tipped arrows and musket fire as the Portuguese leapt out of their boats. Those who made it out of the water ran into a series of trenches Njinga's men had hacked out over the preceding weeks.

The Portuguese took heavy casualties clearing out each trench line in hand-to-hand fighting, but they gradually overran Mapolo. Njinga's men retreated to her headquarters on the forbidding Danji Island as Cardoso's forces regrouped. The two sides, bloodied but far from exhausted, prepared for the next round.

On June 7, Njinga climbed a promontory and surveyed the new Portuguese positions. Her instincts told her both she and Cardoso had something to gain by negotiation. Cardoso had overrun her core territory and captured some of her livestock, but his men must have been short of ammunition. Because a recent wave of smallpox had swept his army like a scythe, carrying off 4,000 *kimbares*, perhaps

---

* Njinga appended to one letter to Cardoso a curious request that the general send her "a hammock, and four rolls of red wool for a cover, a horse blanket, and good wine, and an *arroba* [33 pounds] of wax for candles, and a half dozen lengths of muslin, and two or three lace tablecloths, and some purple, wine-colored, and blue garnets, and a large broad-brim hat made of blue velvet, or the one Your Honor wears, and four measures of paper." She had not given up on diplomacy, and she wanted to stay ahead of next season's fashions.

he would be ready to parlay. She sent word to Cardoso that she would discuss terms if he chose.

Cardoso saw the situation differently. Though far from Luanda, Cardoso could still receive reinforcements from the west, while Njinga was on her own. In a stern reply letter, he insisted Njinga surrender unconditionally.

Through the cool months of June and July, Njinga played for time by promising to capitulate. Cardoso, hoping to end the war without further losses, agreed to a short truce. While he waited for Njinga to walk into his camp, she ordered her best fighters to evacuate the island under cover of night.

Portuguese sentries, detecting movement, fired into the darkness, and Njinga's forces bolted. Cardoso, fully alert, ordered his men to rush the fleeing troops. Njinga got in a few blows of her own during the retreat, managing to burn some of Cardoso's boats and a portion of her own stockpiles before retreating east with a small company of loyalists. She was running for her life.[*]

Njinga spent the next few years as a fugitive in eastern Ndongo and the Matamba highlands. The forest, or *mato*, became her fortress, a barrier as impenetrable as the stone walls of Malta or the Arabian Desert. With no rivers to carry reinforcements and supplies, no European commander would dare follow her into the heart of darkness.

But de Sousa and Cardoso knew she was out there. Somewhere.

Never at a loss for words, the queen sent messengers to the governor expressing her desire to live in peace with the Portuguese. Matters of slave markets and religious accommodations could be worked out, she said. Her one basic condition, from which she never wavered, was that Portugal must accept her as the rightful queen of Ndongo and remove its current puppet, Ngola Hari.

A testy de Sousa did not like what he heard. He could not afford a perception of weakness or indecision among the natives. The Crown depended on him, as Angola's governor, to supply labor for its fields. And slavery was becoming a competitive industry, since the Dutch began picking off Portugal's South American colonies. So de Sousa had the queen's emissaries tortured, beheaded, or sold into slavery, and after several weeks he sent her a final ultimatum: Accept vassalage, accept the lesser position of "sister of the king" to Ngola Hari, or face Portuguese soldiers ordered to kill her on sight.

---

[*] Njinga evaded pursuing cavalry and foot soldiers by abandoning some of her slaves. The Portuguese soldiers placed a higher priority on "pieces" than capturing the fugitive queen, and the hours they spent rounding up abandoned slaves bought Njinga precious time to escape through a network of caves and limb-shrouded trails.

The queen was unfazed by violent threats handed down from the world's second largest global empire. Perhaps Governor de Sousa did not realize that her pleas were not written from a position of weakness, nor were they a ploy for time. She genuinely wanted peace—but Angola would see peace only on the queen's terms. If the Portuguese king could not understand that, then Njinga would emerge from the *mato* to fight, retreat, and fight another day. She would dictate the time and place of battle.

But she needed more allies.

AFTER HER EXPULSION from the Kwanza islands, Njinga rebuilt her power base among the eastern *sobas*. She also won the temporary support of the Imbangala war chief Kasa—the man she had courted until their wedding ceremony went off-script and ended in slaughter. It had been an on-and-off relationship over the years, but now her relationship with Kasa was on, politically at least. And with Kasa came a small but lethal army.

In the summer of 1628, Njinga reoccupied the Kindonga Islands and blocked roads to government slave markets. While her economic tourniquet did not immediately take hold in Luanda, it did tighten the income of Portuguese-leaning *sobas* in central and eastern Angola, and it served notice that Njinga's power was growing.

Feeling the need to flex his muscles, the governor ordered Captain Paio de Araújo de Azevedo, Captain Cardoso's replacement, to renew the war against Njinga. Azevedo marched out of Luanda with a force of conquistadores, cannoneers, and *kimbares*, and in September he closed in on Njinga's resurrected island base.

But when Azevedo's army crossed the river and stormed the islands, the queen was nowhere to be found. She knew, from painful experience, that defending small islands against an army equipped with artillery was a losing proposition. With the public blessing of her dead brother—procured for her by a helpful *nganga*—she declined battle and withdrew east to Matamba.

Njinga hoped Azevedo would turn back when he outran his supply lines, but he surprised her by invading Matamba in force and compelling local *sobas* to swear allegiance to Portugal. In May, Azevedo caught up with Njinga's army and launched a withering attack.

Njinga, with an ear for the music of battle, sensed that she was outnumbered and broke camp, withdrawing as Azevedo's musketeers opened their staccato roll. Retreating through a cliff-walled canyon, she posted rear guards armed with bows and arquebuses. They cut down Portuguese troops traversing the ravine, slowing their pursuit. But the lead musket balls flew, and on came the conquistadores.

The queen and her fugitives crossed seven ravines and four rivers, staying just ahead of a musket detachment careening after her like a pack of bloodhounds. At one point, she took a wrong turn, and Azevedo's company trapped her on a cliff. A squad of Portuguese soldiers rushed to the ledge; several lost their balance and went over, dashing bones and brains on jagged rocks below. As a second group approached more cautiously, Njinga's bodyguards formed a human wall around their queen. They won her a short reprieve, but more Portuguese would come, and she was stranded at the top of a cliff so high voices below couldn't be heard.

With no escape except straight down, the fifty-year-old queen grabbed a vine or rope—the Portuguese could not tell which—and shimmied down the cliff face until she reached the forest floor. Bodyguards followed her, one fighter at a time, while those remaining at the top fended off attacks. By the time her perimeter collapsed, dozens of her men had made it to safety.

Azevedo kept up the search for Njinga and her ragtag followers. On the trail they found abandoned muskets, discarded ammunition bags, clothing, coins, and gunpowder, all thrown down in retreat. Overrunning one of Njinga's war camps, Azevedo's men also bagged two valuable political prizes: Njinga's sisters, Kambu and Funji. Portuguese soldiers stripped the women and paraded them back naked to Luanda, sending a vivid message to *sobas* and villagers on the wages of sin and rebellion.*

With the capture of the royal sisters, Governor de Sousa now had two hostages whose lives meant something to Njinga. But his satisfaction proved short-lived, for winds drifting from the *mato* carried a disturbing rumor: Njinga had joined the Imbangala.

Tribe of Death

As she retreated into Matamba, Njinga's numbers dwindled. She would soon lack the soldiers to rebuild her kingdom, or even protect her from traitors who would sell her, dead or alive, to the Portuguese. So she made her way to a powerful Imbangala chief named Kasanje and asked for his protection. Kasanje agreed, on one condition: She must become his wife.

---

* After months of intense psychological pressure, the defiant sisters broke and agreed to be baptized into the Catholic faith. Kambu was given the Christian name Barbara, and Funji, the older sister, was named Graça. Kambu was later released by the Portuguese around the year 1632.

Njinga's veins pulsed with the blood of a warrior. During the battle for the Kindonga Islands, Captain Cardoso had referred to Njinga as "a woman and queen or king as she called herself because she did not like to admit that she was a woman." She had led soldiers in dozens of battles, and the *lunga*, a bell symbolizing military authority, was one of her most prized possessions. She kept male concubines as status symbols, so the thought of serving another man did not sit well with her.

But Njinga was a practical woman, as most politicians are, and for a short time she would set aside a quantum of pride. She needed allies, not bravado, and when Kasanje laid down his conditions, she threw away her *lunga*, crossed the Kwango River in Kasanje's canoe, and dwelt with him as a subservient, civilian wife.*

Ensconced in the warlord's home, Njinga quietly worked out a new strategy. She would become an Imbangala war chief in her own right, fusing two radically different cultures into a united fighting force to displace the dreaded Portuguese.

THE IMBANGALA reveled in death. Having no permanent home, they moved their *kilombos* (fortified war camps) like steppe herdsmen in search of grass. Roaming central Africa, they sacked villages, carried off slaves and livestock, and left trails of charred and butchered corpses in their wake.

To win credibility with the Imbangala, Njinga participated in the *cuia*, a ritual in which she drank fresh human blood to seal her allegiance to Kasanje. Having entered the world of the cannibal, she then turned to other sacraments that horrified Mbundu traditionalists. She followed in the bloody footsteps of Tembo a Ndumbo, a legendary Imbangala queen who had laid down laws governing her warriors. Ritual sacrifices, infanticide, and cannibalism were all tenets of Tembo's law, and Njinga accepted them without reserve.

Before battle, Imbangala warriors lathered themselves with "holy oil" made by pounding a human corpse into a mortar and pestle until it was a gory, greasy pulp. Priding themselves on growing the tribe's numbers by kidnapping adolescents, Imbangala women sacrificed their babies to create the sacred oil.

Njinga began her transformation to Imbangala war leader by performing a sacrament called *maji ma samba*, which required her to turn her own infant into oil. Since she had no children, she took a baby from one of her female retainers,

---

* Believing a time would come when Njinga would rule again, the queen's followers secretly retrieved the *lunga* and kept it hidden.

crushed it in a pestle, and smeared the oozings over her body. She also took a new name among the Imbangala: Ngola Njinga, Ngombe e Nga ("Queen Njinga, Master at Arms and Great Warrior"). With her authority sanctioned by Imbangala law, she assembled a battalion of female warriors who formed her new bodyguard.

Adopting another custom handed down by Queen Tembo, Njinga took on the trappings of manhood. She acquired a husband and forced him to wear women's clothing. She made him call her king, not queen, and referred to him as her woman or wife. She also ordered her male concubines to dress as women and sleep in the quarters of her female bodyguards, warning them that even accidental contact with her women followers was grounds for prompt execution.

Though she embraced the Imbangala nightmare, Njinga never fully abandoned her Mbundu and Christian beliefs. She had never viewed religion as an exclusive proposition; some of her followers were traditional Mbundu, while others were Catholic. Like any master politician, she was ready to form a bond with any constituents who would follow her, so she communed with her long-dead ancestors and prayed to Christian icons at home.

But at this moment of exile and rebirth, she needed an army, one that only the Imbangala would provide. So she threw herself, publicly and enthusiastically, into the macabre traditions of that militant, death-worshiping tribe.

In 1631, with a new army at her back, she began her second ascent to power by invading Matamba. Her army captured many Mbundu fighters, enslaving some and eating others. Consolidating her hold on central Matamba, she blocked trade routes between the Portuguese-dominated west and major sources of plantation laborers.

As her army captured and killed, stories of her victories spread from village to village like a new religion. One Jesuit working in Kongo heard tales of a semi-mythical woman "[living] an unmarried life just like the queen of the Amazons, [and] she governed the army [like] a warrior female." The queen "offered asylum to their slaves fleeting to her, with a great financial loss of the Portuguese, who had deprived her of her kingdom."

Njinga's conquests attracted young Mbundu men into the ranks of her army as she moved against Matamba's capital. In four years, she conquered Matamba, deposing, branding, and banishing its feckless queen. The conquest of Matamba gave Njinga's Imbangala followers something they had never known: a settled kingdom. Soon enough, they learned to appreciate the blessings of a stable territory with trade goods and recruits, crops and livestock, and the profitable system of selling humans into bondage.

The Imbangala also learned that they needn't worry about their queen dropping their old, gruesome ways when she captured Matamba. Using the language of war—a tongue the Imbangala respected—Njinga referred to her capital as a *kilombo*, or war camp, rather than a city. She blended the cultures of two peoples, honoring both so long as they honored her, and her pluralistic approach sustained broad support among the agrarian and warrior classes.

Njinga's Matamba campaign heralded a ten-year string of regional dominance. She marched her army into the eastern provinces of Portuguese Angola and clawed at the thin popular support claimed by Ngola Hari. Fending off incursions by rival Imbangala clans, she became the dominant power in Angola's lush interior.

The new Portuguese governor, Manuel Pereira Coutinho, had good reason to fear Njinga's alliance with large bodies of Imbangala. As Portuguese rulers had used their fighters as mercenaries for decades, they knew these ruthless people up close, and knew what they were capable of.

But the governor was powerless to stop the warrior queen from Matamba. By mid-1633, Njinga and her grisly troupe had closed down the eastern roads to Portuguese slave markets, savaging the governor's economic base. Annual exports of "pieces," which had numbered 13,000 three years earlier, dropped to zero.

The elimination of Coutinho's prime source of revenue left his colony short of funds to pay its soldiers. "The country does not produce much since markets that were open with lots of slaves are now closed," a report to Lisbon dolefully noted. The unscheduled market closings came courtesy of "the armies that Njinga, who wants the kingdom of Ndongo, brings into the interior and the ones that Jagas [Imbangala] bring."

Coutinho saw no end in sight. Even if he had more men, his soldiers wouldn't have been able to devote their full attention to the havoc Njinga was wreaking in the east. For by the early 1640s, a new threat had arisen from beyond the sea.

A New Player

On the morning of April 20, 1641, lookouts on Luanda squinting into the distance beheld a disturbing sight: Canvas clouds swollen with the Atlantic breeze propelled twenty-two warships flying the red, white, and blue tricolor of the Dutch Republic into Angola's harbor.

The wooden ships dropped anchor and disgorged 2,000 Dutch soldiers, Brazilian recruits, and mercenaries. Marching behind a forest of muskets and pikes, they fanned out through the sparsely defended town, occupying the customs house and government buildings. By nightfall, Luanda, capital of Portuguese Angola, was in Dutch hands. The governor, Portuguese nationals, and Mbundu collaborators fled to the protection of Portugal's inland forts.

Greetings from neighboring kingdoms flowed into Luanda, and seven months after the invasion, smiling ambassadors arrived from Matamba. They recited from memory a lengthy welcome from their mistress, Queen Njinga, who expressed her desire to work in harmony with Luanda's new masters. Her willingness to supply slaves to the Dutch West India Company caught their attention, and they sent envoys to Matamba to discuss trade relations.

The Dutch soon learned that building a coalition around Njinga would be difficult. Many Mbundu were terrified of the queen who had gone Imbangala. Others had become so deeply enmeshed with Ngola Hari that they had no choice but to stand or fall with the puppet king. But Njinga was the most powerful—and most feared—monarch in Southwest Africa. And she was someone the Dutch could do business with.

Over the next year Njinga pressed her advantage against the enemy on the battlefield. Exhorting her warriors to stand up to "these few *mundeles* [whites]," she personally led a relief column to aid a *soba* besieged by a Portuguese force. After a day-long battle, she broke the siege. Imbangala warriors, disregarding the queen's orders to spare the Portuguese captives, gleefully beheaded their prisoners.

For a time, the Dutch alliance worked well. Njinga's domains, Eastern Ndongo and Matamba, produced between 2,000 and 3,000 slaves annually, and she used cash tributes and proceeds from slave sales to buy matchlock muskets, powder, and shot. The Dutch were the anvil, and Njinga was the hammer, landing blow after blow against the hapless Portuguese until Angola's old masters were reduced to a handful of tenuously linked forts.

As her sway over Angola grew, Njinga built lavish *kilombos* and furnished them with rich silks, imported carpets, and bright, patterned cloth. Emphasizing her power and wealth, she received Dutch and Catholic visitors surrounded by attendants wearing brightly colored wraps. Their queen—now in her early sixties—sat adorned with strings of pearls and gem-studded gold necklaces, bracelets, and anklets.

Portugal's new king, João IV, fretted over the collapse of his African colony at the hands of the "infernal woman," as his Overseas Council called Njinga. In January 1646, he sent Francisco de Sotomaior, governor of Rio de Janeiro, to Angola with a company of 260 Portuguese soldiers. His assignment: Assume the governorship, raise a local army, and eject Njinga and the Dutch.

When he set foot in Angola, Sotomaior was appalled by what he found. Portuguese conquistadores had been slaughtered by Njinga's warriors, and the Dutch had deported Portuguese civilians to Brazil. The Crown's forces amounted to no more than 210 garrison troops spread across four hard-pressed forts, supported by around

8,000 *kimbares* of doubtful reliability. The "infernal woman" had won over *sobas* once loyal to Portugal, and its frantic puppet king, Ngola Hari, had been pushed into a small province called Pungo Ndongo, far down the Kwanza River.

Against this force, Njinga fielded a massive army of around 80,000 men and women. And unlike the isolated Portuguese, Njinga's troops lived on a steady diet of food, ammunition, and supplies paid for with a flow of slaves bound for Dutch plantations in Guyana and Brazil.

From her capital at Kavanga, near the Dande River in eastern Kongo, Njinga's spies kept her informed of Governor Sotomaior's war preparations. She planned a spoiling attack before the governor was ready and left nothing to chance, including divine guidance. Consulting her *ngangas*, she had her courtiers pit a white rooster against a black one. When the white bird prevailed, Njinga and her shamans announced that the time for war was propitious.

Occasionally even oracles misread signs, and the white cock may not have been the best one to bet the country's fortunes on. While Njinga's advance guard was in its *kilombo*, feasting on human and animal spoils of a raid, the Portuguese launched a withering surprise attack. Conquistadores and *kimbares* crashed through the camp, cutting down the guard's leader and most of his warriors.

The few survivors straggled back to Njinga's *kilombo* with the bad news, which she did not take well. She promptly beheaded the messengers, telling them they should have died with their men.

Then she prepared for battle.

Governor Sotomaior's strategy had two parts. First, a small force would blockade the Kwanza River, preventing Dutch ammunition, arms, and reinforcements from reaching Njinga's army. With Njinga isolated, his main body would then attack her *kilombo* in the Dembos region of Ndongo. Even if the queen were not killed on the spot, the loss of Dembos would be a body blow to her prestige. Timid *sobas* would return to the Portuguese fold, or at least remain quietly neutral and refuse to actively support Njinga in eastern Ndongo.

To execute Sotomaior's plan, his general-in-chief, Gaspar Borges Madureira, led the largest force Njinga ever faced. Assembled at the Portuguese fort of Ambaca, it included over 400 Portuguese officers and foot soldiers, 200 mulatto musketeers, sixteen horsemen, 2,000 scouts led by Ngola Hari, 30,000 African *kimbares*, plus field artillery, auxiliaries from friendly *sobas*, and slaves freed by the Portuguese to fill their ranks.

The host marched on Njinga's *kilombo* at Sengas de Kavanga, just across the Dande River. Njinga had planned to slow the enemy advance by setting fire to the brush in a scorched-earth defense, but Borges Madureira's fast-moving troops managed to flank her fire line. Portuguese soldiers smashed into a contingent of Dutch allies, and cracks of gunfire popped among the cries and screams of battle.

With Njinga directing the battle from a hill, the armies fought for the better part of the day. Neither side could claim victory, but by late afternoon Portuguese advance lines reached the *kilombo*. Njinga had stationed battalions of fighters around her perimeter, but they were spread too thin to stem the Portuguese tide. Lacking reserves to defend her *kilombo*, the queen and her bodyguards fled, leaving behind 500 firearms, a large store of silks, gems, and fabrics, and, in a nearby palace, Njinga's sister Kambu.

Kambu, who had once been a Portuguese prisoner, was resigned to her fate, and sat serenely with forty ladies-in-waiting as the invaders broke into the *kilombo*. One of her Mbundu captors raped her during the night she was captured, but when handed over to Borges Madureira the next morning, Kambu gave no indication of the affront to her dignity. She appeared before the general dressed in the splendor of a Ndongo queen and was treated reasonably well after that.

Not so for Njinga's other sister, Funji, who was still being held at the Portuguese fortress of Massangano, at the junction of the Kwanza and Lucala Rivers. Secret letters from Funji to Njinga were found hidden beneath a small Catholic altar in Njinga's *kilombo*, letters containing a wealth of military and diplomatic information. When the Portuguese realized their prisoner had been smuggling spy reports to her sister, they dragged her to the Kwanza River and held her under until she drowned.

LICKING HER WOUNDS in northeastern Ndongo, Njinga planned a fresh counteroffensive of 1647, this time in concert with the Dutch. In May, she entered into a contract with the Estates General, the Prince of Orange, and the Dutch West India Company to work together to "exterminate the Portuguese" in southwest Africa. Neither party, they agreed, would negotiate separately with the Portuguese, and in return for military aid Njinga would send the Dutch half the slaves she captured. To underscore their commitment to the bargain, the Dutch seconded Njinga seventy trained musketeers.

In October, the Dutch, Njinga, the Kongolese king, and friendly *sobas* planned a general offensive against the Portuguese, hitting the enemy on all fronts. Njinga's part was to bring an army of 4,000 Imbangala and Dutch to rendezvous with allied *sobas* in Dembos. From there the allies would march south and attack Portugal's main fort, Massangano, before mopping up outposts further west.

Njinga and her army reached Dembos on October 27, two days earlier than expected. Surveying the scene, she found the Mbundus reeling from a Portuguese spoiling attack under General Borges Madureira. Rallying the scattered forces— about 10,000 Dembos, 300 Dutch troops, and her own 4,000 Imbangala—Njinga launched a devastating counterattack. More than 3,000 Portuguese and allies were killed in the battle, including Borges Madureira, felled with a mortal wound to his leg.

Pursuing Portuguese survivors, Njinga led her army south from Dembos toward Fort Massangano. On the march, her army burned more than 200 villages allied with Portugal. Some 1,500 Portuguese fled their homes to seek shelter within the fort's stone walls.

From a central camp, Njinga sent a flying column of Imbangala to overrun the fort and rescue Kambu. But the fort had been strengthened, and the embattled defenders held the walls against the queen's shock troops. The Portuguese blockade up the Kwanza River prevented the Dutch from bringing up heavy artillery to support Njinga's infantry. Stymied for the moment, Njinga was forced to spend a frustrating spring and summer of 1648 chipping away at the provinces around Massangano.

By August, she and the local Dutch commander were ready to launch their final assault on the fort. Then, with victory so close they could taste it, the allies received word from Luanda: The Spanish had landed with a huge army and heavy guns. If they did not rush to Luanda's aid, the Dutch capital city would fall.

Njinga desperately wanted to eliminate Fort Massangano and free her sister, but she grasped the strategic need to keep the Netherlands in the fight. If Luanda were lost, supplies to her army would dry up, and the Dutch might abandon Angola. She lifted the siege and drove to the coast as the Dutch raced ahead of her main force.

When she arrived, the Dutch troops—indeed, every Dutchman in Angola, it seemed—had vanished. Piecing news together over the next day, she learned that the West India Company chief in Luanda had signed a treaty of capitulation with the Portuguese and fled. Angola, it seemed, wasn't worth the fight. Under the yawning guns of Spanish and Portuguese galleons, the erstwhile governor and his men had boarded ships and sailed into the western sea.

Njinga was on her own. Again.

She retreated to Matamba, as she knew she must, and by year's end the Portuguese army had grown too large to destroy in a single campaign. At age sixty-six, Njinga also knew she was running out of time to drive out the Portuguese devils before she joined her ancestors. She was no longer the blood-drinking Imbangala who had slaughtered enemies, dodged poison arrows, and shimmied down cliffs. She focused her energies on securing territories around Matamba and biding her time until the fighting cock, or the bones of her ancestors, or her Christian god, told her to march her army back to Ndongo.

For eight more years Njinga led Matamba through constant warfare on her borders. She launched twenty-nine attacks in two years and laid waste to the lands of *sobas* who did not submit to her. In late 1657, she led a force against the army of Kalandula, an Imbangala chief allied with the Portuguese. She prepared her soldiers by leading them in the standard pre-battle dances, then marched them toward Kalandula's *kilombo*, sending detachments ahead to block escape routes in the night. By morning, she had Kalandula's camp surrounded.

With a knack for theatrics, she dressed for battle and led from the front. "I have seen Njinga dressed as a man, armed with a bow, arrows, and already old and of small stature," wrote one Portuguese witness, adding, "Her speech is very effeminate."

She ordered a soldier to run her flag high up a tree and challenged Kalandula to battle. Kalandula, terrified of the queen's reputation, sent a messenger to pledge his loyalty. But 400 of his men, fearing for their lives, attempted to bolt. Njinga's soldiers captured them and sent them off to the slave markets. Smelling treachery, she led a violent assault on Kalandula's camp.

Not long afterward, Kalandula's sightless, putrefying head arrived in Luanda. It was Njinga's calling card to the Portuguese governor.

Peace at Last

While she would order men into battle for the rest of her life, Njinga gradually accepted the new reality of her forest kingdom: Diplomacy would have to win what bows and axes could not.

She had always been willing to dictate long letters in hopes of winning an honest peace, wearing down her enemies with ink if she could not reach them with her bow. Those efforts ended in disappointment, though, because they contained one immoveable demand: acknowledgment of her rule over her homeland, Ndongo. Portugal would never accept her claim to their colony.

In her seventies, Njinga turned to religion to break the impasse. Having been baptized a Catholic, she had treated Portuguese missionaries well, and priests captured by her warriors were either released or permitted to live at her court in relative freedom. Those who stayed were given private quarters, and she kept an altar to Christ in her *kilombo*. She would not change her polyglot religion, nor her views on violence and sex, but she did tell two padres that she did not consider herself a cannibal and wished to live as a Christian.

It was the Capuchin missionaries who found a breakthrough. The Tuscany-based order had strong contacts in the Vatican and was antagonistic to the Jesuits, whom Portugal sponsored. While the Capuchins weren't sure Njinga was a reliable conversion prospect—she had committed "innumerable cruelties, condemned not only by the law of God but by natural law," they admitted—her repeated offers to let them preach in her lands persuaded the Church to seek inroads. In November 1654, the order dispatched missionaries to establish a prefect in Matamba.

The Church wasn't the only one seeking an accommodation with the Queen of Matamba. By 1654, Portugal's King João concluded that Njinga was best left alone. He did not wish to lose troops he might need to repel another Dutch invasion, and instructed his governor not to provoke Njinga.

Accepting that neither side could break the other, at age seventy-four Njinga sent an envoy with a gift of ten slaves and an offer to buy her surviving sister's release. With that purchase came an implied agreement to accept the Portuguese as masters of the land they called Angola, while Njinga would rule as the *ngola* of Matamba. As a bonus, the Church would be free to practice in her territory, without fear of being enslaved or eaten. By linking her sister's freedom to a Catholic mission in Matamba, Njinga won diplomatic backing from the Vatican.

The sticking point was the number of slaves she would have to pay to ransom Kambu: The governor wanted two hundred, a shocking price even for royalty. Njinga countered with 130 pieces, the first hundred to be delivered upon word her sister was halfway to Matamba, and the rest upon her arrival at Njinga's *kilombo*.

In late 1656, the Portuguese governor accepted Njinga's counteroffer. Kambu, baptized into the Catholic faith as Barbara, was released after ten years in captivity and arrived at Njinga's court on October 12. Reunited, the two women threw their arms around each other. Smiling, laughing, and weeping as they embraced, their cheeks glistened with long tears of joy. Njinga had brought her family—what was left of it—home.

KAMBU'S RELEASE set the two kingdoms on a path to peace. The following year Portugal signed a formal treaty with Matamba. The Lucala River would form the boundary between Angola and Matamba. Njinga agreed to end some of the more odious Imbangala practices, like infanticide and cannibalism, and white priests would be permitted to practice Catholicism in her lands.

The bargain ended more than thirty years of war.

Njinga spent her twilight years shoring up Matamba's political stability, building institutions that would outlive her. Peace with Portugal and the flowering of Christianity were central pillars of her nation's long-term political health. Anointing her sister Kambu as her successor, she nudged Matamba closer to the European model of royal succession.*

But the old warrior spirit never left her. In her last years, she took pleasure recalling her adventures fighting and running, killing and leading. With a broad smile, she regaled Capuchin missionaries with tales of her days ambushing bands of Imbangala, Ndongo, and Portuguese. In her eighth decade, she astonished one priest by rising nimbly from her chair and demonstrating the war dance she had mastered in her childhood, one full of intricate twists, turns, and dodges every Mbundu warrior memorized, so an enemy's poisoned arrows wouldn't find a home between her ribs.

As in 1626, when she first went to war against Portugal, Njinga used mystic spirits to ratify her tilt toward Catholicism. She held a public ceremony where *nganga* priests became possessed by four great Imbangala spirits. These spirits, to no one's surprise, told Njinga that if she wished to live as a Christian, she was free to do so.

With the backing of the spirit world, Njinga prayed daily before a wooden crucifix that had been recovered from one of her old battlefields. She ordered churches built, and renamed her capital Santa Maria de Matamba. She even gave up her forty male concubines, lovers, and spouses, and began corresponding with the Vatican. In June 1660 Pope Alexander VII welcomed Njinga as "Dearest in Christ our Daughter Anna Queen Nzinga." The woman who had reinvented herself as a warrior, baptized Catholic, king, blood-drinking Imbangala, reborn Catholic, and monogamous statesman ruled a kingdom temporarily secure and at peace.

NGOLAS, THEY SAY, do not die; they are death itself, immortal beings who defy time and simply move from this world into the home of their forbears. On December 17, 1663, at the ripe old age of eighty-one, Ana de Sousa, born Njinga, daughter of King Mbande a Ngola, went to live with her ancestors.

A polarizing figure in life, Angola's warrior queen set off convulsions even after death. Though she was an avowed Catholic, her tradition-minded followers expected a wave of human sacrifices to accompany the beloved queen into the spirit

---

* Because their brother had ensured that neither Njinga nor Kambu had any children, Njinga cannily promoted João Guterres Ngola Kanini, from a cadet line of Ndongo royalty, into a senior position that would give him a leg up on his rivals after Kambu's death and preserve the kingdom's stability.

world. At a minimum, a decent send-off required knocking some of her attendants on their heads and burying them with their mistress. Court slaves and ladies-in-waiting—prime candidates for the knocking and burying—nervously pondered their role in the funeral.

They needn't have worried. Njinga wished to die a Catholic, and had left strict orders to follow a Capuchin priest's funeral arrangements. The order of service blended Mbundu and Christian elements, politely skipping the usual sacrifices.*

Yet Njinga's subjects were driven by primal emotion, not a ritualized order of service written by white missionaries for some far-off god. Local Matambans surrounded her corpse as it was carried to the grave and threw themselves onto the dirt in a show of homage and subservience to their queen—their *ngola*.

Which is just what Njinga would have expected.

THE PORTUGUESE EMPIRE Njinga battled for four decades had already passed its zenith when she was driven from Ndongo. The world was changing, and the next hundred years produced an intellectual revolution that would change the way leaders thought about power and their relation to the masses they led.

Yet the personal connection between soverign and conduct of war remained. A century later and half a world away, another warrior queen would lead the largest empire on earth in a power struggle against two empires, two kingdoms—and her husband.

---

* In conformance with Njinga's orders, no humans were sacrificed to mark her death in the capital. In the more conservative, outlying provinces, however, Njinga's death was marked by both animal and human sacrifices. Old habits die hard.

10

PHILOSOPHE WARLORD

Russia's Catherine the Great

"The soul of Caesar with the seductions of Cleopatra."
—DIDEROT ON CATHERINE, 1774

SHE RODE TO POWER on a gray thoroughbred, clad in the bottle-green jacket of the Imperial Guards. Her chestnut tresses, spilling lazily under a tricorn hat, flicked in the summer breeze as her mount, a muscled warhorse named Brilliant, clopped down a tree-lined road.

Bouncing to the rhythm of Brilliant's hooves, the rider's bright blue eyes snapped left and right, scanning the road for musketeers. Or a roadblock. Or cannon.

Yet as far as she could see, the only armed men were marching behind her, not toward her.

The thirty-three-year-old mother led her regiments down the rutted road to a country estate on the Baltic Sea coast. There she planned to arrest her husband, ruler of the largest empire on earth.

❖   ❖   ❖

RUSSIA'S MOST FAMOUS EMPRESS had not an ounce of Russian blood. Eighteen years earlier, Princess Sophia of Anhalt-Zerbst, teenage daughter of an obscure Prussian nobleman, had been summoned from her home in Pomerania and sent on an arduous sled journey to St. Petersburg, the capital of the wild, uninviting country known as Russia. Crossing miles of snow, mud, and gloom, Sophia's coachmen deposited her at a baroque palace where the language, religion, and customs defied penetration.

The invitation couldn't be declined, for it arrived bearing the imperial cypher of Empress Elizabeth. The empress had been evaluating a stable of young noblewomen to marry Russia's heir to the throne, and when Sophie arrived at St. Petersburg, something about her caught the empress's eye. Perhaps it was her sharp chin, oval face, or large, azure eyes. Perhaps it was the curve of her lips, which hinted at a quick wit awaiting permission to reveal itself—a door cracked to sunlight that would snap shut at the first sign of a storm. Whatever she saw in Sophie, Empress Elizabeth chose the German princess as the bride-elect of her nephew, Grand Duke Karl Peter Ulrich.

Under intense pressure from her social-climbing mother, Prussia's King Frederick II, and the empress, Sophie renounced her native Lutheranism and converted to the Russian Orthodox faith. Taking the baptismal name Ekaterina Alexeyevna, Catherine, as she became known, began learning the Russian language. Placing her faith in God and the empress, a year later she married Peter and plunged into the splendor and brutality of the Romanov court.

Empress Elizabeth ruled that court with the rigor of a Guards sergeant. Being watched by spying servants and ruled by an overbearing monarch, court life was enough to make any girl, especially one from a foreign land, skittish and miserable. And as she grew to know the man she married, her years as wife of Grand Duke Peter dissolved into a mélange of tears, abuse, and distress.

Like Catherine, Peter had been snatched from his German home as a child and stuffed under Elizabeth's suffocating wing. The product of a sadistic tutor and poor health, he grew into a scared, bullying, pockmarked teenager with a cruel streak. In his teens he spent his days playing with toy soldiers, his evenings marching servants around his apartment as if they were on a Berlin parade square. His nights he spent drinking.

He reached physical adulthood, but his mind never matured. Graduating from toy soldiers to real ones, he imported a squadron of grenadiers from his native Duchy of Holstein and drilled them in the harsh style of his Germanic idol, Prussia's King Frederick the Great.

In the confines of their royal suite, Peter treated his wife like a detested older sister, and his marriage as if it were a bizarre joke. For the first nine years of wedlock, he seemed entirely uninterested in sexual relations. When his libido finally awoke, his taste ran to a low-class, high-born mistress who, court observers hissed, swore like a soldier, spit when she talked, and displayed the manners of a profane scullery maid. Infatuated with his homely duckling, Peter made no secret of his intent to put Catherine in a convent and marry his mistress as soon as Empress Elizabeth was gone.

Around this time, Catherine fell out of favor with the empress. The cause was her inability—or, Elizabeth suspected, her unwillingness—to produce an heir to the throne, the most basic duty of a royal consort. Elizabeth sensed, correctly, that Catherine found Peter's gawkish looks repulsive, and refused to believe her womb's vacancy was due to lack of cooperation from her husband.

Desperate to recover her standing with the empress, Catherine took her chamberlain as a secret lover, and before long she delivered a son. The empress, delighted to have a grandnephew to carry on the dynasty, named Catherine's baby Paul and snatched him from his mother, to be raised by nurses and tutors.*

Treading water in an eddy of social climbers, Catherine withdrew into a palace of the mind. She spent her days reading Tacitus, Suetonius, and other classical writers. She pored over modern works of French *philosophes* like Voltaire, Diderot, and Montesquieu, electric minds who were revolutionizing western thought. She mastered the Russian language, (although she preferred to correspond in French), and at state banquets she wrapped herself in a stole of gaiety that cloaked the lonely, frightened life she lived.

She also cultivated allies in high places. In 1755 she took a lover: a handsome twenty-three-year-old Pole attached to the British embassy named Count Stanislaus Poniatowski. She kept on good terms with Russia's senior generals, and her devotion to the Orthodox Church won her support within the Patriarch's palace. To royal watchers and ambassadors, Catherine's intellect, interpersonal skills, and instinct for court politics marked her as a woman who might temper Peter's impulses when he became tsar.

Those impulses did not bode well for the Russian state, and the court's wig-and-stocking crowd considered Peter a dangerous fool. Holding aside his bombast, drunkenness, and poor choice of mistress, he had a gift for alienating the men who ran the empire. When Russia was locked in war with Frederick the Great's Prussia, Peter mocked Russian military traditions and exalted everything Teutonic. He dismissed the vast kingdom he was about to inherit as an unsophisticated backwater,

---

* By the time of Paul's birth, Peter had been coaxed into having conjugal relations with Catherine. The parentage of the boy, who would become Tsar Paul I of Russia, is thus uncertain. Catherine later had a daughter by Stanislaus Poniatowski, a Polish count whose story arc would cross Catherine's several times. Like Paul, the Poniatowski baby was deemed to be Peter's child. Also like Paul, the girl was named by the empress and swept away from her mother. When she died at fifteen months of age, the loss left a deep scar on Catherine's heart.

and in the early 1760s, as Elizabeth's health declined, many in court, the army, and the Church feared the new emperor would send Russia staggering backwards.

Peter managed to fall short of even those dreadfully low expectations.

When Empress Elizabeth died in January 1762, Russia and Austria had been fighting Prussia for five years. After shedding rivers of blood, Elizabeth and Austria's ruler, Archduchess Maria Theresa, had finally driven Prussia to the brink of defeat. King Frederick, despondent at the thought of Russian troops marching through Brandenburg, began thinking wistfully of dying a soldier's death on the battlefield.

Inheriting a vast kingdom on the threshold of victory, Peter stunned the world by pulling out of the war and renouncing all Prussian territory his troops had conquered. Turning his back on his Austrian ally, he assembled an army of 40,000 Russian soldiers to march against Denmark, his aim being to overrun the inconsequential province of Schleswig and restore it to his native home of Holstein.

The new tsar's orders cut short a war every Russian wanted to win, and launched a new war no Russian wanted. The imperial *volte-face* was, in the eyes of Russia's officers, a repudiation of their hard-won victories at Gross Jägerndorf and Künsdorf, Kolberg and East Prussia. It also threatened the prestige, promotions, and wealth these triumphs had brought to the up-and-coming officer class.

Adding insult to injury, Peter infuriated his soldiers by ordering them to exchange their traditional, loose-fitting uniforms for uncomfortable powdered wigs, mitre hats, and tight-fitting breeches of the Prussian model. Worse still, he announced plans to disband the traditional Russian Guards regiments—two of them founded by Peter the Great—and replace his personal Russian bodyguard with a Holstein cavalry detachment.

Peter could not have more thoroughly alienated his army if he had spent ten years studying the subject. Officers began quietly talking of a palace coup, and six months into Peter's reign, their vengeance knocked on his gilded door.

Peter

For years, Catherine had borne Peter's insults with the resignation of an early Christian martyr. She showed restraint and grace when confronted with buffoonery, like when he loudly called her an idiot at a large state banquet. When Peter pinned the coveted Order of St. Catherine on the gown of his mistress in a formal ceremony, Catherine watched meekly, uttering not a word of richly warranted protest.

Yet behind the stoic's veil crouched a tiger biding her time, building a power base among a growing regiment of Peter's enemies. She was empress consort and mother of the heir to the throne, a position that commanded respect among Petersburg traditionalists. She had embraced Orthodoxy, endeared herself to court and commons, and solidified support among the police and army. "She is as much loved and respected as the emperor is despised," the French ambassador reported to King Louis XV. Too dull to realize it, Peter was backing the wrong woman into a corner.

In a drunken rage in the spring of 1762, he ordered Catherine's arrest. He rescinded his order on abject pleas of Catherine's uncle, but Catherine knew her time to act was short. "It was then," she wrote afterwards, "I began to listen to the proposals which people had been making to me since the death of the empress."

She did more than listen. In early June she secretly approved a manifesto announcing that Emperor Peter III had abdicated the throne and that Catherine, Empress of All Russias, was ruling in his stead. She won the loyalty of key Guards officers, the most important of whom was Captain Grigory Orlov, a hero of the Seven Years War and Catherine's secret lover. Orlov and his fellow conspirators garnered support among their brother officers, winning goodwill by liberally distributing wine and cash through regimental barracks. Compliments, they said, of their loving empress.

On June 12, Peter left the capital for Oranienbaum, a sprawling palace twenty-five miles west of St. Petersburg. From there he planned to launch his glorious war against Denmark. As a precaution against troublemaking by the empress—though mostly as an afterthought—Peter ordered Catherine to leave the capital and ride to Peterhof, a gilded baroque palace twenty miles down the Baltic coast. Taking her own precautions, Catherine left her seven-year-old son, Paul, in St. Petersburg with his tutor, a reliable court official named Nikita Panin.

Catherine and Peter had moved their opening pawns, and the chessboard was wide open. Catherine, ready to strike, was about to play her knights and rooks. Her husband, knowing nothing of the game they were playing, picked up a violin.

On the evening of June 27, a Guards captain was arrested after rumors swirled of a palace coup. A message was dispatched to the emperor at Oranienbaum, but Peter dismissed the report as an exaggeration. The Russian people, he knew beyond all doubt, could not possibly prefer his idiot wife to himself, God's ordained tsar and emperor.

A second letter, warning of unrest in the capital, arrived at the emperor's chambers while he was playing his violin. Annoyed at the interruption to his music, Peter ordered his servant to leave the unread note on a table. He would get to the letter in good time.

Loose talk.

A ruckus in a barracks.

Rumors.

The window of opportunity was closing for both royals. Years of uneasiness had telescoped into a few breathless hours to act. Peter was separated from his capital and his army, while Catherine was isolated at Peterhof. Neither had the advantage.

Catherine had not yet committed an irrevocable move. But would she? And when? Even Peter would not ignore rumors of a coup much longer, and in a matter of hours the emperor might order her arrest.

AT FIVE O'CLOCK the next morning, as Peter and his mistress slumbered at Oranienbaum, Catherine was shaken from her sleep by Alexei Orlov, brother of Grigory and sergeant in the Preobrazhensky Guards regiment.

"Little mother, wake up!" said Orlov, urgency infusing his rough voice. "The time has come! You must get up and come with me. Everything is ready for your proclamation!"

Seeing Fate's pendulum swinging, Catherine threw on a black dress and leapt into a swift carriage that took her to St. Petersburg. Bouncing along the uneven road, she and Alexei ran into Grigory, who hustled her to the Izmailovsky Guards regimental barracks.

Her first and most crucial job was to win over the three Imperial Guards regiments surrounding the capital, and she began with the unit most likely to come over to her side. At the Izmailovsky barracks, she stepped from her carriage and addressed the soldiers who gathered around her in the camp square.

"I have come to you for protection," she told the men. "The Emperor has given orders to arrest me. I fear he intends to kill me." For the sake of her beloved Russia, for the sake of the heir to the Romanov throne, she placed her life, and the life of her child, under the regiment's protection.

The response was swift and emotional. Burly Slavic soldiers, swept away by the moment, shoved forward and mobbed Catherine, elbowing one another aside to kneel before their queen and pledge their loyalty.

"The soldiers rushed to kiss my hands, my feet, the hem of my dress, calling me their savior," she wrote afterward. "Two of them brought a priest with a cross and started to take the oath."

Catherine had passed her first test.

Sparks of revolt caught tinder at other Guards outposts. She dashed to the Semenovsky Guards barracks, where the outpouring was as passionate as before.

Flushed with support, she rode to the Preobrazhensky barracks and swept them away, too. At the head of her lead companies—many of the men throwing away their wigs and donning their old Russian uniforms—she cantered to the Winter Palace, where her guards fanned out and occupied the city center. She conferred with military and local officials, then moved on to the great Kazan Cathedral a few blocks away, where the Senate and Holy Synod acclaimed her the rightful ruler of Russia, her son Paul heir to the throne.

She had the Guards, the Church, the Senate, and the capital crowds. But, she wondered, whose loyalty did Peter command? What would his next move be? As long as Peter remained at large, he could make his way to Prussia, where the bulk of his army awaited him. If the army followed him back to Russia, a bloody civil war would tear the empire apart.

Catherine's life depended on staying one step ahead of Peter, and she dispatched swift couriers to the island fortress of Kronstadt, ordering the garrison commander to refuse Peter should he demand entry. She sent another rider galloping to Pomerania, where the Russian army waited, and directed Nikita Panin's brother, General Peter Panin, to assume command of the army. She ordered the commanding general of Russian forces in Silesia to bring his men home to Russia; should King Frederick attempt to block their movement home, her orders required the general to "join the nearest army corps of her Imperial Roman Majesty, the empress of Austria."

Peter's reign was about to end. *If* the army followed her orders.

For the next several hours she awaited news, her mood pendulating between anxiety and elation as minutes crawled by. Peter's existential threat grew every hour he remained at large, and Catherine at last concluded that she could not remain at the capital any longer. She must force events, not wait for them.

She took a carriage to the Preobrazhensky barracks and had the adjutant proclaim her the regiment's colonel, an honorary post first held by Peter the Great. She then borrowed elements of the traditional Russian army uniform her husband had so brusquely rejected: a captain's green coat, a black three-cornered hat, a saber, and a sword knot, or *dragonne*, offered by a handsome subaltern named Grigory Potemkin.

To the delight of her troops, Catherine looked the part of a battle queen—not a pompous little *glupetz* like the emperor, but a true Russian war leader. During her years in court she had identified with the fighting men and sought their support, and on this occasion, she dressed like one. "To do a man's work, you needed a man's outfit," she would quip afterward.

Mounting a thoroughbred named Brilliant, she led a column of 12,000 men from St. Petersburg to Oranienbaum. As dust clouds rose over swaying muskets, and the rumble of tramping boots filled her ears, she felt a surge of adrenaline rushing into her brain. Her prison of sorrow and humiliation was about come crashing down.

❖   ❖   ❖

AWAKENING FROM SUPINE STUPOR upon news of his capital's defection, Peter and a tiny retinue made their way by boat to the island fortress of Kronstadt, at the mouth of St. Petersburg's bay. Peter vaguely hoped to rally the fort's garrison, but as his boat approached the fort's gate, the guards shocked him by forbidding him passage in the name of Empress Catherine.

Realizing that he had been stalked and trapped without even knowing it, the brittle little man fell to pieces. He collapsed, sobbing in the arms of his bewildered mistress.

Seeing no way out, Peter resigned himself to his fate. Riding back to Oranienbaum, he dismissed his servants and wrote a letter to Catherine apologizing for his behavior. He offered to share the throne with her. When his letter went unanswered, he wrote a second letter abdicating his throne.

The Emperor of Russia, wrote Frederick the Great, "allowed himself to be dethroned like a child being sent to bed."

Catherine's coup may have been bloodless, but it was not deathless. Peter died eight days after he was arrested, evidently strangled with a scarf by Alexei Orlov or one of the men guarding him. The regicide may have been the result of a drunken argument, but more likely it was a premeditated act committed by Catherine's supporters.

There is no evidence that Catherine ordered her husband's murder, but it could hardly have come as a great surprise. The soldiers guarding Peter knew he would remain a threat to the empress as long as he drew breath, and any political opponent—or foreign power—could throw its weight behind the "rightful ruler of Russia." Catherine's interests required Peter to die. So he died.

Whatever her foreknowledge, Peter's death swept the debris from her path to power. "At last," she wrote, "God has brought everything to pass according to His designs."

And hers.*

---

* In a letter to Poniatowski, Catherine blamed Peter's death on a "haemorrhoidal colic," claiming, "Despite all the help the doctors could give him, he died while demanding a Lutheran priest." Catherine's bald-faced lie became a euphemism for political murder among Russians and westerners. When Catherine later invited French *philosophe* Jean d'Alembert to visit St. Petersburg, he joked to Voltaire that he dared not go since he was prone to piles, which was a very dangerous condition in Russia.

❖   ❖   ❖

CATHERINE'S CORONATION, like every Russian coronation since Tsar Ivan the Terrible's, was held in the Kremlin's gold-domed Assumption Cathedral. The empress wore a silver, off-the-shoulder dress and a train carried by seven gentlemen-in-waiting, trimmed with ermine and emblazoned with gold double-eagle crests. Surrounded by bearded priests, she walked solemnly up crimson-carpeted steps and took the Diamond Throne of Tsar Alexis.

As smoke rose from miters and the crowd gazed in silence, Catherine lifted the nine-pound crown and placed it on her own head. Made with red velvet shaped like a bishop's miter, it was encrusted with diamonds, accented with two rows of large pearls, and topped with a 389-carat ruby. Staring ahead beneath frowns and ecstasies of frescoed saints, she took the imperial orb in her left hand and a scepter in her right.

In that moment, Catherine personified everything Russia looked for in a leader. "She was beautiful, and the blue eyes beneath [her crown] were remarkable for their brightness," a star-struck British ambassador wrote. "The head was poised on a long neck, giving an impression of pride, and power, and will."

The glitter of coronation gave way to the serious business of governing, and Catherine's first order of business was to formalize Russia's exit from the Austro-Prussian war. Though she had been appalled at Peter's decision to betray Austria, she had no intention of renewing the war against King Frederick. For Russia, the war had been a *matrioshka* doll of tragedy within tragedy, and she was not about to plunge into a new bloodbath merely to please Austria's sanctimonious Maria Theresa. She announced the cessation of hostilities and brought thousands of soldiers home.

Relieved of that necklace of millstones, Catherine turned her attention to domestic matters with the same mental energy that had lit up England's Elizabethan court two centuries before. "Time belongs, not to me, but to the Empire," she liked to say, and she made the most of the Empire's time. Waking at six o'clock every morning, she let out her English greyhounds, said morning prayers, then worked in a Russian-style dress with long, comfortable sleeves. She wrote official letters and reviewed reports until late morning, met with ministers through early afternoon, then read, wrote to friends, or held salon discussions until evening. Taking little or no dinner, she ended her workday around 10:30 p.m.

Catherine had learned during her days as grand duchess that political groundwork was a vital part of an autocrat's toolbox. She had what her German countrymen would call *fingerspitzengefühl*—a "fingertip-feel" for the nuances of power—and knew that the ministers and local bureaucrats who run the empire speak of a monarch's "absolute power" with a wink.

"It's not as easy as you think," she once confided to a secretary. "In the first place, my orders would not be carried out unless they were the kind of orders which could be carried out . . . I take advice, I consult . . . and when I am already convinced in advance of general approval, I issue my orders and have the pleasure of observing what you call blind obedience. And that is the foundation of unlimited power."

CATHERINE'S WORLD, 1762

"General approval" by the apparatchiks was not the same thing as the democracy the French *philosophes* mused about in their essays. To Catherine, the core function of government is to maximize the welfare and freedom of its people. But welfare and freedom require limits, and she agreed with John Locke that law and freedom are inseparable. "A civil society requires a certain established order," she wrote. "There ought to be some to govern and some to obey."

As ruler of an empire of 19 million subjects, she politely differed with her high-minded Parisian friends who held no responsibilities for anyone but themselves. After one particularly exasperating day of pushing against the Newtonian inertia of bureaucracy, she lamented to Diderot, "You work only on paper, which suffers everything . . . while I, poor empress, work on human skin that is otherwise irritable and ticklish."

That skin was especially ticklish with the army, to which Catherine owed her throne. Her first tentative efforts at military reform bowed to the respectful but firm demands of the Orlov brothers, and were aimed only at rolling back the most unpopular edicts of her late and unlamented husband. But six months into her rule, she approved more ambitious reforms aimed at modernizing her army's mix of cavalry, artillery, infantry, and support troops.

As her confidence grew, Catherine ordered the country's military think tank, the War College, to report to her on a weekly basis, and made senior officers directly accountable to the throne. These small moves strengthened her hand over the fighting services. Incrementally—almost imperceptibly—she was consolidating her power as a warlord.

SHE WOULD NEED THAT POWER, for beyond Russia's borders lay a nest of coiled vipers. To the west sat the immense Polish Commonwealth, an amalgamation of Polish, Lithuanian, and Ukrainian lands larger than France, with a population half as great as Russia's. Viewed from Catherine's Winter Palace, Poland caused problems whenever it became either too powerful or too weak.

In its heyday, Poland's troops had invaded Muscovy, but by Catherine's time the confederation had slipped into a political coma. Its king lay dying, and its parliament was crippled by the *liberum veto*, a procedural rule requiring unanimity of its 1,000 delegates to pass legislation. Since at least one delegate would disagree with any proposal—or could be bribed to disagree—Poland's government was incapable of governing, and its slow implosion created a power vacuum that drew the attention of hungry empires on its borders.

West of Poland, two kingdoms stood out as Russia's natural rivals: Maria Theresa's Austro-Hungarian Empire, and the Kingdom of Prussia, ruled by Catherine's former liege, King Frederick the Great. Catherine found Maria Theresa to be a humorless, stubborn, illiberal prig too prone to wear her religion on her silk sleeves. Deriding her as "Lady Prayerful," Catherine thought little of Maria Teresa's intellect. The militant Frederick, on the other hand, was a smart, dangerous ruler who had invaded Austria in 1740 and had been at war with Austria or Russia continuously until Peter's ill-timed truce.

To Russia's south spread the vast Ottoman Empire, ruled by Sultan Mustafa III. The Ottoman domains—flotsam of the Islamic tide that crested a thousand years before—jutted into the Balkans, Greece, Romania, eastern Ukraine, and Crimea. Control of the Black Sea and Dardanelles Strait made Mustafa the arbiter of Russian trade with Southern Europe.

With its huge manpower reserves, the "Sublime Porte," as the Ottoman government was called, had for centuries been the bugbear of Europe. But by Catherine's time, the bear's claws, though still long, were getting dull. Two decades of peace under Mustafa had stagnated the sultan's military might, so only around the Black Sea, home of Cossack and Tatar, did the Porte darken Catherine's borders.

This brought everyone back to Poland, the tragic buffer state for the great eastern powers. Because Poland was the obvious battleground for any future wars among those powers, four cunning monarchs—Catherine, Mustafa, Maria Theresa, and Frederick—kept watchful eyes on Warsaw as it descended into paralysis.

WHILE WAR WAS NOT ON CATHERINE'S MIND when she took up the scepter, managing a vast empire necessarily risks bloodshed. Her turn to draw the sword came two years into her reign, when Poland's ailing King Augustus died. Seizing the moment, she replaced him with her former lover, Stanislaus Poniatowski.

The regime change cost her 100,000 rubles and the backing of 14,000 Russian troops, but it gave Russia the perfect client king. The cash-strapped "sovereign" who had once shared Catherine's bed was now beholden to his former mistress for his political and financial future.

Catherine's airburst over Warsaw rattled court windows from Paris to Istanbul. If she married King Poniatowski, as court-watchers thought likely, then Russia's reach would extend to Berlin's doorstep in the north and to the Ottoman frontier in the south. Polish nobles and commoners seethed at Russian intervention, and in early 1768 the country burst into revolt. Catherine dispatched an army to prop up her puppet king, and her veterans put down waves of unrest.

But Polish resentment refused to die. Local wars between Russian Orthodox bandits and Polish confederates flared up, spilling into Ottoman lands. Atrocities were committed by both sides, and in one Crimean town a thousand souls were massacred by Orthodox Cossacks.

From Constantinople, Sultan Mustafa and his viziers watched with alarm. Ottoman policy in Europe required Poland to form a bulwark against the northern bear. The sultan's French allies, also wary of Russian expansionism, advised the Sublime Porte to strike, and on October 2, 1768, the Porte delivered an ultimatum to Catherine's ambassador: All Russian troops must leave Polish territory at once, or the Ottoman Empire would declare war on Russia.

The ambassador refused, and four days later the sultan threw him into prison. For the first time in her six-year reign, Catherine found herself at war.

Mustafa

Because her coup had been bloodless, Catherine entered the Russo-Turkish War with no experience in battle management—a fact that did not escape the notice of Prussia's King Frederick, who privately dismissed the war as a fight between "the one-eyed and the blind."

Catherine had lived through the Seven Years War, though, and she knew the ministers who shaped Russian strategy. For years she had cultivated relationships with the officers who led the army, two of whom she would take to her bed. But she knew nothing of drills and tactics beyond the absurd demonstrations of her late husband.

Perhaps that didn't matter. Her job was not to lead battalions, but to assemble them, arm them, and find them competent leaders. That required a different skill set—one capable of creating a sound military organization.

For Catherine, war began in the Winter Palace. Diplomacy and battle, two sides of one political coin, required balance. That balance could only be managed from St. Petersburg, and foreign policy was a king's prerogative. She wisely resolved to make all major decisions herself and leave tactics to the professionals.

For advice on strategy, Catherine reconstituted the *Voennyi Soviet*, or War Council. She stacked the council with men of conflicting factions who could be relied upon to oppose each other, reasoning that whatever course of action the antagonists actually agreed upon was probably the right one. She met with the council on Mondays and Thursdays, carefully reading and listening to their reports, sifting in her mind the ideal and the possible.

From these reports she learned that the Ottoman army, though not the terror it used to be, was still large and formidable. The sultan controlled the Crimean Peninsula, giving him a base to strike into southern Russia, and his command of the Black Sea allowed his field marshals to choose the place of attack. The sultan's foothold in Transylvania and Wallachia, south of the Danube River, gave the Turks a second potential approach to Russia, leaving Catherine to react to Ottoman attacks at any number of points.

The War Council began by studying Russia's war with Turkey thirty years earlier, during the reign of Empress Anna. Catherine and her advisors debated at length what went right and what went wrong as they honed Russia's strategy for the current war. They also studied dispatches from ambassadors in Stockholm, Paris, London, Warsaw, Berlin, Vienna, and Copenhagen, looking for signs that Europe's other kingdoms might move against Russia once her troops were locked in battle with Turks in the south. They folded these contingencies into their war plans.

Grand strategy has an ebb and flow that can be measured, just as a nurse monitors a patient's vital signs. Catherine and her inner circle knew that for this war, they would have to adjust the medicine over time to find the right dose. If Russia suffered too many battlefield defeats, a neighbor, or combination of neighbors, might pounce on a weak, ineffectual Russia. On the other hand, too many victories might stir up an anti-Russian coalition—say, among France, Britain, or Prussia—to check the power of the Romanov bear.

After considering the war from all angles, Catherine expressed her views on what Russia hoped to gain from fighting. Foremost was expansion into the Black Sea, with the free right of Russian vessels to sail its waters. Second, the borders of Poland and Lithuania should be free of Turkish influence. To these goals, the council added the incitement of an anti-Ottoman revolt in Dalmatia, the liberation of Georgians in the Caucasus, and the deployment of a fleet into the Mediterranean.

Strategy was, of course, just the beginning. What might look wise and effective in St. Petersburg could seem bizarre a thousand miles away on a smoking battlefield. A clear picture of the battlefront lagged far behind at a time when communications were delivered by rider or sled, making any detailed management extraordinarily difficult. Understanding her limits, Catherine intended to give broad instructions to her field commanders, leaving ample room for discretion to the man on the scene.

Having settled on Russia's war aims, the War Council's next task was to amass enough soldiers to do the job. Calculating the size of an army necessary to defeat the Turks, the council settled on a conscription rate of one soldier for every three hundred souls. Accounting for likely rejects, sick, and garrison soldiers, the draft rate would yield an annual muster class of about 33,000 soldiers.

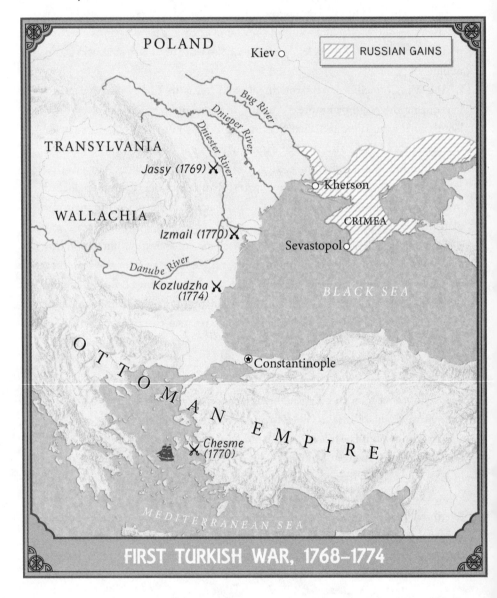

POLAND

Kiev o

RUSSIAN GAINS

Bug River

Dnieper River

Dniester River

TRANSYLVANIA

Jassy (1769) ✕

o Kherson

WALLACHIA

Izmail (1770) ✕

CRIMEA

Sevastopol o

Danube River

Kozludzha ✕
(1774)

BLACK SEA

O T T O M A N   E M P I R E

⊛ Constantinople

✕ Chesme
(1770)

MEDITERRANEAN SEA

FIRST TURKISH WAR, 1768–1774

Catherine and her council calculated that the new levies, when added to the standing army of 186,000, should be enough to move south, spread out, and subdue the Ottoman army. By early 1769, Russia was ready for war.

To offset the Ottoman advantage in numbers, Catherine seized the initiative. Before the Turks could launch a major offensive, she sent her 80,000-man First Army south along the Dniester River under command of General Alexander Golitsyn.

The result was not what Catherine hoped for. Golitsyn, not an energetic man at the best of times, moved slowly, and it took his army five months to capture its first major objective. Tiring of Golitsyn dragging his boot heels, in August Catherine stepped in and replaced him with General Peter Rumyantsev, a tall, spare man who, it was rumored, was a bastard son of Peter the Great.

The change of commanders flipped the war's dynamics. In a lightning campaign, Rumyantsev smashed Turkish and Tatar forces east of Transylvania, and his cavalry subordinate, Major General Grigory Potemkin, knifed through Wallachia like Vlad the Impaler. Rumyantsev then drove south toward the Danube River mouth. By August 1770, Rumyantsev had pushed back the enemy nearly two hundred miles from Russia's European borders.

Catherine's delight with the war's progress on land was tempered by her inability to make headway at sea. She began the war with no Black Sea harbor, so she had no Black Sea fleet. But she did have a navy in the Baltic Sea, on the north side of Europe, and acting on a suggestion by her lover, Grigory Orlov, she ordered her Baltic fleet of fifteen large warships—640 guns in all—to sail through the English Channel, around France and Spain, through the Mediterranean, past Italy and Greece, and into the Aegean Sea.

As her navy called at Spithead, Port Mahon, Livorno, and other anchorages on Europe's coast, Catherine envisioned a grand wheeling attack against Turkey that would let all of Western Europe know what Russia was capable of. In a playful mood, she wrote her ambassador to the Court of St. James, *"Et voilà qu'on a reveille le chat qui dormoit, et voilà que la chatte va courir sur les souris, et voilà que vous alles voir ce que vous verres, et voila qu'on parlera de nous, et voilà qu'on ne s'attendoit pas a tout le tintamare que nous ferons, et voila que les turcs seront battus . . ."**

In the summer of 1770, Catherine's admirals reached the Aegean and launched a violent attack against a larger Turkish fleet. They sank the Ottoman flagship in

---

* "And here we wake up the cat that slept, and here is the cat who will run on the mice, and here you go see what you see, and here we will talk of ourselves, and here the Turks will be beaten . . . "

open water and drove the rest into the small harbor of Chesme on the Turkish coast. The Russians followed up with a fireship attack against the tightly packed Turkish galleons. The cannonade and fireships lit the outer line of galleons, which erupted in spectacular orange balls as flames reached their powder magazines. Chesme, wrote a French observer, "became a volcano that engulfed the whole naval force of the Turks."

By the time the smoke drifted off Chesme's harbor, fourteen Turkish ships of the line had disintegrated, along with six frigates and fifty auxiliary ships. The blood of 11,000 Ottoman sailors ribboned the lapping waters; the Russians lost thirty men.

Chesme threw the Ottoman leadership into a panic. Overnight, the Aegean had become a Russian lake, and Catherine's commanders threw a loose blockade on Turkish merchant shipping. In St. Petersburg, the empress celebrated the victory with medals, the building of a beautiful pink-façade church, and cash awards to her senior commanders.

After two years of war, Catherine controlled a long swath of the Black Sea's northern shore. The next year, she sent her Second Army into the Crimean, and by the summer of 1771, her troops had driven the Turks off the peninsula. "At the risk of repeating myself or becoming a bore," Catherine wrote to Voltaire, "I have nothing to report to you but victories."

Yet those victories were in far off places. She did not tell Voltaire that at home the emotional lift of Chesme, the Danube, and Crimea was dampened by the war's gnawing cost. Troop levies were becoming a sore spot for Catherine's subjects, especially in the south, where conscription rates rose to feed the pyre. Her ministers drafted one out of every 300 subjects in 1768, then one in 150 over the next two years, then one in 100 in 1771, the war's third full year.

She also didn't advertise the embarrassing fact that her finances were growing thin. Field armies and fleets cost the empire between 12 and 21 million rubles per year to maintain—two-thirds of her government's revenues—and soldier pay was in arrears, which is never a healthy thing for an autocrat.

To meet these demands, Catherine was forced to replace coins with paper currency. Prices inevitably rose, and her finance ministers were compelled to borrow 4.8 million rubles from Flemish and Genoese bankers. Catherine took a deep breath and gambled that she could repay the loans from the spoils of war.

For a time, it seemed as if those spoils might soon be collected, for in July 1772, Sultan Mustafa opened peace talks with Russia. But sensing uneasiness in Vienna over Russia's resurgence, Mustafa dragged out negotiations while he secretly tried to persuade Maria Theresa's co-ruler and son, Emperor Joseph II, to declare war on

Russia. Joseph briefly considered going to war, but Catherine called his bluff by sending reinforcements into Poland. He thought better of it, and backed down.

The Austrian emperor was not the only one worrying about Catherine's designs on the south. Prussia's King Frederick, dreading the prospect of Russian troops massing near Berlin, proposed a compromise: The empires would keep the sultan's European borders intact, satisfy Catherine's right to spoils with Polish territory, and give a little something to the blessed peacemakers, Prussia and Austria. Catherine, he proposed, would take the eastern, heavily Orthodox portion of Poland. For staying out of the war, Austria would receive the southern Catholic portion, while Frederick would have the northwestern Lutheran part. Poland would be permitted to keep Warsaw, Krakow, and the middle two-thirds of its lands.

Frederick's pact required Austria to abandon her strategic ally, Turkey—a requirement the pious Maria Theresa claimed deep moral misgivings over even as her troops crossed Poland's southern border. Catherine and Frederick thought the archduchess more than a little hypocritical. Frederick told a friend, *"Elle pleure, mais elle prend toujours."* * Catherine dryly remarked, "My dear worthy Lady Prayerful has taken a bite out of Poland. It seems that in Poland one has only to stoop and help oneself."

Having invested so much in a Polish puppet king, Catherine was loath to dilute her returns by doling out pieces to Germans who had sat out the war. But as a German herself, she was sensitive to feelings in Berlin and Vienna, and power politics sometimes requires sharing slices of pie. When it is not one's own pie, it usually pays to be generous.

So, a deal was struck. Poland lost 81,000 square miles and a third of its population. Austria received the most populous share in the south. Prussia took East Prussia and other territories in the north, while Catherine acquired Livonia, Belorussia, and eastern Lithuania, adding about 1.3 million subjects to her empire. Poland's vivisection enabled the three sovereigns to breathe a little easier, and it made everyone happy except for the Turks. And the Poles.

Finalizing peace with Turkey proved frustrating. The sultan dug in his slippered heels and refused to agree to terms commensurate with his battlefield defeats. When he demanded heavy concessions, such as Ottoman sovereignty over Black Sea trade routes, his audacity roiled the Russian empress. "On no account do I wish that the Turks should dictate to me what ships I may or may not have on the Black Sea," she wrote her state council. "The Turks are beaten, it is not for them to lay down the law to us."

----

* "She cries, but she always takes."

Mustafa may have been beaten, but he wouldn't admit it. With the peace process stalled, in June 1774, Catherine sent another army over the Danube to break the deadlock. Leading a 10,000-man division, an eccentric major general named Alexander Suvorov shredded the sultan's main army at Kozludzha. Suvorov's victory placed a Russian army deep inside the Balkans, behind the sultan's main battle line, and nothing but a long march stood between Catherine's bayonets and Constantinople.

Sultan Mustafa died as Catherine unleashed Suvorov, and his successor, Sultan Abdul Hamid, had no interest in prolonging his brother's war. After Kozludzha, he resumed peace talks in earnest, and Catherine streamlined the negotiation process by giving General Rumyantsev authority to negotiate within broad parameters. With the long delays between the Danube and St. Petersburg eliminated, the envoys signed a treaty.

The sultan paid a stiff price for peace. His empire surrendered three Black Sea ports, opening a Russian trade route into the Mediterranean. The Crimean Khanate, an ancient Ottoman outpost, became an independent Russian protectorate, and the Porte agreed to pay Catherine a war debt of 4.5 million rubles.

Though long and expensive, the war with Turkey had been a smashing success. Catherine had conquered the Black Sea's north shoreline, swallowed up eastern Ukraine, and expanded her Polish holdings. And in defeating an ancient enemy, Catherine had restored prestige and honor to Russian arms on land and at sea.

As her ministers negotiated peace with Turkey, Catherine saw a time of tranquility just around the corner. But a band of illiterate, rough-hewn Cossacks, fired by a brutal life of virtual slavery, was about to give her a rude shock.

Pugachev

While Catherine lavished attention on the ideals of the Enlightenment, her subjects, far from the splendors of St. Petersburg, toiled in squalor. Peasants chafed under harsh rule of brutal landowners and petty nobility. Work in the fields, work in the mines, the knout, the lash—it made for a miserable life that seemed it could get no worse.

But it did. When war with Turkey forced the government to raise taxes and conscription rates, much of the blow fell on the broad backs of the peasantry. As Catherine fixed her eyes on her Danube and Black Sea campaigns, the steppes began to smolder.

In October 1773, in the southeastern province of Orenburg, a Cossack peasant from a Yaik River village rode among hamlets claiming to be Tsar Peter III, Russia's no-longer-dead emperor and Catherine's no-longer-dead husband. "Tsar Peter," whose real name was Yemelyan Pugachev, was an illiterate populist who won rural support by vowing to free the serfs, end taxation, and crush the nobility. "If God permits me to reach St. Petersburg," he announced in a dictated manifesto, "I shall put my wicked wife Catherine into a convent. Then I will free all the peasants and exterminate the nobles down to the last man."

The peasants liked what they heard, and Cossack tribes of the lower Volga flocked to Pugachev's crude banner. With 3,000 fighting men, he laid siege to the fortress town of Orenburg and established his base there. Serfs in local mines and factories seized metalwork and casting shops and killed their owners. By early 1774, nearly 6,000 armed peasants were on the march.

In St. Petersburg, Catherine and her ministers heard of the unrest, but did not take it seriously. Her eyes fixed on ending the war with Turkey, Catherine spared only a small battalion to put down the ruffians. Her detachments were overwhelmed and slaughtered by the rebels.

Victory begets confidence, and flushed with confidence, Pugachev's army moved through southern Russia like a plague of locusts, looting homes and murdering land-owners, families, and servants. Mothers and daughters, raped before the dying eyes of husbands and fathers, were carted into sexual servitude, only dimly thankful their own throats hadn't been slit. Prisoners were forced to swear fealty to "Tsar Peter" on pain of death, and Pugachev's army of willing and unwilling conscripts ballooned to nearly 15,000.

When the gravity of Pugachev's revolt finally dawned on Catherine, she had few soldiers to spare. Her victories over the Turks had been purchased with overstretched resources, and Pugachev had gathered momentum before she could scrape together a large body of troops, which she placed under General Alexander Bibikov.

In keeping with her command philosophy, Catherine gave Bibikov wide latitude to battle, arrest, investigate, and punish insurrectionists, so long as he did not resort to torture. The practice, in Catherine's view, was not only morally repugnant, but a notoriously inefficient means of finding the truth. "What need is there to flog during investigations?" she wrote Bibikov. "For twelve years the Secret Branch under my own eyes has not flogged a single person under interrogation, and every single affair has been properly sorted out."

Armed with these instructions, Bibikov moved rapidly against Orenburg, and in a set-piece battle he routed Pugachev's force. The pretender fled with his court of "nobles" to the Ural Mountains as Bibikov swept up rank and file subordinates.

Catherine treated captured rebels with as much leniency as she dared. She had a few minor ringleaders put to death, but most peasants were sent home with safe conduct passes and fifteen kopeks for travel expenses.

She saw no need for a wave of blood. To a friend from Hamburg who urged her to take harsh reprisals, she wrote, "Since you like hangings so much, I can tell you that four or five unfortunates have already been hanged. And the rarity of such punishments has a thousand times more effect on us here than on those where hangings happen every day."

❖   ❖   ❖

THE SOUTH REMAINED QUIET for three months, but like a ghost from the fog, Pugachev returned. In July 1774, he materialized outside the Volga city of Kazan with an army of 25,000. His rebels stormed the city and burned it to the ground, reveling in another orgy of rape, murder, torture, and looting. Pugachev boasted that he would soon be marching on Moscow and set his sights north.

The sack of Kazan shocked Catherine and her ministers. Two centuries earlier, its capture had been the crowning victory of Ivan the Terrible. Now it looked as though another bloodthirsty tsar would be marching in the opposite direction. Terrified Muscovites began packing their bags, while local leaders organized citizen brigades to prepare earthworks and muster militia to defend the ancient capital.

Catherine's most urgent need was to find a general who could stop Pugachev. Unfortunately, General Bibikov, her first choice, had died of fever and lacked Tsar Peter's evident powers of resurrection. As she cast about for Bibikov's replacement, her senior foreign policy advisor, Nikita Panin, suggested his retired brother, General Peter Panin. The general agreed, so long as he was given absolute power, military and civil, in southern Russia.

Catherine wasn't sure General Panin was the right man. A talented, occasionally brilliant military commander, he was also an eccentric prima donna who had been known to show up at headquarters wearing a gray satin nightgown and tall French cap with pink ribbons. Of deeper concern was his oft-expressed opinion that Russia would be better served with a man on the throne than a woman. After Panin retired, grumbling that his services in the Turkish war had not been adequately rewarded, Catherine had quietly ordered the Secret Branch to place him under surveillance.

Now the strange man who spoke so contemptuously of his queen wanted command of all military and civilian power in the south. Catherine winced at the thought of swallowing the bitter medicine.

Yet the needs of the empire trumped the sovereign's personal feelings, and sometimes leaders must work with people they despise. "Before the whole world, frightened of Pugachev, I commend and elevate above all mortals in the empire a prime big-mouth who insults me personally," Catherine grumbled to Grigory Potemkin.

She elevated the big-mouth, but managed to limit his authority to the areas directly affected by the uprising. She also kept the commission investigating the causes of the revolt under her personal control, lest its conclusion be tainted by Panin's chauvinist views.

Like cockroaches in a kitchen, Pugachev's band seemed impossible to destroy. When Panin's flying column defeated the rebel army at Kazan, Pugachev reappeared at the head of a new army. When that army was defeated, "Tsar Peter" fled down the Volga with a cadre of followers to rally a new mob.

Catherine knew she could not rest until Pugachev's head was separated from his shoulders, and she authorized Panin to assure local nobles that their privileges and safety would be guaranteed by Her Imperial Majesty if they would provide foot soldiers and supplies for Panin's army. The nobles, who were likely to be found hanging from trees if Panin lost, enthusiastically contributed, and Panin's veterans crushed another of Pugachev's mobs. Three weeks later, the pretender's remaining sycophants betrayed him and delivered Pugachev in chains to Panin, hoping to win clemency.

Panin locked Pugachev in an iron cage too small to stand in, then carted him over hundreds of bumpy miles to Moscow for trial. From St. Petersburg, Catherine quietly monitored the investigation into Pugachev's treason—refusing, as before, to condone torture. Interrogators concluded that Pugachev was a simple rogue, not the pawn of any foreign government, and Catherine wrote Voltaire that the evidence suggested Monsieur Pugachev was just a coward who, she promised, would die like one.

There was no doubt that Catherine would keep her promise. But she was acutely conscious of how her response to the rebellion would be interpreted at home and abroad. She publicly distanced herself from the trial of Pugachev and his lieutenants, and wrote to the official in charge, "Please help to inspire everyone with moderation both in the number and in the punishment of the criminals. The opposite will be regrettable to my love for humanity. We do not have to be clever to deal with barbarians."

The trial did not take long, and the court sentenced Pugachev to quartering while alive, followed by beheading. For Moscow officials, the sentence was complicated by Catherine's attitude toward capital punishment. "As regards executions, there must be no painful ones, and not more than three or four people," she had instructed her procurator general in Moscow.

But traitors are born to suffer, and when Pugachev's deputy received a similar sentence, one of the judges objected that Pugachev, as ringleader, should receive a harsher penalty than his lieutenants. Instead of keeping Pugachev's sentence at quartering and reducing the deputy's sentence to, say, a simple beheading, the judges went in the other direction and increased Pugachev's punishment to breaking on the wheel.*

The revised sentence ran contrary to Catherine's desire to avoid barbaric executions, and it took a great deal of persuasion by her procurator to get the local magistrates to leave Pugachev's sentence at quartering. Knowing Catherine would be furious if they made a grisly public spectacle over the rebel, the procurator quietly arranged to have the executioner "bungle" the sentence by chopping off Pugachev's head first, then lopping his hands and feet after he was dead.

Muscovites who came to watch Pugachev scream and flail as blood sprayed from his limbs were naturally disappointed, for quality entertainment was hard to come by. But Catherine wanted the sparks of rebellion stamped out without stirring up fresh ones. After four of Pugachev's top lieutenants were quartered, she issued a general amnesty, commuted several death sentences to hard labor, and exiled or pardoned the rest. She ordered Pugachev's home on the Don River burned to the ground, its ashes scattered, and forbade Pugachev's brother from using his family name. For good measure, she even changed the names of the capital, river, and Cossack tribe from whence Pugachev hailed.

In crushing Pugachev's revolt, Catherine had beaten back the most serious challenge to her authority. But the uprising convinced her that the serf class was an unstable element, oppressed for centuries and ready to rise up against even well-intentioned lawgivers. The monarchy, more than ever, must back benevolence with unchallengeable authority.

From now on, she would deal with threats from a position of strength.

Potemkin

Grigory Potemkin, the handsome Guards officer who offered Catherine his sword knot during her palace coup, had been her confidante and lover since early 1774. Catherine was thirty-three years old at the time, Potemkin ten years her junior. Blessed with thick reddish hair, an impish smile, and large, penetrating eyes, the

---

* Breaking on the wheel entailed smashing the condemned's arms and legs between spokes of a wagon wheel with a sledgehammer, sometimes threading the shattered limbs in and out of the spokes before training the hammer on the pelvis and chest. Usually, but not always, decapitation brought the victim's misery to an end.

"wittiest and most original eccentric of this iron century," as Catherine called him, captured the mind and heart of the empress and would hold both until his last breath.*

Potemkin's brilliant exploits as a cavalry commander in the Turkish War stood out, and after the first war ended, Catherine would appoint him as her viceroy of the south, prince of the empire, field marshal of the Russian Army, commander of the Black Sea fleet, and president of the War College. His responsibilities centered on the Black Sea and Danube regions, and in southern Russia he ruled as a king in all but name.

Of all Catherine's lovers entrusted with power, Potemkin was by far most talented. One Austrian visitor penned a vivid description of the frenetic prince: "I behold a commander-in-chief who looks idle and is always busy; who has no other desk than his knees, no other comb than his fingers; constantly reclined on his couch, yet sleeping neither in night nor in daytime," he wrote.

> *Easily disgusted, morose, inconstant, a profound philosopher, an able minister, a sublime politician, not revengeful, asking pardon for a pain he has inflicted, quickly repairing an injustice, thinking he loves God when he fears the Devil; waving one hand to the women who please him, and with the other making the sign of the cross, embracing the feet of a statue of the Virgin or the alabaster neck of his mistress.*

The womanizing, cross-signing prince shook up the strategic picture around the Black Sea four years after the war with Turkey ended by building a port and shipyard at Kherson on the lower Dnieper River, twenty miles from the Black Sea. A year later, he began laying down warship hulls. By 1782, Kherson boasted stone buildings, a fortress, barracks for 10,000 soldiers, and a mass of Greek merchant ships from the Aegean and Mediterranean Seas.

Potemkin did not stop with Kherson. He pleaded with Catherine to bring Crimea into the Russian Empire, writing her that if she would annex the region, "You will achieve immortal glory such as no other Sovereign of Russia ever had . . . With the Crimea will come domination of the Black Sea; it will be in your power to blockade the Turks, to feed them or to starve them."

---

* While Catherine acknowledged at least twelve lovers during her lifetime, her relationship with Potemkin was special. She referred to him as her husband in surviving letters, and it is possible the two were secretly married. For a year or more, until about 1776, they were physically intimate, and their emotional bond held until death parted them in 1791.

Though Catherine's religion and anti-Turkish policy aligned Russia with the Orthodox Greeks—her Aegean expedition in 1770 was partly to spur Greek revolt—she was skeptical of Potemkin's promises. She didn't need a second war with Turkey, and didn't want to attract the interest of western powers by upsetting the balance in the east. Watching and weighing the odds of intervention, her finger-feel for diplomacy told her to tread cautiously this time. For months, she refused to act.

Then, in late 1782, Potemkin showed up in St. Petersburg to plead his case. Crimea, he argued, would remain Russia's bleeding ulcer, an invitation to invasion, if she did nothing. And who in the world would stop Russia? The British were still at war with the French and Americans, while Constantinople was distracted by riots and plagues at home.

Catherine and Potemkin argued over the subject as only long-time lovers can, but eventually he met his burden of persuasion and won the jury's verdict. He had barely left for Kherson when a courier caught up to him with a letter that read, "We hereby declare our will for the annexation of the Crimea and the joining of it to the Russian Empire with full faith in you and being absolutely sure that you will not lose convenient time and opportune ways to fulfill this."

Potemkin occupied the Crimean Peninsula within a few months, and no sooner was the Romanov flag flying over the region than Potemkin launched one of history's greatest real estate developments. Recruiting thousands of immigrants, he built cities, roads, farms, shipyards, and government offices along the peninsular coast. In just over a decade, Crimea's population swelled from 52,000 to 130,000.

In a move the Ottoman Porte could hardly ignore, Potemkin built a second naval base on the peninsula's tip, called Sevastopol, and he commenced work on a seaport Catherine would later christen Odessa. By 1787, Russia's Black Sea fleet boasted twenty-four frigates and ships of the line. Catherine now commanded the world's fourth greatest naval fleet.*

THE EMPRESS HAD ALWAYS BEEN SHREWD at counting cards held by other rulers. When she first annexed Crimea in early 1783, she calculated that France and Britain were too preoccupied with the end of the American Revolution to oppose

---

* The three larger fleets, of Great Britain, Spain, and France, were preoccupied competing for dominance in the Atlantic and western Mediterranean.

her. Sweden, she guessed, would not move against Russia without French support, and Prussia would remain quiet so long as Austria supported Russia. Without the active support of one of the other major powers, Constantinople would have to swallow the humiliation of the Crimea's loss.

By 1786, however, the picture changed. The war between Britain, America, and France had ended. Prussia, Britain, and the Netherlands—all wary of Russia's rise—began forming an anti-Romanov alliance. If one or more great powers backed the Turkish sultan, the Ottoman Empire might react violently to Catherine's provocations of the last three years.

Catherine nonetheless felt a show of support for Potemkin was called for, so she decided to take a grand tour of the lands she, Potemkin, and the Russian people had spent blood and treasure developing. Perhaps she would even see a few guests along the way.

On the second day of 1787, Empress Catherine departed a snow-swept St. Petersburg in a large, ornately painted sledge. The salon's iron runners slid over snow in a convoy of 14 sled carriages, 124 sledges, and 560 fresh horses stationed at intervals along her route.

When ice on the Dnieper River broke in the spring, she and her entourage of 3,000 boarded a fleet of lavishly appointed barges and rode the Dnieper's lapping waves south. Prince Charles de Ligne, a roguish *bon vivant* among the cortege, dubbed the flotilla "Cleopatra's Fleet," and while Catherine had no Marc Antony to impress, she was aware that other kingdoms would be watching her. She obliged them with a show of wealth and power.

Arriving at Kaniev, an old city on the Polish-Ukrainian border, she met with Poland's King Stanislaus, her onetime lover and longtime puppet. It would be an awkward meeting, as she had once refused to give the king what he wanted most—her love—and forced him to accept a consolation prize he had no interest in: the Polish throne. Although Stanislaus's desires were now less ambitious, Catherine had little interest in substantive discussions and kept their meetings ceremonial. The two spoke cordially, Catherine said her goodbyes with embarrassing haste, and she moved on to see a more important guest.

Catherine and Austria's Emperor Joseph II traveled together to Kherson, Potemkin's port near the Black Sea, where they conferred in private about the Turkish menace, the Polish question, and the state of Austro-Russian relations. During their diplomatic arabesque, the two rulers christened three Russian warships, including one named the *St. Josef* after Catherine's royal guest. Lying at anchor nearby were another hundred or so merchant vessels whose cargo, when taxed, added considerable wealth to Russia's coffers.

Catherine's new battle squadron, plus a much larger fleet at Sevastopol, were berthed a two-day sail from the Ottoman capital of Constantinople, a city known to the ancients as Byzantium. Over Kherson's entrance, Potemkin erected an arch with a Greek inscription reading "This is the way to Byzantium."

The sultan in Byzantium found the statement ominous.

What did Catherine have in mind?

Abdul Hamid

Shortly after her return to St. Petersburg, Catherine was stunned to learn that her Crimean gambit had backfired. The Ottoman sultan, Abdul Hamid, issued an ultimatum: If Russia did not withdraw her troops from Crimea, the Ottoman Empire would declare war on Russia.

With her powerful Black Sea fleet and highly publicized meetings with the Austrian and Polish heads of state, Catherine had expected the Porte to tread lightly. But her fleet, which could reach Constantinople, had backed the Turkish tiger into a corner. The Turk was doing what cornered tigers do.

Unwilling to let the sultan strike first, in August 1787, Catherine declared war and placed Potemkin in command of all Russian forces in the south. Potemkin's primary objective would be to capture the massive Turkish fortress of Ochakov, whose guns controlled the mouth of the Dnieper River and prevented Catherine's fleet from debauching into the Black Sea. After taking Ochakov, Potemkin would march southwest, extending Russia's hold on the sea's western coast.

To shorten his lines and provide more troops along the Dnieper, Potemkin sent Catherine a letter proposing to evacuate the Crimea. While she usually deferred to her military experts, on this occasion political considerations, of which she was mistress, trumped military strategy. She rejected Potemkin's plan: A withdrawal from Crimea, even if militarily prudent, would make Russia look weak. With Vienna, Berlin, and Warsaw staring intently at a second Russo-Turkish war, she could not afford to appear impotent. They had to hold the Crimean.

The Turks struck first, but, fortunately for Catherine, the Ottoman generals botched the job. They sent troops by boat against the Russian fort at Kinburn, but when the sultan's men jumped from their barges and slogged onto the beach, they found General Suvorov and his men waiting for them. With a wicked bayonet charge that left the surf pink, Suvorov's infantry drove the invaders into the sea.

While Kinburn was a heartening win, a violent gale ripped through the Russian fleet as it weighed anchor from Sevastopol. One of Potemkin's prized warships went to the bottom; others lost masts, yards, men, and guns in the blow.

The gale also blew the mercurial Potemkin into a black pool of depression, and in a fit of despair he wrote his queen to offer his resignation. "Lady Matushka, I've become unlucky," he moaned.* Because lucky commanders are more valuable than good ones, he urged her to give command in the south to someone else.

Catherine and Potemkin had a special dynamic, and she sensed the prince's letter was more for effect than genuine. In a long letter she shook Potemkin to his senses. "You are impatient as a five-year-old child," she scolded him. "Affairs of which you are now in charge require an imperturbable patience." He should let the dust settle before concluding that the sky was falling.

Catherine's intimacy with Potemkin allowed her to be blunt. But she also knew her sullen prince, like any man, needed a pep talk from time to time, and this was one of those times. To her letter she added a hopeful guess—correctly, it turned out—that the sea storm had been just as devastating to the Turkish fleet. Before closing her letter, she assured him, "My friend, neither time nor distance, nor anyone in the world will change my thoughts of you and about you."

Catherine's faith in her distant friend was rewarded at the end of 1788, when Suvorov and Potemkin took Ochakov in a storm of bayonets and grapeshot. Russian troops breached the walls and massacred the inhabitants "like a strong whirlwind that in a moment tossed people onto their hearses," Potemkin wrote.

The capture of Ochakov opened the Black Sea's northwest coast to Russian advance, and Suvorov and Potemkin made the most of their opportunity. Under Potemkin's strategic direction, Suvorov drove down the Danube River to Izmail, the most heavily defended fortress in Europe. Laying siege with 30,000 men, he stormed the walls in a furious attack. Streams of blood marked lines where defenders clashed with attackers, and the fortress, with its 40,000 men, women, and children, fell to Suvorov's dripping bayonets.

Gustavus

As she waited for Ochakov to fall, Catherine received a nasty shock from an unexpected quarter. King Gustavus III of Sweden, her first cousin, had long dreamed of recovering Scandinavian lands Peter the Great had conquered in the early 1700s.

---

* "Little Mother."

Unpopular at home and egged on by ministers from Britain, Prussia, and the Netherlands, Gustavus saw his moment of military glory while Catherine's troops were fighting the Turks in the south.

He began by sending St. Petersburg an ultimatum demanding that Russia return Finland, accept Sweden's mediation of the Second Turkish War, and give all territory won in the First Turkish War back to the sultan. If Catherine refused, Sweden would invade Russia and seize St. Petersburg. Gustavus boasted to his court that he would eat breakfast at Peterhof, Peter the Great's gilded palace, then dictate peace terms from Peter's throne.

To a puzzled Catherine, the king's message was almost grotesque in its arrogance. Coming from a peacock whose own throne was wobbling, Gustavus's demand seemed surreal. Shaking her head in wonder, she wrote Potemkin, "What have I done that God should choose to chastise me with such a feeble instrument as the king of Sweden?"

With a sigh, she summoned the War Council and went back to her maps. Another war it would be.

Though Catherine had little regard for her Swedish cousin, a war to the north was no laughing matter. The bulk of her armies were a thousand miles away, and her capital, on the Baltic seacoast, lay vulnerable to amphibious attack. Power is a matter of perception more than might, and a solid defeat outside St. Petersburg would threaten Catherine's hold on the Russian empire, perhaps even her life.

But Gustavus was no master of war, and his first major attack in July of 1788 ended in a draw. For two years neither monarch wrested any strategic advantage. Catherine held Finland, but at one frightening moment the Swedish fleet sailed through the Neva River estuary and anchored within cannon range of St. Petersburg. Keeping her composure, Catherine began one letter to an officer at Potemkin's headquarters, "Amidst the roar of cannon, which shakes her windows, your Imperturbable writes to you."

Every day Catherine remained Imperturbable plucked another leaf from Gustavus's laurel wreath. His war of opportunism was deeply unpopular at home. His government was racking up huge war debts, and the Danes, egged on by Catherine's diplomats, were preparing to attack his western border. Gustavus had run out of time to make good his boast of breakfasting at Peterhof, and he began looking for a way out.

Catherine wished to press her advantage, but the strategic picture was turning against Russia. Her successes against the Turks and Swedes had shaken the balance of power in Eastern Europe. The Poles longed to drive out Catherine's puppet government, and Prussia's King Frederick Wilhelm II, the dough-faced successor to Frederick the Great, moved his forces east in an implied threat to Catherine's Polish holdings. British ministers, trying as always to preserve the power balance, bribed Sweden to remain in the war and promised the Ottoman Porte that Britain would deploy a fleet to keep Catherine pinned down in the north. But as the great powers lined up against Catherine, she remained defiant.

Potemkin returned to St. Petersburg and pleaded with Catherine to accept the diplomatic reality. Russia, though militarily powerful, was strategically isolated. At the very least, she should ensure peace with Prussia, perhaps by offering Frederick Wilhelm more of Poland's lands. A treaty with Berlin, Potemkin argued, would free up Russia's northern garrisons and force the sultan to end the war in the south. After those wars were over, Catherine could return to Poland and Prussia at her leisure.

Catherine refused. Sweden had gained nothing in the north, and she had been living with victories for so long she had little concept of a real thrashing—or what one might mean to the empire. At a personal level, she also could not stand the thought of bowing to a fat, dim-witted upstart like Frederick Wilhelm.

Her refusal to take Potemkin's medicine sparked bitter rows with her former lover. In the royal apartments they argued like an old married couple. Catherine shed bitter tears and took to her bed, while Potemkin threw tantrums, slammed doors, chewed his nails, and threatened to resign.

But Catherine and Potemkin were consummate political actors, even with each other, and neither outburst was entirely sincere. Looking over maps and military reports in the privacy of her chambers, Catherine glumly admitted to herself that Russia could not take on Turkey, Sweden, Britain, Poland, and Prussia simultaneously. She would have to choose her battles. And her treaties.

She spurred her ministers to carry Stockholm across the peace threshold. Her agents bribed Denmark into declaring war on Sweden, and under the pressure of two-front wars, in August 1790, the royal cousins concluded a peace. Both sides agreed to return to the boundaries of June 1788. With that, a rather pointless war was consigned to history's dustbin.

"We have pulled one paw out of the mud," a relieved Catherine wrote Potemkin. "As soon as we pull out the other, we'll sing 'Hallelujah.'"

She extracted her other paw in January 1792, when Sultan Selim III, Abdul Hamid's successor, signed his own peace treaty. The Porte acknowledged Catherine's hegemony over Crimea and the northern Black Sea coast, and ceded territory to Russia between the Bug and Dniester Rivers.

Russia could now boast a warm-water port, a naval presence in the Black Sea, and a dominant hand in Eastern Europe.

But domination invites challenge, as Catherine was about to relearn.

Kosciuszko

Catherine's standard strategy was to push her enemies into declaring war, then win the war and extract concessions at the peace table. Knowing the limits of her power, she avoided entanglements outside Eastern Europe or the Caucasus, both of which she considered Russia's natural sphere of influence.*

But in 1789, the revolutionary fever Catherine had feared since the Pugachev revolt began infecting Europe. A year after the Americans ratified their republican constitution, French radicals toppled King Louis XVI and his wife, Marie Antoinette, and established a constitutional monarchy. Three years later, Sweden's King Gustavus was assassinated—by revolutionaries, Catherine believed—and in Paris a mob seized and imprisoned the deposed royal couple.

The collapse of monarchy in the home of the Enlightenment hit Catherine like a blow to the chin. "It's a veritable anarchy," she wrote as flames of revolution spread through France. "They are capable of hanging their king from a lamppost!" The Jacobin leaders, she said, "set in motion a machine which they lack the talent and skill to control."

The idealistic young *philosophe* who corresponded in French now saw her intellectual homeland become a nest of hissing cobras. The once-respected kingdom, she wrote, had fallen prey to "a crowd of lawyers, fools masquerading as philosophers, rascals, young prigs destitute of common sense, puppets of a few bandits who do not even deserve the title of illustrious criminals."

As the rascals and prigs debated what to do with the imprisoned Louis and Marie Antoinette, a new test of wills flared over Poland. Frederick Wilhelm of Prussia, worried as always about Catherine's designs, signed a defensive treaty with Warsaw pledging to come to Poland's aid in the event of Russian invasion. Wilhelm backed his pledge with an 88,000-man army that would remain on the Prussian side of the border until needed.

---

* She once declined requests by England's King George III for Russian soldiers to help put down rebels in his American colonies—a decision vindicated when France recognized American independence and the colonists drove out the redcoats.

The pact heartened Polish nationalists, and the following year emboldened Poles rolled back the weak constitutional system that Catherine had forced on King Stanislaus. Like the early French revolutionaries, they declared Poland a constitutional monarchy. Slowly, clumsily, Poland was struggling out of its winding sheet.

But Polish timing was terrible, as its chief backers, Prussia and Austria, were turning their attention to revolutionary France, a fixation Catherine encouraged. "I am breaking my head to push the courts of Vienna and Berlin to involve themselves in the affairs of France," she confided to her private secretary. "I have much unfinished business, and it's necessary for them to be kept busy and out of my way."

In April 1792, the French revolutionary government declared war on Austria. Studying the angles like Archimedes, Catherine concluded the moment to invade Poland had come. Prussia and Austria would howl, but they would do nothing while bloodthirsty Jacobins were pounding at their western doors. Austria's new king, Francis II, would be fighting for his life, and Frederick Wilhelm would likely renege on his promise to defend Poland and shift his army to support Austria. The "half wills" of the German states, she said, "will only oppose us with a pile of written paper and we will finish our affairs ourselves."

A month after the French launched their war, Catherine sent 65,000 Russian troops across the Polish frontier. The Prussian king did exactly as Catherine had predicted: He protested vigorously, but found a loophole in his treaty that permitted Prussia to sit out the war.

Poland stood alone.

A shaken King Stanislaus assured his subjects that he intended to fight for the new constitution. But he had few soldiers and knew he could not win a war against his former lover. He sent a secret emissary to Catherine, offering to abdicate in favor of her grandson if she would call off her invasion.

Catherine had no interest in a Russian puppet king in Warsaw. She wanted a Polish puppet king, which she had, and refused to accept Stanislaus's resignation.

Again Russians marched into Warsaw. Again Poles laid down their feeble arms. Again Catherine's army occupied Poland, and again she relieved the commonwealth of prime land. In January 1793, she and Frederick Wilhelm signed a secret treaty, helping themselves to yet more slabs of rich Polish soil.

With another quill stroke, and 65,000 troops, Catherine acquired over 100,000 square miles of eastern Poland, swallowing parts of Belorussia, Lithuania, and western Ukraine. Another 3 million Poles became subjects of the Romanov crown.

❖   ❖   ❖

THE POLES did not make happy Russian subjects, and like a wolf stalking through the forest, the revolutionary fervor that Catherine dreaded crept closer to Russia's door. Less than two years after her partition with Prussia, the Polish tinderbox again burst into flames. Thaddeus Kosciuszko, a Polish officer who had fought with George Washington, raised 6,000 soldiers and declared an end to foreign dominance in Poland. He routed 7,000 of Catherine's troops near Krakow, killing or capturing 3,000. Dead Russians were stripped, their naked bodies thrown into the streets, while Kosciuszko denounced Catherine as an enemy of the Polish people.

A truculent Catherine wrote Frederick Wilhelm that the time had come "to extinguish the last spark of the Jacobin fire in Poland." She persuaded the Prussian king to invade Poland from the west, and sent General Suvorov to crush the revolt from the east.

In the fall of 1794, Suvorov's corps of 13,000 men annihilated Kosciuszko's army. Kosciuszko was captured and sent to Schlüsselburg Fortress. Reinforced from the east, Suvorov moved against Praga, a suburb of Warsaw, defended by Poland's main force of 30,000 soldiers and 104 cannon. Four hours after launching his assault, Suvorov emerged victorious. Blood flowed through Praga's gutters as 20,000 Poles were massacred by Russian troops or drowned trying to cross the Vistula River to safety.

With the brutal lesson of Praga reverberating through the countryside, Warsaw meekly surrendered, and the embers of revolt were coldly doused. Suvorov's report to Catherine consisted of three words: *"Ура, Варшава наша!"* ("Hurrah, Warsaw is ours!"). Catherine undercut her favorite general by one word in her reply announcing his promotion: *"Ура, фельдмаршал!"* ("Hurrah, Field-Marshal!").

From the war's first shots, Catherine had concluded that Poland could no longer be permitted to exist. In the past it had quietly supported Sweden, Turkey, Prussia, and other anti-Russian belligerents, and any republican ideals that took root in that ill-governed land might infect her subjects to the east.

She negotiated the final partition of Poland with her old partners, Prussia and Austria. This time, she took Courland, the rest of Lithuania, the rest of Belorussia, and the rest of Ukraine. Austria received Poland's remaining southern regions, and Prussia occupied Warsaw and western Poland.

Poland ceased to exist.*

---

* It would be more than a century before Poland reemerged from the ashes of the First World War. A child of the Treaty of Versailles, Poland would again suffer a Russo-German partition in 1939, when Josef Stalin and Adolf Hitler carved up the forlorn country.

Agha Mohammad

By age sixty-seven, Catherine's old fire had mellowed to a warm, amber glow. The chestnut hair of her coup had turned white, her waist had grown thick, and dentures filled gaps in her teeth. Plagued with headaches, flatulence, colds, and rheumatism, the lioness in winter squinted through reading glasses as she read reports and wrote correspondence. Echoing George Washington's famous words, she apologized to a secretary, "Our sight has been blunted by long service to the State, and now we have to use spectacles."

Yet her mental rapier remained sharp, and the years had done nothing to blunt her work ethic. She still began each morning at six o'clock by taking her English greyhounds outside. Working from her writing desk, in the course of each morning she drank four or five cups of black coffee, each pot brewed from a pound of beans. Well into the afternoon she blunted quill tips over sheaves of official papers, correspondence, and replies to confidential reports.

Catherine's last military adventure was typical of her warmaking style. Back in 1783, the empress had taken advantage of instability within the Persian kingdom to expand Russia's hand in the Caucasus. She and the king of Georgia had signed a treaty making Georgia, a Persian tributary, into a Russian protectorate. But in 1794, a new Persian shah, Agha Mohammad Khan, ascended the Peacock Throne. The following year he launched a savage invasion of Georgia, laying waste to the kingdom's villages and burning its capital, Tbilisi, to the ground.

Catherine was treaty-bound to defend Georgia, but she sensed an opportunity to do more than mechanically eject the Persian raiders. She had cultivated a Persian puppet, the shah's half-brother, and sent a 50,000-man army through Georgia and Azerbaijan with the object of installing a new shah in Tehran.

On November 4, 1796, as her army was poised to invade Persia, Catherine's servants found the empress unconscious, the victim of a sudden, massive stroke. She lingered *in exteremis* and her breath came in short, labored gasps. Doctors informed her son Paul that the end was near, and the long-faced metropolitan of St. Petersburg arrived to administer the empress her last rites.

"Gentlemen," announced a courtier to a group gathered in Catherine's antechamber a short time later, "the Empress Catherine is dead and His Majesty Paul Petrovich has deigned to mount the throne of all Russias."

❖   ❖   ❖

IN THE CENTURIES TO COME, few outside Russia would recognize the name Sophia of Anhalt-Zerbst, the young Pomeranian girl torn from her family and hurled into a world of palace intrigues and family feuds. Indeed, the woman in the marble tomb marked "Ekaterina II" would have hardly recognized the young, abused woman.

But all Europe knew the name she carried into history, a sobriquet she refused in life: Catherine the Great. Her indirect approach to grand strategy, drive to expand her empire, and gambler's instinct would leave a defining mark on Russia's psyche as the rest of the world lurched into an era Catherine fundamentally distrusted: the rise of democracy.

ACT IV

MAPS AND LEGENDS

❖   ❖   ❖

And Man knows it! Knows moreover, that the Woman that God gave him,
Must command but may not govern—shall enthrall but not enslave him.
And She knows, because She warns him, and Her instincts never fail,
That the Female of Her Species is more deadly than the Male.

—Kipling

Warrior queens of the nineteenth century tended to be rebels with short careers. Yaa Asantewaa of Ghana's Ashanti tribe and Rani Lakshmibai of Jhansi, India, broke their spears against a British Empire armed with large-caliber Martini-Henry rifles and the Maxim gun.

The machine against which these latter-day Boudicas raged was led by men. Queen Victoria, the dominant empress, had transferred most of her warmaking authority to a constitutional system dominated by gentlemen in dark suits and top hats. Russia, Germany, Austria, France, Japan, the United States: the same. Men voted, women did not. Men led, women followed. In war's newfangled horseless carriage, men still crowded the driver's seat.

But the world was changing, and so was war. The armies of Catherine the Great had marched no faster than those of Alexander the Great. Then the telegraph, railroad, assembly line, rifle cartridge, and high explosives magnified the speed, complexity, and cost of nineteenth-century warfare. Wars became enormously expensive ventures in which entire nations mobilized their human and material capital, subjecting their leaders to new stress tests that oft exceeded their abilities.

As the twentieth century dawned, the old empires found themselves stretched like prisoners on history's rack. In India, southern Africa, Ireland, and the Far East, Britannia found herself pelted with speeches, strikes, spears, and bullets. If the Ottoman Empire was the sick old man of Europe, Maria Theresa's Austria-Hungary, torn by ethnic violence, was its sick old matron. Catherine's Russian empire died a violent death in 1917, to be reborn as the *enfant terrible* of Lenin and Stalin, while the would-be empires of Bismarck and Louis Napoleon withered in the heat of the First World War. The order of a thousand years was giving way to a new, dynamic, and uncertain world.

From the seismic upheavals of a global depression and two World Wars, leaders of the late twentieth century—a time of independence movements, terrorism, women's liberation, technology, and democracy—began picking up pieces of the *ancien regime*. Democracy resculpted the power of a female leader by creating a succession plan that did not pivot on the fertility of her womb. Transition of power became routine, and lineage, at least in theory, didn't count. By the late 1960s, a woman from a middle-class family could succeed a man from an aristocratic line without inflicting serious harm on the realm.

As a result, women born outside royal lines enjoyed an upward mobility that Manduhai, Elizabeth, and Njinga would have found disturbing. The new breed had not been trained from childhood to commune with gods or command legions. Cleopatra ruled as Isis; Tamar's throne was her birthright. But Indira Gandhi, Golda Meir, Benazir Bhutto, and Margaret Thatcher—women leading nuclear-armed states—as well as regional leaders like Corazón Aquino of the Philippines, Yugoslavia's Milka Planinc, Germany's Angela Merkel, Nicaragua's Violeta Chamorro, Ukraine's Yulia Tymoshenko, and Liberia's Ellen Johnson-Sirleaf, took power through the ballot box.

As the rules governing power changed, so did norms of warfare. Principles of self-determination and human rights elbowed their way into the *realpolitik* of Metternich and Bismarck. By the late twentieth century, nations could still launch attacks outside their borders, but they could not sustain violence for long without the patronage of a superpower and a cloak of diplomatic legitimacy. War was not exactly a dead relic of our unenlightened past, but after the Second World War it could only be used sparingly, and in the right circumstances.

As dust settled over the graves of Hitler, Tojo, and Stalin, three women found their moments of decision on the battlefield. The wars of a yoga practitioner, an almond farmer, and a plastics chemist follow in our final act.

11

RED DURGA

India's Indira Gandhi

"In a war it is not possible to vacillate or to be weak or to play the role of Hamlet. One has to be really ruthless if the need arises."
—INDIRA GANDHI, 1972

BELOW CALCUTTA'S BLAZING SUN her hazel eyes swept a sea of dark faces. Twenty thousand Hindis of every age and caste packed the parade ground to catch a glimpse of the woman who ruled the land of the rajas.

Standing before a bulbous microphone, draped in a patterned *sari*, Indira Nehru Gandhi launched into a speech praising the people of neighboring Bangladesh. Lauding their resistance to West Pakistan's campaign of rape, terror, and genocide, she vowed to back their cause with the support of the world's biggest democracy. Bangladeshi refugees who had been flooding over India's eastern border would soon have homes to return to, she promised.

Indira knew the risks she was courting, and asked her people to accept those risks. "India stands for peace," she declared. "But if a war is thrust upon us we are prepared to fight."

As the throng roared in approval, an aide stepped to her side. Indira leaned away from the microphone as the aide slipped her a note. She paused, looking down at the message as the cheers faded.

The aide stepped away and she resumed her speech. Hastily wrapping up her remarks, she left the podium with a smile and a wave, then ducked into a waiting car with a worried-looking entourage.

❖   ❖   ❖

INDIRA GREW UP the skinny, lonely daughter of Jawaharlal Nehru, a leader in the independence movement led by India's spiritual father, Mahatma Gandhi. Socialist and anti-colonial activism landed her parents in prison several times, leaving scars on their daughter they seemed not to notice.

"If you only know what it did to me to have lived in a house where the police were bursting in to take everyone away!" she told an interviewer years later. "I was a thin, sickly, nervous little girl. And after the police came, I'd be left alone for weeks, months, to get along as best I could."

Her mother, plagued by poor health, died when Indira was eighteen. With no mother and a father in and out of British jails, Indira's family packed her off to attend school in England. She studied at Oxford's Somerville College and returned to India four years later with a fiancé: Feroze Gandhi, a student from her hometown of Allahabad.*

Indira and Feroze married in 1942 and plunged into anti-colonial activism under the leadership of Mahatma Gandhi—"Bapu," or "Father" to his followers—and Indira's father Nehru. The newlyweds were promptly arrested by British officials, and Indira spent eight months in an Allahabad jail. But after their release the couple settled down and began raising two sons, Rajiv and Sanjay.

The convulsions of the Second World War, and the nonviolent protests of Bapu and Nehru, forced Prime Minister Clement Atlee's British government to recognize Indian independence in 1947. Nehru, India's first prime minister, brought Indira to the capital of New Delhi, and from the center of the world's largest democracy Indira received her education in power politics.

As independence fever matured and the business of running government took root, Nehru led India's ruling political faction, the socialist-leaning Congress Parliamentary Party. In Parliament's lower house, the *Lok Sabha*, Nehru worked the levers of power, standing out in crowded hallways, a red rose threaded through a buttonhole of his trademark *sherwani* suit. If Bapu was India's spiritual father, Nehru's image as its secular father was enhanced by the presence of his attractive, intelligent daughter.

Indira served as her father's hostess, personal assistant, and eyes and ears beyond the capital. Her voice, melodic and low, offset two deep, umber eyes and an

---

* Feroze Gandhi was no relation to Mahatma Gandhi. He changed the spelling of his last name of "Ghandy" to conform to that of the Indian leader after joining the Indian independence movement. The name coincidence would serve Indira well.

intriguing smile. Her ink-black hair, pulled up in a Jacqueline Onassis–style bouf-
fant, hinted at a modern, feminine look that complemented her father's old-
school persona.

Her energy bloomed when visiting Hindu and Muslim refugee camps in India's
northwestern regions, where she assisted workers in managing food distribution to
the hungry. An exacting administrator, she found her voice speaking to people facing poverty, disaster, and death. Her calm, no-nonsense bedside manner revealed a
woman who could show empathy without developing a crippling attachment to
victims of ill fate.

Though she was an appealing foil to her father, for most of her life Indira had
been pushed off the political ladder because of her youth and gender. But she cultivated a political base during her father's premiership and adopted the persona of
dutiful but reluctant daughter, disclaiming an ambition she inwardly nursed. Following the death of her husband in 1960, and of her beloved father four years later,
Indira firmly placed her small foot on the ladder's first rung.

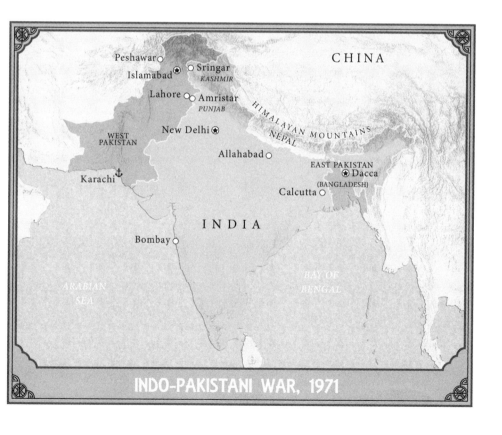

INDO-PAKISTANI WAR, 1971

❖   ❖   ❖

THE LAND OF RAJAS had embraced Hinduism since the time when Homer recounted the fall of Troy. But the Muslim tide of the Middle Ages left eddies that pooled in India's western and eastern regions. In those eddies, temples were destroyed, rebuilt, and destroyed again. Indian faithful, encouraged by their colonial rulers, formed into camps where religion, as in the days of Queen Elizabeth, dictates one's identity. And one's grievances.

When the British acceded to Indian self-rule in 1947, they carved the subcontinent into sections like meat on a bull. Lines drawn by an English barrister who had never previously been east of Gibraltar created borders based on the two prevailing religions, paying little thought to subtle differences or to other faiths, such as Sikh, Buddhist, or Christian.

India's far west—Baluchistan, Sind, the Punjab, and the Northwest Frontier—were mostly Muslim, so the British amalgamated them into a region called West Pakistan. India's eastern extreme was also predominately Muslim, so it became East Pakistan. To keep Muslims and Hindus together, the British combined West and East Pakistan into a single nation consisting of two Muslim regions 1,300 miles apart, separated by a land inhabited by millions of Hindus.

In Kashmir on the northwest, home to 12 million inhabitants living on the windswept slopes of the Himalayas, the British left the border dangerously vague. The mystical region was subject to conflicting claims by China, Pakistan, and India, and it rumbled with ethnic violence that claimed a half million lives after partition.

In 1962, Chinese troops redrew Kashmir's borders with the barrel of an AK-47, occupying fifty kilometers of Indian territory. The invasion forced Nehru, a pacifist at heart, to modernize his military establishment, and he purchased large stocks of modern weapons from the Soviet Union. While he remained "nonaligned" between the capitalist and communist worlds until his death in 1964, he knew that in the bipolar world of the Cold War, India's growing population and economy would create irresistible pressures to declare for either the Soviet Union or the United States.

In the spring of 1965, a series of Indo-Pakistani border skirmishes in the Kashmiri mountains led India's second prime minister, Lal Bahadur Shastri, to launch a full-scale offensive in West Pakistan. When war broke out, Indira was serving as Minister of Information and Broadcasting. While her role in the month-long war was largely symbolic, it elevated her public profile. She toured the front, gave defiant speeches, visited wounded soldiers, and served as the face of Indian resolve.

With the fire of independence a thing of the past, India was undergoing a time of malaise, and voters were dissatisfied with their hidebound ministers. Indira stood out as the energetic, enthusiastic exception. The Indian press began referring to her as "the only man in a cabinet full of old women," and the adulation heaped on Indira infuriated Prime Minister Shastri.

The feeling was mutual. To Indira, the moderate Shastri was a scrunch-faced caricature of a middle-aged Indian man who erased her father's legacy with every step he took away from socialism and nonalignment. In public, she played the carefully scripted role of India's loving mother, but behind the scenes a circle of supporters—many of them major political figures—fed her belief that she, not Shastri, held the key to India's future.

When the doors closed and the microphones were flipped off, she could be a ruthless political competitor with little interest in compromise or winning friends. As one of her political foes put it, "She would ally herself with the Devil if she thought it served her purpose."

Some of this impression stemmed from Indira's refusal to engage in idle chat. Her long pauses and sharp, sometimes condescending stare rattled her conversation partners, putting them off-balance. "I don't waste time in flowery small talk, as people do in India, where the first half hour is spent in compliments," she admitted to an interviewer. "When I say, 'Hurry up, let's get to the point,' they feel hurt."

Her secular humanism also put off many constituents, who felt she overlooked the role of religion in India's pluralistic society. She did not wholly disagree with them. "I don't go to temples and pray to the gods or anything like that," she explained. "If by religion we mean a belief in humanity rather than the gods, an effort to make man better and a little happier, then yes, I'm very religious."

But to traditionalists, praying to gods in temples was a core value that brought together the land of 1,600 dialects and a half-billion people.

Indira didn't serve under Shastri much longer, for reasons no one but the god Yama would have predicted. In January 1966, the exhausted prime minister suffered a massive heart attack and shuffled into his next life, leaving a power vacuum in New Delhi that Indira quickly leapt into. Yanking supporters into her coalition, Indira's train gained steam, and the Congress Party elected her as its leader, making her prime minister of India.

"LONG LIVE THE RED ROSE!" chanted a huge crowd that greeted her as she emerged from the parliamentary building. The reference to her father's famous boutonniere hinted at a new period of energy at home and respect abroad.

But in the first months of her premiership, it was unclear whether Indira would survive the next general election. Food shortages plagued the country and religious riots scarred cities like New Delhi, Ludhiana, and Bhiwani. Stabilizing a nation struggling to crawl out of postcolonial mire required Indira to beg for food aid abroad and make difficult choices over food production at home.

Indira made her first official trip to the United States in March 1966. The intriguing woman with the white-streaked hair took Washington by storm and wowed the American press and public. She also thoroughly charmed President Lyndon Johnson. Beaming for the cameras, she returned to New Delhi with a promise of 3.5 million tons of badly needed wheat and over $200 million in foreign aid.

"India is a good and deserving friend," President Johnson told Congress in his Texas Hill Country drawl. "Let it never be said that bread should be so dear and flesh and blood so cheap that we turned in indifference from her bitter need."

But Johnson's helping hand cost Indira among the leftist Indian press that viewed America, then mired in Vietnam, as a neocolonial empire little better than the British. Critics denounced Indira for cozying up to the American imperialists, forcing her to do some backtracking. But when she publicly called the United States an imperialist power, President Johnson, feeling personally betrayed, slapped tight restrictions on future US foreign aid, erasing much of the victory she had won in Washington.

Indira made another unforced error that year. To help feed her people, she brushed off calls from religious leaders to outlaw the slaughter of cows, which are sacred to Hindus. Failing to appreciate the backlash her beef policy would unleash, riots among the devout caught her flat-footed. When a caste Hindu mob threatened to storm the Lok Sabha, she reluctantly sent in troops to put down the demonstrations. Seven rioters and a policeman were killed, and the popular outcry forced Indira's Home Minister to resign.

Part of Indira's way of coping with the challenges of governing was to adhere to a strict personal regimen. "I am very fit," she told a journalist. "The first thing in the morning, at five o'clock, I do my yoga exercises for fifteen or twenty minutes." When she put on weight, she lost it. After menopause, she adhered to a healthy diet, took vitamins, and abstained from alcohol. She dyed her hair when it went gray, although her Parisian hairdresser left a distinctive white streak rising from her brow. That shock of white became as much her trademark as Winston Churchill's cigar or John F. Kennedy's Ray-Ban sunglasses.

The weakness in her health regimen, if any, was lack of sleep. She rarely slept more than five or six hours a night before getting up to practice yoga and begin another exhausting workday. But she refreshed herself throughout the day by taking short catnaps, the sort Napoleon, Salvador Dalí, and Albert Einstein were famous for. She renewed her mind by drawing herself inward, away from the pressures of the outside world.

Indira once asked an interviewer if he had seen newspaper reports of "large voids in the universe" that scientists were discovering. "I have always felt that within you, within a person, you have such voids, and you can retire into them without disrupting yourself," she mused. "You may be having a conversation or you may be in a crowd. But if you want to retire into yourself, you can retire and you can do almost anything you like . . . That is why you can't get tired, because you are automatically relaxing yourself."

She did a lot of retiring into herself as she spent her next few years fighting to survive domestic and political unrest. Her work paid off in the national elections of March 1971, when her wing of the Congress Party swept nearly two-thirds of the Lok Sabha's seats—a sea change for which Indira, a tireless election campaigner, received the lion's share of the credit.

The landslide allowed Indira to make policy decisions without looking over her shoulder. A coterie of northwestern loyalists, nicknamed the "Kashmiri mafia," formed a kitchen cabinet that dominated domestic and foreign policy. Centralizing military decision-making, Indira abolished the Defence Committee of the cabinet and directly consulted with General "Sam" Manekshaw, chairman of the Chiefs of Staff Committee, whenever she needed advice on military matters.

She would need that advice, for during the month of her electoral masterstroke, a fresh threat rose. Muslim Pakistan's two lands, clamped on India's borders like an unbalanced vise, were breaking apart.

PAKISTAN, AS NOVELIST SALMAN RUSHDIE alluded, was "two Wings without a body, sundered by the land-mass of its greatest foe, joined by nothing but God." East Pakistan, off India's eastern border, was home to a slight majority of Pakistan's population, yet it was dominated by the politicians and generals of West Pakistan, 1,300 miles away. The shorter, darker East Pakistanis spoke Bengali, while their lighter-skinned countrymen to the west spoke Urdu or Punjabi. The western minority siphoned rupees from the east as if it were a colony. Eighty percent of government jobs, and 90 percent of army ranks, were held by West Pakistanis.

In time, East Pakistani dreams of independence found their voice in the charismatic Sheikh Mujibur Rahman and his nationalistic party, the Awami League. "Sheikh Mujib," as he was affectionately known to his followers, agitated for Bengali rights, setting the stage for a breakaway from West Pakistan. But it took a natural disaster to set both Muslim exclaves on a collision course.

In the autumn of 1970, history's deadliest cyclone tore through the East Pakistani coast, creating a storm surge that killed as many as half a million Bengalis. A slow and ineffective response from Pakistan's western capital, Islamabad, infuriated East Pakistanis, who clamored for radical change.

Then, in December, Pakistan held its first democratic election in decades, and the Awami League opposition won a narrow majority in the national assembly. By rights, Sheikh Mujib was poised to become Pakistan's next president, but General Agha Muhammad Yahya Khan, Pakistan's military dictator, refused to seat the president-elect, setting off a wave of strikes, civil disobedience, and demonstrations in an enraged East Pakistan.

For a while, Indira and her inner circle believed General Yahya would reach an accommodation with Mujib's Bengalis. Bargaining, after all, flowed through the blood of every Indian, whether Muslim or Hindu. Pakistanis negotiate, Indians negotiate. Even the British negotiated with Gandhi, their worst enemy on the subcontinent. It made sense to wait for Yahya and Mujib to work out a shared power arrangement.

Yahya, a heavy-set man with upswept eyebrows and a pendulous jaw, had other plans. His clumsy efforts to accommodate Bengalis simply whetted their appetite for independence, while hard-liners in his regime left him little room for flexibility. With geography, ethnicity, and politics conspiring against him, Yahya reached for a military solution to a problem that had no military solution.

In March 1971, he launched Operation Searchlight, a crackdown on East Pakistan's swelling insurgency. Pakistan's 14th Infantry Division and several independent army brigades—about 40,000 troops in all—spread throughout the country, murdering and raping civilians, burning homes, and imprisoning suspected dissidents. Riflemen in fatigues torched a university women's dorm, then machine-gunned students as they fled the inferno. Children's arms were hacked off, girls were raped, and when the scythe stopped swinging, hundreds of thousands of Bengalis had been killed. Many more fled their homes.*

Searchlight was not just a messy leverage play to help Islamabad negotiate with Mujib. Islamabad wanted Mujib and his followers out of the way. Permanently. The army arrested the Bengali sheikh, flew him to West Pakistan, and scheduled him for

---

* Indira's government, driven by political concerns, estimated that West Pakistani forces murdered three million East Pakistani citizens. Other sources claim the number killed was in the 300,000 range.

trial by a specially convened military court. Mujib's verdict and sentence were a foregone conclusion.

Fleeing a blood monsoon, East Pakistani families poured over India's border into West Bengal. Up to 150,000 came each day on foot, or by oxcart, rickshaw, or automobile. By May 1971, over 3.5 million Bengalis had abandoned their homes and flooded into refugee camps in India.

East Pakistan coughed, and India caught the flu. Refugees spread panic, cholera, and Marxist radicalism through West Bengal and adjacent Indian states. Indian soldiers and volunteers erected 335 temporary camps, and the government commandeered schools and hospitals to cope with the disaster.

It was not enough. The tide of hollow-eyed, famished families overwhelmed the Indian good Samaritans. West Bengal was shackled to a corpse, and the corpse was dragging India under.

As the refugee crisis worsened throughout April, Indira summoned General Manekshaw, the Indian Army's chief of staff, to a cabinet meeting. She wanted to know what the army could do to stop the crackdown, so Bengali refugees could return home.

When Manekshaw walked into the room and took his seat, he found Indira in a terrible mood, having just read a fistful of telegrams from eastern officials. The cables painted a pitiful picture and warned of social breakdown in India's east.

"Look at this! So many are coming in," she fumed. "What are you doing about it?"

"Nothing," replied Manekshaw. "What has it got to do with me?"

Her face flushed. "Can't you do something? Why don't you do something?"

"What do you want me to do?"

"I want you to march in."

"That means war," said the general.

She paused.

Taking counsel of fears did not come naturally to Indira. "If what seems right involves danger . . . well, one must risk the danger," she once said. "I've never thought of the consequences of a necessary action. I examine the consequences later, when a new situation arises, and then I face the new situation. And that's it."

Now she was facing a new situation—a most dangerous one.

"I don't mind if it is war," she said at last.

"It is My Job to Fight"

New Delhi disliked drawing attention to its military services. Although India maintained the third largest standing army in the world, Indira was the daughter of pacifists. Except for fleeting references to "heroic sacrifices" in stump speeches, she rarely paid homage to her fighting men the way British or American politicians do.

But now she saw valid reasons for deploying the army into East Pakistan. For one thing, the refugees were destabilizing the eastern Indian states. For another, the enormous financial strain of caring for a projected 10 million humans was stoking a national economic crisis. And strategically, if East Pakistan broke off from the west, West Pakistan would have no interest in staring across India. It would likely turn its focus to the Islamic nations of Western Asia and the Middle East.

Indira was a shrewd judge of how other nations would likely react, and as she looked around the globe, she concluded that no great power would help India solve its refugee problem—or stop India if she went to war. Relations with the Soviet Union were good. The United States had no vital interest in the region, and President Richard Nixon was busy trying to extricate America from Vietnam. Western Europe and the United Nations would make noise but do nothing.

That left China, Pakistan's ally. China was a tiger when it wished to be, but diplomatic and military intelligence led Indira to believe that Chairman Mao would watch but not act, especially if the Soviets supported New Delhi. In time, she grew so confident in China's neutrality that she had her defense minister transfer six of the army's ten divisions from the China border to the East Pakistani front.

If the superpowers refused to act, India would take up the sword and liberate Bangladesh.

❖   ❖   ❖

IN HIS CABINET ROOM CHAIR, General Sam Manekshaw stiffened when Indira told him, *"I don't mind if it is war."*

General Sam was a living legend in the Indian Army. Sporting a handlebar mustache and enormous nose, he was fond of gardening, cassette mixtapes, and Scotch whisky. During the Second World War, he had been stitched with nine bullets from a Japanese machine gun and was dragged, half dead, to a field hospital. When the surgeon was about to give up on the bullet-riddled mess, he asked his half-conscious patient what had happened to him. Sam mumbled, "I was kicked by a donkey." Seeing real toughness behind the humor, the doctor stuck by Sam's side and saved his life.

Sitting before the prime minister and her cabinet, it was Sam's turn to give the prognosis.

"Have you read the Bible?" he asked calmly.

"What has the Bible got to do with it?" snapped the foreign minister.

"God said, 'Let there be light, and there was light.' And you say, 'Let there be war,' and there is war? Are you ready? I certainly am not ready."

Turning to Indira, he said, "It is now the end of April. In a few days' time, 15–20 days' time, the monsoons will break and in East Pakistan, when it rains, the rivers become like oceans . . . I would be confined to the roads. Due to weather conditions, the Air Force will not be able to support me, and the Pakistanis would thrash me."

Cheeks flushed, Indira glared at Sam as he told her his only armored division was on the wrong side of the country. During the summer months, the Himalayan passes would also be free of snow, inviting Chinese intervention in Kashmir while India was entangled to the south.

Turning to the agricultural minister, Sam continued: "We are now harvesting. I will require every vehicle, every truck, all the road space, all the railway space to move my soldiers and you will not be able to move your crops. If there is a famine in India, they will blame you. I won't be there to take the blame."

The minister squirmed, saying nothing.

Back to Indira. "I am telling you what the problems are. If you still want me to go ahead, Prime Minister, I guarantee you 100 percent defeat. Now give me your orders."

Indira once told a journalist that she never dissembled. "If I'm happy, I look happy; if I'm angry, I show it." Now she showed it. She held power over a half-billion Indians, and was not used to being told "no" by a mere general. And a mere general was telling her those half-billion Indians couldn't defeat an isolated army on their own border.

She ordered everyone out of the room except Manekshaw.

When the ministers filed out and the door closed, Sam stood at attention and spoke to her before she could open her mouth. He asked if she would prefer his resignation to be given on mental grounds or for physical health.

The tension broke like a fever. As Indira recovered from the shock of his message, her lips spread into an unfeigned smile. "Sit down, Sam," she said. "Everything you told me, is it true?"

"Yes," said Sam. "It is my job to fight. It is my job to fight to win." India would win the war in December, but would lose it in April. As agonizing as the refugee crisis was, she had to be patient.

"All right, Sam," she said at last. "You let me know when you are ready."

As war's tympani rumbled, Indira laid diplomatic groundwork for Bangladesh. She called on western and communist nations to stop the carnage, and worked telephones in her wood-paneled office to win something more than prayers and sympathy from abroad. In early July, she met with Henry Kissinger, President Nixon's national security advisor, to discuss the western response. Kissinger was stopping in New Delhi on his way to Islamabad, and Indira asked him to have breakfast with her to discuss the Bangladeshi crisis.

The night before her breakfast, Indira telephoned Sam Manekshaw and asked him to meet her for breakfast with an unnamed guest. She had an unusual request of the informal general: She asked Sam to wear his full-dress military uniform, medals and all. A bit puzzled, Sam showed up as ordered, his broad chest covered with military orders as he and Indira sat down with their distinguished guest.

Over breakfast, Indira asked Kissinger to plead with Nixon to rein in West Pakistan. The insufferable conditions in Bangladesh, as the Bengalis were calling East Pakistan, was driving human waves over her borders and creating a humanitarian and political crisis for India. The United States was a major supplier of weapons to the Yahya regime and was Islamabad's biggest ally. If anyone could force Yahya to stop the repression, it was Nixon.

Preoccupied with his upcoming meetings, the dough-faced Kissinger offered nothing. He said he didn't see how the United States could bring much pressure on Islamabad. It had suspended a few military shipments, but doing so reduced its leverage over Yahya.*

Then, almost offhandedly, he asked Indira what she intended to do. Pointing to the bemedaled Manekshaw, she replied, "If the US government and US president cannot control the situation, then I am going to ask him to do the same."

Kissinger's refusal to discuss any US commitments—or even show much interest—convinced Indira that the United States would do nothing to alleviate either the refugee crisis or the repression that inflamed it. Nixon's announcement of a rapprochement with China the next month, and continued military sales to Pakistan, signaled a tilt toward Islamabad and brought Indo-US relations to a new low.

Fearful of encirclement by the United States, Pakistan, and China, a month later Indira walked back from her father's policy of nonalignment and signed a formal treaty of "peace, friendship and cooperation" with the Soviet Union. She was realigning superpower interests in South Asia. And raising the stakes.

---

* Although Kissinger's next official stop was to Islamabad, his real destination was a tightly guarded secret. After leaving Delhi, he flew to Pakistan and crossed the border into western China for secret talks with Chou En-lai to open diplomatic relations. Rapprochement with China became one of the cornerstones of Nixon's foreign policy.

Over the hot summer of 1971, Bangladeshi rebels, armed and trained by the Indian army, fought government troops occupying East Pakistan. At first the Pakistani army crushed the separatists, but the rebels proved quick learners. Armed with obsolete British rifles and grenade launchers, they staged hit-and-run operations under cover of the monsoon season, when Pakistani tanks and troop vehicles were immobilized by mud-choked roads and swollen rivers—just as General Manekshaw had predicted.

The histrionic Yahya saw Indian hands behind the separatist rebels and began complaining loudly to his allies. To send New Delhi a warning, he also mobilized his reserves and began making contingency plans for war.

Yahya didn't know it, but his mobilization played into Indira's strategy. Since April, she had intended to mobilize her reserves for a war she knew was coming. Yahya's mobilization gave her a convenient excuse to call up troops without looking like an aggressor to the world community.

In September, as the military engine revved, Indira began cashing in on India's ties to its new patron. She traveled to Moscow to solidify Soviet backing and delivered a speech at the Kremlin setting out her view of the crisis at her doorstep. "What has happened in Bangladesh can no longer be regarded as Pakistan's domestic affair," she announced. She left Moscow with a secret promise of military aid in the event of war with Pakistan, a pledge that might help keep the Chinese in check.

After enduring a summer of unrest, Indira set out on a tour of Western Europe and the United States. She aimed to stoke an international peace effort of something more than soothing diplomatic bromides. But at every stop, she hit a wall. In Belgium, Austria, France, West Germany, and Britain, ministers welcomed her but refused to make any real commitments.

Falling short in Europe, in late October she ruled out peace talks with Pakistan, declaring, "We certainly will do nothing to provoke an attack or start any hostilities, but we have to be alive to our interests and safeguard our security."

In one interview, a British reporter asked her, "Is there a situation in which you might attack Pakistan?"

"Well, I hope not," Indira replied, her lips forming a sly smile. "India has always tried to be on the side of peace and negotiations. But of course we can't endanger our security in any way."

"Do you frankly expect to see war with Pakistan soon?"

"I don't really think I can give an answer."

Her fingers fidgeted with the shoulder fold of her sari.

"One thing you must remember is that we have never, never attacked anybody," she added. "But we have been attacked three times."

"The refugees are coming over, and you have this enormous problem in India," the reporter asked. "How much longer can you sustain it?"

"We can't sustain it now. Longer is . . . it's now for some months, it's really something that's been water going higher and higher."

"What are you going to do about it?"

Indira looked down. "Something will have to be done."

❖   ❖   ❖

SHE PLAYED HER LAST CARD in November 1971, pitching the United States for support. Unlike her mission for food aid in the Lyndon Johnson years, this time Indira had no need to beg. Her party controlled the Lok Sabha, she had the backing of the Soviet Union, and her army outnumbered Pakistan's. She would meet with the leader of the free world, and she would ask for his help. But she would not grovel.

Nixon and Indira, Kissinger wrote with understatement, "were not intended by fate to be personally congenial. Mrs. Gandhi's assumption of almost hereditary moral superiority and her moody silences brought out all of Nixon's latent insecurities." The meeting would be Nixon's worst with a foreign leader.

To a frowning Richard Nixon, India and the Soviet Union were getting chummier with each new phase of the crisis. Indira's government publicly exaggerated the level of US military aid to Pakistan—Nixon had stopped sending weapons to Yahya, and US nonlethal aid was small—and she accused the United States of supporting genocide. Indira's rejection of UN observers and her anti-US diatribes rankled Nixon, confirming his belief that Indira wanted to dismember Pakistan.

Smiling through gritted teeth, Nixon rolled out the red carpet for Indira on November 4 when she arrived in Washington. On camera, it was all smiles; off camera, things went sour. When Nixon met with her in in the Oval Office, Indira told him that India could no longer tolerate the instability of ten million refugees spreading disease and unrest within her borders. The United States had to force Yahya to pull his troops back and let the refugees return home.

As Nixon replied, Indira stared at him in that cool way often perceived by Indians and Westerners as condescension. Nixon kept up a stream of civil conversation, promising nothing. Indira said little, implying much. Inwardly fuming at her directness, Nixon asked her to meet with him the next day.

The next morning at the White House, Nixon and Kissinger met in the Oval Office to discuss the president's meeting with Indira later that day. The goal, they agreed, was to refuse her, but not in a way that would let her go back to New Delhi harping about American discourtesy, which might sting India into invading West Pakistan.

"This is just the point when she is a bitch," said Nixon as his secret tape recorder rolled.

"Well, the Indians are bastards anyway," agreed Kissinger. "They are starting a war there. It's—to them East Pakistan is no longer the issue. Now, I found it very interesting how she carried on to you yesterday about West Pakistan."

"Now I've talked to her, told her everything we're going to do. Now it's up to her," said Nixon, leaning back in his chair.

"Mr. President," added Kissinger, "even though she was a bitch, we shouldn't overlook the fact that we got what we wanted, which was we kept her from going out of here saying that the United States kicked her in the teeth . . . You didn't give her a goddamn thing . . . I mean, if you had been rough with her—"

"Yeah."

"—then she'd be crying, going back crying to India. So I think even though she is a bitch, I'd be a shade cooler today, but—"

"No, no," said Nixon, his gravelly baritone growing animated. "I mean, 'cool' in terms of, like yesterday, as you noted, I tried to carry the conversation."

"No, I'd let her carry it."

"And was sort of saying," continued Nixon, "'Look, we're being as good as we can in dealing with Pakistan. What else can we do?'"

What could he do? Nothing, Nixon said emphatically. When it was time for the meeting, he kept her waiting forty-five minutes, to repay her condescension of the day before. She returned the favor by pointedly asking about US policy toward every part of the globe except South Asia. And she left the United States empty-handed.

But as she had warned Kissinger in July, if the US would not rein in Pakistan, her generals would.

Battle for Bangladesh

Through the final weeks of November, Indira's covert war in Bangladesh grew in violence and scope. It reached its crescendo on November 21, when the Indian Army began attacking border regions with armor and artillery support. Claiming they were acting in self-defense, Manekshaw's troops crossed the border and established jumping-off points for an assault on Dacca, the Bangladeshi capital.

The battle for Bangladesh—approved by Indira, Sam, and the eastern Indian commander, Lieutenant General Jagjit Singh Aurora—would commence under a new moon on the night of December 6. At Indira's insistence, the offensive would be a joint operation under command of General Aurora and retired Colonel M.A.G. Osmani, Bangladesh's highest-ranking rebel army leader.

On India's western border, army and air force bases braced for Pakistani retaliation and planned counterattacks. Military units went on full alert, and key Indian landmarks and waypoints, including the famed Taj Mahal, were draped in burlap or camouflaged to deny their use to Pakistani fliers as reference points.

Three days before the invasion's scheduled launch, the Pakistani Air Force struck fifteen air bases in northwestern India. Coming on a weekend, the attacks caught the Indian leadership scattered across the country: Indira was speaking in Calcutta, the defense minister was traveling to Bangalore, and the finance minister was in Bombay.

On a hurried flight back to New Delhi, Indira learned the extent of Yahya's air strike from her foreign affairs advisor, D.P. Dhar. "The fool has done exactly what one had expected," he told Indira.

The air strikes turned out to be a bolt of phenomenal political luck. The attacks were bungled and damage was minimal, yet the level of destruction was beside the point. On the eve of India's invasion, New Delhi could credibly claim that Pakistan had drawn first blood and that it was merely defending itself. This was Yahya's war, not Indira's.

Heading immediately to the Operations Room at India's defense ministry, Indira received a full briefing from generals, air chiefs, and their staffers. Looking around the room, her eye caught a bottle of scotch next to a pair of highball glasses. She gave General Manekshaw a stern look, then looked pointedly at the bottle.

"Madame, the brand name of that whiskey is Black Dog," said the general. "It's the whiskey that Yahya Kahn drinks. I am quite sure that I shall overdrink him and outfight him, so please do not be angry."

Indira let Sam get back to work. She was the politician, he was the general, and partners work best when they trust each other enough to do their jobs. He had promised her a victory if she waited until December, and December had come. Like Abraham Lincoln's favorite general, she would let him fight the way he thought best—and drink whatever he wanted—as long as he won.

Shortly before midnight, a grim-faced Indira Gandhi took to the airwaves and addressed the nation from her blacked-out capital. "I speak to you at a moment of great peril to our country and our people," she began.

Today a war in Bangladesh has become a war on India . . . I have no doubt that by the united will of the people, the wanton and unprovoked aggression of Pakistan should be decisively and finally repelled . . . Aggression must be met and the people of India will meet it with fortitude, determination, discipline, and utmost unity.

The next morning Indira convened an emergency cabinet meeting to discuss India's war aims in light of the Pakistani attack. Defense and finance ministers argued vehemently for a major attack against West Pakistan, which should be eliminated as a future threat. At the very least, Pakistan's armored forces should be destroyed, and Pakistani-held portions of Kashmir should be "liberated."

But the nature of war had changed since the old days when a raj could slaughter his neighbor anytime he had an army large enough to do it. In the modern era, superpower patrons, secret diplomacy, and the United Nations dictated how deeply a country could drive its spear, even when its cause appeared just. Mohandas Gandhi had defeated the British Empire's bayonets with a walking stick and bag of salt, all because politics intruded on war far more than in ages past.

Recognizing these limits, Indira would not permit either the United States or Pakistan to paint India's fight as a war of conquest or dismemberment. The war's prime goal was to liberate Bangladesh so the refugees could return home, and after conferring with her military leaders, she told cabinet ministers that the military would take a few strategic points in Kashmir and wreck Pakistan's western force from the air. That should deter Yahya from launching a full ground invasion from the west, and that would be enough for Indira's purposes.

Faced with a crisis they could no longer ignore, the superpowers moved military assets into the region like high-stakes chess players in a Fischer-Spassky match. In the White House, Kissinger privately told Nixon, "We can't let a friend of ours get screwed in a conflict with a friend of Russia's." Nixon responded with a naval task force led by the nuclear aircraft carrier USS *Enterprise*. Within days, *Enterprise* and her consorts steamed through the Strait of Malacca to the Bay of Bengal with a heavy implied warning to Indira—and to the Kremlin.

The Kremlin was just as determined not to let its friend get screwed by America's friend. It vetoed UN Security Council resolutions calling for an immediate cease-fire in East Pakistan and kept missiles, artillery ammunition, and vital equipment flowing to New Delhi. In response to Nixon's deployment of the *Enterprise*, USSR Politburo chairman Leonid Brezhnev sent a Soviet flotilla to Bengal. For a time, it seemed possible that the next world war could begin off the coast of India.

Indira's cabinet spent two days debating a response to the alarming presence of US and Soviet navies off India's shores. Worried ministers proposed slowing the drive on Dacca to appease the Americans and let tensions die down. But Indira took the opposite approach. After consulting with military leaders and Soviet diplomats, she deduced that the safest response would be for General Manekshaw to push faster and take Dacca before the United States could move more forces into the region. As soon as the Pakistani army in the east surrendered, she would announce the liberation of Bangladesh and declare a cease-fire, reassuring Washington and Peking that she had no designs on West Pakistan.

So, she ordered Sam to move on the Bengali capital as fast as he could. A swift battlefield victory would solve her political and diplomatic problems at a stroke—she hoped.

Triumph

The weight of war's grindstone has wrecked many national leaders. King George III, Frederick the Great, Franklin Roosevelt, and Adolf Hitler suffered physical or mental breakdowns under the stress of death and destruction for which they shared responsibility. Other leaders, like Napoleon, Abraham Lincoln, Josef Stalin, and Lyndon Johnson, survived their wars but aged visibly under the psychological toll.

Not Indira. Her ability to set aside the cares of the moment and rejuvenate her mind by turning inward enabled her to remain sharp and focused. Time had taken but a modest price from the woman of fifty-four years, and she rode over the crisis with the confidence of Durga, the Vedic war goddess to whom the Indian press now compared her. She began wearing saris in red patterns—an edgy color for an Indian widow—and told a friend, "The color red suffused me throughout the war."

Indira, better than most, understood the irrationality of worry. If a problem could be solved, she would solve it, eliminating the source of her disquiet. If the crisis were beyond her abilities, then why should she spend time worrying about it?

She later explained how her mindset helped her withstand the war's hammer blows. A western reporter once asked her, "What is this Hindu philosophy, which is often regarded as passive and acquiescent?"

"No, it isn't," she corrected him.

It just faces reality. It's something that gives you an inner strength. I don't get uptight, as the Americans would say. In a situation of war you must face the situation as it comes. You give it your all. You do your very best. That's all you can do. You can't do better than that, and then you shouldn't be bothered about the rest.

To ensure she was giving her best, she met with her military chiefs each morning at 8:30 a.m. for breakfast. Sometimes she made decisions, but more often she simply kept abreast of the fighting at the front.

Occasionally, she played the role of team cheerleader. A week into the war, a glum Manekshaw reported heavy losses among his troops in slow, painful fighting outside Dacca.

"Sam, you can't win every day," Indira reassured him. She said she had complete confidence in her top general and his strategy, and sent him away in better spirits.

It helped that the war was, on the whole, progressing well. In the west, the Indian Air Force commanded the skies over West Pakistan and kept Islamabad's armor from debouching from the roads to India. At sea, the Pakistani submarine *Ghazi* washed ashore—the victim of a lucky mine hit—and in the Bay of Bengal her navy reported that the Americans were taking no hostile actions. In Bangladesh, the equivalent of ten Indian infantry divisions under the command of General Aurora closed in on Dacca.

Badly outnumbered, surrounded by a hostile populace, and over 1,300 miles from home, Pakistani military resistance crumbled. Casualties piled up in field hospitals, and Bangladesh partisans murdered civilians who tried to help them. When Indian troops reached the outskirts of Dacca, Pakistani commander Lieutenant General Amir Abdullah Khan Niazi saw the end. Cut off and with no hope of reinforcement, on December 16, Niazi surrendered unconditionally to General Aurora.

Meeting his opposite number at Dacca's football stadium, Niazi put his pen to the surrender document, signed his name, and handed a .38 caliber pistol to Aurora.

The war for Bangladesh was over.

At five o'clock that afternoon, Indira was giving an interview to a Swedish television team when an aide slipped her word of Niazi's surrender. She politely excused herself, then headed to the Lok Sabha.

Indira could barely contain herself as she made her way to the assembly hall. Her aide, Karan Singh, recalled, "Mrs. Gandhi was not a woman who would give away her emotions easily in front of others, but that was the first time in my life that I saw her so very excited."

With quick steps, she walked down the parliamentary chamber's center aisle, an emerald blue wrap pulled tight as her hands pressed a *namaste* greeting to the members. When the legislators took their places, her voice rang out, clear and dignified:

I have an announcement to make. The West Pakistan forces have unconditionally surrendered in Bangladesh . . . Dacca is now the free capital of a free country. This House and the entire nation rejoice in this historic event. We hail the people of Bangladesh in their hour of triumph. We hail the brave young men and boys of the Mukti Bahini for their valor and dedication. We are proud of our own Army, Navy, Air Force and Border Security Force, who have so magnificently demonstrated their quality and capacity.

A rolling thunder of applause swept the chamber. Cheers went up: The Congress Party, the opposition, every member of every faction, every caste, went wild. Outside the columned building, crowds began pouring into the wide Sansad Marg boulevard to raise their voices with their leaders. The sword that had been hanging over India for nine months had fallen and missed them. The fever of tragedy had broken.

Of course, surrender in Bangladesh only ended fighting in the east. To the west, the Indian Army sent troops several miles over the Pakistani border, their deepest penetration in the disputed Kashmir region. When Dacca surrendered, many of Indira's advisors insisted that India should wheel west and launch a knockout blow while Yahya and his forces were reeling.

But Indira had assured the Soviets she would halt as soon as Bangladesh was free. An invasion of West Pakistan would might draw China into the war. Besides, the fighting in the west would be very different from the walkover in Bangladesh. West Pakistani troops were amply supplied, enjoyed local air cover, and were supported by a population deeply hostile to India. A major city like Karachi might cost 30,000 casualties, and Indira saw no strategic prizes to be won by taking a few impoverished border towns in the Punjab.

Like a gambler raking in her winnings, Indira quit while she was ahead. As she told an aide, "I must order a cease-fire on the western front also. For if I don't do so today, I shall not be able to do it tomorrow."

That evening, she announced an end to hostilities on the western front. The war was over. Nearly 8,000 Pakistanis had been killed, joining 1,500 Indians in death.

Operation Blue Star

Indira emerged from war's kiln a national heroine. Newspapers and parliamentarians drew comparisons to the goddess Shakti, a feminine deity of energy and strength, or Durga, the battle goddess. Encomia like "Empress of India" —a name her father would have been horrified to see linked with the family—began turning up in the foreign press, and "Indira" became one of the most popular baby girl names that year. A Gallup poll in the United States identified her as the most admired person in the world.

Even her western antagonist, Richard Nixon, confessed grudging admiration. In a private conversation with NBC's John Chancellor, he admitted, "She is an enormously able woman. I have great respect for her. But she's tough."

Traipsing down this conversational path, Nixon added, "Women's Lib contends that if only we had women in positions of power we'd have no war. You look at the history of nations, and when you have had women in positions of power, women are really tougher than men. Very curious, isn't it?"

Indira's Congress Party, not surprisingly, reaped a political windfall in 1972, capturing 70 percent of all contested seats in Parliament. Indira's hold on government seemed unassailable.

But political winds never blow in one direction for long. Monsoons failed two years in a row, and the resulting drought made food scarce. Social unrest rocked India, political violence escalated, and in 1975, Indira declared a state of emergency. She ruled as a dictator for nearly two years.

Dogged by charges of corruption, despotism, and failing to address food and job shortages, in 1977, voters turned out the Congress Party. Indira and her son Sanjay lost their seats in the Lok Sabha, and for the next three years she languished in the political wilderness. The new government put her on trial for election fraud and other political crimes, which landed her in jail for a week.

Riding the highs and lows of politics, she remained undaunted. "I go on taking difficult paths, and between a paved road and a footpath that goes up the mountain, I choose a footpath," she used to say. "To the great irritation of my bodyguards," she added with a smile.

Fortune's pendulum swung back in 1980, when Indira Gandhi returned to power in a landslide victory. This time, she inherited another crisis that was, to her, both new and old: a sporadic border war with Pakistan in Kashmir's mountainous north.

Relations with Pakistan, never good at the best of times, had gone downhill since the two nations signed a vague agreement ending the 1971 war. The "line of control" in Kashmir they agreed on hadn't become a recognized border, and tensions between the two neighbors simmered. In 1974, she had authorized the test detonation of a nuclear bomb, and the explosion spurred Pakistan to develop its own nuclear weapon. Observers in Moscow, Washington, Islamabad, and New Delhi would lie awake at night, calculating the odds of a nuclear war between two South Asian enemies.

Three years after her return to office, Indira was no closer to a solution. The old peace agreement did not specify how far into the glaciers one stretch of border ran—no one had thought to map out a border on a moving sheet of ice—and in

1983 Indian Army uniform purchasers were startled to receive a call from a London outfitter that supplied mountain gear for the Indian Army. The Pakistani Army, the company manager said, was ordering large stocks of Arctic weather gear, including parkas, hats, wool socks, and mittens. The acquisition of cold-weather clothes could only mean one thing: Pakistan was going to war in the mountains.

Predicting a Pakistani move onto Kashmir's Siachen Glacier, running between 12,000 to 19,000 feet above sea level, Indira authorized Operation Meghdoot ("Cloud Messenger"). The Indian Air Force ferried a brigade of troops by helicopter to the glacier's peak. Those troops set up gun positions in the critical passes, effectively lopping off another thousand square miles of territory claimed by Pakistan. The "War at the Top of the World," as *Time* magazine called it, resulted in an Indian victory of minor bloodshed and dubious significance.*

INDIRA'S LARGER PROBLEM in the early 1980s was not Pakistan, but rather Sikh separatists. As followers of gurus who revealed divine teachings, this religious sect comprised only two percent of India's population, but they were heavily concentrated in the Punjab. Led by Jarnail Singh Bhindranwale, a demagogue warlord, they demanded a separate Punjabi state. To put teeth into their demands, Sikh militants embarked on a vicious campaign of terror and assassination.

In late 1983, Bhindranwale's soldiers overran the Golden Temple of Amritsar, the holiest of Sikh religious sites. They converted the place of worship into an armed camp, lining the walls with sandbags and automatic weapons. From the temple they sent death squads to murder local Hindus and unreliable fellow Sikhs, including Amritsar's police chief. Mutilated bodies of torture victims began turning up in ditches outside the sacred temple.

Indira would not allow an armed terrorist group to establish itself in Punjab's heart. But how could she eliminate the militants without setting off a wave of violence among the larger Sikh community?

After dithering over whether to use force—she privately told confidantes she feared attacking a "house of God"—Indira gave in to her military advisors and approved Operation Blue Star, a plan to take the Golden Temple by storm.

---

* In 1987 and 1989, Pakistan would launch futile attempts to retake the barren glacier. To this day, both sides still occupy their positions, though fighting is rare. Altitude and cold claim far more lives than bullets or shrapnel.

On the evening of June 2, 1984, troops of India's 9th Infantry Division surrounded the temple and cut off communications with the outside world. Commando raids whittled down the temple's outer defenses, and, under withering fire from temple militants, they launched their assault.

Bullets flew in thick swarms, and on June 6, the temple fell. The militant leader and thirty-one of his followers lay dead.

Separatists took with them over three hundred soldiers who charged into the temple, along with half the commando squad sent to spearhead the attack. An additional number of dead pilgrims—faithful who happened to be in the wrong place at the wrong time—was never fully tallied.

Having no deep religious beliefs herself, Indira had nothing against the Sikhs or their religion. She had made reasonable efforts to accommodate each of the land's major faiths and counted among her trusted bodyguards a number of practicing Sikhs. So, three days after the battle, Indira sent India's president, Zail Singh, to visit the temple as a goodwill gesture.

President Singh spent an afternoon touring the complex amidst chants, shouts, incense, and the smell of death. As he walked along pockmarked temple walls, a rifle cracked, and a bodyguard standing next to the president spun around, a bullet in his shoulder.

In late summer, Indira removed Kashmir's chief minister, Farooq Abdullah, for collaborating with militants and turning a blind eye toward their pipeline of Pakistani aid. But like the hydra of Lerna, India's sectarian monster grew a new head every time Indira hacked one off. Farooq's dismissal flushed a new wave of anger in Punjab and Kashmir, and Indira's standing there plummeted.

"No Hate is Dark Enough"

Indira was not a woman cowed by violence. While giving a campaign speech in her early days, someone in the crowd threw a rock at her face. The missile broke her nose and split her lip, but she refused to leave the stage and used a fold of her sari to hide her bleeding mouth.

"I am not afraid," she told an interviewer after Amritsar. "I am frequently attacked. Once a man poked a gun at me. Another time in Delhi someone threw a knife at me. And then, of course, there are always the stones, the bricks, the bottles, especially at election time." She would soldier on.

At the end of October, Indira sat in her home in New Delhi, pondering her country's future. Wearing a saffron sari with a hand-woven black border, she sat placidly as makeup artists finished brushing her up for a spot on a BBC documentary directed by actor Peter Ustinov.

She began the short walk to her press office, surrounded by her usual entourage, including her longtime bodyguard, a Sikh named Beant Singh. By his side stood Satwant Singh, a young constable who would accompany the prime minister to her interview.

Indira broke off her conversation briefly to acknowledge her bodyguards with a *namaste* greeting. As she did, Beant drew his revolver and leveled it at her. He stood motionless, a blank look on his face as Indira stared at him, puzzled.

"What are you doing?" she asked.

The pistol cracked. A hole flashed in the sari over Indira's abdomen.

She instinctively raised her hands to protect her face. Beant fired four more shots into Indira's body, staggering her. A few feet away, Satwant Singh drew his Sten submachine gun but froze in indecision.

Beant barked an order, and Satwant emptied the Sten's 32-round clip into Indira's body. Thirty bullets shredded her liver, splintered bones, cut her spinal cord, penetrated a lung. As they laced her body, she spun and dropped to the ground in a blood-soaked heap.

Emerging from shock, Indira's entourage leaped at the assassins. Beant was shot and killed by his captors, while Satwant, also shot, recovered and lived to receive his punishment four years later.*

Indira's eyes stared without seeing as frantic men rushed her to the hospital. They fought with transfusions and scalpels, but the battle was unwinnable. On the morning of October 31, Indira Nehru Gandhi's soul took wings and flew into the cool Delhi sky.

Keeping with Hindu tradition, Indira's body rendered up her soul on a funeral pyre of sweet-smelling sandalwood. As orange and yellow flames engulfed her, her son Rajiv tapped his mother's head with a bamboo pole, releasing her spirit into the heavens.

Her ashes were scattered over the Kashmir Himalayas.

---

* On the second anniversary of the storming of the Golden Temple, Beant Singh's widow, Bimal Kaur Khalsa, led a guerrilla force of 200 militants on an attack against the temple. One guard was killed, but the attack was repulsed. The wife of Indira's assassin later won a seat in the Lok Sabha. Satwant Singh, the surviving bodyguard, was hanged in 1989.

As a child, Indira Nehru had been transfixed by the story of Joan of Arc, the French heroine who died at the stake after fighting the English. "I don't remember where I read about her, but I recall that she immediately took on a definite importance for me. I wanted to sacrifice my life for my country," she told an interviewer. "It seems like foolishness and yet . . . what happens when we're children is engraved forever on our lives."

In the weeks following Indira's death, aides sifted through the late minister's papers. They catalogued and sorted them: some for the archives, some for her family's safekeeping, some for the fire pits.

As they leafed through a life scarred by tragedy, war, and triumph, they found one note in Indira's handwriting, written in the last autumn of her life:

> *If I die a violent death as some fear and a few are plotting, I know the violence will be in the thought and the action of the assassin, not in my dying—for no hate is dark enough to overshadow the extent of my love for my people and my country; no force is strong enough to divert me from my purpose and my endeavour to take this country forward. A poet has written of love—"how can I feel humble with the wealth of you beside me." I can say the same of India. I cannot understand how anyone can be an Indian and not be proud—the richness and infinite variety of our composite heritage, the magnificence of the people's spirit, equal to any disaster or burden, firm in their faith.*

Indira was the leading edge of a new wave of women war leaders—women who understood the primacy of politics and diplomacy in a nuclear age. Her work with Brezhnev, Nixon, and Kissinger was as much a part of her war strategy as her collaboration with General Manekshaw.

Other women leading nuclear-armed states were watching Indira and learning from her. Two years after the Indo-Pakistani armistice was signed in a Dacca football stadium, another woman—like Indira, an old-school icon—made a decision in war that would change the fate of three ancient enemies.

12

BABUSHKA

Israel's Golda Meir

"You cannot decide whether we should fight or not. We will . . .
You can only decide one thing: Whether we shall be victorious."
—GOLDA MEIR, 1948

NO MATTER HOW MUCH SHE FOUGHT IT, the dream kept coming back.

"Suddenly all the telephones in my home start to ring," she once told a friend. "There are a lot of phones, located in every corner of the house, and they don't stop ringing. I know what that ringing means, and I'm afraid to pick up all the receivers. I wake up covered in a cold sweat . . . I breathe a sigh of relief, but I can't get back to sleep. I know that if I fall back to sleep, the dream will return."

Golda knew what the voice at the other end of those subliminal phones would tell her. She had instructed her military attaché to call her whenever an Israeli citizen was killed by Arab fighters, no matter what hour of the day or night. Some nights, the aide called to report a few deaths from Egyptian shelling in the Sinai, or Fedayeen mortar rounds dropped on Jewish settlements.

Some nights, nothing. That's when the dream returned.

❖   ❖   ❖

GOLDA MABOVICH'S EARLIEST childhood memory was a fuzzy image of her father boarding up their Ukrainian home on rumors of another anti-Jewish pogrom. In 1903, when she was five, her father emigrated to the United States to find work, and two years later Moshe Mabovich brought his family to live with him in Milwaukee, Wisconsin.

Golda reveled in the freedom America offered. A headstrong adolescent, she ran away to Denver to live with her older sister, Sheyna. Sheyna and her husband, both social activists, were closely connected to Denver's Zionist community and hosted dinners to discuss political and social issues facing the scattered Jewish community. Listening to the grown-ups talk, Golda soaked up radical ideas about women's suffrage, rights of workers, and the injustices of capitalism. The raven-haired teenager found herself swept away by the romance of Zionism, and would carry that torch until she drew her last breath.

After a few years in Denver, Golda reconciled with her parents and returned to finish high school in Milwaukee, where she graduated valedictorian of her class. In 1917, she married a mild-mannered sign painter named Morris Meyerson and began raising funds for the Jewish homeland.

Golda wore the pants in her marriage, and in 1921 she convinced Morris to move with her to Palestine. The couple settled at the kibbutz Merhavia in the Jezreel Valley, along with other European and Middle Eastern settlers who called themselves the Yishuv. Worried that her fellow Yishuv would look down on her as a "soft American," she made a point of outworking everyone in the almond fields, the kitchen, the chicken coops, and the storehouse.

Her work ethic and blunt, outspoken leadership made Golda a central figure in the Merhavia community. Before long, her fellow kibbutzim elected her to the Histadrut, Palestine's Jewish labor federation. Golda's political work took her, Morris, and their two small children to Tel Aviv, and from there to the legendary city of Jerusalem.

Golda once reflected, "There is a type of woman who does not let her husband narrow her horizon." She saw family life as an obstacle to her true calling: public service. Acknowledging that her heart wasn't in the marriage, she and Morris separated. Freed from her domestic responsibilities, she plunged into political work, sparing personal time only for a series of affairs with prominent Histadrut officials.

Independence

With the death of Hitler's Third Reich in 1945, thousands of Jews languished in liberated concentration camps throughout Europe. Golda and other Palestinian leaders funneled this flotsam to a new homeland they were calling Israel. Fearing an Arab backlash, British officials in Palestine froze Jewish immigration, and in response, militant Jewish gangs launched a campaign of terrorism against British authorities.

Defusing crises caused by radicals, like Irgun faction leader Menachem Begin, became a full-time job for mainstream Jewish leaders like Golda and Jewish Agency head David Ben-Gurion. Bombings and assassinations by Begin's men brought British retribution at home and created public relations nightmares for Zionists abroad.

Golda was no radical. She looked for political solutions and had no patience with home-grown terrorists, Jewish or otherwise. For hotheads like Begin, she offered Ben-Gurion a cold-blooded solution: The establishment must put an end to their violence "in every manner."

"Does putting an end to them mean destroying men?" Ben-Gurion asked her.

"All right then, even to destroy men," Golda replied. "I have no moral constraints in regard to this group."

Ben-Gurion was appalled. "Jews will not slaughter one another in the Land of Israel."

"They have already slaughtered Jews," Golda retorted. "I know that it is very bad to shoot people from the Irgun or Stern group, but if they bring it to that point . . . we have to do everything to make them stop."

It didn't stop. Jewish attacks grew bolder, and Britain's government deployed 17,000 soldiers to Palestine to herd the Yishuv into line. In a sweep known as Black Sabbath, British military officials rounded up and arrested Jewish leaders. Golda, one of the few not on government target lists, stepped into the power vacuum left by the arrested men.

The British would regret not arresting Mrs. Meyerson. She hectored bureaucrats into releasing prisoners and kept a firm hand on the Jewish Agency helm until Ben-Gurion and his deputies were released. "As long as Golda's outside [detention]," settlers joked, "the only man in the Jewish Agency is still free."[*]

As she climbed Palestine's rickety political ladder, conservative Jews took a dim view of a woman running their affairs. "Kudos to a smart and energetic woman," read an editorial in one Orthodox daily. "But it is impossible to put Golda at the head of the most important thing of the Jewish people. This is not a position for a woman."

Golda wasn't aiming for the "most important thing," but she had three priceless qualities that the shadow government needed: She could outwork any man, she wouldn't take "no" for an answer, and she grew up in America. To Ben-Gurion, that made her a natural choice for a special assignment.

---

* Golda hated the "best man in the cabinet" shtick, which had been tossed around since the time of Artemisia. "I've always found [the remark] irritating, though men use it as a great compliment," she grumbled. "Is it? I wouldn't say so. Because what does it really mean? That it's better to be a man than a woman, a principle on which I don't agree at all."

As the British prepared to relinquish their unpopular mandate over Palestine, Arab attacks on Jewish residents jumped. In December 1947, Golda scrambled onto a bus after her car was ambushed on Jerusalem's outskirts. She recalled a man firing his rifle at the attackers, then slumping over after being hit by a bullet. Powerless to save him, Golda cradled the man as the blood drained from his body. He died in her lap.

By 1947, the Jewish Agency was desperately short of weapons, food, ammunition, and the countless other mundane commodities that allow an independence movement to survive. Tapping into Golda's American connections, Ben-Gurion sent her back to her adoptive homeland to plead for funds that would put Israel back on the map.

Touring the United States in a plain blue dress, her dark hair torqued into a plump bun, the socialist from Milwaukee launched a speaking tour, haranguing American capitalists to open their wallets. Speaking extemporaneously, she told crowds it was up to the Americans of Chicago, of Dallas, of New York, to keep the Jewish state alive in the face of British repression and Arab violence.

"The Yishuv in Palestine will fight in the Negev and will fight in Galilee and will fight on the outskirts of Jerusalem until the very end," she declared, echoing words of Winston Churchill.

> *You cannot decide whether we should fight or not. We will . . . You can only decide one thing: whether we shall be victorious in this fight or whether the Mufti will be victorious. That decision American Jews can make. It has to be made quickly, within hours, within days. And I beg of you—don't be late. Don't be bitterly sorry three months from now for what you failed to do today. The time is now.*

Before leaving Palestine, Golda had been told that if she were lucky, Americans might donate as much as $8 million. She flew back to Jerusalem with more than $50 million in donations. An awed Ben-Gurion later remarked, "When history will be written, it will be said that there was a Jewish woman who got the money which made the state possible."

WHEN ISRAEL DECLARED INDEPENDENCE on May 14, 1948, Golda was one of thirty-eight signatories to Israel's declaration. The beleaguered British government, happy to wash its hands of Palestine, brought its soldiers home. Once British troops were out of the way, Israel's neighbors declared war on the new nation.

For Golda, the war for independence was a blur of blood, crises, and adrenaline as she raised funds and organized the new government's labor ministry. She smoked pack after pack of cigarettes, drank two pots of coffee each day, and spent her hours shuttling from one disaster to the next.

One day, while riding a commuter bus, shrapnel and bullets began flying in all directions among the passengers. Golda remained in her seat, stock-still, covering only her eyes.

When the shooting stopped, a passenger asked her why she covered her eyes. Was she afraid of what she saw?

She shook her head. "I'm not really afraid to die," she said. "Everyone dies. But how will I live if I am blinded? How will I work?"

The war ended after nine convulsive months, and for seven years Israel used its breathing room to organize a proper government. Golda spent the nation's early years working as ambassador to the Soviet Union, labor minister, and foreign minister. She forged ties with emerging West African nations, kindled a faint dialog with the Soviet Union, and ably defended Israel's position abroad.

But her blunt candor, which resonated so well with American audiences when she was out schnorring for funds, alienated staffers who worked for her.

"Golda entertained strong convictions," recalled one ministry official. "She believed she possessed an inner truth. On certain issues, she simply could not be swayed. She demonstrated little interest in being liked or approved. She believed in remaining steadfast to the truth as she saw it. This trait made it difficult for her to change her mind."

Women who worked for Golda found not an ounce of feminist solidarity in their leader. "Many people thought that she hated women," a female Foreign Ministry staffer remarked. "I don't know whether that was true, but she certainly wasn't a friend to us."

Golda had little interest in mentoring the next generation of leaders or building a smooth, harmonious organization. Solving problems with direct solutions was Golda's way. If the kibbutz needed chickens, she learned how to breed them, then bred them. If Israel needed money, she took a plane to New York and hit the speaking circuit. In her late fifties, she had cut too many Gordian knots, smashed too many locked doors, to care whether women saw her as a role model or team player. Shaping her life around what other people thought simply didn't interest her, never had.

The friction within Israel's government was fueled by a generation gap widening between Israel's tectonic plates. Fidgeting behind Golda and Ben-Gurion were younger men like Moshe Dayan, Shimon Peres, and Menachem Begin—terrorists during British rule and hotheaded fighters in the War of Independence. After being relegated to the radical fringes for so long, they had tasted the power of the political mainstream. They believed it was time for the old guard to step aside and make way for the new.

At age sixty, Golda Meyerson—her name now Hebraized to "Meir"—made no concessions to her physical or political mortality. But like water seeping through a rock, time permeated her once-young body. Her ink-black hair waged a rear-guard stand against a tide of gray, and decades of politics, work, and war had left battle scars on her face. The lithe frame of Milwaukee had softened into a plump trunk carried on slow, swollen legs hinged on thick cankles. Plagued with migraines, shingles, nervous exhaustion, a troubled gallbladder, phlebitis, and lymphoma, her doctors repeatedly ordered her to stop smoking.

"There's no point in my giving up cigarettes now," she would tell them. "I won't die young."

Yet her eyes retained the raptor-like look of her youth. Green and deep, they held a focus that grew sharper as the years passed.

Two Decades, Two Wars

Golda's first great crisis as foreign minister rushed at her in July 1956, when Egyptian president Gamal Nasser nationalized the Suez Canal and closed the Gulf of Aqaba to Jewish shipping. The colonial powers, Britain and France, opposed Nasser and assembled a military force to eject Egypt from the Sinai Peninsula and Canal Zone.

Without waiting for Egypt to make the next move, the Israeli Defense Force (IDF) launched a preemptive strike, overrunning the Sinai Peninsula and smashing the Egyptian army. British and French troops drove to the canal while Israel occupied the Sinai from the Negev Desert in the north to Sharm el-Sheikh at the peninsula's southern tip.

In the United Nations, Golda defended Israel's decision to shoot first. Egypt's government was infiltrating Israel with irregular fighters, and Nasser had threatened the nation's economy by shutting down Aqaba and the canal. Israel had a right to defend its national interests, even if that meant drawing first blood and occupying the Sinai.

She felt morally right, but to Golda's dismay the superpowers aligned against Israel. The Soviet Union, looking for an opening into the Middle East, threatened to intervene on the side of Egypt. US president Dwight Eisenhower, facing reelection and hoping to be seen as an honest broker between Arabs and Israelis, turned his back on Britain and France and threated economic sanctions unless Israel withdrew its troops.

Under intense pressure, Israel withdrew from the Sinai on condition that a United Nations peacekeeping force secure Israel's border against further Egyptian aggression. The UN agreed.

As foreign minister, Golda had a front-row seat to a drama that underscored her credo: War is political, and should be tailored to political ends. It is useful, sometimes, but if the diplomatic foundation is not carefully laid, ambassadors and politicians could snatch defeat from the jaws of victory.

The 1956 war had been such a crushing military victory that war strategists like the one-eyed general Moshe Dayan confidently predicted the Arabs would not be ready for another war until at least the 1970s.[*] But in 1967, Egypt's President Nasser prepared to take another run at his perennial foe. In May, he ordered United Nations peacekeeping troops out of the Sinai.

To the surprise of everyone, Secretary General U Thant promptly complied with Nasser's demand, abandoning the UN's commitment to protect Israel's border and clearing the way for an invasion of southern Israel.

Israel was on its own.

Nasser closed the Suez Canal to ships sailing to Israel, and Jordan's King Hussein signed a military pact with Egypt and Syria, menacing Israel from three sides. By June 1967, 465,000 Arab troops, 2,800 tanks, and 800 aircraft were poised to lunge over Israel's borders.

As the country teetered on the fulcrum between peace and war, Golda held no official government title. The year prior, she retired from government. Tired of criticism, tired of the long days, tired of her fight with lymphoma and chemotherapy, she claimed, unconvincingly, that she was done with politics.

But she was one of Israel's most experienced elder statesmen. Like the ancient judge Deborah, who held court under a date palm tree and worked through battle plans against the Canaanites, Golda's views were widely respected. As war looked inevitable, Prime Minister Levi Eshkol invited her to sit with the cabinet as its members debated whether to launch a preemptive strike.

As always, Golda was blunt. When the prime minister asked her views, she told the cabinet to strike first.

"I don't see how war can be avoided. Nobody is going to help us," she said. "I understand the Arabs wanting to wipe us out, but do they really expect us to cooperate?"

The cabinet agreed, and the government turned matters over to the Israeli

---

[*] Dayan had lost his left eye in World War II while serving with an Allied reconnaissance brigade in Syria and Lebanon.

Defense Force. French-built Mirage attack jets launched a devastating strike against Egyptian air bases on June 5, wrecking 204 Egyptian warplanes on the ground. Flying home at top speed, they refueled and rearmed, then unleashed renewed fury on air bases in Jordan and Syria, destroying another 200 planes. In an afternoon, Arab air power was broken.

Beneath this aluminum umbrella, Israeli ground forces charged forward. On the Syrian border, an Israeli division captured the Golan Heights, a launch site for rocket attacks on northern Israel. To the south, the Israeli Defense Force rolled up the Sinai Peninsula to the Suez Canal. To the east, it drove as far as the Jordan River's West Bank and captured Old Jerusalem. In six days, Israel had decisively beaten three enemies who outnumbered her. The IDF also captured more than three times Israel's original land, home to a million Arab residents.

Visiting the Western Wall, a Jerusalem landmark taken during the war, Golda followed an old Jewish tradition by stuffing a folded piece of paper with her wish into one of the wall's cracks.

Shalom, the paper read.

Peace.

The Six-Day War showed her, once again, that Israel's security would turn on its military might, not the opinions of others or the fleeting goodwill of the United Nations.

"We don't want wars. We want peace more than all else," she told a fundraising crowd in New York's Madison Square Garden a few weeks later. Yet Israel had to defend itself, violently if necessary. "Those that perished in Hitler's gas chambers were the last Jews to die without standing up to defend themselves," she vowed. She later remarked, "If we have to have a choice between being dead and pitied and being alive with a bad image, we'd rather be alive and have the bad image."

The war also taught Golda that she could not remain inactive. Politics was in her blood. She had become addicted to the adrenal surge that comes from controlling events and being needed, driving a young nation through the perils of Middle Eastern politics. It had become her animating force, her drug of choice, something her body and mind craved like caffeine and tobacco.

Now almost seventy years old, she returned to Tel Aviv to form a new coalition party. Using her force of personality, and intelligently aligning splinter groups on key issues, she spot-welded a new political base that made her Israel's latest kingmaker.

Like Indira Gandhi, Golda could be ruthless with her political enemies. "Golda knew what power was and how to wield it," recalled one advisor. "She was a hard politician. Either she liked you or she didn't. And woe betide you if she didn't."

Another opponent described her style in down-to-earth terms: "She comes clumping along with that sad, suffering face drawn with pain from her varicose veins and God knows what-all. You rush to help her to your seat. She thanks you kindly. The next thing you know, you're dead."

In February 1969, it was Prime Minister Eshkol who was dead, though not due to any scheming by Golda. He died in his sleep, the victim of a heart attack, and party leaders asked Golda to succeed him as prime minister.

Golda had long yearned for the "most important thing," but her drawn face was no act. She had been in the room where it happens for thirty years, and her body was breaking down from age and overwork. She had no desire to leave office the way Eshkol had—lying in state, gawked at by blank-faced ministers and party bosses, each holding one eye on the corpse and the other on the corpse's successor.

So before accepting the premiership, she paid her physician a visit. With an unblinking eye, she asked how long she could expect to live.

"Ten years," came the answer.

Ten years.

She went home and thought it over.

Ten years would be enough time, she concluded. Enough to finish her part of Israel's epic.

"Nourished by the Blood of Her Children"

She took the helm of a nation in changing seasons. The pioneer spirit of the *kibbutzim* had faded a bit as a softer, more indulgent middle class took root. Ashkenazi labor was being supplanted by low-wage Arab immigrants in construction and agricultural jobs. Among the nation's young people, Hebrew folk songs were giving way to Beatles tunes, and an African Jewish group calling itself the Black Panthers protested ethnic discrimination by their European-born countrymen. Long hair, short skirts . . . to a salt-of-the-earth socialist like Golda, it was hard to accept that the nation she helped build was moving on. Like the rest of the world.

Her job was no easier for being a woman of seventy. Newspapers grumbled that she was too old for the post of prime minister, while ultra-Orthodox Jews still carped about a female premier violating God's law.

To Golda, age and gender didn't matter. The world worked the way it did, and she would not waste a minute defending either the theology or ideology behind women in government. At this moment, Israel needed her, so Israel got her. It was that simple.

"I became prime minister because that was how it was, in the same way that my milkman became an officer in command of an outpost on Mount Hermon," she later wrote. Like the chickens at Merhaven, if there was a problem to solve, she would solve it.

The pragmatist in her found self-proclaimed feminists annoying. As an individualist who believed anyone could make their mark through hard work and self-sacrifice—not quotas or special treatment—Golda had little patience for the women's rights movement that was finding its voice in the early 1970s. She dismissed activists of her day as "those crazy women who burn their bras and go around all disheveled and hate men." When asked about women's liberation, the woman who had cradled a dying man on a bullet-ridden bus snorted, "What do they have to be liberated from? Are they bored?"

Golda's plain speaking and shrewd ways of twisting American arms for Phantom jets dispelled fears of the soft "feminine government," which comforted Israel's establishment. It was a dangerous world, and Israel needed a leader who could be ruthless.

As a Zionist, national security was Golda's obsession. "Golda Meir was an original," remembered Nixon's Secretary of State, Henry Kissinger. "Shrewd, earthy, elemental, she saw herself as a mother to her people. To her every square inch of the territory of Israel had been nourished by the blood of her children . . . The idea of returning territory was almost physically painful to her."

The idea of fighting for that territory was also painful. She knew many who had fallen in Israel's wars, and the government kept a five-volume journal of every combatant who died in action. As she told journalist Oriana Fallaci, "We don't like to make war, even when we win. After the last one, there was no joy in our streets. No dancing, no songs, no festivities. And you should have seen our soldiers coming back victorious. Each one was a picture of sadness."

Golda accepted that sadness as a part of life in the ancient, war-torn land. As with chickens, as with coalition governments, she saw war in practical terms. "We don't thrive on military acts. We do them because we have to," she told *Vogue* magazine in 1969. "And thank God we are efficient."

That efficiency sometimes required blood. She had favored assassinating Jewish terrorists during the years of British rule, and she authorized Mossad to hunt down Black September terrorists involved in the 1972 Munich Olympics massacre of Jewish athletes.

Yet she had no regrets. "Are we supposed to sit here with our hands folded, praying and murmuring, 'Let's hope that nothing happens?'" she once asked. "Praying doesn't help. What helps is to counterattack. With all possible means, including means that we don't necessarily like."

Golda understood the moral trade-off between violence and security, and accepted the responsibility that goes with leading a nation in wartime. Her orders went out from behind closed doors in Tel Aviv, but she never deluded herself about what those neat, typewritten slips of paper meant. The blood was on her hands.

"There's no difference between killing and making decisions by which you send others to kill," she said, a somber look on her face. "It's exactly the same thing. And maybe it's worse."

Flipping through a book on America's war in Vietnam, she reflected through sad eyes:

I've so often found myself having to make certain decisions: for instance, to send our soldiers to places from where they wouldn't come back, or commit them to operations that would cost the lives of who knows how many human beings on both sides. And I suffered . . . I suffered. But I gave those orders as a man would have given them. And now that I think of it, I'm not at all sure that I suffered any more than a man would have. Among my male colleagues I have seen some oppressed by a darker sadness than mine. Oh, not that mine was little! But it didn't influence, no, it didn't influence my decisions.

Another of those decisions lay just around the corner.

IN SEPTEMBER 1970, Egypt's President Nasser died of a heart attack, and his successor, Anwar Sadat, stepped onto the world stage. A bald, brown man with a warm smile, Sadat, like many of Golda's associates, had been jailed by the British back in the 1940s. Moderate by Egyptian standards, he distanced himself from Soviet manipulations and quietly felt around for a *modus vivendi* with Israel.

Sadat's problem was that any compromise with Israel would be wildly unpopular among his hardliners, both in and out of government. Too many concessions, and he could end up with a smoking grenade in his lap. Too few, and Egypt would bleed for another generation. So he announced that if Israeli armed forces would withdraw behind the Gidi and Mitla passes in the Sinai and agree to return all land captured in the 1967 war, Egypt would open talks to confirm Israel's right to exist on borders to be negotiated.

Seeing Sadat's offer as a step toward permanent peace, President Nixon and Henry Kissinger pressed Golda to respond favorably. But Golda saw no reason to trust Cairo's good faith. Borders drawn in 1947 hadn't prevented an Arab invasion in 1948. Victory in 1948 didn't prevent war in 1956. UN guarantees in 1956 did not stop war in 1967. Arab leaders had showed no interest in allowing Jews to live in peace; why should Sadat be any different?

To Golda, the unsentimental reality was that neither Egypt nor Syria would invade Israel for one reason, and one reason only: Israel was too strong. Its Sinai line and forces on the Golan Heights were the keys to lasting peace—not Arab goodwill.

"If the Arabs felt that they could have a war and win, we would have had another war a year ago," she told a reporter from *U.S. News & World Report*. "They aren't deterred because they don't like war . . . If they don't attack us in an outright war it is because they know exactly what is going to happen."

Buoyed by her faith in the IDF, Golda refused to withdraw Israeli troops from the occupied territories. In capturing the Sinai, Israel had turned the haunt of jackals into a land of reed and papyrus; Golda would not hand it back to the jackals.

Her determination looked like short-sighted stubbornness to many in the foreign diplomatic corps. "Meir was more interested in receiving Phantom jet fighters from Washington than in listening to what Sadat was offering," a foreign ministry official remembered. "The Israeli political leadership at the time could not accept the symbolic presence of even a mere token Egyptian police force on the Israeli-occupied east bank of the canal."

As Golda held her ground, rhetoric from Arab capitals escalated. She kept up a secret dialog with Jordan's King Hussein, a moderate whom Golda had supported when his kingdom was invaded by Palestinian radicals driving Syrian tanks. She and Mossad, Israel's spy agency, also closely watched Egypt's moves through a highly placed spy code-named "In-Law."*

They watched, but saw nothing. The standard "no peace" and "year of decision" slogans still rippled from Cairo's press ministry throughout 1971 and 1972, but, as usual, the front lines remained quiet. As 1973 opened, Golda saw no reason to think this year would be any different.

---

* In an appalling breach of security protocol, "In-Law" was a code-name used for Ashraf Marwan, President Nasser's son-in-law, a close advisor to President Sadat.

She still carried the old flame of independence, but time was slipping through her glass. Golda's public approval rating held at an enviable 73 percent, two points below her age, but she knew she could not hold the reins much longer. In November 1972, she told a reporter, "I can't go on with this madness forever. If you only knew how many times I say to myself: To hell with everything, to hell with everybody, I've done my share . . . Yes, many don't believe that I'll leave. Well, they'd better believe it, and I'll even give you the date: October 1973."

AS THE OCTOBER 1973 elections approached, optimism suffused Israel's voters. The economy was setting growth records, and Israeli currency reserves reached $1.2 billion, an all-time high. Even security seemed, for once, a safe bet: Since the end of 1971, Nixon had sent Israel sixty-six Phantoms and 104 Skyhawk ground attack planes, giving Tel Aviv the dominant air force in the region. Its intelligence community could provide enough warning to mobilize a 240,000-strong reserve pool, and the Israeli Air Force could hold back the Arabs until reserves took their places on the front lines.

On the far side of the Suez Canal, Egypt didn't seem to be spoiling for a fight. President Sadat expelled his Soviet military advisors, a sign that the Egypt-Soviet relationship was cracking. Golda's defense minister, Moshe Dayan, told army officers that Arab military dysfunction "derives from factors that I don't believe will change quickly: the low level of their soldiers in education, technology, and integrity; and inter-Arab divisiveness which is papered over from time to time but superficially and for short spurts."

Israel's generals had drunk from the cup of victory many times, and victory, like liquor, weakens inhibitions. A joke running around Tel Aviv war offices had a bored Moshe Dayan grousing over a cup of coffee with Lieutenant General David "Dado" Elazar, the IDF's chief of staff.

"There's nothing to do," complained Dayan.

"How about invading another Arab country?" asked Dado.

"What would we do in the afternoon?" Dayan muttered.

THE JOKES ABRUPTLY STOPPED when an unmarked Bell helicopter landed at a Mossad safe house north of Tel Aviv on the night of September 25, 1973. The doors slid open, and a short, mustachioed man in a Western business suit emerged. Israeli operatives ushered him inside the house.

Waiting for him in an anteroom was Golda Meir. With a pleasant smile, she stood, extended her hand, and welcomed Jordan's King Hussein.

Hussein was an old-school Arab ruler, but he had quietly explored peace with Israel since the early 1960s. He had expelled the Palestinian Liberation Organization, and his relations with Syria had grown frosty after Syrian-backed PLO forces invaded his country. Having lost a big slice of the Hashemite Kingdom in the Six-Day War, he didn't wish to lose any more, and his foreign policy turned on good relations with Israel. He would cheerfully help his official enemy whenever it was in his kingdom's interest.

Garrulous by nature and unsure how to begin, the king started off making small talk with the Israeli leaders. Golda, nodding patiently, let the king prattle on for nearly an hour until he came to the real reason for his visit. His soft words hit Golda like a kick in the stomach: The Syrians were going to war.

At midnight, Hussein walked out of the safe house and disappeared into a helicopter that was swallowed up in the night sky. Golda immediately rang up Moshe Dayan. The defense minister was unruffled. Like many influential thinkers in Aman, Israel's defense intelligence agency, Dayan subscribed to "The Concept," a syllogism the intel wizards practically inscribed on a stone tablet from Mount Sinai. According to The Concept, Syria would not attack Israel without Egypt's help, and Egypt would not help Syria without Soviet bombers and "Scud" ground-to-ground missiles. The Egyptians had no such bombers or missiles. *Ergo*, no help. *Ergo*, no war.

Dayan had been the IDF's chief of staff during the heady days of the Suez War, and received much of the credit for Israel's victory in the Six-Day War. Golda saw no reason to second-guess the nation's top military expert, and she deferred to the collective wisdom of the men in "the Pit," the nickname of the IDF command center.

Troubled but reassured, Golda flew to Strasbourg, where she was scheduled to give a speech to the Council of Europe. As she worked the diplomatic halls, her close advisor, Israel Galili, telephoned with a warning that the border situation was growing ominous. He asked Golda to come home immediately, but she insisted on stopping in Vienna on the way home to browbeat the Austrian chancellor on matters of Jewish immigration and anti-Semitic terrorism.*

---

* In September 1973, a year after Palestinian terrorists massacred Jewish athletes at the Munich Olympic village, Palestinians took three Soviet Jews and an Austrian customs official hostage and demanded that Austria close a transit camp processing Soviet Jews immigrating to Israel. Austrian Chancellor Bruno Kreisky closed the camp, setting himself up for a tongue-lashing from Golda for caving in to terrorist demands.

Galili's phone call had been prompted by darkening clouds to the southwest. Anwar Sadat had called up 120,000 reservists, and an Egyptian division was moving toward the Suez Canal. Hostilities along the Suez, even local ones, might be the critical signal Syria needed to launch another war on Israel's northern border.

Yet Eli Zeira, the respected head of Aman, along with Dayan, General Elazar, and Zvi Zamir, Mossad's director-general, still did not see war as imminent. Dayan was still smarting from a political spanking the newspapers had given the government earlier in the year. When Egypt's army began unusual troop maneuvers that spring, Dayan persuaded Golda to call up Israel's military reserves—at a $35 million price tag—while Zeira held to his belief that nothing would happen. Zeira turned out to be right.

After the call-up incident, no politician wanted to defy Aman and wind up with egg on his face. With a population of three million, Israel lacked enough workers to keep a quarter million men and women under arms indefinitely; the economy could not afford those absences for long. So Israel's strategy required the IDF to hold back the enemy long enough for the reserves to take up their positions.

Of course, that strategy assumed the enemy could not deliver a knockout blow quickly or without warning.

Which was exactly what Sadat and Assad were planning.

Day of Atonement

Israel's northern border with Syria ends at the Golan Heights, a plateau occupied by the IDF since the Six-Day War. Strategists referred to the Heights as "the eyes and ears of Israel," because it provides a window into Syrian war preparations. Through field glasses, Israeli observers picked out a first-line armor brigade and reinforcements shuffling into forward positions. Most worrisome of all was the thick belt of Soviet SAM-6 antiaircraft missiles—first-rate batteries that threatened to neutralize Israel's priceless advantage in the air.

If Syria meant to launch a war, it was making all the right moves.

To the southwest, along the Suez Canal, reconnaissance photos showed the Egyptian army massing bridge-building and pontoon equipment—precisely the sort of preparation for a lunge over the canal. While Egypt's government publicly called the movement a simple military exercise, Israeli sources identified stockpiles of fuel and ammunition, and reported that personal leave recently granted to officers had abruptly been canceled.

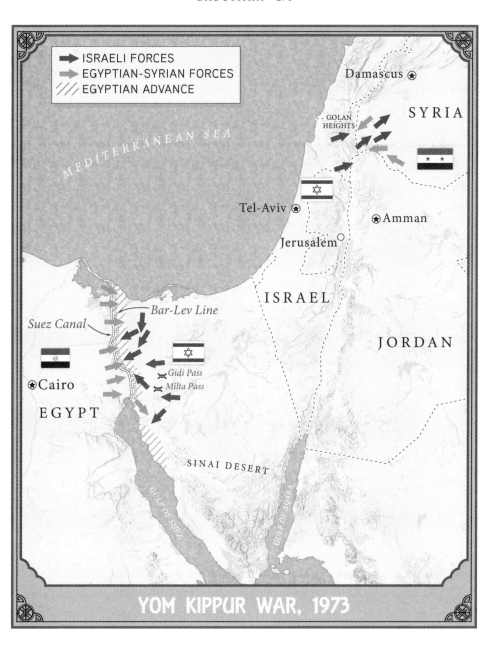

ISRAELI FORCES
EGYPTIAN-SYRIAN FORCES
EGYPTIAN ADVANCE

MEDITERRANEAN SEA

Damascus

SYRIA

GOLAN HEIGHTS

Tel-Aviv

Amman

Jerusalem

ISRAEL

JORDAN

Bar-Lev Line

Suez Canal

Gidi Pass

Milta Pass

Cairo

EGYPT

SINAI DESERT

GULF OF SUEZ

GULF OF AQABA

YOM KIPPUR WAR, 1973

If the Egyptians were only planning an exercise, why did they need to top off their ammunition stocks? And why had they given officers leave, only to cancel them without notice?

Early warning of a shooting war was critical to Israel's defense, because on the ground the IDF would be outnumbered at least 3-to-1. The Egyptian army fielded 650,000 combat troops, the Syrians another 150,000. Counting contingents from Jordan, Iraq, and other aligned nations, the Arabs mustered some 900,000 men willing, or resigned, to die in the struggle against Zionism.

To hold back this tide, General "Dado" Elazar commanded about 135,000 front-line troops.

On Wednesday, October 3, Dayan informed Golda of abnormal troop movement on both fronts. Her pulse quickened as she listened, but Zeira's deputy assured her that nothing was imminent. Dado concurred, explaining with the confidence of a seasoned prophet that Syria would not go to war without Egypt, and Egypt wasn't ready for a full-scale war.

What about a diversionary attack by Egypt? Golda pressed.

The experts calmly replied that Egypt wouldn't dare expose its tanks to the fighter-bombers of the Israeli Air Force.

Troubled, she remarked to Galili, "There's a contradiction between signs on the ground and what the experts are saying." But the old bubbie would not overrule generals and intelligence experts who spent their lives studying war.

Besides, Yom Kippur, the highest of Jewish holy days, would begin in three days: Saturday, October 6. Golda loathed the thought of calling the nation to war before the last shofar was blown. At least, not without something definite she could point to.

The next day things became definite. On Thursday afternoon, Zeira's cryptographers picked up an uncoded radio message from Moscow referring to the evacuation of families of Soviet troops from Egypt. General Elazar canceled military leaves for the holiday and put the IDF on its second-highest state of alert. He moved tank units up to the Golan Heights and laid the groundwork for another reserve call-up if needed.

As the crisis deepened, Golda's ministers waded through a bog of indecision. Dayan insisted he saw no unequivocal signs of war, and Galili cautioned Golda that a call-up of reserves might provoke the Arabs into striking first. General Elazar, who had been burned by the false alarm that spring, hesitated to demand full war preparations. Yet everyone in the high command knew that Israel could be blindsided if the worst case turned out to be right.

As a compromise, Golda's cabinet recommended against calling up the reserves, at least for the moment. But before leaving for Yom Kippur services, the cabinet authorized Elazar to begin a call-up, even on the holiday, if war appeared imminent.

Like Roosevelt before Pearl Harbor, Golda was staring at shards of data that pointed in different directions. Clarity in the Middle East had always been obscured by the routine "Death to Israel!" scimitar-rattling by Syria, Egypt, and Iraq that came to nothing. A Soviet armor brigade moving to the West German border would have set off alarm bells all over Europe; on the Israeli border, it was just another day at the office.

As Jewish families warmed their stoves for Yom Kippur Eve meals, most had no idea of the sandstorm rising beyond their borders. East of the Suez Canal, a thin chain of Israeli pillboxes and firebases known as the Bar-Lev Line was manned by a tripwire force of 475 infantrymen, 300 tanks, and 50 artillery pieces. They faced over 100,000 Egyptian troops, 1,350 tanks, and 2,000 artillery pieces. To the north, Israel had two small infantry regiments and 177 tanks facing 45,000 Syrian troops, 1,500 tanks, and 942 heavy guns.

No Israeli, from the prime minister to the lowest IDF private, knew what would happen next. As the land fell silent on Friday evening, Golda went to bed, letting her subconscious sift through yesterday's horrors and tomorrow's dreams.

AT 3:50 IN THE MORNING of Saturday, October 6, the telephone of Golda's nightmares rang. This time, the phone was real, and the voice at the other end wasn't a specter from a dream. It was her military secretary, conveying a message from Zvi Zamir, Mossad's top man. In-Law had spoken, he said: Egypt and Syria would launch their attack before Yom Kippur was over.

An ashen-faced prime minister summoned Dayan and General Elazar for an 8:00 a.m. conference. Whether to fight was no longer the question. The question was whether to strike first.

As she shuffled into her office to meet the brass, Golda looked like hell. Her head was bent and her eyelids drooped over deeply etched cheeks. Her gray-streaked hair, usually pulled into a tight bun, was wild and disheveled, giving her the look of a crazed witch from a Ukrainian fairy tale. She listened, she nodded, but her only normal aspect was her granite-hard voice.

Assuming that the Arab attack would not take place before late afternoon, "Dado" Elazar recommended a preemptive air strike, the first move in the IDF playbook. He pointed out that defense of the Suez and Golan areas would require at least 50,000 additional ground troops, and at the moment those troops were fasting and praying with their families. But the Air Force was ready now, and

Dado recommended smashing Syrian air bases at noon, Syrian missiles at three o'clock, and Syrian armor columns two hours later. Hitting now could save many Israeli lives.

As she watched her generals debate tactics, Golda shuffled cigarettes from pack to lighter to lips like a nervous blackjack dealer. For all her intimacy with war, she was out of her depth on planning military operations. The seventy-five-year-old babushka had no idea how many soldiers made up a division, and she knew nothing of "defense in depth" or spoiling attacks. Once, when a reporter asked her to comment on a military exercise she was observing, she guffed, "Do you think that an old lady like myself would have anything to say about things like this?"

But the old lady had a head for decision-making, and after a few minutes of wavering, she reached a decision that startled every man in uniform. In this war, the world had to know beyond all doubt who the aggressor was. The United States, Israel's best ally, would not let World War III begin over a Middle East border skirmish. Kissinger, recalling Pakistan's preemptive air strike against India, had repeatedly warned Golda not to strike first.

Israel couldn't defy the United States on this fundamental issue, she explained. War required mass stockpiles of weapons and ammunition, and Israeli stocks would run low in a matter of days. If President Nixon proved reluctant to send missiles, jets, and air-defense systems to Tel Aviv, the tide of battle could turn against Israel before week's end.

"None of us knows now what the future has in store for us," she told her generals. "But there is always a possibility that we'll need someone's help, and if we strike first, no one is going to help." The IDF's thin green line would have to bear the storm's brunt until the reserves could be mobilized.

If Golda were going to show restraint, she would make certain Nixon and Kissinger appreciated the sacrifice they were asking. She summoned US Ambassador Kenneth Keating to her office and told Keating that war appeared imminent. It must be a miscalculation on the part of Damascus and Cairo, she said. Israel was at peace and wished to remain that way. She urged Keating to call Washington right away and ask Nixon to persuade Sadat and Assad to stand down.

Next, Golda summoned the cabinet to a noon emergency meeting. Many of her ministers would be furious over her decision to forego a preemptive strike. By refusing to blunt the Arab attack with one of her own, she could very well condemn an unknown number of their countrymen to death. Golda could tell herself it was a calculated risk to preserve a vital strategic relationship, but she sagged under the weight of the decision.

"You can defend it to the Cabinet," a friend reassured her before the meeting started.

"Yes," she said wearily, "but it is a terrible responsibility."

Two hours later, as Golda was telling cabinet ministers that war was imminent, warning sirens blared through Jerusalem, Tel Aviv, and every major city in Israel.

"What is this?" she asked, her face scrunched in confusion.

"It seems the war has begun," a stenographer remarked.

She nodded. "So, they did surprise us after all."

Couriers drove cars and motorcycles recklessly through empty holiday streets to find unit commanders and distribute mobilization orders. Corporals and privates tapped the shoulders of young men as they sat in temples. Whispered messages and small folded notes sent them quietly home to fold prayer shawls and strap on revolvers. On their day of atonement, these men and women would defend their homeland.

On the other side, Syria and Egypt began their atonement for the humiliation of the Six-Day War.

FROM BEHIND EGYPT'S BORDER, attack jets climbed, then screamed down on Israel's Bar-Lev Line. Spraying missiles and dropping bombs, the warplanes banked and disappeared into the western sky as pillars of smoke rose above the desert.

On the ground, orange flashes knifed from 2,000 Egyptian artillery pieces. Soviet-built tanks revved engines and clattered forward under the artillery barrage, while 4,000 riflemen and commandos paddled over the canal in rubber boats. The desert fire was lit.

In planning sessions at "the Pit," Israeli leaders had been confident that their tanks could repel the enemy on the ground. But Egyptian antitank units popped out from cover and fired Soviet-built missiles with surprising accuracy, turning steel machines into fireballs. In the first fifty-six hours of fighting, Israel would lose 400 tanks and forty-nine fighter-bombers. Nearly 32,000 Egyptian troops moved onto the Sinai Peninsula, and the strategic blueprint revered by Golda's generals burned like a scroll.

In the north, where the front lines were close to Israel's major cities, the situation looked grave. Syrian troops lunged into the Golan Heights. Soviet SAM missiles were dropping Israeli Phantom jets like desert flies. Assad's tanks and armored personnel carriers lumbered forward, firing high explosive shells, spraying bullets, pushing back the thin line of defenders.

By Sunday, October 7, the fog of war had lifted enough to give Golda and her commanders a glimpse of the disturbing picture of the IDF being forced back. Lines of Soviet-built tanks, trucks, and personnel carriers snaked across the Golan Heights, while Soviet SAM missiles held off Israeli jets.

When Moshe Dayan visited the front, the sight of carnage hit him square in his sharp jaw. His confidence badly shaken, Dayan ordered bridges over the Jordan River prepared for demolition and muttered to the Israeli Air Force chief that destruction of the Third Temple—a metaphor for modern Israel—might be at hand.

In the south, things looked worse. The Egyptians shot their way across the Suez Canal and were rolling up the Bar-Lev fortifications. Israelis planned a stand at the Mitla and Gidi passes, but if Sadat's troops reached those passes before reserves arrived to save the day, the IDF would have only two small divisions standing between Egyptian tanks and Israel's heartland.

In a tense forty-five-minute meeting in Golda's office, General Elazar outlined Sunday's crumbling picture. The Syrian penetration threw the IDF command into an uncharted minefield. In the Sinai, Egyptians had pierced the Bar-Lev Line. Long used to attacks and victories, Golda's lieutenants had never weathered a life-or-death setback, and Elazar was forced to tell Golda that the Israeli Army had no practical experience in large-scale retreat. "We know how to do it from the books," he said, "but we've never actually done it."

Everyone in the room knew how serious the threat had become. If the Syrians broke through before the reserves were deployed, Assad's men might overrun the country. The Egyptians were further back, but they had more men. And neither would be satisfied with simply recovering the occupied territories. The goal of Assad and Sadat was to drive the Jews into the sea, Dayan said. "They have come to fight us for the Land of Israel."

Golda nodded. Her objectives were limited, but the enemy's were not. If Assad held the advantage, he would drive as far into Israel as their tanks would go. "There is no reason why [the Arabs] would stop," she said. "They already tasted blood."

Moshe Dayan, the minister nominally responsible for the disaster, admitted that he and the high command had misjudged the Arabs. Their fighting skills had improved since the last war, and the IDF had planned for the last war—not the war the Arabs were currently winning.

That afternoon, Dayan came to Golda's office and offered to resign.

Golda wouldn't hear of it. She didn't much like Moshe, but he was a hero to the Israeli people and had engineered victories since World War II. His stern face and black eye patch had become a symbol of Israeli strength; his resignation now would be a body blow to public morale.

Besides, it had been Golda's decision to refrain from the preemptive strike. So, she told Moshe to forget the idea of resigning.

She also told him to forget another idea. As the meeting broke up, Dayan began walking to the door between Golda's office and the hallway. Placing his hand lightly on the doorknob, he casually turned to Golda and fumbled for his words, saying, "I thought, since the situation is so bad, [as] we just heard for half an hour from Dado, that we should . . . since we don't have a lot of time . . . we should prepare for a demonstration, also a nuclear option." Shalhevet Freier, the head of Israel's Atomic Energy Commission, was sitting outside Golda's office, Dayan said. With Golda's approval, he offered to order the commissioner to begin preparations for a nuclear attack.

Golda's chief advisors, Israel Galili and Yigal Allon, vehemently opposed the suggestion. Even in self-defense, the use of nuclear weapons would make Israel a pariah among nations. The United Nations, possibly even the United States, would line up against it.

Golda agreed with them. "Forget it," she told Dayan.

With a bright and untroubled eye, Dayan said he accepted Golda's decision. But as soon as he left the room, Galili warned Golda that Dayan might "forget" to tell the AEC commissioner the nuclear option was off the table. Golda quickly summoned Freier into her office and told him in no uncertain terms that Israel would not prepare for nuclear war. The nuclear option would never be exercised. The nation would stand or fall on its conventional skill.

Dayan, Israel's one-eyed Jeremiah, peppered Golda with prophecies of doom as Sunday wore on. His pessimism was contagious. Gray-faced and shaken, Golda emerged from a war cabinet meeting mumbling, "Dayan is speaking of surrender."*

She hadn't seen the cobra's fangs before it struck, and she began to contemplate her own death in an overrun capital. As she later told Dado's bureau chief, "On the second day of the war, I decided to commit suicide."

But her mind, wracked by anxiety and physical stress, bounced back. Jews, she liked to say, did not have the luxury of pessimism. They would fight to win, for they had no other option. Any thoughts of abandoning her post, even in disaster, even at age seventy-five, flew as she contemplated the job she had to finish.

---

* Golda, herself badly shaken, was being unfair to Dayan. Though his confidence had taken a blow during his first visits to the front, he hadn't used the word "surrender" and quickly dropped talk of the Third Temple's destruction.

Blood returned to her cheeks, and her eyes brightened. She told herself events were not wholly out of her control. The next move would be up to her generals, but the move after that was hers alone.

"Get Simcha," she told an aide.

THOUGH DAYAN SOUNDED DESPONDENT, General Elazar did not. True, they were outnumbered, and they were fighting two wars on opposite ends of their country. But their lines had not been broken, and trained reserves were streaming to assembly points, checking out their old weapons and readying for the counterattack.

"Today we hit bottom," Elazar told Golda on Monday, the war's third day. "Tomorrow I predict that we'll be able to get our chins above water."

By noon on Tuesday, their chins were still below the tide. Elazar's limited counterattack in the Sinai went off the rails, costing his army seventy scarce tanks. To the north, the Syrians had been reinforced and were launching a fresh offensive. Gloom still pervaded the Pit, which the bitter Air Force commander dubbed the "Holocaust Basement."

Dayan, scheduled for a television announcement that night, spoke histrionically with newspaper editors of Egypt's "unlimited equipment" and the terrible odds facing Israel. When unnerved editors passed Moshe's remarks to Golda's office, she canned his television appearance and substituted a former Aman head, who presented a somber but more balanced picture of what was to come.

As the war's first shocks began to fade, businesslike faces cramming the Pit's tables looked a little brighter. These men in olive green knew how to spot the high and low tides of battle, and they thought they saw the water's edge receding just a bit.

In the south, the Egyptians reached the limit of their antiaircraft umbrella; to push any further would expose their tanks to ecclesiastical punishment from the Israeli Air Force. General Elazar dispatched General Chaim Bar-Lev, the father of the Sinai defense line, to take command of the southern front. Bar-Lev's firm hand brought stability, then slow improvement.

On the Syrian front, the IAF made steady inroads. Fighter-bombers managed to neutralize enough SAM sites to permit bombing of Syrian command posts, oil refineries, power plants, and radar stations deep inside Syria. Setting its sights on the Syrian capital of Damascus, the IAF warmed up its bombers for the long-awaited retribution.

When the IAF proposed bombing Damascus, Golda initially refused. She worried that bombing the Syrian capital might be seen as widening the war. At worst, it could nudge the United States into a neutral stance at a time when Israeli munitions were running low and Nixon's help was needed more than ever.

But the generals urged Golda to seize the tactical advantage. They argued that hitting Damascus would take the fight out of Syria, and send a warning to Jordan, Iraq, or any other Arab nation that might think of piling on.

Weighing risks on both sides, Golda concluded her generals were right. She had refused to permit her commanders to strike first, but now that the war had begun, she would press any advantage she could find. She nodded, and soon Phantom and Mirage fighters were shrieking over Damascus skies.

On the ground, Israeli troops on the Syrian frontier launched a fierce counterattack toward the Purple Line, the prewar Israeli-Syrian border. When they reached it on Wednesday, October 10, they dropped another thorny question into Golda's lap: Should Israel push beyond the Purple Line toward Damascus, or shift its armor south, to the Sinai front, and recapture territory lost to Egypt?

That night, a divided military command trooped into Golda's office with opposing recommendations. Dayan and Elazar favored throwing Israel's reserves against the Purple Line and driving on Damascus. That would leave Egypt with the upper hand in the Sinai, but a big push north might knock Syria out of the war before Iraqi troops could reinforce them.

On the other side, Elazar's headstrong deputy, Major General Israel Tal, argued that the Egyptian front was the more important of the two. The Egyptians were at the edge of their SAM protection, he argued, so the Air Force should ready a massive strike for the moment the turtle stuck its head out of its shell. That would require the IDF to concentrate its might in the south, leaving nothing for a push toward Damascus.

The military question was pregnant with political implications, and once again the final decision was left in the weathered hands of an elderly grandmother.

Golda's mind spun through the ramifications of both approaches. If the IDF captured Syrian territory, Israel might trade that land for Sinai territory captured by Egypt—a sort of ransom of dirt. But a drive on Damascus might also scare Iraq into bailing out its Arab neighbor. It could also prompt an anxious Soviet Union to send bigger weapons to Syria, or perhaps intervene directly.

Working through military and political factors like a math teacher solving an equation, Golda announced her decision. She pointed out that it would take four days to shift tanks, guns, and soldiers from Syria to the Sinai. During those four days, the UN and superpowers would try to broker a cease-fire. That pressure could be resisted, but not for long. If the war ended with Israel holding less territory than when the war started, Arab nations would take away a new lesson: War, though expensive, paid dividends. They might slumber for a season, but eventually they would awaken, fresh for another conflict, intent on conquering Israel one slice at a time. Peace would become unattainable.

So Golda directed the generals to cross the Purple Line and drive into Syria. They would take whatever land they could before the rest of the world ordered them to stop. The Sinai army would have to make the best of what it had.

It didn't strike any of the officers in uniform that day—men who killed, who ordered men to kill, who studied violence for a living—as odd that they should ask a frumpy old babushka for orders on air strikes and strategic troop movements. But some Israelis outside the Pit were perplexed to see Moshe, Dado, and other career officers soliciting military instructions from Golda. As the defense editor of the Israeli newspaper *Haaretz* wrote, "It was strange to see a warrior of seven campaigns and brilliant past chief of staff of the IDF bringing clearly operational subjects to a Jewish grandmother for decision."

AS THE TIDE OF BATTLE turned, Golda and her warlords cast nervous eyes toward their munitions warehouses. Modern war is enormously expensive, and in the first three days of fighting, the IDF had lost five hundred tanks, one-eighth of its air force, and thousands of rounds of missile and artillery ammunition.

The only source of replacement materiel was the traditional Arsenal of Democracy, the United States, and Golda ordered her ambassador, Simcha Dinitz, to press Henry Kissinger for help. She even offered to make a lightning trip, incognito, to Washington to meet with President Nixon face-to-face.*

Richard Nixon, a staunch supporter of Israel, would be *hors de combat* for most of the crisis. On the day Golda's forces reached the Purple Line, his vice president, Spiro Agnew, was forced to resign over a financial scandal. Democrats were talking

---

* Golda believed her friendship with Nixon would tip the balance. Kissinger turned down the request, reasoning, "For her to leave the country leaderless for forty-eight hours in the middle of a war was a sign of panic. If it got out, the entire Arab world would become so confident that nothing could work."

impeachment over the Watergate break-in, special prosecutor Archibald Cox was fighting him in court over secret White House tapes, and Nixon would soon fire Cox, the Attorney General, and the Deputy Attorney General in what the press dubbed the "Saturday Night Massacre."

Crippled politically, Nixon spent most of the crisis brooding, drinking, and wallowing in self-pity at his Florida retreat in Key Biscayne. That left American strategy in the hands of his secretary of state.

Henry Kissinger understood the danger facing Israel. A non-practicing Jew who had lost thirteen family members to the Holocaust, he was personal friends with many Israeli leaders. In the superpower game between the US and Soviet Union, the American client, Israel, could not be allowed to emerge from the Yom Kippur War as the loser.

Yet Kissinger was savvy enough to know that long-term peace in the Middle East, for Jews or Arabs, required both sides to anchor their security interests to a stable foundation, yet feel enough risk to force them to the bargaining table. He privately told Nixon that the best result for long-term peace would be "if Israel came out a little ahead but got bloodied in the process."

As Kissinger saw it, the Yom Kippur War was not an end in itself. It was a small component of a larger goal: a negotiated end to the Cold War. That required delicacy and Machiavellian discretion. The United States had sent Golda artillery rounds, Sidewinder missiles, and other small things that would repel the invasion without enabling the IDF to roll into Cairo. If the Israelis drove too deep into Egypt, Sadat might ask the Kremlin to save him, which would require a strong American countermove. The escalation would spin into a confrontation between Washington and Moscow that would ruin the *détente* Nixon and Kissinger had painstakingly built over the last four years.

To keep America's larger involvement a secret, Kissinger demanded that anything flown to Israel must go in the few available Israeli transport planes, limiting what Israel could acquire. The big items—tanks, fighter jets, and the like—would not be shipped, as long as the Soviets stayed out of the conflict.

The Soviets didn't stay out long, however. US intelligence reports showed the Red Air Force airlifting a modest amount of fuel and ammunition to Syria. When Nixon learned of Moscow's involvement, he exploded and ordered his defense secretary to open the aid pipeline—*all the way*. The United States would replace everything Israel lost on the battlefield, and everything on Golda's wish list would be granted.

Even with a presidential blank check, the aid pipeline valve proved rusty. At Kissinger's insistence, the US government spent three futile days trying to persuade commercial airliners to fly military equipment into Israel in an effort to keep the American hand shrouded.

As bureaucrats at State, Defense, and the White House wrangled with charter lines, Golda squirmed and watched her war stocks run low. Desperate, she ordered Ambassador Dinitz to keep up the pressure on Nixon's men, day after day, night after night.

After excruciating delays, US Defense Secretary James Schlessinger finally ordered the US Air Force to do the job. A week into the fighting, the Air Force launched Operation Nickel Grass, a massive American arms airlift. High above the waves and shouts of the people of Tel Aviv, flocks of giant Galaxy and Starlifter transports soared over blue Mediterranean skies and landed at Tel Aviv's Lod Airport. From their holds, American loadmasters disgorged fighter-bombers, cluster bombs, howitzer ammunition, tanks, antitank missiles: 26,000 tons of the mitochondria of battle.

When Golda learned of the scale of the airlift, she broke down in tears of relief. Her gamble in the hours before the war started—a gamble that cost the lives of hundreds of her countrymen—had paid off. Her lieutenants would no longer have to hoard equipment against future losses. With America's blank check, they could hit back with everything they had.

❖   ❖   ❖

AS THE AMERICANS struggled to mount a resupply mission, Golda, Dayan, and Elazar paid a visit to the Golan Heights. They wanted to see the war zone and give the international press a taste of the fighting engulfing Syria and Israel.

Emerging from a helicopter at a tank supply depot, Golda heard the thump of howitzers in the distance. "The stench of death, cordite, diesel, and exhaust was overwhelming," her press aide later wrote, exaggerating slightly.

In a parking lot filled with tanks taking on fuel and ammunition, her chief of staff threw a map of the front over a tank's deck and outlined the battle with a pen. Eyes reddening with sorrow, she borrowed Dayan's binoculars for a look at the land beyond the Heights.

Squinting into the eyepieces, Golda saw the carnage of decisions made far behind the battle lines. The valley, nicknamed the Vale of Tears, was strewn with the wreckage of war. Twisted armored personnel carriers, burned-out trucks, and dead tanks littered the valley like animal carcasses.

She passed back the binoculars and, with fumbling hands, she reached into her black purse for a pack of cigarettes and tapped out a smoke. Dado struck a match. She took a deep, melancholy drag.

Walking over to a makeshift *sukka*—a religious booth thatched with palm fronds—Golda waded into a crowd of soldiers whose knit caps had been yarmulkes, their field jackets prayer shawls, just a week before. She chatted with the dirty, exhausted young men and asked if they had any questions.

A soldier in his twenties, coated with black dust from head to boot, stepped forward.

"My father was killed in the war of '48, and we won," he said. "My uncle was killed in the war of '56, and we won. My brother lost an arm in the '67 war, and we won. Last week I lost my best friend over there"—pointing to the Vale of Tears—"and we're going to win." Eyes boring into Golda, he then asked, "What's the use of our sacrifice if we can't win the peace?"

A sad half-smile creased Golda's face.

"I weep for your loss, just as I grieve for all our dead," she said.

I lie awake at night thinking of them. And I must tell you in all honesty, were our sacrifices for ourselves alone, then perhaps you would be right. I'm not at all sure they would be worthwhile. But if our sacrifices are for the sake of the whole Jewish people, then I believe with all my heart that any price is worthwhile . . . Our sacrifices are not in vain.

Golda's words came straight from her heart. But within her heart, she knew the soldier was right. Her troops could win this war, and probably would. But what good was another victory if ten years from now a new war sprouted like a noxious weed? What did Israel think she was buying with the lives of her sons and daughters, if not a lasting peace?

To win that peace, they first had to win the war. In the afternoon, Golda and her commanders gathered back in her Jerusalem office to discuss the conflict's next phase. The Syrians had been pushed behind the Purple Line, and Israeli tanks were closing to within thirty miles of Damascus. As long as there were no fresh disasters, including Soviet intervention, Syria would be knocked out of the war.

Another question was tougher to answer: What to do about Egypt?

Death of an Army

The Sinai battle was grinding into a stalemate, with both sides trying to grab bits of land before the superpowers made them stop. Sadat desperately wanted the Sinai's Mitla and Gidi Passes. But his Third Army, the pride of Egypt's armed forces, couldn't reach the passes without leaving its protective SAM umbrella and exposing its tanks to the dreaded Israeli Air Force.

On the other hand, Israel couldn't push the Egyptians back across the Suez Canal.

The answer lay in an audacious move that Golda, Dayan, and Elazar turned over in their minds when the front lines hardened. They would send a force over the Suez Canal into Egypt to cut off Third Army from its food, ammunition, and water.

Crossing the Suez was an enormously risky gamble. General Bar-Lev only had two depleted armored divisions—about 350 tanks—to throw against the Egyptian line. Beyond the canal lay two fresh Egyptian armored divisions, and any deep thrust courted the risk of the invader being cut off from its supplies and starved or annihilated.

But the rewards might justify the risks. If the IDF could get a foothold on the Egyptian side of the canal, Egypt's Third Army would be isolated, Cairo would be threatened, and Sadat would probably sue for peace.

On October 13, Sadat made Golda's decision easier by making a crucial blunder. He moved his two reserve armored divisions over the canal and launched his Third Army toward Mitla Pass. General Bar-Lev countered with Operation Stouthearted Men, the kind of set-piece battle the IDF brass had been waiting for.

With 2,000 tanks committed to battle on both sides, Egyptians and Israelis fought one of history's largest armored vehicle battles. Egypt lost 250 tanks, while the IDF lost twenty. General Ariel Sharon's infantry shattered the hinge linking Egypt's Second and Third Armies and tore a hole in the Egyptian line.

That night, a chipper Bar-Lev rang up Golda. "We are back to being ourselves, and they are back to being themselves," he quipped. Buoyed by Bar-Lev's report, Golda ordered her generals to cross the Suez Canal.

Monday, October 15, fell in the middle of Sukkot, a Jewish holiday dating back to the time when Moses led the children of Israel through the Sinai Desert. Back then, the Hebrews were running east, fleeing Pharaoh's chariots. Now the chariots, steel and emblazoned with the Star of David, were hurtling west as Bar-Lev's men broke through the canal's central defenses and pushed into Egyptian territory.

To General Elazar's disappointment, his stouthearted men made little progress once they crossed into Egypt, and their commanders considered withdrawing back across the canal.

As the battle for a bridgehead over the Suez hung in the balance, an inexcusable security breach by Golda kept the drive in play. While General Elazar was planning an evacuation from the canal's west bank, Golda, without consulting him, gave a pep talk to the nation before the Israeli parliament. "Right now," she announced, "as we convene in the Knesset, an IDF task force is operating on the west bank of the Suez Canal." Members of parliament exploded in cheers.

Dayan and Elazar also exploded when they heard about the speech, but not in cheers. Their numbers on the canal's west side had been too small for the Egyptians to realize what they were up to, and Israel's bridgehead was still vulnerable to a mass counterattack. The prudent course would be to retire to the canal's east bank. Golda's speech transformed a small, tactical crossing into an issue of national prestige, so they could not evacuate their men without severely damaging public morale. Golda had unwittingly boxed in her generals, and the generals would have to double down.

Elazar's renewed push across the canal, made on a shoestring budget, wasn't exactly the invasion of Normandy. But it kept the bridgehead alive. His numbers grew, and he began pushing south to cut off Egypt's Third Army from supplies and reinforcements. When Moshe Dayan phoned Golda a few days later, he casually mentioned that he had visited the African side of the canal.

"You were there?" she asked, her voice rising.

"Yes," said Dayan, his confidence in bloom. "There are a thousand soldiers there now. Tomorrow morning the whole state of Israel will be there."

The whole state of Israel didn't retrace Joseph's ancient footsteps, but the irony of Israelites invading Egypt was lost on no one, least of all Soviet chairman Leonid Brezhnev. When Egypt and Syria had the upper hand in the war's first days, Brezhnev pushed for a UN cease-fire resolution that would let them keep the land they had won. Now the Soviets were pushing for a cease-fire to save their clients from a rout. And when Henry Kissinger informed Golda that a truce proposal was gaining traction in the UN Security Council, she knew her time to punish Sadat was running out.

Kissinger had done his best to hold UN activity to a snail's pace, but on October 19, he warned Ambassador Dinitz that, at best, Israel might expect three more days before a cease-fire resolution went into effect.

Three days, thought Golda, would be enough. Having entered Egyptian territory, the IDF would soon surround, starve, and annihilate Sadat's Third Army. With a disaster on that scale, Sadat wouldn't be in any hurry to invade Israel.

Playing his own game, Kissinger didn't want to see Golda's troops humiliate Egypt. Another brilliant Israeli win might make Golda so intransigent that a negotiated peace with Egypt would be impossible. Moreover, the *threat* of Israeli tanks driving on Cairo kept Sadat dependent on the United States, the only nation that could call off Israel. So long as a sword was hanging over his vaunted Third Army, the Egyptian president would have no choice but to follow America's lead.

Kissinger liked being in that position.

To buy time, he tried to stall talks with the Soviets by offering an American-drafted UN resolution the Soviets would probably haggle over for a day or more. But Brezhnev quickly agreed to American terms, leaving Kissinger no choice but to accept his own proposal.

Kissinger forwarded the long-awaited cease-fire draft to Golda. The resolution, he said, would be adopted by the UN Security Council the next day and would require the parties to stop shooting by 6:52 p.m. on October 22. The resolution also provided that Egypt would negotiate directly with Israel for a "just and permanent peace."

Desperate to save his army, Sadat accepted the resolution on the spot. Golda, now in the driver's seat, balked. She hadn't pushed very far into Egyptian territory, and Sadat's Third Army, though surrounded and starving, was still under arms on the Israeli side of the canal. Halting now would give the Arabs an opportunity to rewrite history and convince themselves they hadn't been beaten.

"For God's sake, [Sadat] started a war, our people are killed, his in the many thousands are killed, and he has been defeated," she complained to a *CBS News* interviewer. "Sadat must, I think, be given time to enjoy his defeat and not to immediately, by political manipulations, turn it into a victory."

On the other hand, the US-Soviet proposal offered Golda something no Arab nation had ever conceded: direct peace negotiations with Israel. A chance at formal recognition was an opportunity Golda found hard to pass up.

After a cabinet meeting lasting until three o'clock in the morning, the Israeli government said it was inclined to accept the proposal on one condition: Secretary Kissinger must get on a plane and fly from Moscow to Tel Aviv immediately to discuss the terms with Golda.

Kissinger hopped a plane and arrived in Tel Aviv on October 22. As soon as he sat down with Golda, she leaned forward in her chair and scolded him with that gravelly tone she used on wavering party members. She berated the United States for not including her in negotiations over critical truce details and demanded amendments to the cease-fire documents, including a provision for the exchange of prisoners.

Kissinger tried placating Golda with "off the record" promises to work out her objections. He told her, for instance, that he and Brezhnev informally agreed that a prisoner exchange would quickly follow the cease-fire.

Golda's eyes narrowed. *What else did you and Brezhnev agree to that I don't know about?*

She pointed to vague references in the resolution about "negotiations toward peace," the one thing Israel really wanted from a truce. Scowling, she asked Kissinger what "negotiations" would be commenced, and why the resolution did not specify where or when.

She then called in General Elazar to explain to Kissinger the military picture in the Sinai. Egypt's Third Army was all but cut off. The IDF was poised to smash it, and just needed a little more time to finish the job.

After her withering cross-examination, she turned to Kissinger for a response.

Kissinger was fond of saying, "Do unto others as they do unto you. Plus ten percent." He told her that the United States was willing to let Sadat twist a little bit longer, even if hostilities spilled past the official cease-fire time. "In Vietnam," he said, "the cease-fire didn't go into effect at the exact time that we agreed upon." Israel could push a little more. A *very* little more.

But he warned Golda not to derail the peace process. "Madam Prime Minister," he said, "You didn't start the war, but you face a need for wise decisions that will protect the survival of Israel." She must accept the world's terms.

Golda nodded. While not officially accepting the cease-fire yet, she agreed in principle that the cease-fire terms would be honored, more or less on schedule, and agreed to sell the cease-fire to the cabinet.

Thanking her, a tired Henry Kissinger boarded his plane and flew home to Washington.

As Kissinger winged his way home, Israel's army severed the last link between Cairo and its Third Army. In Tel Aviv, Moshe Dayan urged Golda to block food, water, and medical supplies from reaching the trapped men. The IDF stood poised to bag a 40,000-man army and compel Sadat to admit that Egypt had been beaten. Such a victory would deter the Arabs from opening a new war, perhaps for another generation.

Though sympathetic, Golda felt Dayan was wrong. It may not have been fair for Kissinger to ask Israel to stop shooting at the moment of triumph, but the US had sent forty Phantom jets, thirty-two Skyhawks, and ton after ton of munitions, missiles, and badly needed equipment. If the price of an epic battle victory was US support, then the price was too high for the woman who drove the decision.

"There is only one country to which we can turn," she told the Cabinet. "Sometimes we have to give in to it—even when we know we shouldn't. But it is the only real friend we have and it is a very powerful one. We don't have to say yes to everything. But there is nothing to be ashamed of when a small country like Israel, in this situation, has to give in sometimes to the United States."

Israel would accept the cease-fire on Henry Kissinger's terms.

❖   ❖   ❖

THE SOLDIER ON THE FRONT LINES sees the landscape differently from the minister in the capital. A lethal explosion on the front may appear as nothing more than a footnote in an intelligence report. A raging battle might take the form of a tiny grease pencil bulge on a situation map in the capital city.

The grease lines did move slightly after the cease-fire took effect. Desperate soldiers of the once-mighty Third Army tried to break out of their trap. Israeli troops responded with a withering fire that drove the Egyptians back behind their lines. In the process, the IDF pushed forward and took new ground.

When he learned of the firefight the next morning, Kissinger was furious with Golda. Cranky and jet-lagged, he rang up Tel Aviv and demanded that she announce Israel's immediate formal acceptance of the cease-fire resolution. Should she refuse, America would distance itself from Israel and cut off arms shipments. She must also withdraw her forces to their positions at the time the cease-fire went into effect, at 6:52 p.m. the night before.

Golda told Kissinger things were more complicated than he knew. Troop positions had been jumbled since the initial UN resolution was adopted, and it was possible the Israelis had moved forward in the confusion of Third Army's breakout attempt.

Satisfied that Golda was not going back on the larger cease-fire issue, Kissinger shrugged off the point. The exact stop line was a detail, nothing more, he said. He suggested Golda simply pull her troops back a few hundred yards and say that's where they were when the cease-fire went into effect.

"How can anyone ever know where a line is or was in the desert?" he asked.

"They'll know all right," said Golda.

Hanging up, Golda made the announcement. The war was over.*

When news of the cease-fire was broadcast from Tel Aviv, militants like Menachem Begin, head of the conservative Likud Party, turned their fury on Golda. Israel lost over 2,600 men and women, and the aura of Israeli invincibility had been broken. If Golda fought on, dictating peace terms in the shadow of the pyramids, the protective spell might be recast.

Golda, however, realized the spell could not last forever. The IDF could beat back the Arabs a dozen times or more, and still they would come. For Israel, even a single loss would mean the destruction of the nation she helped build.

No—she was reaching for a prize that had eluded Israel for three thousand years: a permanent peace with an ancient enemy. Direct talks with Egypt might lead her people to a new era of coexistence with her neighbor to the west, and she stood by her decision.

She was finished with war.

ON OCTOBER 28, three weeks after the war's opening shots, commanders of Egyptian and Israeli armies met under a canvas roof stretched over the guns of four parked tanks. Their orders, to work out a "military disengagement" in the Sinai, opened a new phase in Israeli-Egyptian relations.

"For the first time in a quarter of a century there is direct, simple, personal contact between Israelis and Egyptians," Golda told the Knesset. "They sat in tents together, hammered out details . . . and shook hands."

The scope of those details grew. Chairs moved from tents to conference rooms. Faces changed. Hammered by her opponents for failing to mobilize for war quickly enough, Golda stepped down as prime minister in 1974.† She was replaced by

---

* Although fighting virtually ended by Wednesday, October 24, the dire situation of Egypt's Third Army—starving and short of water—moved Sadat to ask for American military assistance, which prompted Moscow to prepare to airlift soldiers to break the blockade. In response, Kissinger, acting without presidential knowledge, had US nuclear and conventional forces put on high alert. The Soviets backed down, and escalation to superpower war was averted.

† An investigating commission chaired by Supreme Court Justice Shimon Agranat exonerated Golda of blame for Israel's failure to prepare for the war. The greater share of the blame was placed on Aman, General Elazar, and several Sinai commanders. One week after the commission's report was released, the seventy-five-year-old prime minister tendered her resignation.

Labor's Yitzak Rabin, then by Menachem Begin, one of the hotheaded Irgun boys Golda had wanted to liquidate back in the 1940s. In November 1977, under the beaming smile of US President Jimmy Carter, Sadat and Begin, two former terrorists, signed the Camp David Accords in Washington, putting an end to the long state of war between Egypt and Israel.

A legacy, the song goes, is planting seeds in a garden you never get to see grow. But Golda was lucky enough to see her garden sprout shoots. After the Camp David talks concluded, she was on hand to greet President Sadat for his historic visit to Tel Aviv. The two former enemies sat together and shared a few enjoyable moments. As old warhorses who did their duty as they saw it, they had earned their season of peace.

In 1969, before accepting the mantle of interim prime minister, Golda's doctor had given her ten years to live. He was close. Golda Meir passed into night on December 8, 1978, as Begin and Sadat prepared to receive their Nobel Peace Prize for the Camp David Accords. Published on the front pages of newspapers around the world, the death of Israel's mother overshadowed the historic award.

Even in death, Golda had the last word.

GOLDA CEMENTED a pattern of modern warfare that would affect the way nations fought in succeeding decades. The Indira-Golda strategy of triangulating the United Nations, the superpowers, and the local battlefield taught other leaders—both men and women—that alliances and diplomacy were as much a part of national war strategy as tanks and fighter planes.

The lessons of the old Jewish socialist reverberated far beyond her homeland. The year after Golda's death, another woman took the helm of a nuclear-armed nation. Like Golda, she was strong-willed and didn't shy away from using force. Unlike Golda, she fought not for survival, but for a deeply held belief in right and wrong.

13

CROSSFIRE HURRICANE

Britain's Margaret Thatcher

"How do you actually run a war?"
—MARGARET THATCHER, 1982

THE PRIME MINISTER'S ROOM was crammed with long-faced men. Westminster men, whose expressions ran the full gamut of bureaucratic emotions, from grimacing despair to sour resignation. Men who told the woman sitting before them what she refused to hear: The Falkland Islands were a lost cause.

Argentine warships, planes, and soldiers were converging on Britain's colony in the South Atlantic, they told her. Those forces would overrun the islands in a day or two. The British Empire was about to endure the humiliation of another possession torn from its hands, and there was nothing anyone could do about it.

The strawberry blonde at the table's center knew disaster, for disaster had nipped at her heels these last three years. London's stock market had crashed, interest rates hovered at sixteen percent, factories gathered rust, and three million Britons were out of work. Opinion polls rated her the least popular prime minister in recorded history. As the rock band Pink Floyd prepared to record an album savaging her stewardship, prospects of reelection the next year—or even surviving a no-confidence vote—looked bleak.

But the image of Argentina's blue and yellow flag rippling over the Falkland Islands was a new low, even for self-effacing Britain. It announced that Queen Victoria's global empire had become so moribund that a banana republic could seize its possessions with impunity. Britannia's transition from world empire to paper empire was nearly complete, and after three hundred years, the sun was finally setting on the Union Jack.

The sun was also setting on the career of Prime Minister Margaret Roberts Thatcher.

❖   ❖   ❖

SHE GREW UP believing in the old-fashioned notion of British exceptionalism. A middle-class grocer's daughter from Grantham, England, Margaret Roberts was fourteen years old when Britain, hammered by German bombers, drew its power to resist Nazism from the defiant words of Prime Minister Winston Churchill.

Hanging on Churchill's sonorous phrases as they marched over the radio waves, she was mesmerized by the way the great bulldog recruited the language of Shakespeare, Shelley, and Shaw into the war effort. In the years after the guns fell silent, the impressionable teenager practically worshipped the old PM, enduring rolled eyes and snide remarks whenever she affected familiarity with "Winston," as she liked to call him.

The pretty, blue-eyed girl studied chemistry at Oxford's women-only Somerville College during the war. Life there refined her conservative theories, and she joined the Oxford University Conservative Association, an outlet to debate serious political issues facing Britain.

Unlike many of her classmates, college did not shake Margaret's religious faith. She read C.S. Lewis—"Who has ever portrayed more wittily and convincingly the way in which Evil works on our human weaknesses?" she later wrote—and attended services at the local Methodist chapel. Her Christianity, in some ways more a product of the Old Testament than the New, solidified a rigid view of right and wrong, of good and evil. She would enter adulthood believing there was no room for compromise between the two.

After graduating, Margaret Roberts went to work for a plastics company, but donning a white coat and experimenting with emulsifiers struck no intellectual spark. Political science submerged natural science as her passion, and she absorbed the conservatism Churchill had preached. In 1950, the twenty-five-year-old chemist ran for a parliamentary seat as a Conservative Party candidate from Dartford, a working-class Labour stronghold.*

---

* The musically inclined son of a Dartford Conservative Party supporter, seven-year-old Michael Jagger, grew up to symbolize opposition to the establishment Thatcher represented. Later in life, Mick Jagger expressed his respect for Thatcher's willingness to stand up for her beliefs, even when they proved unpopular.

Margaret lost three elections over the next few years, but reveled in the thrill of campaigning. Along the way, she fell in love with and married Denis Thatcher, a successful businessman who had served in Italy and France during the Second World War. Two years later, the failed local politician and ambitious Kentish housewife gave birth to twins.

As she raised her young children, Thatcher reinvented herself. She earned a law degree and transplanted her family to Finchley, a prosperous North London suburb that was fertile ground for a Conservative Party candidate. Garnering the support of Finchley's Tories, in 1959 she overcame voter reluctance to elect a woman and defeated her Liberal and Labour Party opponents. It had taken four tries, but she finally won her seat in Parliament.

Over the next two decades, Thatcher worked her way up the Conservative Party ladder, serving as loyal backbencher when the Tories lost their majority in 1964, and as Education Secretary when they won it back in 1970. Five years later, when conservatives were trounced at the polls, party MPs set aside traditional prejudices and elected Margaret Thatcher the first female leader in the Conservative Party's 141-year history.

In one of her first overseas trips as opposition leader, Thatcher flew to India to meet Indira Gandhi, a fellow Somerville alumna. The unlikely pair—an Indian socialist whose family detached Britain's largest colony, and a British capitalist committed to the empire's ideals—hit it off from the start. Thatcher treasured her friendship with the Indian nationalist and drew from her example. Confident and capable, both understood that the road to power was a rocky, perilous path for anyone, man or woman. Especially a woman.

But Thatcher knew it could be done, even by a woman, even in England, even among conservatives. She had climbed power's slippery ladder in high heels for twenty years and enjoyed the occasional off-color joke over a whiskey with "the boys." Like Golda Meir, she could not understand why other women—at least, women willing to work endlessly, sacrifice family time for career, and trade the perfect life for the productive life—couldn't make it without handouts from men.

Once, when touring the United States as opposition leader, a Chicago reporter asked Thatcher whether she felt she owed a debt to the women's liberation movement. "Some of us were making it long before women's lib was ever thought of," she snapped.

In the free-wheeling, mud-slinging world of British politics, Thatcher's gender opened a wide defilade of attacks from her opponents. In the 1970s, "Ditch the Bitch!" became a rousing chant among Labour MPs, and her cuts in government spending on school milk programs drew the slogan, "Thatcher, Milk-Snatcher." Sharp-tongued Liberal MP Clement Freud dubbed her "Attila the Hen," while French president François Mitterrand described her as having the eyes of Stalin and the voice of Marilyn Monroe. The caricature of a latter-day shrew bludgeoning ministers with a swinging purse stuffed with memoranda gave rise to the political term "handbagging," a dig no other major politician had to endure.*

Politicians get used to attacks. Insult and hate are part of the hostile underbrush they dwell in, and like rhinos, they grow a thick hide to ward off stings as they lumber through the savannah. But Thatcher's school lunch program lingered like sour, snatched milk in the public nostrils, and personal attacks cut her deeper than she would let on in public. Like Churchill, she did not believe in holding back tears, at least in private, and more than once, pent-up frustration and bitterness burst into a choked rush of sobs into her husband's shoulder.

"Why go on?" Denis once asked her, consoling her sweetly as tears ran down her cheeks.

Why go on?

To Thatcher, the question had a strange, almost foreign ring. She stopped, drew a breath, then looked at Denis through wet, defiant eyes.

"I'll see them in hell first," she said flatly. "I will never be driven anywhere against my will."

HELL WOULD HAVE TO WAIT, for Margaret Thatcher brought more to the job than bottle-blonde hair and thick skin. She had a prodigious work ethic, serious-minded practicality, a rigid view of right and wrong, and an ambitious streak. Coming of age in the right place, at the right time, she espoused free-market economic thinking and social traditionalism that had gained currency with the British voter of the late 1970s.

With the 1980s hanging just around the corner, Labour Party dominance was giving way to an undertow of middle-class resentment the papers dubbed the "Winter of Discontent." Conservative and moderate voters bristled at Britain's retreat from traditional values and the erosion of its empire. Inflation was cutting swaths

---

* Coming from Mitterrand, who supported Thatcher during the Falklands crisis, the "eyes of Stalin" remark might have been meant as a compliment. Other versions of Mitterrand's quip include, "The eyes of Caligula and the mouth of Marilyn Monroe" and "Bridgitte Bardot with Caligula's eyes."

into family savings, Northern Ireland was gripped by terrorism, strikes rocked the country, and crime and pornography were rampant in the cities. Britain's youth—the empire's future—were particularly disaffected as they slam-danced their way into post-Beatles pop culture. The Sex Pistols screeched of "no future" in "England's fascist regime" through cassette players, while anarcho-punk fashion spread through nightclubs and record shops, energizing a sex-and-drugs counterculture that horrified parents from Dover to Inverness.

Thatcher tapped into that horror with an unapologetic brand of conservatism. She called for a return to traditional values at home and resistance to communism abroad—a message that resonated with the public.

If her message was well received, her style piqued voter uneasiness. It was not that she wasn't tough enough for the job; by the late 1970s, it was an old chestnut for conservatives to call Margaret Thatcher "the best man among them."

No, it was just the opposite: Thatcher's uncompromising approach sounded more like Queen Boudica than Queen Victoria, and her take-no-prisoners style was costing her party votes.

To broaden her appeal, Thatcher softened her image. "Maggie" hit the television and print interview circuits portraying herself as an ordinary housewife with traditional English values. She wore the same string of pearls her husband Denis had given her on the birth of their twins—a trademark she would keep throughout her life—and carried a purse with old-fashioned white gloves. She consulted voice coaches like Sir Laurence Olivier, who taught her to how lower her voice, speak slowly, stop hectoring audiences, and above all, speak from the heart.*

Margaret also cloaked her hard-edged economic views with the sort of comfortable, old-sweater ideals men and women don't find threatening. "What people don't realize about me is that I am a very ordinary person," she told London's *Daily Mirror*. "I enjoy it, seeing that the family have a good breakfast. And shopping keeps me in touch."

She was, of course, no ordinary person. Thatcher's method was to master a game men invented, reserving for herself a quantum of femininity. Meticulous with her makeup—Clinique was her favorite brand—she and her personal assistant pored over issues of *Vogue* for fashion tips on dress, perfume, and hairstyle. Yet she also had to look the part of the Empire's first minister. Anticipating executive womenswear

---

* Her consultants also advised her to lose her pearls, which looked too suburban for city voters, but Thatcher declared the pearls non-negotiable. "I don't know why the bloody hell I shouldn't wear these pearls," she fussed to friends. "They were a present from Denis."

of the 1980s, she ditched bright sleeveless dresses and garden-fête hats for a disciplined blonde coiffure and dark blue power suit. Carefully selecting her battle armor for important occasions, she and her assistant developed a wardrobe shorthand, referring to her "conference blue" or "Gdansk green" suits when planning her look for upcoming meetings. As a clothing expert from Christie's put it, "She was the ultimate power dresser. She was very aware of the power of television and the power it could have, and she dressed accordingly."

Style mattered, and Thatcher saw nothing phony about an image makeover. To the contrary, she felt it a measure of her drive and ambition. She later wrote, "Every politician has to decide how much he or she is prepared to change manner and appearance for the sake of the media. It may sound grittily honourable to refuse to make any concessions, but such an attitude in a public figure is most likely to betray a lack of seriousness about winning power."

Thatcher's blend of down-home appeal and Sheffield-steel principles kept supporters in her camp as they trudged into voting booths for the May 1979 elections. When they emerged, the conservatives had won a twenty-one-seat majority, and the grocer's daughter took the reins of Her Majesty's Government.

To Die for Ireland

Elected on a platform of economic conservatism, Thatcher began slashing taxes and government spending. Her budget cuts unleashed seismic disruptions in Britain's labor force, and traditional industries like steel and coal cratered. Unemployment skyrocketed, small businesses floundered, and inflation, her Public Enemy Number One, refused to budge.

Her favorability among voters followed the economy, dropping to 23 percent, but Thatcher stayed the course. When urged to dial back by moderate cabinet ministers—"wets," she called them—she brusquely retorted, "The lady's not for turning." The slogan became her political mantra.

Though a foreign policy hawk, Thatcher did not spare the military. Her cost-conscious defense minister, John Nott, saw little need for a large, ocean-going navy and wrung from Thatcher reluctant approval to sell one of Britain's three aircraft carriers to Australia and find other ways to trim a fleet that once ruled the waves. Those other ways included cuts in the Royal Navy's missile frigate and destroyer fleet, the elimination of three submarines, the removal of a survey vessel from the Falkland Islands, and the sale of two large assault ships. She might preach the gospel of anticommunist defense—her second great commandment—but her first commandment was, "Thou Shalt Not Overspend."

Tests of will flew at her almost as soon as she took office, when the Provisional Irish Republican Army stepped up its sixty-year campaign of violence to wrest Northern Ireland from the United Kingdom. In August 1979, when Thatcher had been in power only three months, the IRA assassinated Lord Louis Mountbatten, Queen Elizabeth's cousin and hero of the Second World War. The shocking death of a beloved public figure was a lethal message directed to the new government and the woman at its head.

Thatcher responded swiftly, reinforcing British garrisons in Belfast and other key points around Northern Ireland. Flying to the Irish border, she visited troops at Crossmaglen and was photographed wearing a combat jacket and beret of the Ulster Defence Regiment.

The images, which made front pages in UK newspapers, infuriated Irish nationalists. Thatcher didn't care. Northern Ireland, she insisted, was British, and would remain so until its people voted of their own free will to leave the Union. "No democratic country can voluntarily abandon its responsibilities in a part of its territories against the will of the majority of the population there," she declared, articulating a principle that would become the unmoving North Star of her foreign policy.

Faced with an aggressive British response, the IRA turned to a new tactic: moral blackmail. In March 1981, an imprisoned IRA gunman named Bobby Sands began a hunger strike to force the government to grant political status to all IRA prisoners. Other inmates joined Sands. As strapping young Irishmen in their twenties grew thin and frail, sympathy for the Irish cause flowered. Photos of a boyish, smiling Bobby Sands were printed on IRA recruiting posters and tacked onto phone poles and pub walls across Ireland. The British government, claimed Sinn Féin, had criminalized Northern Ireland's struggle for independence.

Despite domestic and international pressure, Thatcher refused to budge. Northern Ireland became a matter of principle for her, and on matters of principle she could be stubborn to the point of messianic.

When Sands died after a sixty-six-day fast, she told the public that the IRA prisoners were pawns of a larger evil. "It would seem that dead hunger strikers, who have extinguished their own lives, are of more use to the IRA than living members," she told one audience. "Such is their calculated cynicism."

Enemies denounced Thatcher as heartless and irrational, inflexible and criminal. But she won. After an agonizing six months, the IRA gave in to public pressure and called a halt to its hunger strike campaign. Violence would fester, bombs would kill—a hotel explosion in 1984 nearly took Thatcher's life—but Margaret Thatcher had showed the world she would not back down.

Gipper and the Iron Lady

As a disciple of free-market economics, Thatcher made the struggle against communism a cornerstone of her foreign policy. Perceiving how badly the Soviet Union's reputation had sunk after its 1979 invasion of Afghanistan, she supported the anti-communist Solidarity workers movement in Poland and exhorted British athletes to boycott the 1980 Summer Olympics in Moscow.

Closer to home, she offset cuts in conventional forces by boosting Britain's contribution to NATO and purchasing state-of-the-art Trident nuclear missiles from America. Her hawkish stance brought out cries of warmongering by the political Left, and Soviet state-run newspapers derided Thatcher as the "Iron Lady." She took the nickname as a compliment.

The other cornerstone of her foreign policy was Britain's relationship with the United States, and her personal relationship with its president, Ronald Reagan. Reagan had been elected in 1980 on the same conservative tide that had swept Thatcher into office. Genteel and affable, Reagan lacked Thatcher's attention to detail, but his dedication to free-market democracy mirrored Thatcher's. They would become life-long friends.

Fortunately for Thatcher, Reagan had no aversion to strong-minded women, few of whom could match his wife Nancy for sheer willpower. Once, when Thatcher called Reagan on a secure line and began haranguing him on an issue, he held the phone receiver at arm's length so others in the room could hear the cacophony. Smiling broadly, he quipped, "Isn't she marvelous?"

Their personal rapport flowed from shared beliefs and the "special relationship" handed down as a legacy of Franklin Roosevelt and Winston Churchill. In correspondence, they dropped titles and referred to each other as "Ron" and "Margaret." On her first visit to Washington after Reagan's inaugural in 1981, Thatcher echoed the words of Roosevelt's envoy to Churchill, Harry Hopkins, forty years before: "We in Britain stand with you . . . Your problems will be our problems, and when you look for friends, we will be there."

A beaming Reagan responded, "In a dangerous world," there would be "one element that goes without question: Britain and America stand side by side."

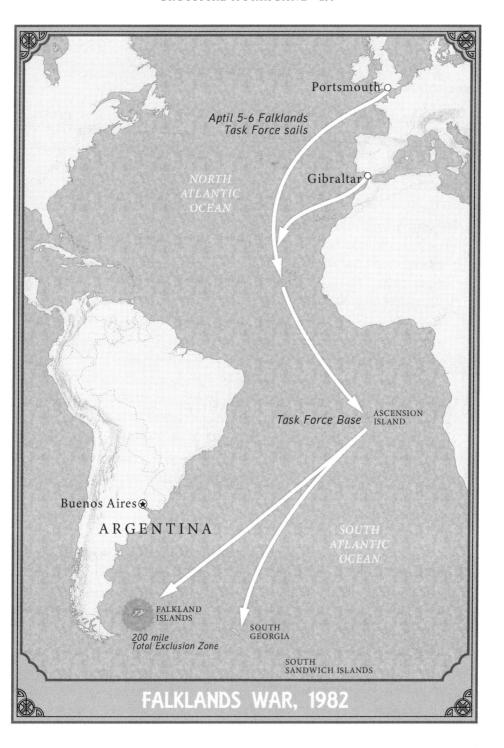

Portsmouth

Aptil 5-6 Falklands
Task Force sails

NORTH
ATLANTIC
OCEAN

Gibraltar

Task Force Base   ASCENSION
ISLAND

Buenos Aires

ARGENTINA

SOUTH
ATLANTIC
OCEAN

FALKLAND
ISLANDS

200 mile
Total Exclusion Zone

SOUTH
GEORGIA

SOUTH
SANDWICH ISLANDS

FALKLANDS WAR, 1982

It may have been a dangerous world, but in early 1981 the two nations were at peace, and it was easy to stand side by side in peace.

Standing side by side in war would be a different story.

Las Malvinas

Amid crises foreign and domestic, in March 1982 military intelligence reports drew Thatcher's eye to a storm brewing over a speck of land she could not locate on a map: the Falkland Islands.

Three hundred miles off the Argentine coast in the South Atlantic, the Falklands had been claimed by Great Britain since 1833. Its 1,820 inhabitants were overwhelmingly ethnic Britons who, like their Northern Irish counterparts, saw the Empire as their guarantor of security and freedom against a hostile South American majority.

Title to the islands was not uncontested. *Las Malvinas*, as the Argentines called them, had been a focal point of anti-imperialist indignation for nearly a century and a half. They also provided a ready-made distraction for any Buenos Aires administration under fire at home when the public mood soured, as it often did.

In 1982, the Argentine public mood was especially sour, which was *muy mal* for its military junta, led by the army's General Leopoldo Galtieri. The Argentine government had spent a fortune on weapons purchases over the previous half-decade, but the people couldn't eat weapons. Facing a collapsing economy, political upheaval, and uproar over its habit of making political opponents disappear, the regime found itself buffeted by a string of conspiracies and crises. As 1982 opened, the junta desperately needed a rallying cry to unite its people.

To Galtieri, a middle-aged general with the distinguished look of an elder Mafia don, Las Malvinas seemed tailor-made for Argentine unity. The sun had set on the Union Jack in Palestine, Egypt, India, Rhodesia, the New Hebrides, and Belize, and the British lion's toothlessness became more apparent every time another former colony was wrenched from the Queen's hands. In 1976, the Argentine military sent fifty soldiers to occupy a deserted British island in the South Sandwich chain. The Labour government had responded with only token diplomatic protest.

Now, in 1982, the time seemed right for another bite at the dying empire. Under Thatcher the United Kingdom was cutting its military budget, and by June the islands would be entering the worst of the notorious South Atlantic weather. Dreaming of the adulation his people would shower on him if he won back lands stolen 150 years before, Galtieri prepared to expel the imperialists.

Galtieri's junta tested Britain's resolve in March 1982 by moving a handful of civilian contractors onto the island of South Georgia, a speck of rock populated by thousands of penguins, a few tumbledown sheds, and several members of the British Antarctic Survey. Without asking permission from the British government, the contractors were deposited at the island's harbor and raised the Argentine flag over a rusty generator casing. A local British survey official demanded the Argentines leave, but the head of the contracting party refused.

Thatcher approved a sortie by the survey vessel HMS *Endurance* to shadow the trespassers but warned the Royal Navy not to take any hostile action. Galtieri responded by sending a marine detachment to South Georgia, and followed up his move with two missile corvettes that anchored off the island.

To the high-minded British Foreign Office staff, the South Georgia drama was what Macbeth would call sound and fury, signifying nothing. Unwilling to bruise diplomatic relations, Foreign Office ministers persuaded Thatcher to stand down. That, they advised, would give Galtieri a breathing spell in which to reconsider his actions.

What it gave Galtieri was reason to believe the British wouldn't fight. And time to prepare an invasion of Las Malvinas.

ALTHOUGH NO ONE in Her Majesty's Government liked to acknowledge it, the Falkland Islands were an albatross hanging around the nation's neck. Lying nearly 8,000 miles from London, their *homo sapien* inhabitants were outnumbered more than 300-to-1 by sheep, to say nothing of the five species of penguin that fished the rocky island coasts. Unless the Panama Canal was unexpectedly shut down, the Falklands offered Britain no economic or strategic advantages—just "miles and miles of bugger-all," as Thatcher's husband Denis described them.

The problem lay with the islanders. Like their fellow subjects in Northern Ireland, the Falklanders dreaded Argentine persecution if the junta displaced the Crown. Their opposition to British withdrawal and effective lobby in Westminster Hall tied the hands of every government, liberal or conservative, that sought to scale back Britain's commitment.

While she hoped to de-escalate the standoff in South Georgia, a worried Margaret Thatcher recognized that the incident might escalate into a crisis requiring military options. On March 25, she ordered the Ministry of Defence to begin contingency planning for naval operations in case diplomacy failed. She also quietly ordered the ministry to deploy three attack submarines around the Falklands.

Defence dispatched the submarines, but cautioned Thatcher that her "scope for effective military action in response to whatever Argentinians may do is extremely limited, and that almost anything we could do would be too late and/or extremely expensive." Britain's war fleet, concentrated in northern Europe, was on the wrong side of the world. Argentina's navy, with a 7,700-mile head start, boasted one aircraft carrier, a cruiser, four submarines, and nine destroyers, plus five marine battalions capable of mounting an amphibious invasion.

The British garrison on the main island of East Falkland, eighty Royal Marines, were armed with light infantry weapons and could offer no more than token resistance. Reinforcements from the UK would take a month to arrive, so there was no question that if Argentina acted soon, the islands would be lost, and Britain would be forced to wrest them from an entrenched, prepared enemy. And given Thatcher's legendary aversion to spending, nearly every assessment her ministers gave her included the caveat that any task force large enough to turn back an invasion would be "expensive."

In the waning days of March, Argentine newspapers announced that the junta would be sending a naval force to "protect" oppressed Argentine citizens on South Georgia. The aircraft carrier *Veinticinco de Mayo* put to sea, and on March 30 the British embassy in Buenos Aires reported that two Argentine destroyers, two corvettes, and one submarine were steaming toward the Falklands.

Thatcher had been elected to cut spending and stand up to Soviet communism. She never expected to fight an old-style colonial war for one of Britain's last possessions.

Squinting into the oracle's cave, she could see two dark and dangerous paths. Backing down to a South American junta would herald the worst national disgrace since Britain's loss of the Suez in 1956. It might even encourage other petty dictators around the world to take what belonged to the British Empire. But standing firm might mean war, and war would mean death. And regardless of right or wrong, much of the world—and surely all of Latin America—would turn against Britain.

The box Galtieri had put Thatcher in wasn't lost on British observers. Enoch Powell, a Conservative MP, predicted to his colleagues on the floor of Parliament that Thatcher's response would define her premiership. Rising from his green upholstered bench, he declared,

The Prime Minister, shortly after she came into office, received a sobriquet as the "Iron Lady" . . . In the next week or two this House, the nation, and the Right Honourable Lady herself will learn of what metal she is made.

On the last afternoon of March, an anxious Margaret Thatcher called her advisors into the Leader's Room at the House of Commons to discuss Britain's military options. Canvassing the Whitehall mandarins in their dark suits and ties, she heard risks, disadvantages, and dangers.

Defence Secretary John Nott, a lanky, bald man with thick spectacles, bluntly told her that the islands, if taken by Argentina, could not be recaptured.

Thatcher looked at him in shock.

We are talking about Great Britain, one of the greatest powers in human history. And it cannot stand up to a bankrupt South American clique?

It was, she later reflected, "the worst moment of my life."

But she recovered from the blow, and with a stern look she shot back, "If they are invaded, we have got to get them back."

"We can't," Nott said.

"You'll have to," she insisted.

She had no idea how to conduct a military campaign, much less plan a complex amphibious operation against a wind-buffeted clump of guano-strewn rock 8,000 miles away. She groped for a response.

Into this sea of gloom stormed Admiral Sir Henry Leach, who had arrived from Portsmouth by helicopter. Speaking directly to the prime minister, Leach declared that if Argentina took the Falkland Islands by force, the Royal Navy could take them back. It would take three weeks before the fleet could arrive, and the soldiers would be thin on air cover. The weather, that perennial enemy of amphibious operations, would be dodgy. But the needle could be threaded.

Thatcher's pulse quickened as she absorbed the admiral's words. She had walked into the room a military neophyte, but her impulse to fight, not surrender, had been seconded by a respected naval veteran.

"Now my outrage and determination were matched by a sense of relief and confidence," she wrote later. "Henry Leach had shown me that if it came to a fight, the courage and professionalism of Britain's armed forces would win through."

Carved above the old fireplace in Thatcher's Parliament office was the Norman French motto *Fais Bien Craigns Rien* ("Do Good and Fear Nothing"). Her own fears receding, Thatcher ordered Nott to assemble a task force. If the crisis were defused before the fleet arrived at the Falklands, it could always turn back; that's what rudders were for. But without the fleet, diplomacy would accomplish nothing.

The valor of ignorance buoyed Margaret Thatcher that day. Had she known the risks of war as intimately as Admiral Leach, as Secretary Nott—as even her own husband, Denis—she might have hesitated before mounting Boudica's chariot. One minister remarked, "She wouldn't have done it if she'd been a man and if she'd been in the armed forces during the war. Then she'd have been aware how dreadfully wrong everything was likely to go."

But in her narrow visual spectrum of black and white, Thatcher saw only the need to vindicate a moral principle. She would not admit the slightest chance that Britain could lose.

A few days later, an interviewer asked her, "If you fail, would you feel obliged to resign?"

"I am not talking about failure," she answered firmly. Her blue eyes locked on her questioner.

"I am talking about my supreme confidence in the British fleet . . . superlative ships, excellent equipment, the most highly trained professional group of men, the most honourable and brave members of Her Majesty's service. Failure? Do you remember what Queen Victoria once said? 'Failure—the possibilities do not exist.'"

Sixteen years after his death, Winston Churchill's fighting spirit had found its voice through the lips of a grocer's daughter.

Operation Rosario

The Argentines were menacing the islands, but they had not yet invaded, and the crisis was not beyond diplomatic redemption. Thatcher directed her foreign secretary to ask US Secretary of State Alexander Haig for help. She also fired off a telegram to President Reagan, asking him to pressure Galtieri for assurances that Argentina would not invade the Falklands.

Reagan telephoned Galtieri and spent fifty minutes trying to persuade the junta leader to call off his soldiers, but the general had whipped his countrymen into a nationalistic furor. Demonstrators were pouring into the streets of Buenos Aires, chanting support for the government, swelling the junta's bravado and making it impossible to back down. Galtieri had let slip the dogs of war and could not call them back.

In the early hours of April 2, Argentine conscripts fanned out to begin Operation Rosario: the invasion of the two main islands, East Falkland and West Falkland. Launching grenades and firing machine guns, thousands of soldiers converged on the Royal Marines barracks, the airport, and the Government House at the island's capital, Port Stanley. As word spread of villages being overrun, the island's governor dolefully remarked, "It looks as if the buggers mean it."

The buggers meant it. By day's end, Argentina's sun banner fluttered over Port Stanley, leaving the commander of HMS *Endurance* to sum up events to fleet command: "This has been a humiliating day."

IN LONDON, Thatcher's first jobs were to voice the outrage Britons were feeling and to provide them with a sense of firm leadership at the top. For this, she knew where to find inspiration. She kept copies of speeches by Winston Churchill, whose "Fight on the Beaches" and "Finest Hour" declamations were some of the most memorable in the English language. In wartime there was no better mentor for a British leader to follow.

Wrapping herself in the bulldog's mantle, Thatcher stood before members of the House of Commons. Men who once heckled her with catcalls, hoots, and howls of "Ditch the Bitch!" weren't heckling her now.

Chin out, eyes beaming above the old wooden pulpit of Gladstone, of Pitt, of Asquith and Churchill, Thatcher gave voice to the rule of law among nations in a voice low and controlled. No high-pitched rage, no hysteria, no flaunted gesticulations. A look of determination was all she needed.

In emphatic but controlled language, she expressed a principle she believed worth fighting for:

> *The people of the Falkland Islands, like the people of the United Kingdom, are an island race. Their way of life is British; their allegiance is to the Crown. They are few in number, but they have the right to live in peace, to choose their own way of life and to determine their own allegiance. It is the wish of the British people and the duty of Her Majesty's Government to do everything that we can to uphold that right.*

When she finished, Tory MPs rose to their feet and cheered her. Shouts from Westminster rippled over the island as public support swung to the embattled minister. From Belfast and Falmouth, from Cardiff and Dover, from the Highlands and the Midlands, the lion in winter was telling the world it had awakened and was clearing its throat for a roar.

Two days after Thatcher's speech, the vanguard of a Royal Navy task force weighed anchor and steamed from Portsmouth under command of Rear Admiral John "Sandy" Woodward. The carriers *Invincible* and *Hermes* left on April 5, to be joined by a squadron of eleven destroyers and frigates, three submarines, and the amphibious assault ship HMS *Fearless*.

Those were only the first-line fighting ships. For every warship, there were tankers, supply tenders, minesweepers, and medical ships sailing behind in support, carrying everything from bombs to beans, magnifying the operation's scope, cost, and risk.

"It was not always understood that to sail a large task force with troops halfway round the world, with the intention of making opposed landings, required an enormous logistical operation," Thatcher later wrote. "In the end we sent over 100 ships, carrying more than 25,000 men."

Counting his cards in Buenos Aires, General Galtieri believed he had created a *fait accompli*. His invasion would be met by howls from London, bloviated UN resolutions, weak economic sanctions, and nothing more. As he told US military envoy Vernon Walters, he was supremely confident that "that woman" wouldn't dare try to take back Britain's former islands.

Thinking of the IRA hunger strikers, Walters said he wasn't so sure. "'That woman,'" Walters replied in Spanish, "has let a number of hunger strikers of her own basic ethnic origin starve themselves to death without flickering an eyelash. I wouldn't count on that if I were you."

Inching to Battle

As the British fleet inched its way down Atlantic naval charts, "that woman" had plenty of time to reflect on the human consequences of her decision. She was painfully aware that she had never trained for war. She was a chemist, tax lawyer, and politician whose career had been built on cost-cutting. She had ordered the sale of ships now steaming to the island's rescue. It had been thirty years since Britannia had been challenged like this, and the last time ended in disaster.

She knew she would need plenty of help, and sought the advice of men who had been there.

"How do you actually run a war?" she asked defense undersecretary Sir Frank Cooper over a gin during a Sunday lunch. Cooper, a Spitfire pilot in World War II, thought that one over.

"First, you need a small War Cabinet," he said at last. "Second, it's got to have regular meetings come hell or high water; thirdly you don't want a lot of bureaucrats hanging around." No treasury men, for instance, putting cost ahead of success.

Borrowing ideas from Cooper, former Prime Minister Harold Macmillan, and a few other old soldiers, Thatcher formed a war cabinet, ponderously dubbed the

"South Atlantic Sub-Committee to the Overseas and Defence Committee." Composed of herself and four senior ministers, the War Cabinet met in Thatcher's first-floor study of No. 10 Downing Street every morning at 9:30, where they charted the Empire's response to the Argentine gauntlet.

As with every war, destruction is but a means to an end, and those ends are set by political leaders. Thatcher's generals, admirals, and air marshals pressed her to articulate Britain's aims and priorities. Was it important, for instance, to minimize Argentine casualties? Would Her Majesty's Government support military action against the Argentine mainland? Would Britain tolerate "significant loss of life" among islanders as an acceptable price of victory?

These political questions bore down on Thatcher with each nautical mile the task force sailed.

As critical as the political aims were, tactical details were nearly as important, and much thornier. When would attack submarines be permitted to engage Argentine surface vessels? Would the task force sail at the speed of the slowest vessel, or should the faster ones race ahead? Would Britain send land-based bombers to assist? And where would they refuel those planes?

The War Cabinet would spend hours debating military subjects and seeking input from Whitehall's admirals, generals, and air marshals.

On tactical matters, Margaret Thatcher's ineptness was near-absolute. She would offer suggestions that elicited stifled chuckles or patronizing smiles from Whitehall advisors, three-quarters of whom had served in uniform. In response to Argentine air attacks, for instance, she asked, "Couldn't we put up a smokescreen?" Her men patiently explained why a smokescreen was impractical. When she suggested occupying Tierra del Fuego, they explained why it was not worth the risk. When a helpful naval aide spread out maps of the Atlantic, she confidently pointed out the location of the Falkland Islands. The aide discreetly directed her to the correct spot on the map.

But she was a quick study, and military inexperience compelled her to defer to military professionals. She later explained her thinking in terms the German war theorist Carl von Clausewitz would have appreciated: "The rules of engagement are the means by which the politicians authorize the framework within which the military can be left to make the operational decisions," she said.

They have to satisfy the objectives for which a particular military operation is undertaken. They must also give the man on the spot reasonable freedom to react as is required and to make his decisions knowing that they will be supported by the politicians. So the rules have to be clear and cover all possible eventualities.

"All possible eventualities" covered a lot of ground, and each question her ministers asked carried an unspoken warning: Winter was coming, the seas were billowing, and failure lurked behind every icy wave.

And failure in the Falklands meant the HMS *Margaret Thatcher's Government* would sink like a bloody stone.

Accepting the risks, Thatcher refused to back down. "All these considerations were fair enough," she conceded later. "But when you are at war you cannot allow the difficulties to dominate your way of thinking; you have to set them out with an iron will to overcome them." Two years into her administration, the lady was still "not for turning."*

FOR SEVEN CENTURIES, England's security had pivoted on the actions of her allies, and Thatcher hoped she could count on Britain's strongest ally, the United States. But the American public did not respond with the outrage Britons had expected. Most had never heard of the Falkland Islands and saw the conflict as a kind of comic-opera episode worthy of a *Doonesbury* cartoon. Ronald Reagan expressed surprise that Britain and Argentina would actually go to war over "that little ice-cold bunch of land down there."

Behind closed doors, Reagan's advisers were divided. United Nations ambassador Jeane Kirkpatrick feared that backing Britain would open a US–Latin America rift that communists in Central America would exploit. Reagan's defense secretary, Caspar Weinberger, believed America's alliance with Britain trumped its relations with Argentina, and he quietly allowed the Royal Navy to use a US base on Ascension Island in the South Atlantic. He also gave the British access to a wealth of US military intelligence.

At Foggy Bottom, Secretary of State Alexander Haig, a former NATO general, was torn between the communist menace in Latin America and the need to support America's most important ally. Playing the honest broker, Haig had to remain publicly neutral.

The man living at 1600 Pennsylvania Avenue gave no public hint of what he wanted. "It's a very difficult situation for the United States, because we're friends with both of the countries engaged in this dispute, and we stand ready to do anything we can to help them," Reagan told reporters on April 5. "What we hope for

---

* Thatcher never declared "war." Her advisors cautioned her that a declaration of war would automatically make every other nation neutral—and unable to assist Britain—unless they took the affirmative step of disclaiming neutrality, which they would be reluctant to do. "Conflict" was the word she chose.

and would like to help in doing is have a peaceful resolution of this with no forceful action or no bloodshed."

If forced to choose sides, Reagan knew he must uphold the "special relationship." But he hoped it wouldn't come to that. In a White House meeting with his national security team, he reiterated, "The main thing we have to do is to get these two brawlers out of the bar room."

To close the bar room, he asked Secretary Haig to broker a compromise. Haig's plan, to arrange a cease-fire and then negotiate over sovereignty, horrified Thatcher. She considered his proposal a "conditional surrender," since it would end the fighting with Argentina in possession of the islands and give the Argentines presumptive governing power. The hostage-taking of fifty-two American diplomats by Iranian radicals during Jimmy Carter's presidency had left a deep impression on the British public about superpower shame. Her Majesty's Government had no intention of allowing 1,800 Falklanders to remain hostages to the Galtieri junta, no matter what its best friend and ally might think. She would make that crystal clear when Haig arrived in London.

Thatcher welcomed Haig and a small entourage to 10 Downing Street, where she opened the meeting by showing him a pair of recently hung oil portraits—one of the Duke of Wellington, who defeated Napoleon at Waterloo, the other of Lord Nelson, hero of Trafalgar.

Her point wasn't lost on the secretary of state, but Thatcher was not a subtle woman, and her remark about Wellington's military victory was just her way of warming up a history lesson.

Haig winced when Thatcher compared the American proposal—an Organization of American States commission to address military withdrawal—to appeasement of Hitler before World War II. Her blue eyes hardening, she lectured Haig, "I beg you to remember that in 1938 Neville Chamberlain sat at this same table discussing an arrangement which sounds very much like the one you are asking me to accept . . . We in Britain simply refuse to reward aggression. That is the lesson we have learned from 1938."

When excited, Thatcher's voice grew rapid. She would stick out her chin and lean into her listener, her open hands stabbing the air as she emphasized one point after another. With Haig, she was in full form as she preempted any discussion of a solution that included Argentine rule over the islands.

Thatcher's advisors, including Foreign Secretary Francis Pym, sat quietly. Haig sensed they did not fully back their PM, and at one point an uncomfortable-looking Pym urged Thatcher to hear Haig out. She blazed back, "The good Lord did not put me on this planet so that I could allow British citizens to be placed under the heel of Argentine dictators."

Pym shrank into his chair.

Haig pressed for a compromise, but he knew he had run into a woman who was not merely talking for public consumption. She was a true believer.

"The prime minister has the bit in her teeth, owing to the politics of a unified nation and an angry parliament, as well as her own convictions about the principles at stake," he cabled Reagan after the meeting. "She is clearly prepared to use force."

Thatcher left the meeting roiled at Haig's awkward efforts to play peacemaker. She understood America's balancing act and was prepared to make some minor concessions that would not reward Argentina or sell out the islanders. But the US and Britain were the world's closest allies, and she felt she could ask Reagan to treat her like one.

"Please don't take this amiss," she told Haig in a telephone call. There was "considerable disappointment at the US position in a way—that the full difference between democracy and dictatorship is not appreciated, and that we are both treated the same."*

She wouldn't settle for less than the withdrawal of all Argentine forces. But she was also unwilling to break with the Americans publicly, and had to keep diplomacy in play while her task force steamed south. Acting on a suggestion from John Nott, she parried Haig with a diplomatic gambit: She asked him to get Galtieri's commitment to Washington's peace proposal first, calculating that the junta could not afford to compromise any more than she could.

She was right. Believing it had the upper hand, the junta was deliberately rude to Haig's entourage and refused to compromise on Argentine sovereignty over the islands. Galtieri even threatened to ask for help from Cuba, which might pull in Soviet naval forces to sink the carrier *Invincible*, giving Argentina credit for the kill.

Unable to make Galtieri budge, the Reagan Administration came down off the fence and finally agreed to back Britain. Weapons and materiel flowed out of US ordnance depots on a massive scale, and on May 6, a relieved Margaret Thatcher could tell the House of Commons, "We now have the total support of the United States, which we would expect and which I think we always expected to have."

---

* After giving Haig a good dressing-down, Thatcher echoed sentiments Churchill expressed to Franklin Roosevelt thirty-seven years earlier during an argument over Berlin. "I hope you realize how much we appreciate and are thankful for your presence here, and how the kind of candor we have displayed could only be possible among the closest of friends," she told Haig. "With everyone else we're merely nice!"

Death of the *General Belgrano*

Thatcher would need American support in late April, when the war of words became a war of missiles. On April 25, a British commando unit recaptured South Georgia, taking 180 Argentine prisoners and the sub *Santa Fe*. Admiral Woodward radioed London of the mission's success, adding that there were no British losses.

Elated to have something good to report, Thatcher immediately went to Queen Elizabeth at Windsor Castle to deliver the news in person. Returning to No. 10 Downing from the palace, she had Defence Secretary Nott announce the minor victory to reporters in the street outside the residence's front door. Tilting his large glasses and bushy eyebrows toward the written message, Nott read Woodward's radiogram to reporters with all the drama of a BBC cooking show recipe for shepherd's pie. But the night's emotion radiated from Margaret Thatcher. Standing straight as a broadsword, her war face aloof and determined, she betrayed a hint of a smile when Nott reached the part about no British casualties.

When Nott finished, a reporter shouted a question: "What happens next?"

Thatcher frowned. During Her Majesty's moment, Britain's moment, the question came off like a scratch on a vinyl record.

"*Just REJOICE AT THE NEWS, and CONGRATULATE our armed forces and the Marines!*" she bellowed, her soft chin stabbing out each syllable.

Her abruptness startled the reporters. As she began marching back to her door, another called out, "Are we going to declare war on Argentina, Mrs. Thatcher?"

"*REJOICE*," she repeated, striding into No. 10 without a second look.

There would be more to rejoice, yet more to mourn. On May 2, Admiral Woodward radioed London to report that the Argentine cruiser *General Belgrano*, escorted by two Exocet missile-armed destroyers, was hovering just outside Britain's 200-mile "exclusion" zone. *Belgrano* and her escorts, Defence feared, were making a pincer attack against the British main fleet. The British sub HMS *Conqueror* had been shadowing *Belgrano*, Woodward said, and her commander requested permission to attack.

The Argentine move put Thatcher in a tight spot. Sinking *Belgrano* would invite condemnation from the Soviet Union and Argentina's allies. But if they let her go, they might lose her in the Atlantic's swirls. The next they might hear of her could be the whoosh of an antiship missile bearing down on a British troopship.

To Thatcher, there was only one answer. "[The *Belgrano*] posed a very obvious threat to the men in our task force," she told the Commons the next day. "Had we left it any later it would have been too late and I might have had to come to the House with the news that some of our ships had been sunk."

The War Cabinet agreed. A coded message went out, three torpedoes flew, and *Belgrano*, gouged and broken, receded into the Atlantic's dark depths. She carried 321 Argentine sailors into her silent crypt.

Stung by *Belgrano*'s sinking, Argentina's navy refused to sail out of port and remained there for the duration, but its air force still posed a formidable threat. Two days after *Belgrano*'s destruction, an Argentine attack plane launched an Exocet missile into the side of the destroyer HMS *Sheffield*, killing twenty-one British crewmen.

The *Sheffield* attack was the first loss of a British warship to enemy action since 1945, and the news hit Thatcher like a thunderbolt. When she was told the news, she retreated to her private room at Commons, tears rolling down her cheeks.

"Don't let anyone in," a kindly minister told the bodyguard at her door. "She wants to be alone."*

With the loss of warships on both sides, Thatcher and the British public were done with contorted plans for a half-baked peace. It was war, and Britain would fight to win. Yet Thatcher would still have to fight well-meaning but soft men bent on a compromise that would, she feared, legitimize Argentine aggression.

She was most suspicious of her Foreign Office, whose strongest weapon against foreign aggression, the papers joked, was the "preemptive cringe." It was on those men her ire was unleashed. One envoy who had brought her several peace proposals from Haig scribbled in his diary,

Mrs T has not yet consigned me to the Tower; but I am told that her voice drops two dangerous decibels when she goes through my telegrams during inner Cabinet meetings. How much lower it would sink in patient but intolerant wrath if I included in my messages all Haig's pleas.

Seven weeks of negotiation had gone nowhere. Winter was setting in, and like the railway schedules of 1914, war's timetable could not be postponed much longer. Time was approaching for Albion's guns to do what diplomacy could not.

Five days after the *Sheffield* sinking, the War Cabinet approved Operation Sutton, Admiral Woodward's plan for an amphibious landing on the western coast of East Falkland. If all went right, the Union Jack would come ashore at San Carlos Bay on May 21.

---

* In a show of black humor only British servicemen can pull off, as *Sheffield*'s now-orphaned crew were carried away on a rescue ship, they gathered on the rescuer's deck and bade goodbye to the sinking *Sheffield* by singing the campy Monty Python anthem "Always Look on The Bright Side of Life."

As D-day approached, Thatcher's nerves frayed. On a normal peacetime day, she rarely slept more than five hours a night. Now that the decisions were made and she had nothing to do but wait, she barely slept at all. After fidgeting at No. 10 for a day, she finally asked the War Cabinet's secretary, "You couldn't find me some decisions to make, could you? I find all this waiting around very difficult."

Though twisted in knots on the inside, Thatcher knew she must keep the appearance of "business as usual" for the sake of home front morale. The day the landings took place, she gave a speech at the opening of a warehouse in her home district of Finchley. After delivering her address, riding on a forklift, lunching with the workers, and looking untroubled for photographs, she returned to Downing Street to await Fate's verdict.

Battle for the Beaches

The tip of Britannia's trident, Admiral Woodward's task force, included the carriers *Hermes* and *Invincible*, twenty Harrier attack jets, the destroyer *Glamorgan*, and the missile frigates *Broadsword*, *Yarmouth*, and *Alacrity*. This vanguard was followed by the stately *Queen Elizabeth II*, a luxury ocean liner that, like her World War II aunts, was packed with British soldiers—in this case, 3,000 men of the Welsh and Scots Guards who would support landings by paratroops and Royal Marines.

The risks were formidable. The Royal Navy was mounting a seaborne invasion in uncertain weather on a tight budget. The task force had fewer than two dozen Harrier "jump jets" to face over one hundred Argentine combat aircraft. And time was on Galtieri's side: by mid-June, winter would set in.

Nature, it seemed, was turning her back on Britain. Just before the landings, a Sea King helicopter carrying a crack team of SAS commandos hit an albatross, whose ungainly body flopped into the engine intake, sending the helicopter into the swirling ocean. The freak accident killed twenty-two elite fighters even before the fighting began.*

Yet the weather that made flight so hazardous for the British also cloaked the landing fleet from the eyes of Argentina's flying raptors. On May 21, the fleet arrived off East Falkland's San Carlos harbor under a canopy of clouds and gunfire. As tracer

---

* Another Sea King helicopter pilot serving aboard HMS *Invincible* was Prince Andrew, Duke of York and second son of Queen Elizabeth II. The Ministry of Defence suggested transferring the prince off the ship, but the queen insisted her son remain at his post.

rounds arced and shellbursts plumed the island's shore, landing craft were lowered from ships and turned toward the coast.

As if to make amends for the albatross incident, Neptune stayed his hand during those critical minutes, and the water remained complacent as landing boats waddled into San Carlos Bay. Moments later, marines and paratroopers swarmed the island's western beaches. The landing went smoothly, and by nightfall Woodward's lieutenants had put 5,000 paratroopers, commandos, and marines ashore.

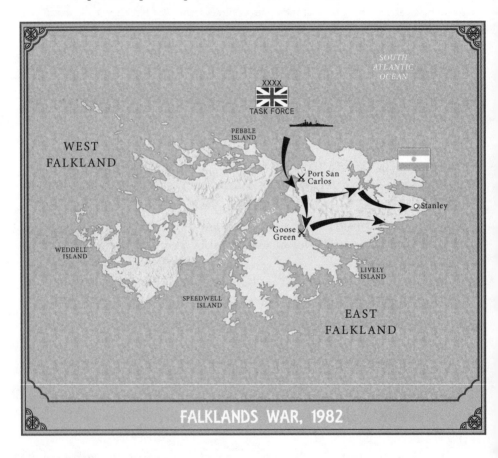

FALKLANDS WAR, 1982

Argentina's navy remained cowed by the sinking of *General Belgrano*, but its air force had not. American-built Skyhawks set upon the destroyer *Coventry* and sank her, killing nineteen. The frigate HMS *Ardent* went up in flames during another air strike—twenty-two dead—while the frigate *Argonaut* and destroyer *Brilliant* were badly damaged.

Argentine fighter-bombers circled the beach like Patagonian hawks, bombing British infantry on the beachhead. The pounding grew so vicious that Admiral Woodward kept his carriers safely out to sea, which limited the time the precious Harriers could spend over East Falkland defending the men on the ground. Grumbling British soldiers, bereft of air cover, hunkered down at San Carlos in what they bitterly dubbed "Bomb Alley."[*]

The Royal Navy's worst loss was not a warship, but the 18,000-ton transport *Atlantic Conveyer*, which went to the bottom with three of the four big Chinook helicopters Woodward had earmarked to ferry troops to Port Stanley, on the island's east side. Without those helicopters, commandos would have to "yomp"—British slang for a foot march—fifty-six rugged miles, with each soldier carrying eighty pounds of weapons, food, water, and ammunition step after rocky step. With the Argentines holding air superiority over the island's eastern and central regions, a slow line of marching men was an invitation to slaughter.

Echoing her fantasized connection with Winston Churchill in her younger days, Margaret Thatcher had a deep, personal bond with the young men in field green who put their lives on the line for Queen and Country. "Maggie" kept an excellent rapport with these men who lived on the spear's tip, and few residents of Downing Street commanded the fighting man's loyalty as she did.

But there was a darker side to this coin. Because she saw the war as a personal crusade, its losses were personal, too. The night *Coventry* went up in flames, she retreated to her upstairs room at No. 10 and wrote letters in longhand to the parents of each man who died. When *Atlantic Conveyer* was hit on May 25, she received the bad news, along with a false report that the carrier *Invincible* had also been hit. Her husband Denis walked into the bedroom to find her sitting on the edge of the bed, crying.

"Another ship! All my young men!" she sobbed.

Sitting beside her, Denis said quietly, "That's what war's like, love. I've been in one. I know."

Before the war was over, Margaret Thatcher would write letters to the families of 255 men who would never come home. It was a heart-wrenching burden sustained by her unshakable sense of right and wrong, of good and evil. Of principle. Muddled

---

[*] The death toll in Bomb Alley could have been greater, for many of the American-made bombs dropped from Argentine planes failed to explode when used at low altitudes. The bomb manufacturers had prepared a manual explaining how to re-fuse the bombs to explode on impact, fixing this problem, but the US government didn't forward the manual to Argentina. The Argentines were furious with the Americans over what they considered shoddy customer service.

questions of peacetime democracy—financial cost, poll numbers, criticism by the press—meant nothing to her. In her heart, Thatcher knew she was fighting a righteous cause against naked aggression, in the name of a people she had sworn to defend.

To her, that was all that mattered.

While her men were being pounded on the sands of San Carlos, Thatcher swallowed an almost-irresistible urge to call her ground commander, Brigadier General Julian Thompson, and order him to break out from his beachhead. Forcing herself to be patient, she told an audience of Tory women, "We must expect fresh attacks upon them, and there can be no question of pressing the force commander to move forward prematurely. The judgment about timing must be his and his alone, and we have confidence in his judgment."

As British casualties mounted, Argentina made some crucial mistakes. Its navy, keeping its submarines safe in port, allowed British ships free reign of the combat zone. Argentine air commanders, bitten by the impressive performance of the nimble Harrier jets, grew gun-shy and declined to risk their Skyhawks in an all-out battle to destroy the beachhead. The Argentine Army was left on its own.

Argentine infantrymen—most of them one-year conscripts from the country's warmer north—had no more enthusiasm for the cold weather and hot British projectiles than their sister services. Nearly all the original invading force had been pulled back to Argentina, and those left behind had no desire to give their lives for a forlorn pile of rocks and sheep.

A thousand defenders dug in at Goose Green, a key point south of San Carlos. But after putting up moderate resistance, the Argentines there surrendered to British paratroops. As June opened, Argentina was pushed back to the high ground around Port Stanley.

As the scales tilted in Britannia's favor, diplomats and heads of state pressured Thatcher to declare a cease-fire and accept a mediated settlement. Pope John Paul II called for a truce, while German Chancellor Helmut Schmidt criticized Britain for widening the war.

Thatcher brushed off this noise. Her Majesty's Government would not, as she later put it, "snatch diplomatic defeat from the jaws of military victory." Even if the request came from her closest ally. Though they were friends, Thatcher was not hesitant when talking to the US president. She spoke the language of war, while Reagan remained reticent. When he called her on May 31 to urge a cease-fire, Reagan quoted Churchill's words about "magnanimity in victory."

Unimpressed, Thatcher told him she would not consider "magnanimity" until "victory" had been won.

"Just supposing Alaska was invaded," she lectured Reagan. "Now you've put all your people up there to retake it and someone suggested that a contact could come in [and mediate]. You wouldn't do it."

"No, no," Reagan conceded, "although Margaret, I have to say I don't quite think Alaska is a similar situation—"

"More or less so," she interrupted. "Ron, I'm not handing over the islands now . . . I can't lose the lives and blood of our soldiers to hand the islands over to a contact. It's not possible. You're surely not asking me, Ron, after we've lost some of our finest young men, you're surely not saying that after the Argentine withdrawal, that our forces, and our administration, become immediately idle? I had to go immense distances and mobilize half my country."

Reagan said nothing, for he knew he would do the same. "Margaret, I . . . Yes, well . . . Well, Margaret, I know that I've intruded, and I know how—"

"You've not intruded at all, and I'm glad you telephoned," she interrupted cheerfully. Quickly appending British niceties, she hung up.

Thatcher had the ability to listen past diplomatic dissonance and hear notes that rang true. In this case, it was the sound of military victory.

But she could not fend off the cherry bombs forever. Pressured by peace proposals, it was clear she would need a decisive battlefield win—namely, the capture of the island's capital, Port Stanley—to end the war on her own terms. If her soldiers couldn't yomp across East Falkland and take that capital, and quickly, a cease-fire would end the British campaign as effectively as a thousand-missile barrage.

"Ferrous Matter of the Highest Quality"

As troops prepared for the final assault on Port Stanley, the Argentine Air Force dealt Britannia another blow. On June 8, attack planes destroyed two landing ships, *Sir Galahad* and *Sir Tristram*, killing forty-nine and wounding 115, most of them from Britain's storied Welsh Guards Regiment. Three days later, as British paras and marines launched a night attack against Port Stanley's outer defenses, another destroyer, HMS *Glamorgan*, was hit by an Exocet missile. In minutes, another thirteen men died.

"It is impossible for me to describe the depth of feeling at these times," Thatcher wrote afterwards. "In fights for liberty—we lose our bravest and best. How unjust and heartbreaking."

But death is the coin of war's realm, and Thatcher stayed her course, waiting up late for news announcements and snatching military dispatches from her duty clerk as soon as he brought them in. "Like everyone else in Britain, I was glued to the radio for news—strictly keeping to my self-imposed rule not to telephone while the conflict was under way," she remembered.

Finally, on June 14, Argentine Brigadier General Mario Menendez surrendered the 5,000 men of his Port Stanley command. At a cost of 255 British soldiers, sailors, and airmen, 649 dead Argentinians, and three Falkland civilians, the Union Jack again fluttered over the Falkland Islands.

When news of the surrender reached London, a wave of relief washed over the exhausted prime minister. She struggled to process all she had been through. "As I went to sleep very late that night I realised how great the burden was which had been lifted from my shoulders," she later wrote. "A feeling that whatever problem I have to go through now, at least I won't have to go through that terrible period when every time the phone rings, every time the door opens, you worry."

At the PM's room in Westminster, where she had first made the decision to fight, advisors gathered, glasses in hand, to toast the Iron Lady of Britain.

"I don't think anyone else but you could have done it," said a beaming Willie Whitelaw, her deputy prime minister. Antony Acland of the Foreign Office, who had butted heads with her many times, recalled, "She wept, out of sheer relief."

Her husband Denis, grinning with pride, put his arm around his tear-stained wife and simply said, "Well done. Have a drink."

❖   ❖   ❖

THE FALKLANDS VICTORY transformed Margaret Thatcher from besieged one-termer to iconic war leader. As she returned to Downing Street after news of the surrender at Port Stanley, she mixed with crowds that had gathered on the street, singing "Rule Britannia!" Her approval rating skyrocketed, and two days after the Argentine flag came down, the Member of Parliament who had asked of what metal the "Iron Lady" was made took to the floor to answer his own question:

> *Is the Right Honourable Lady aware that the report has now been received from the public analyst on a certain substance recently subjected to analysis and that I have obtained a copy of that report? It showed that the substance under test consisted of ferrous matter of the highest quality, that it is of exceptional tensile strength, is highly resistant to wear and tear and to stress, and may be used with advantage for all national purposes.*

John Nott, her beleaguered defense secretary, later mused about the headstrong woman and her circle of male advisors: "Above all, she had a woman's courage. A different type of courage from a man's. She had more courage and more obstinacy than a man. She really did believe that all men were 'wet' and in particular the species called 'gentlemen,'" he wrote. "She was confronted with a crisis for her government and she shut her mind to the risks of conducting such an adventure 8,000 miles away. It was a woman's war—and the woman in her won."

Britain's military reputation soared. British paras and Royal Marines became war's premier artisans, in sharp contrast to the Red Army's Afghan quagmire and US fiascos in Iran and Lebanon. Traveling to the Falklands the following January, Thatcher spent several hours with "the boys," quizzing them about their victories, asking them to share stories of Tumbledown and Top Malo and Goose Green and Port Stanley.

Thatcher reveled in her role as a victorious war leader. Three years later, a photographer snapped a picture of the prime minister perched in the turret of a British Challenger tank, her face wrapped in an incongruous white head scarf. The photo instantly drew comparisons to her chariot-mounted predecessor, Queen Boudica, whose statue sits across the street from Parliament and its iconic clock tower.

The legacy of the Falklands War loomed large in British politics for more than a decade. The first woman to lead England in war in 250 years easily won reelection. Margaret Thatcher would not release the reins of her chariot until 1990, laying down the mantle of office as Britain's longest-serving prime minister. The high-heeled footsteps of the Iron Lady would echo loudly as Britain yomped into the twenty-first century.

EPILOGUE

The Final Argument of Queens

IT TAKES A FIRM HAND and strong stomach to play the game King Louis XIV called "the final argument of kings." Some women become pawns, others are knights, and a few even flip the board.

Viewed from the reverse, the tapestry woven by war queens assaults the eye with random thread lines. Manduhai's rough weave points to a decrepit empire she stitched back together. Catherine's elegant strands reflect the rational thoughts of an enlightened despot. Boudica's scarlet lines splay in many directions, like jets of blood running dry before her scene is complete.

Sewn over the centuries by different hands, the fibers defy coherence. But when we flip the tableau to the front and take a few steps back, we can make out repeating patterns, some of them revealing surprising truths about women holding wartime power. For all their cultural differences, most sisters of the sword shared several distinct traits.

First, the stereotype of the nurturing, violence-averse mother figure is rarely borne out in moments of crisis when the question of war is dropped at a leader's feet. Successful war leaders are often cold, calculating, swift, and decisive—even cruel— when faced with an existential threat. Indira Gandhi planned a preemptive strike against Pakistan, while Golda built her foreign policy around air and armor power. Tamar sent armies to slaughter and enslave neighboring Muslims and Byzantines. Catherine the Great used war to gain a foothold on the Black Sea and tear away parts of Poland. The female of the species may not be the deadliest by far, as Kipling claimed, but she can be deadly enough to do the job.

Second, a relentless work ethic is a prerequisite. Governing is hard work; wartime governing is exponentially harder. There are no shortcuts, no avoiding strenuous, around-the-clock effort. Elizabeth Tudor, Cleopatra, and Catherine the Great devoted long, tedious hours each day to managing domestic and military agendas, most of which were neither glamorous nor fun. Thatcher's daily schedule rivaled that of her workaholic idol Winston Churchill, and Golda Meir made it her mission to outwork any man or woman in Israel's government. Successful commanders-in-chief are comfortable being work horses, not just show horses.

Third, knowing the limits of one's expertise is absolutely essential. Though successful at managing grand strategy, Indira Gandhi and Golda Meir would have made inept brigadiers. Golda didn't know how many soldiers were in an army division, and Indira insisted on an invasion of Bangladesh at the worst possible time. Catherine the Great spent her hours in salons and at writing desks, not at field headquarters or barracks.

A woman's lack of familiarity with the nuts and bolts of warfare will not, by itself, affect her success as a commandress-in-chief. Tactics, said General George Patton, belong at the battalion level, not in the supreme commander's palace. "No general officer and practically no colonel needs to know any tactics," Patton once told his diary. "If generals knew less tactics, they would interfere less."

The successful women teamed up with seasoned military advisors, like General Manekshaw, Marc Antony, Prince Potemkin, or Admiral Leach, and they generally stuck to what they knew best: strategic aims, diplomacy, and politics. A commander who is willing to listen to the right professionals on tactics, patiently accepting hard limits while keeping a tight grip on top-level objectives, has the makings of a successful war leader.

Fourth, women war leaders should not be afraid to requisition traditional male imagery to instill confidence in their commanders and troops. Soldiers risking their lives for warrior queens—"monstrous regiments of women," John Knox might have called them—sometimes need visual evidence of stone-hearted competence at the top. Women who appear comfortable with the look and accoutrements of war can meet this need by making a visual connection with both soldiers and legislators who support them. Njinga was the most enthusiastic practitioner of this approach (drilling with her men, wielding weapons, carrying the *lunga* bell), but to a lesser degree, Caterina Sforza (falchion sword and engraved cuirass), Elizabeth Tudor (silver breastplate and marshal's baton), Manduhai (bow, quiver, and helmet), Thatcher (military beret, riding a tank), and Catherine the Great (sword and jacket of the

Preobrazhensky Guards) proved surprisingly comfortable shifting their image from *regina* to *rex* as circumstances demanded.

Finally, statesmanship is another quality that drives wartime success. When the passions of war inflame parliaments, generals, and the public, a leader must know when to play the long game, even if it means giving up a short-term advantage. Cleopatra, Indira Gandhi, Golda Meir, and Catherine the Great—all students of retail diplomacy—were far-sighted internationalists who simultaneously played on two or three chessboards. Catherine's decisions to push the Ottoman Empire into war, or to partition Poland, followed a careful survey of the attitudes and capabilities of other great powers. Indira flew to meet with leaders in Moscow, Washington, and London before launching her war in Bangladesh. Golda's vetoes of a preemptive air strike, and the use of nuclear weapons, are particularly significant; the first decision ran counter to the advice of her military professionals, and the second preserved humanity's taboo against using nuclear weapons in anger. Both decisions were driven by diplomatic considerations. Golda may have been a hardline Zionist to her Arab neighbors, but when superpowers were involved she played it down the middle, never straying more than an octave from middle-C.

HISTORY'S *GENERALISSIMAS* LEFT a unique footprint on war's great map. But they are also subject to wartime rules that apply equally to kings and queens.

First and foremost, a national leader's military options are fundamentally shaped by the economic and geographic cards in her hand. Strategy follows resources, not the other way around. Elizabeth I and Margaret Thatcher, whose finances were never flush, were anxious to avoid open-ended military expenditures, so it was natural for them to insist on limited wars. Conversely, Cleopatra, lacking good native armies but richer than Croesus, levered Egypt's economic power to subsidize Roman legions in the same way that Pitt the Younger fought Napoleon with British gold and foreign blood.

The best war leaders also capitalize on their nation's technological resources. While most technological advantages affect the battlefield—big-gun galleons in Elizabeth's wars, muskets in Njinga's wars, Harrier jump-jets in Thatcher's—leaders like Indira and Golda made good use of air travel and communications technology to keep strategic allies on their side or acquire useful military intelligence. They understood these advances enough to use them as force multipliers in war, but never made the mistake of relying on technology as a substitute for sound strategy.

Because war's DNA is encoded in the map, geography also plays a starring role. Good war leaders harness space and time when setting military objectives. Gandhi, Catherine, and Golda, fighting two-front wars, used their central positions to shift hard-pressed forces north or south, east or west, to the scene of trouble in the same way that Napoleon, Jefferson Davis, Hindenburg, and Hitler used interior lines to forestall the inevitable. In her one-front war with Portugal, an outgunned Njinga adopted a hit-and-run strategy that capitalized on the interior forests of Matamba to protect her base, in the same way that George Washington, Alexander I, and Ho Chi Minh avoided the battle royale against foreign juggernauts.

The second lesson is that gambles are unavoidable. In war, leaders can be forced to jump into a chasm without knowing, as General Dwight Eisenhower wrote, whether the bottom is lined with feathers or brickbats. In these cases, a seconds-long bolt of good luck or bad can make the difference between a head wearing a crown or rolling in a basket.

War leaders must also be willing to accept risk. Artemisia rammed an allied warship in full view of King Xerxes, not knowing whether he would see her fratricide for what it was, or whether any Calyndian survivors would swim ashore and rat her out to the king. In the South Atlantic, seasonal gales should have spelled disaster for Margaret Thatcher, while the timely appearance of a Dutch fleet in Angola (and its untimely disappearance six years later) radically altered Njinga's fate. As with Napoleon at Marengo, Houston at San Jacinto, or Patton at Casablanca, Fortune, though notoriously fickle, is as decisive for women as for men. She can be estimated, she can be seduced, but she can never be commanded.

Finally, failure is one of war's occupational hazards. *Almost* is one of the most disappointing words in any language, and it turns up with depressing regularity in war diaries and after-action reports. As Tolstoy might have put it, successful wars are all alike; failed wars are lost in their own ways. Some Valkyries, like Cleopatra, lost by making the strategic error of battling large, resource-rich empires with the political will to fight to the end. Others, like Njinga, entrusted their hopes to allies who proved unequal to the task.

Most decisive failures, however, were of the prosaic, "want of a nail" sort. Driven by blind rage, Boudica was long on passion but short on logistics; with food and water running low, her poorly trained horde was forced to give battle against the Romans on unfavorable ground. Caterina Sforza lost at Forli when she gambled on immobile defenses. Cleopatra, following Antony's lead, persisted in fighting a war of attrition in Greece when her navy lost its lifeline to Egypt. Women are no more immune than men to defeat through scant resources, subordinate incompetence, or failure to master fundamentals like planning, provisions, and training.

VALHALLA'S QUAGGLE OF QUEENS left behind a mixed bag of personalities, strategy, tactics, and experiences. Taken together, they contributed upper-octave sonatinas to Mars's long and violent symphony, and bequeathed insights about future conflicts whose commanders will emerge from the next generation of Thatchers, Catherines, and Njingas.

ACKNOWLEDGMENTS

Any book spanning 2,500 years of women leading Egyptians, Celts, Mongolians, Greeks, Britons, Turks, Jews, Italians, Russians, Mbundus, and Caucasians requires a lot of help. Preeminent expertise was generously shared by some of the world's top experts in their respective fields of history, and we are inestimably grateful to Oxford University's Dr. Susan Doran, Yale University's Dr. Erica Benner, UCLA's Dr. Kara Cooney, Stanford University's Dr. Joel Beinin, Cardiff University's Dr. Miranda Aldhouse-Green, Macalester College's Dr. Jack Weatherford, Sam Houston State University's Dr. Stephen Rapp, Jr., University of North Georgia's Dr. Timothy May, and biographer Claire Berlinski.

We are also indebted to a "monstrous regiment of friends" who offered editorial, creative, and moral support during the book's endless rewrites. Our heartfelt gratitude goes to Ambassador Jonathan Addleton, literary agent Suzy Evans, Sally Jordan, Samantha Holt, Allegra Jordan, Sarah Primrose, Austin Jordan, Sarah Borders, Shannon Baur, Jim Hornfischer, Leia Shermohammed, Dr. Julie Pace, Zachary Mullis, Hal Elrod, Thad Wilson, Connor Walden, Rachel Jordan, Elizabeth Lally, Galina Cramer, Virginia McGuffey, Jennifer Elrod, Nadia Saleem, Kate Jordan, Andy Jordan, the sisters of Kappa Kappa Gamma, and editor *par excellence* Melanie Madden for literary advice, draft commentary, encouragement, and willingness to listen to endless debates over which leaders to include, or leave out—and what we can learn from these remarkable women.

With love and thanks,
Emily Anne Jordan
Jonathan W. Jordan

BIBLIOGRAPHY

Books

Abadi, Jacob. *Tunisia Since the Arab Conquest: The Saga of a Westernized Muslim State*. Reading, UK: Ithaca Press, 2012.

Abun-Nasr, Jamil M. *A History of the Maghrib in the Islamic.* Cambridge University Press, 1993.

Adcock, F.E. *The Roman Art of War Under the Republic*. Barnes & Noble Books, 1995.

Aitken, Jonathan. *Margaret Thatcher: Power and Personality*. Bloomsbury, 2013.

Aldhouse-Green, Miranda. *Boudica Britannia*. Pearson, 2006.

Avner, Yehuda. *The Prime Ministers: An Intimate Narrative of Israeli Leadership*. Toby Press, 2010.

Beard, Mary. *Women & Power: A Manifesto*. Liveright, 2017.

———. *SPQR: A History of Ancient Rome*. Liveright, 2015.

Behan, Mona, and Jeannine Davis-Kimball. *Warrior Women: An Archaeologist's Search for History's Hidden Heroines*. Warner Books, 2002.

Benner, Erica. *Be Like the Fox: Machiavelli In His World*. Norton, 2017.

Berlinski, Claire. *There Is No Alternative: Why Margaret Thatcher Matters*. Basic Books, 2011.

Biran, Michal. *The Empire of the Qara Khitai in Eurasian History: Between China and the Islamic World*. Cambridge University Press, 2005.

Breisach, Ernst. *Caterina Sforza: A Renaissance Virago.* University of Chicago Press, 1967.

Burkett, Elinor. *Golda*. Harper, 2008.

Caminos, Ricardo A. *The New-Kingdom Temples of Buhen*. Egypt Exploration Society, 1974.

Campbell, John. *The Iron Lady:Margaret Thatcher, From Grocer's Daughter to Prime Minister.* Penguin, 2011.

Castor, Helen. *She-Wolves: The Women Who Ruled England Before Elizabeth*. Harper, 2011.

Clark, Emily, and Mary Laven. *Women and Religion in the Atlantic Age, 1550–1900*. Ashgate, 2014.

Clarke, George S. *Russia's Sea-Power, Past and Present.* John Murray, 1898.

Clausewitz, Carl von. *On War*. Penguin, 1982.

Cline, Eric H., and David O'Connor, eds. *Thutmose III: A New Biography*. University of Michigan Press, 2006.

Cooney, Kara. *The Woman Who Would Be King:Hatshepsut's Rise to Power in Ancient Egypt.* Crown, 2014.

———. *When Women Ruled the World: Six Queens of Egypt*. National Geographic, 2018.

Coughlan, Robert. *Elizabeth & Catherine*. G.P. Putnam's Sons, 1975.

Custine, Marquis de. *Empire of the Czar*. Doubleday, 1971.

Dale, Iain, ed. *Memories of Margaret Thatcher: A Portrait, by Those Who Knew Her Best.* Biteback Publishing, 2013.

Dando-Collins, Stephen. *Cleopatra's Kidnappers: How Caesar's Sixth Legion Gave Egypt to Rome and Rome to Caesar.* Wiley, 2005.

Darnell, John Coleman, and Colleen Manassa. *Tutankhamun's Armies: Battle and Conquest in Ancient Egypt's Late 18th Dynasty.* Wiley, 2007.

Davies, Brian. *Empire and Military Revolution in Eastern Europe: Russia's Turkish Wars in the Eighteenth Century.* Bloomsbury, 2013.

———. *The Russo-Turkish War, 1768-1774: Catherine II and the Ottoman Empire.* Bloomsbury, 2016.

De Pauw, Linda Grant. *Battle Cries and Lullabies: Women in War from Prehistory to the Present.* University of Oklahoma Press, 1988.

Delbrück, Hans, and Walter J. Renfroe, Jr., trans. *Warfare in Antiquity: History of the Art of War.* University of Nebraska Press, 1990.

Dhillon, B.S. *A History and Study of the Jats.* Beta Publishers, 1994.

Dixit, J.N. *India-Pakistan in War & Peace.* Routledge, 2002.

Dixon, Norman. *On the Psychology of Military Incompetence.* Pimlico, 1994.

Dodge, Theodore Ayrault. *Caesar: A History of the Art of War Among the Romans.* University of Nebraska Press, 1990.

Doran, Susan. *Elizabeth I and Her Circle.* Oxford University Press, 2015.

———. *Elizabeth I and Foreign Policy, 1558–1603.* Routledge, 2000.

Duffy, Christopher. *Russia's Military Way to the West: Origins and Nature of Russian Military Power 1700-1800.* Routledge, 2015.

Dunn, Jane. *Elizabeth and Mary: Cousins, Rivals, Queens.* Vintage Books, 2005. Earenfight, Theresa. *Queenship in Medieval Europe.* Macmillan, 2013.

Eastmond, Antony. *Art and Identity in Thirteenth-Century Byzantium: Hagia Sophia and the Empire of Trebizond.* Routledge, 2017.

———. *Royal Imagery in Medieval Georgia.* Penn State Press , 2010.

Edgerton, Robert B. *The Fall of the Asante Empire:The Hundred-Year War for Africa's Gold Coast.* Free Press, 1995.

Elfasi, M., ed. *Africa from the Seventh to the Eleventh Century.* Heinemann Educational Publishers, 1995.

Falki, Hanadi. *Field Marshal Sam Manekshaw.* Prabhat Prakashan, 2011.

Fallaci, Oriana. *Interviews with History.* Houghton Mifflin, 1976.

Farrokh, Kaveh. *Shadows in the Desert: Ancient Persia at War.* Osprey, 2007.

Frank, Katherine. *Indira: The Life of Indira Nehru Gandhi.* HarperCollins, 2001.

Fraser, Antonia. *The Warrior Queens: The Legends and the Lives of the Women Who Have Led Their Nations in War.* Alfred A. Knopf, 1989.

Fuller, John F.C. *Julius Caesar: Man, Soldier, and Tyrant.* Da Capo Press, 1991.

Fuller, William C. Jr. *Strategy and Power in Russia, 1600–1914.* Free Press, 1992.

Gabriel, Richard A. *The Military History of Ancient Israel.* Praeger, 2003.

Gaddis, John Lewis. *On Grand Strategy.* Penguin UK, 2018.

Gera, Deborah Levine. *Warrior Women: The Anonymous Tractatus de Mulieribus.* Brill, 1997.

Goldsworthy, Adrian. *The Complete Roman Army.* Thames & Hudson, 2003.

Green, Peter. *The Greco-Persian Wars.* University of California Press, 1996.

Gristwood, Sarah. *Blood Sisters: The Women Behind the War of the Roses.* Basic Books, 2013.

Guy, John. *Queen of Scots: The True Life of Mary Stuart.* Mariner Books, 2005.

Hammer, Paul E.J. *Elizabeth's Wars.* Macmillan, 2003.

Hannoum, Abdelmajid. *Colonial Histories, Post-Colonial Memories.* Heinemann, 2001.

Harmatta, Janos, ed. *History of Civilizations of Central Asia.* UNESCO Publishing, 1994.

Hartley, Janet M. *Russia, 1762–1825.* Praeger, 2008.

Hastings, Max, and Simon Jenkins. *The Battle for the Falklands.* Norton, 1983.

Hay, David J. *The Military Leadership of Matilda of Canossa, 1046–1115.* Manchester University Press, 2008.

Herzog, Chaim. *The War of Atonement.* Casemate, 2009.

———, and Mordechai Gichon. *Battles of the Bible.* Greenhill Books, 1997.

Herzog, François, and Janet Lloyd, trans. *The Mirror of Herodotus.* University of California Press, 1988.

Heywood, Linda M. *Njinga of Angola: Africa's Warrior Queen.* Harvard University Press, 2017.

———, and John K. Thornton. *Central Africans, Atlantic Creoles, and the Foundation of the Americas, 1585–1660.* Cambridge University Press, 2007.

Hölbl, Günther. *History of the Ptolemaic Empire.* Routledge 2001.

Hrbek, Ivan. *Africa from the Seventh to the Eleventh Century.* University of California Press, 1992.

Hutchinson, Robert. *The Spanish Armada: A History.* St. Martin's Press, 2013.

Ilahiane, Hsain. *Historical Dictionary of the Berbers.* Scarecrow Press, 2006.

Isaacson, Walter. *Kissinger: A Biography.* Simon & Schuster, 1992.

Jacob, J.F.R. *Surrender at Dacca: Birth of a Nation.* Manohar Publishers, 1997.

Jackson, Guida M. *Women Rulers Throughout the Ages.* ABC-CLIO, 1999.

Jagchid, Sechin. *Mongolia's Culture and Society.* Westview Press , 1979.

James, Liz, ed. *Women, Men and Eunuchs: Gender in Byzantium.* Routledge, 1997.

Jansen, Sharon L. *The Monstrous Regiment of Women: Female Rulers in Early Modern Europe.* Palgrave MacMillan, 2002.

Jayakar, Pupul. *Indira Gandhi.* Pantheon, 1988.

Johnson, Linda Cooke. *Women of the Conquest Dynasties: Gender and Identity in Liao and Jin China.* University of Hawai'i Press, 2011.

Jones, Prudence J. *Cleopatra: A Sourcebook.* University of Oklahoma Press, 2006.

Kellner-Heinkele, Barbara, ed. *Altaica Berolinensia: The Concept of Sovereignty in the Altaic World.* Harrassowitz, 1993.

Kissinger, Henry. *Years of Upheaval.* Simon & Schuster, 1982.

Klagsbrun, Francine. *Lioness: Golda Meir and the Nation of Israel.* Schocken Books, 2017.

Kleiner, Diana E.E. *Cleopatra and Rome.* Harvard University Press, 2009.

Kuhrt, Amélie. *The Persian Empire.* Routledge, 2013.

Laughton, John Knox, ed. *State Papers Relating to the Defeat of the Spanish Armada, Anno 1588.* 2 vols. London: Navy Records Society, 1894.

Lee, Lily Xiao Hong, and Sue Wiles, eds. *Biographical Dictionary of Chinese Women: Tang Through Ming, 618–1644.* M.E. Sharpe, 2014.

Lee, Wayne E. *Empires and Indigenes.* New York University Press, 2011.

Lev, Elizabeth. *The Tigress of Forli.* Houghton Mifflin Harcout, 2011.

Levin, Carole. *The Heart and Stomach of a King.* University of Pennsylvania Press, 2003.

Loewe, Michael. *Everyday Life in Early Imperial China During the Han Period.* Hackett Publishing, 1968.

McDermott, James. *England and the Spanish Armada.* Yale University Press, 2005.

McMahon, Keith. *Women Shall Not Rule.* Rowman & Littlefield, 2013.

Mansingh, Surjit. *India's Search for Power.* Sage Publications, 1984.

Marcus, Leah S., et al., eds. *Elizabeth I: Collected Works*. University of Chicago Press, 2000.

Massie, Robert K. *Catherine the Great: Portrait of a Woman*. Random House, 2012.

Mathur, K.P. *The Unseen Indira Gandhi*. Konark Publishers, 2016.

Mattingly, Garrett. *The Armada*. Houghton Mifflin Harcourt, 1959.

Maurer, Helen E. *Margaret of Anjou: Queenship and Power in Late Medieval England*. Boydell, 2003.

McKnight, Kathryn Joy, and Leo Garofalo, eds. *Afro-Latino Voices: Narratives from the Early Modern Ibero-Atlantic World, 1550–1812*. Hackett Publishing, 2009.

Meir, Golda. *My Life*. Putnam, 1975.

Met'revelli, Roin, and Stephen Jones, eds. *Kartlis Tskhovreba: The Georgian Chronicle*. Artanuji, 2014.

Meuwese, Mark. *Brothers in Arms, Partners in Trade*. Brill, 2012.

Mikaberidze, Alexander. *Historical Dictionary of Georgia*. Rowan & Littlefield, 2015.

Minns, Ellis Hovell. *Scythians and Greeks*. Cambridge University Press, 2010.

Montefiore, Simon Sebag. *Catherine the Great & Potemkin*. Vintage, 2016 .

Monter, William. *The Rise of Female Kings in Europe, 1300–1800*. Yale University Press, 2012.

Moore, Charles. *Margaret Thatcher*. Alfred A. Knopf, 2013.

Mote, F.W. *Imperial China, 900–1800*. Harvard University Press, 2003.

Müller, Karl Otfried. *The History and Antiquities of the Doric Race*. 2 vols. London: John Murray, 1834.

Murray, Williamson, et al., eds. *The Making of Strategy*. Cambridge University Press, 1994.

Naylor, Phillip C. *North Africa: A History from Antiquity to the Present*. University of Texas Press, 2009.

Nelson, Arthur. *The Tudor Navy*. Conway Maritime Press, 2001.

Nelson, Sarah Milledge. *Ancient Queens: Archaeological Explorations*. AltaMira Press, 2003.

Newitt, Malyn, ed. *The Portuguese in West Africa, 1415–1670*. Cambridge University Press, 2010.

Nicholas, Sir Harris, ed. *Proceedings and Ordinances of the Privy Council of England*. Commissioners of Public Records, 1837.

O'Neill, Kelly. *Claiming Crimea: A History of Catherine the Great's Southern Empire*. Yale University, 2017.

Ogden, Chris. *Maggie: An Intimate Portrait of a Woman in Power*. Simon & Schuster, 1990.

Panthaki, Behram, and Zenobia Panthaki. *Field Marshal Sam Manekshaw*. Niyogi Books, 2016.

Pasolini, Pier Desiderio. *Caterina Sforza*. 3 vols. Ermanno Loescher & Co., 1893.

Peddie, John. *The Roman War Machine*. Combined Books ,1996.

Pelley, Patricia M. *Postcolonial Vietnam*. Duke University, 2002.

Phaf, Ineke, and Tiago de Oliveira Pinto, eds. *AfricAmericas*. Iberoamericana, 2008.

Rabinovich, Abraham. *The Yom Kippur War*. Schocken Books, 2008.

Randall-MacIver, D., and C. Leonard Wooley. *Eckley B. Coxe Junior Expedition to Nubia*. Vol. VIII: Buhen. University Museum, 1911.

Rashba, Gary L. *Holy Wars: 3,000 Years of Battles in the Holy Land*. Casemate, 2011.

Roberts, Andrew. *Leadership in War: Essential Lessons From Those Who Made History*. Viking, 2019.

Ray, Meredith K. *Daughters of Alchemy*. Harvard University Press, 2015.

Rayfield, Donald. *The Literature of Georgia: A History*. Routledge Books, 2013.

———. *Edge of Empires: A History of Georgia*. Reaktion Books, 2012.

Rodgers, W.L. *Greek and Roman Naval Warfare*. Naval Institute Press, 1937.

Roehrig, Catharine H., ed. *Hatshepsut: From Queen to Pharaoh*. Yale University Press, 2005.

Rudolph, Lloyd I, and Susanne Hoeber Rudolph, eds. *Making U.S. Foreign Policy Toward South Asia: Regional Imperatives and the Imperial Presidency.* Indiana University Press, 2008.

Schiff, Stacy. *Cleopatra: A Life.* Back Bay Books, 2011.

Shephard, Gillian. *The Real Iron Lady: Working with Margaret Thatcher.* Biteback Publishing, 2013.

Sicker, Martin. *The Islamic World in Decline.* Greenwood Publishing, 2001.

———. *The Rise and Fall of the Ancient Israelite States.* Greenwood Publishing, 2003.

Singh, Arvindar. *Myths and Realities of Security and Public Affairs.* Ocean Books, 2008.

Sisson, John Richard, and Leo E. Rose. *War and Secession.* University of California Press, 1990.

Smith II, Andrew M. *Roman Palmyra.* Oxford University Press, 2013.

Southern, Pat. *Empress Zenobia: Palmyra's Rebel Queen.* Continuum Books, 2008.

Standen, Naomi. *Unbounded Loyalty: Frontier Crossings in Liao China.* University of Hawai'i, 2007.

Stapleton, Timothy J. *A Military History of Africa.* 3 vols. ABC-CLIO, 2013.

Steinberg, Blema S. *Women in Power.* McGill-Queens University Press, 2008.

Sun Tzu. *The Art of War.* Tuttle, 1996.

Suny, Ronald Grigor. *The Making of the Georgian Nation.* Indiana University Press, 1994.

Tanner, Harold M. *China: A History.* Hackett Publishing, 2009.

Taylor, Keith Weller. *The Birth of Vietnam.* University of California Press, 1983.

Thatcher, Margaret. *Margaret Thatcher: The Autobiography.* HarperCollins, 2010.

Thomas, Hugh. *The Slave Trade.* Simon & Schuster, 1997.

Thornton, John K. *Warfare in Atlantic Africa, 1500–1800.* Routledge, 1999.

Thornton, Richard C. *The Falklands Sting: Reagan, Thatcher, and Argentina's Bomb.* Brassey's, 1998.

Troyat, Henri. *Terrible Tsarinas: Five Russian Women in Power.* Algora Publishing, 2001.

Tyldesley, Joyce. *Cleopatra: Last Queen of Egypt.* Basic Books, 2008.

Upham, Edward. *History of the Ottoman Empire.* 2 vols. Constable & Co., 1829.

Van de Ven, Hans. *Warfare in Chinese History.* Brill, 2000.

Vickers, K.H. *Humphrey Duke of Glouster.* Archibald Constable & Co. Ltd., 1907.

Volkovskii, N.L., and D.N. Vokovskii. *Russkaya Voennaya Cila.* Polygon, 2006.

Wagner, John. *Encyclopedia of the Wars of the Roses.* ABC-CLIO, 2001.

Wallinga, H.T. *Xerxes' Greek Adventure: The Naval Perspective.* Brill, 2005.

Wang, Yuan-Kang. *Harmony and War: Confucian Culture and Chinese Power Politics.* Columbia University Press, 2013.

Warry, John. *Warfare in the Classical World.* University of Oklahoma Press, 1995.

Watson, Alaric. *Aurelian and the Third Century.* Routledge, 1999.

Weatherford, Jack. *The Secret History of the Mongol Queens.* Crown, 2010.

Webster, Graham. *The Roman Imperial Army.* Barnes & Noble Books, 1994.

Weir, Alison. *The Life of Elizabeth I.* Ballentine, 2008.

———. *Queens of the Conquest.* Ballentine, 2017.

Wyatt, Donald J. *Battlefronts Real and Imagined: War, Border, and Identity in the Chinese Middle Period.* Palgrave Macmillan, 2008.

Other Sources

Adams, Ryon F. "Outfought and Outthought: Reassessing the Mongol Invasion of Japan." Master's thesis, U.S. Army Command and General Staff College, 2009.

Bedrosian, Robert, trans. *Kirakos Ganjakets'i's History of the Armenians.* http://rbedrosian.com /kgtoc.html.

Boyd, John. "Destruction and Creation." Thesis, U.S. Army Command and General Staff College, 1976.

Blythe, J.M. "Women in the Military: Scholastic Arguments and Medieval Images of Female Warriors." *History of Political Thought* (Summer 2001).

Carey, Brian Todd. "Cyrus II of Persia: Great Before Alexander." *Strategy & Tactics* (May–June 2016).

Carney, Elizabeth D. "Women and Military Leadership in Pharaonic Egypt." *Greek, Roman and Byzantine Studies* 42 (2001).

Clothier, Stephen. "Greek Perspectives on Cyrus and his Conquests." Open Access Dissertations and Theses, Paper 6824, 1997.

De Vries, Joyce. "Caterina Sforza: The Shifting Representation of a Woman Ruler in Early Modern Italy." *Lo Sguardo: Riviista di Filisofia* 13, no. 3 (2013).

Donvito, Filippo. "The Lioness of the Caucasus." *Medieval Warfare* 4, no. 2 (2014).

Frye, Susan. "The Myth of Elizabeth at Tilbury." *The Sixteenth Century Journal* (Spring 1992).

Gabriel, Richard A. "Israel's First Great General." *Military Chronicles* (December 2010).

Gupta, Jessica, dir. "The Life of Field Marshal Sam Manekshaw, MC." Film, UNESCO Parzor Project, 2002.

Hairston, Julia L. "Skirting the Issue: Machiavelli's Caterina Sforza." *Renaissance Quarterly* (Autumn 2000).

Heywood, Linda. "Njinga and Memory in Colonial Angola." Presentation, Harvard University Center for African Studies, November 28, 2016. https://vimeo.com/194683568.

Hine, Douglas O. "The 1982 Falklands-Malvinas Case Study." Study No. 1036, U.S. Naval War College, June 4, 2010.

Husby, Tristan K. "Justice and the Justification of War in Ancient Greece: Four Authors." http://digitalcommons.conncoll.edu/classicshp/1.

Jhutti, Sundeep S. "The Getes." *Sino-Platonic Papers* (October 2003).

Johnson, Charles C. "Thatcher and the Jews." *Tablet* (December 28, 2011).

Kak, Kapil. "India's Grand Strategy for the 1971 War." *CLAWS Journal* (Summer, 2012).

Kaye, Steve, "Finding Boudica," www.bandaarcgeophysics.co.uk/arch/boudica_logistics.html

Mallowan, Max, "Cyrus the Great." *Iran* 10, 1972.

Marcus, Joyce, "Breaking the Glass Ceiling: The Strategies of Royal Women in Ancient States." *Gender in Pre-Hispanic America*, Dumbarton Oaks Research Library and Collection (2001).

Margaret Thatcher Foundation Archives. www.margaretthatcher.org.

Mitchell, Lynette G. "The Women of Ruling Families in Archaic and Classical Greece." *The Classical Quarterly* (May 2012).

Moore, General Sir Jeremy, and Admiral Sir John Woodward. "The Falklands Experience." *Royal United Services Institute for Defense Studies* (March 1983).

Nichter, Luke A. and Richard A. Moss. "Superpower Relations, Backchannels, and the Subcontinent: Using the Nixon Tapes to Examine the 1971 India-Pakistan War." Nixontapes.org. http://nixontapes.org/india-pakistan.html.

Nixontapes.org. nixontapes.org/transcripts.html.

Özer, Abdürrahim. "The Ottoman-Russian Relations Between the Years 1774–1787." August 2008.

Reece, Stuart. "Voltaire's Correspondence with Catherine II." Master's thesis, State University of Iowa, 1914.

Rhee, Jong Min. "Empress Wu of the Tang Dynasty: Becoming the Only Female Emperor in China." Master's thesis, University of Southern California, December 2008.

Richard Nixon Presidential Library. www.nixonlibrary.gov/virtuallibrary/tapeexcerpts.

Roberts, Andrew. Lecture, New York Historical Society, April 30, 2015.

Seawright, Caroline. "The Process of Identification: Can Mummy KV60-A Be Positively Identified as Hatshepsut?" www.thekeep.org.

Thompson, A.A. "The Appointment of the Duke of Medina Sidonia to the Command of the Spanish Armada." *The Historical Journal* (June 1969).

Thornton, John K. "Legitimacy and Political Power: Queen Njinga, 1624–1663." *Journal of African History* 32 (1991).

Ward, Simeon L. "The Falklands War April–June 1982: Operation CORPORATE." Master's thesis, U.S. Marine Corps Command and Staff College, April 3, 2008.

Yener, Emir. "Ottoman Seapower and Naval Technology During Catherine II's Turkish Wars 1768–1792." *International Naval Journal* 9, no. 1 (2016).

Zosimus. *New History*. London: Green and Chaplin, 1814. Reprinted. www.tertullian.org /fathers/zosimus01_book1.htm.

SOURCE NOTES

Chapter One: Tomyris

Background on the Massagetae and their culture comes from A. Abetekov and H. Yusupov, "Ancient Iranian Nomads in Western Central Asia," in Harmotta 484; Herzog 33 n. 84; Jhutti 2; Gera 189–90, 203; Herodotus 1:215, 1:216 ("If a man," "This they consider"); Minns 441. The battle between Tomyris and Cyrus, and Cyrus's fate, comes from Herodotus 1:204 ("There were many"), 1:205 ("for the queen"), 1:206 ("King of the Medes"), 1:207 ("Apart from"), 1:211, 212–13 ("Glutton as you are"), 1:214 ("After the battle"); Abetekov and Yusupov, in Harmotta 44; Gera 199–200, 203; Carey 32; Kuhrt 99–102; Muhammad A. Dandamayev, "Cyrus the Great," *Encyclopedia Iranica Online*; and Mallowan 14. Other versions of Cyrus's death are found at Ctesias, *Persica*, book 7 (died fighting the Derbices), and Xenophon, *Cyropaedia,* 8.7.25 (died peacefully at Pasargadae).

Chapter Two: Artemisia

The setting for the Greco-Persian Wars, and Caria's kingdom, is found in Herodotus 7:65, 87, 99 ("There is no reason"), 184; Polyaenus, *Strategems*, 8:53.2; Muller 2:460; Wallinga 45; and Gera 205. The Battle of Salamis, and Artemisia's actions preceding and during the battle, are described in Green 174–76, 180–82, 189–90, 196; Aeschylus, *The Persae* (331 triremes), 338–401 ("An echoing"), 418–21 ("Crushed hulls"); Warry 28; Fraser 33; and Herodotus 8:44–48 (371 triremes), 67–69 ("Tell the king"), 87–88 ("My men"). *But see, e.g,* Wallinga 69, 147, n.38, who views Herodotus's version as improbable. The aftermath of the battle, and Artemisia's advice to King Xerxes, are at Herodotus 8:100 ("It is not"), 101–02 ("Under the present"), 103, and Polyaenus, *Strategem*s, 53.2, 53.3–.5.

Chapter Three: Cleopatra

The backstory of the Ptolemies, Rome's involvement in Alexandrian politics, Cleopatra's rift with Ptolemy XIII, Pompey's death, and Cleopatra's flight from Alexandria are documented at Plutarch, *Antony*, 25:3, 27:2 ("not so"), 27:3–4 ("Her tongue"); Schiff 11–12, 19–26, 28, 58–59, 248; *The Godfather* ("Blood is a big expense," Virgil Sollozzo); Lucan, *Pharsalia*, book VIII; Plutarch,

Pompey, 79; Cassius Dio, *Roman History*, xlii, 4; Livy, *History of Rome*, cxii, 2; Tyldesley 48; and Dando-Collins 6, 41–45, 50. Cleopatra's liaison with Caesar, the palace siege, and the end of the Alexandrian War, are described in Caesar, *De Bello Civili*, 3:112; Plutarch, *Antony*, 25:3 ("This little"); Dando-Collins 4–5, 42, 53, 55–56, 61–67, 69–71, 73, 95, 108–10, 125–28, 136–44; Schiff 14, 42–45, 64–65; Dodge 598-603, and Fraser 36. Cleopatra's rule in Egypt, Caesar's return to Rome, Caesar's assassination, and the opening of the Republican War are found in Suetonius, *Caesar*, 76.3; Schiff 70–71, 94–97, 102–05, 108–09, 115, 123, 138–40, 144; Kleiner 84; Fuller 257; Beard, *SPQR* 346-47; and Fraser 37. The end of the Republican War and the description of Antony come from Philostratus, *Life of Apollonius*, 1.7 (trans. Conybeare); Dando-Collins 41, 233–34; Schiff 144, 147, 150–52, 167–69, and Plutarch, *Antony*, 25:4–26:1, 36:4 ("did not confine"). Cleoptra's meeting with Antony in Tarsus, their joint rule, the Parthian campaign, and Antony's relationship with Octavian are found in Plutarch, *Antony*, 26:1–3 ("gilded," "revel"), 29:1, 36:3, 37:3, 38:1–3, 51:1; Dando-Collins 65, 236–37 ("There are two"); and Schiff 170–80, 187–90, 208–21, 224. The Donations and Antony's break with Octavian come from Plutarch, *Antony*, 53:3–5, 54:3–9, 60:1; Holbl 245; Jones, *Cleopatra: A Sourcebook*, 99 ("Because Antony"), and Schiff 226, 231–32, 241–46, 258. The campaign in Greece and the Battle of Actium are described in Dio 50:17:3 ("You yourselves"), 19:5; Plutarch, *Antony*, 56:1–2, 60:3, 61:1, 64:1, 65:1; Rodgers, 521, 523–25, 527–30, 532–35; Schiff 246, 260–61, 268–70, 272, and Warry 185. Octavian's pursuit, and the deaths of Antony and Cleopatra, come from Rodgers 536; Schiff 279–80, 284–88, 290, 293–97, 300–01; Plutarch, *Antony*, 71:4–5,73:1, 74:1, 76:4–5 ("Never was"), 77:3, 78:3, 79:2–3, 81:1–2, 84:2, 85:4 ("A fine"); Dando-Collins 238–39.

Chapter Four: Boudica

Boudica's lashing is described at Tacitus, *Annals of Imperial Rome*, trans. Michael Grant (Penguin Books, 1992.), 14.30; Aldhouse-Green 177–79, and Fraser 61-62. The Celts, Iceni, and their customs are documented in Strabo, *Geographica*, 246–47, 257; Caesar, *De Bello Gallico*, 4:33, 5:21 ("great Iceni"), 6:16; Aldhouse-Green 22–28, 71, 87, 173–77; Fraser 43, 45–49, 52–53, 64–66; Tacitus, *Agricola*, 15 ("We gain nothing," "Nothing is"); Tacitus, *Annals*, 328, and Wester 61. Roman depredations and the commencement of the revolt are discussed at Tacitus, *Annals*, 328; Tacitus, *Agricola*, 16 ("admit no" "kingdom"); Aldhouse-Green 67–73; Schiff 119–20, 125 ("The greatest"); Fraser 5, quoting Petruccio Ubaldini, *Le vite delle Donne illustri del regno d'Inghilterra, e del regno di Scotia . . .* (1591) ("Tyranny"), 55–57, 59, 61 ("kingdom"). The destruction of Camulodunum is found at Tacitus, *Annals*, 14.32–14.33; Aldhouse-Green 180–85; Fraser 67, Fraser 70–71, quoting John C. Overbeck, "Tacitus and Dio on Boudica's Rebellion," *American Journal of Philology*, vol. 40 (1969) 136 n. 27, 74–76, and "Dig Uncovers Boudicca's Brutal Streak," *The Guardian*, 12/3/00. The destruction of Londinium and Verulamium is found at Tacitus, *Annals*, 14.32–33, in Grant 328–29; Aldhouse-Green 187–91; Peddie 35, and Fraser 78–87, quoting Dio, LXII, 7.2 ("Those who were taken"), 90–93. Boudica's clash with Suetonius and her death are described at Tacitus, *Annals*, 14.35–37, in Grant 329, 330 ("Just keep," "We British"), 331; Cassius Dio, *Roman Histories*, 62:12; Aldhouse-Green 138–39; Delbruck 412–28; Webster 229, citing Dio, 62:12; Goldsworthy 52–53; Webster 112 n. 6, 229; Beard, *SPQR*, 513-17; Fraser 93–100; Kaye, "Finding Boudica." The aftermath of the rebellion comes from Tacitus, *Annals*, 331; Aldhouse-Green, 210–14, and Fraser 102–03.

Chapter Five: Tamar

Chapter quote is from Eastmond 93 ("Though she"). The opening scene comes from Zakaria Machitadze, *Lives of the Georgian Saints*, trans. David and Lauren Ninoshvili (St. Herman Press, 2006); Mariam Lordkiphanidze – "Georgia in the XI–XII Centuries," (Tblisi: Ganatleba 1967), reprinted in English at georgianweb.com/history/mariam/index.html. Tamar's ancestry, Georgi's wars, her accession to the throne and battles with Church and nobility comes from "History and Eulogy of the Kings," in Met'reveli 236, 239, 241–43; Basili Ezosmodzghvari, "The Life of Tamar, the Great Queen of Queens," in Met'reveli 287–91 ("She began to sharpen," "Nobody was sorry"); "The Chronicle of Giorgi Lasha and His Time," in Met'reveli 202–03 ("fortunate and God-fearing," "she was fond"); *Psalms* 124:6 ("Blessed be the Lord"), *Psalms* 124:7 ("the snare"); Suny 37–39; Eastmond 94, 101–02, 106–08, 111; Rayfield 107–09. Tamar's marital difficulties are in "History and Eulogy of the Kings," in Met'reveli 243, 245; "History and Eulogy of the Kings," in Met'reveli 244; Basili Ezosmodzghvari, "The Life of Tamar, the Great Queen of Queens," in Met'reveli 290 ("He subjected"); Rayfield 109–10 ("God save," "the Russian"); Fraser 174. Her divorce from King Yuri and marriage to Davit Soslan are detailed in "History and Eulogy of the Kings," in Met'reveli 247 ("of medium build"), 248 ("God is my witness"); Basili Ezosmodzghvari, "The Life of Tamar, the Great Queen of Queens," in Met'reveli 290; "The Chronicle of Giorgi Lasha and His Time," in Metrreveli 203; Rayfield 110. Her wars with Yuri are found in Basili Ezosmodzghvari, "The Life of Tamar, the Great Queen of Queens," in Met'reveli 300; "History and Eulogy of the Kings," in Met'reveli 241, 249–50, 254; Eastmond 112 ; Rayfield 111. Tamar's war and the Battle of Shamkor are detailed at Rayfield 111–13 ("in the name"); "The Chronicle of Giorgi Lasha and His Time," in Met'reveli 204; "History and Eulogy of the Kings," in Met'reveli 252–53, 255–57 ("Their arrows"), 259 ("In the places"); Basili Ezosmodzghvari, "The Life of Tamar, the Great Queen of Queens," in Met'reveli 292–95 ("Let not your hearts"), 296 ("She did not allow"), 308 n. 38; Rayfield, *Literature of Georgia*, 89. The Battle of Basiani and her capture of Trebizond are at "History and Eulogy of the Kings," in Met'reveli 268–69 ("The battle began"), 271–72; Basili Ezosmodzghvari, "The Life of Tamar, the Great Queen of Queens," in Met'reveli 297 ("took counsel with them"), 298; "The Chronicle of Giorgi Lasha and His Time," in Met'reveli 203; Mikaberidze 655–56; Eastmond 153; Fraser 178. The end of Tamar's reign and her legacy are detailed at Eastmond 96, 101; Suny 40 ("peasants were like"); Basili Ezosmodzghvari, "The Life of Tamar, the Great Queen of Queens," in Met'reveli 291 ("We know"); Fraser 178.

Chapter Six: Manduhai

The opening scene and description of Manduhai's options when she spoke to the shrine are documented in Weatherford 157, 159–60, 186–88, quoting *The Mongol Chronicle Altan Tobci*, Charles Bawden, trans. (Otto Harrassowitz 1955), § 102 ("You will"), 197–99, 202. The background of the Mongol empire, the decline of Mongol unity, and the nadir of Borijin fortunes comes from Weatherford 82–83, 129, 148 ("If it is a girl"), 155–56, 219. The short life and death of Bayan Khan and the marriage of Manduhai is found at Hidehiro Okada, "The Khan as the Sun, The Jinong as the Moon," in Kellner-Heinkele 186; Weatherford 77–79, 157, 156, 159–65, 177–85, 216. Manduhai's campaign in Zavkhan is found in Weatherford 212–13, 214–15 (quoting *Altan Tobci*, verse 101) ("Queen Manduhai"), 218, 219–20, citing *Altan Tobci*, verse 102, 220–21 (citing *Yellow Chronicle of the Oirat*), 226–272, and Adams 27–41. China's trade war with Mongolia, its war with Beg-Arslan, and Manduhai's vengeance on Beg-Arslan and Ismayil are described at Lungfei Feng, "Tumu Crisis and the Weaknesses of the Military System of the Ming

Dynasty," *Asia Social Science* (June 2009); Wang, Yuan-Kang, *Harmony and War* (Columbia University Press 2013); Arthur Waldron, "Chinese Strategy From the Fourteenth to the Seventeenth Centuries," in Murray 107; and Weatherford 223–28, 236, 241, 243–44 ("They caught up"), 248–49. The joint reign of Manduhai and Dayan Khan, and the succession of their dynasty, is recounted at Weatherford 256, 253–54, 258–61, 269.

Chapter Seven: Caterina

Chapter quote is taken from Jansen 40. The opening scene was described in Niccolò Machiavelli, *Discourses*, 3:6; Lev 139–40. The Sforza family background and Caterina's early life are documented in Hairston 687; Lev 2–6, 14–18, 19, 21–23, 26–28; Benner 97–99; Fraser 197. Her marriage to Girolamo during the reign of Pope Sixtus is described in Lev 37–38, 47–49, 53, 59, 62–64, 221; Jansen 40–41; and Hairston 688. Caterina's capture of Castel Sant'Angelo and showdown with the cardinals comes from Lev 91–92 ("So he wants"), 93–94; and Jansen 40–41. The joint rule of Forlì by Girolamo and Caterina are described at Maike Vogt-Lüerrsen, "The Identification of Caterina Sforza in Renaissance Paintings through Symbolism," at www.kleio.org /en/books/caterina_symbols/cs_en/; Lev 107–08; "Mona Lisa Revealed as an Adventurous Beauty," *The Guardian*, 3/14/02; "Lorenzo di Credi," in Virtual Uffizi Gallery, at www.virtualuffizi . com/lorenzo-di-credi.html; Lev 102–04, 105 ("You don't know"), 110, 112–14, 116–18; Jansen 41. Girolamo's assassination and Caterina's revenge are described at De Vries, quoting Machiavelli, *The Prince*, ch. 20:6 ("In our days"); Machiavelli, *Florentine Histories*, 8:7 ("As soon as she was"); Hairston 688–89, 695, 699–709 (quoting Machiavelli, *Florentine Histories*); Lev 120–24, 128–29 ("don't you," "Give the fortress"), 132–33 ("Do it then"), 134 ("She will fight"), 135–40, 142–43 ("My people"), 145–47; Benner 99; Jansen 43; Fraser 199. Caterina's love of Giacomo is described at Breisach 131–32, 136–39; De Vries, "Shifting Representation of a Woman Ruler," 176; Lev 164, 166, 175. The shifting geopolitical picture of the late 15th century is found at Jansen 47; Lev 170–78. Caterina's relationship with Giovanni de Medici is found at Jansen 45–47; Lev 178–80 ("The countess"), 182–85, 186 ("unheard-of "), 188–89. The siege of Ravaldino and Caterina's capture are detailed at Breisach 218–29, 250–51, 335, n. 78; Lev 198, 200–01, 204–05 ("daughter"), 213–15, 217–19 ("All of Italy"), 221–22, 225 ("This is Sunday"), 226 ("wounded many men"), 227 ("Madame"); Jansen 47–48, quoting Caterina to Ludovico, 1498 ("If I have to lose"), 49 ("Signor duke"); and Fraser 200. Caterina's imprisonment, her abortive trial, and her release are found at Lev 228, citing Machiavelli, *On the Art of War*, Book VII ("The poor defenses"), 230 ("She defended"), 231 ("Although this woman," "Under her feminine body"), 238, 240, 242, 247 ("If I could"), 326; Benner 109; Machiavelli, *The Prince*, 20:6 ("The best possible"); Breisach 238, 243–44. Her later years are outlined in Lev 252–56, and her death and legacy are described at Breisach 251–53, 255–56; Jansen 50; Ray 14–15; Frazer 200; Lev 246–50, 252–56, 266–69.

Chapter Eight: Elizabeth

Elizabeth's background, childhood, and life under Queen Mary are documented in Doran, *Circle*, 14–42, Weir 1, 3, 16, 41, and 59. The early years of her reign and life at court come from Weir 14–18, 35, 43–53, 56, 59, 222 ("It is," "Although"), 224, 234, 431. The economics of war and Elizabeth's early attitude toward war come from Doran, *Foreign Policy*, 6; Weir 62; Hammer 28–29, 31–34, 44–53. Geopolitics of Spain, France, and the Catholic-Protestant nations are described in Hammer 54, quoting Calendar of State Papers 2:3 ("a bone"), 55–56; Weir 62. Elizabeth's military engagements in Scotland are chronicled in Doran, *Foreign Policy*, 17–19; Doran, *Circle*, 66, Weir 89, 91, 269; Hammer 55–59 (quoting A. Clifford, ed., *The State Papers and Letters of Sir*

Ralph Sadler (2 vols., London: 1809) 1:438-39), 60–62. Her support of Huguenots, repulse from the Continent, and budget cuts are found in Doran, *Foreign Policy,* 11; Weir 20, 57–59, 91, 116, 131–33, 141, 144 ("God help"), 167–68; Hammer 62–67, 78. Her rivalry with Spain, privateer war, naval increases, assassination plots and problems with Mary, Queen of Scots are detailed at Doran, *Foreign Policy,* 13–16; Hammer 69, 78–79, 80–86, 89–91, 93–94, 96–97, 105–06, 107, quoting Parker, *Grand Strategy,* 4–5, 164–67 ("Even Christ"), 111; Doran 65–89; and Weir 193, 202, 210–11, 213, 282–84, 278–88, 309, 334. The introduction of a national lottery comes from the British Library, "The Great Lottery," bl.uk/learning/timeline/item102765.html. Elizabeth's intervention in the Dutch revolt and Philip's decision to proceed with the Enterprise of England are described at Hammer 116–17, 120–27, 132, 135 ("rather to make"); Weir 345–46, 349–50, 357–59 ("hazard a battle"), 370–71. The description of Elizabeth at midlife comes from the Hillard miniature (1572), the "Phoenix" portrait (1575), the Darnley portrait (1575), the Ermine Portrait (1585), and the Plimpton "Sieve" portrait (1579). The Babington Plot, execution of Mary, and Spanish plans are found in Hammer 137, quoting Parker, *Grand Strategy,* 157, 181 ("to fight"), 138; Weir 224, 276, 367–68, 377–78. The Armada Campaign is recounted at Burghley to Andreas de Loo, 7/18/1857, in Robert Leng, *Sir Francis Drake's Memorable Service Done Against the Spaniards in 1587* (1963 reprint), 43; Philip II to Medina Sidonia, 5/4/1587, Library of Congress; Drake to Privy Council, 3/30/1588, in Laughton 1:123 ("With fifty"); Dr. John Rogers to Elizabeth, 4/1/1588, *Calendar of State Papers: Elizabeth 21, part 4*; Weir 388–89 ("For the love"); Drake to Elizabeth, 4/13/1588, in Laughton 1:148 ("The advantage"); Medina Sidonia, fleet instructions, 1588, Library of Congress; Adams, Robert, *Expeditionis Hispanorum in Angliam* vera description (1588), Library of Congress; Laughton 1:liii; Valentin Dale to Walsingham, 7/25/1588, Library of Congress; Nelson 124–25, 128; Hammer 138–40, 145, 146–48, 152, citing Martin and Parker 179 ("riddled"); Mattingly 347 ("It is a comfort"); Doran, *Circle,* 141; Hutchinson 111–12 ("so great a danger," "For the love of God"), 121 ("time to finish the game"), 122–25, 127–28, 137–60, 164–70, 212; Weir 382, 384, 388–90; McDermott 262-64, 268-72. The aftermath of the Armada battle and the Tilbury speech are recounted at McDermott 280; Weir 392–394 ("had so inflamed," "lost her presence"), 399 ("She is only," "would compare"); Doran, *Circle,* 141; Hammer 152; Hutchinson 136 ("subdue, slay or kill"), 174–80, 215; Frye, 95-114; and Marcus xvii, 325. Elizabeth's intervention at Rouen, naval wars with Spain, and troubles with Essex are described at Weir 394, 403–04, 410, 415, 420–21, 423 ("If any man"), 426–27, 428 ("You vex"), 429 ("I will never"); Hammer 156–61, 164–65, 172–81, 193, 194 ("I know"), 195–204; Hutchinson 229–41, 246–48. Elizabeth's war in Ireland, the death of Essex, and the death of Elizabeth come from Weir 434 ("the Antichrist"), 435–39, 442 ("If you compare"), 443–47 ("We absolutely"), 449–66; Doran, *Circle,* 185–89, 289; Levin 153–54; Hammer 204–05, 207–08, 211–15, 217–19, 230–31.

Chapter Nine: Njinga

Chapter quote comes from Heywood 140, quoting Cavazzi, *Istorica Descrizione,* book 6 para. 32 ("When I was young"). Background on Ndongo is documented at Thornton, *Warfare*, 115; Thomas 128–31; Heywood 4–5 (map), 9–14, 18, 25–32; Thornton, "Legitimacy," 29–30; Cadornega, *Historia Geral*, in Newitt 143 ("not only useful for commerce"). Njinga's youth is recounted at Heywood 35–44, 45, quoting Cavazzi, MSS Araldi, 2:23 ("while boiling"), 50, 55–60. Njinga's mission to Luanda is described at Cadornega, *Historia Geral*, in Newitt 143; Thornton, "Legitimacy," 31–32; Thornton, *Warfare*, 100–02; Heywood 37–40, 49–50, 51–64, quoting Cavazzi, MSS Araldi, 2:24 ("He who is born free"); Heywood and Thornton 124–25. Njinga's rise to power is at Thornton, "Legitimacy," 38; Heywood 22, 54–55, quoting Cadornega,

Historia Gerao, 1:161 ("helped him to die"), 61, 64–65, 76; Heywood and Thornton 127. Njinga's wars with Hari and the Portuguese are found in Njinga to Cardoso, 3/3/1626, in McKnight 43 ("Nothing is accomplished"); Heywood 67, quoting De Souza to government, 8/22/1625, in Antonio Brasio, ed., *Monumenta Missionaria Africana: Africa Ocidental* (15 vols., Lisbon: Agencia Geral do Ultramar, Divisão de Publicoes e Biblioteca, 1952–1988) 7:365–68, 68–69, quoting De Souza to government, 3/19/1625 and 7/8/1626, in Beatrix Heintze, ed., *Fontes para a Historia de Angola do Secula XVII*, (2 vols.; Weisbaden: Franz Steiner 1985–1988), 1:364 ("the war and the uprising"), 2:129 ("she would give them," "better off"), 69–71, quoting de Sousa to king, 2/21/1626, in Antonio Brasio, ed., *Monumenta Missionaria Africana: Africa Ocidental* (15 vols., Lisbon: Agencia Geral do Ultramar, Divisão de Publicoes e Biblioteca, 1952–1988), 7:417 ("a woman"), 72, 79, quoting "Governador a Seus Filhos," in Beatrix Heintze, ed., *Fontes para a Historia de Angola do Secula XVII* (2 vols.; Weisbaden: Franz Steiner 1985–1988), 1:245 ("necessary and just"); and "Carta de Fernao de Sousa a El Rei," 2/21/1626, in Antonio Brasio, ed., *Monumenta Missionaria Africana: Africa Ocidental* (15 vols., Lisbon: Agencia Geral do Ultramar, Divisão de Publicoes e Biblioteca, 1952–1988), 7:418–19 ("for God"), 79, 80–82, citing "Governador a Seus Filhos," in Beatrix Heintze, ed., *Fontes para a Historia de Angola do Secula XVII* (2 vols.; Weisbaden: Franz Steiner 1985–1988), 1:242–43; quoting Njinga to Cardoso, 3/3/1626, in ibid, 1:244–45; and quoting Bento Banha Cardoso to Njinga, 3/15/1626, in ibid 1:245 ("God protect"), 83–84; Thornton, "Legitimacy," 37–38; Thornton, *Warfare*, 105–07, 114–16, quoting Catornega, Istoria, 2:283 ("all their defense"), 115; Filippo Pigafetta, *Relatione del Reame di Congo et Delli Circonvicine contrade tratta dalli scritti and ragionamenti di Odoardo Lopez Portoghese (1591)*, in Newitt 140–41 ("These people go."); Heywood, in *Afro-Latino Voices*, 40–41; Lee 183. Her battles with Azevedo are found in E.G. Ravenstein, ed., *The Strange Adventures of Andrew Battel* (reproduced at gutenberg.org/files/41282/41282-h/41282-h.htm), 166; Heywood 83, quoting "Governador a Seus Filhos," in Beatrix Heintze, ed., *Fontes para a Historia de Angola do Secula XVII* (2 vols.; Weisbaden: Franz Steiner 1985–1988), 1:252 ("woman and queen"); Heywood 107, 166; Heywood 87–90, 101, 104–07, 110. Her immersion into Imbangala society comes from Thornton, *Warfare*, 110–12; Thornton, "Legitimacy," 32, 38, Heywood 75, 84, 119–25, 127, quoting Cavazzi, MSS Araldi 2:38, and Heintze, *Angola non Seculos XVI e XVII*, 344, 348 ("a vassal of the Portuguese"); Joseph Conrad, *Heart of Darkness* (nightmare of her choice). Her wars through 1640 are described at Heywood 121–30, quoting Antonio Franco, *Synops Annalium Societais Jesu in Lusitania* (Augsburg: Wieth 1726) doc. 1632 par. 7, p. 260 ("an unmarried life"); Heywood 129, quoting Carto de Padre Goncalo de Sousa en Nome da Camara de Luanda, 7/6/1633, MMA 8:242–43 ("The country does not produce much," "the armies that Njinga"); Heywood and Thornton 134. Her alliance with the Netherlands comes from E.G. Ravenstein, ed., *The Strange Adventures of Andrew Battel*, 171; Heywood 133–35–41, quoting Louis Jadin, *L'Ancien Congo et l'Angola, 1639–1655* (Brussels: Institut Historique Belge de Rome, 1975) 1:416–17 ("the persecutions"), and Cadornega, *Historia Geral*, 1:352, 404 ("these few whites"). The 1646 campaign and capture of Kambu are described at E.G. Ravenstein, ed., *The Strange Adventures of Andrew Battel* 173; Heywood 142–47, 152, 160, quoting "Avis du Conseile d'Outre-mer sur le Rapport au Roi d'Antonio de Abreu de Miranda," 7/23/1644, in Jadin, *Ancien Congo*, 1:556 ("infernal woman"), and citing "Carta de Francisco de Sotomaior a El-Rei D. Joao IV," 12/4/1645 and 12/18/1646, in Antonio Brasio, ed., *Monumenta Missionaria Africana: Africa Ocidental* (15 vols., Lisbon: Agencia Geral do Ultramar, Divisão de Publicoes e Biblioteca, 1952–1988), 9:402–06, 471, and Cadornega, *Historia Geral*, 1:393–432. The loss of her Dutch allies is described at Meuwese 218–24, and Heywood 151–56. Her battles through 1657 are found in Heywood 157–61, quoting Cavazzi, MSS Araldi, 2:76 ("cleverer with a distaff"), and *Informazione sopre la Regina Jinga*, Ambaca, 10/20/1650, Congo,

Angola Documenti, 1646–1653, 2:234 ("I have seen Njinga"). Her peace with Portugal is described at Njinga to Luis Mendes de Sousa Chicorro, 12/13/1655, in McKnight 45–51; Thornton, "Legitimacy," 32–33; Heywood 165–67, 171, 174–78, 181, 189–91, citing Cavazzi, MSS Araldi, 2:71–73, and Cavazzi, *Istorica Descrizione*, book 6, para. 2. Her old age and death are documented at Thornton, "Legitimacy," 32, and Heywood 192–93, 197–98, 200–01, 226–30, 235–44.

Chapter Ten: Catherine

The chapter quote, opening scene, and childhoods of Catherine and Peter are drawn from Montefiore 160 ("soul of Caesar"); Madariaga 9, 10 ("In spite of "), 11, 12 ("madcap childish"), 13–17; Massie 28, 52–57, 72–88, 95–118, 125–33, 151–65; Coughlan 172–74, 178, 265. Peter's short reign and Catherine's coup come from Madariaga 1, 23–24, 29–33; Montefiore 44–52, 60 ("Our philosophy"); Fraser 254 ("For a man's work"); Coughlan 177, 180–84, Coughlan 185 ("I have come") ("The soldiers rushed"), 186–87, 280; Massie 241–65; Massie 252, quoting Bain, *Peter III*, 130 ("She is"); Massie 254, quoting Bain 192 ("It was then"); Massie 261 ("join the nearest"); Massie 266 ("He allowed"); Massie 275, quoting Catherine to Poniatowski ("At last"). Her coronation is described in Madariaga 187, 287–88, quoting Scott Thompson, 85–86 ("a woman of "). Her early reign and foreign policy comes from Montefiore 60 ("I felt certain"), 61 ("Time belongs," "not as easy"); Madariaga 151–52, 153 ("The first"), 155–56 ("a civil society"), 157 ("liberté est"), 187, 327–29, 339 ("You work only on paper"); Davies, *Russo-Turkish War*, 92–94; Coughlan 207-08, 235 ("Lady Prayerful"); Massie 305, 322-37, 343-52, 355-61. Her Polish adventure is described at Madariaga 188–89, 201–04; Montefiore 77; Coughlan 228–31, 233; Davies, *Empire and Military Revolution*, 250–52; Massie 363–64, 370–73; Upham 2:272–73; Fuller, *Strategy and Power*, 146. The First Turkish War was described at Montefiore 77–83, 84 ("became a volcano"), 85–91, 217–18; Madariaga 205–36, 224, 228–29 ("On no account"); Fuller, *Strategy and Power*, 141–46, 156; Hartley 8; Coughlan 234–37; Davies, *Russo-Turkish War*, 105–08, 172–77; Davies, *Empire and Military Revolution*, 251–58, 266–77, 284; and Massie 374–75, quoting Catherine to Voltaire, in Haislip 182 ("At the risk"), 376–85. Her handling of the Pugachev Revolt comes from Montefiore 97–98, 100, 128–35; Massie 397–410, 403 ("If God"), 405–06, quoting Catherine, in *Alexander,* 174 ("Since you like"); Madariaga 239–68, 249 ("What need is there"), 267 ("As regards executions"); Coughlan 246–51. Potemkin's expansion into the Black Sea region comes from Davies 234–35 ("creates a breach"); O'Neill x ("You will achieve"), 38, 44–46; Montefiore 105 ("wittiest and most original"), 123–24, 138–39, 220–22, 232–34, 248, 249 ("We hereby declare"), 250, 252–56, 274–76, 278–80, 293, 345 ("Easily disgusted"), 354–56, 363–65, 370–71; Coughlan 289–311; Madariaga 262–63, 364–98; Massie 495–96 ("Cleopatra's Fleet"), 498–500 ("This is the way"), 508–09, quoting de Ligne to Ségur ("I behold"); Fuller, *Strategy and Power*, 142. The Second Turkish War was described in Montefiore 385–86, 387 ("Lady Matushka"), 388, 396–97, 404–11, 412 ("like a strong whirlwind"), 413–15, 411–43, 448–53, 472 ("If you want to take"); Sicker, *The Islamic World,* 78; Coughlan 315–18; Madariagra 395–98 ("You are impatient"); Massie 503–05. The Russo-Swedish War was recounted in Montefiore 402–03, 411–18, 425–29, 441, 442 ("We've pulled"), 463–65; Massie 507 ("this insane note"), 514–15; Duffy 189 ("I would be prepared"); Fuller, *Strategy and Power*, 145 ("extricated ourselves"); Coughlan 317 ("Amidst the roar"), 325; Madariaga 414 ("We have pulled"). Her repression of the Polish uprising is found at Montefiore 146–47, 440–41; Massie 336 ("Our Lady"), 484–85, 488–89, 537–49; Madariaga 421 ("It's a veritable"), and Gooch 100 ("set in motion"); Clarke 47. Her anti-democratic policies and the final Polish partition are found in Montefiore 438–39, 462–63, 472–73; Madariaga 428 ("I am breaking"), 430 ("half wills"), 446 ("the whole"), 447; Massie 555–58 ("to extinguish"), 560 ("now reunited");

Coughlan 328–29. Her invasion of Persia and death come from Montefiore 495–96; Coughlan 254, 319; Massie 560–62, quoting Cronin 289 ("Our sight"), 570–71.

Chapter Eleven: Indira

The chapter quote comes from Jayakar 185, quoting Indira Gandhi, interview, 3/72 ("In a war"). The opening scene is documented in Jacob 101; Frank 338 ("India stands"); Amir Hossain, "Crucial 3rd December 1971," Dakha, *Bangladesh Daily Sun*, 12/3/14, at www.daily-sun.com /print/editorial/2014/12/03/776; Jayakar 176. Indira's childhood and rise to power are found in Mansingh 19–21, 26; Steinberg 17–23, 48 citing Malhotra, *Indira Gandhi*, 37; Fallaci 173 ("If you"). Her rise to prime minister come from Frank 212, 281–82 ("We shall," "swerved"), 283–84, 290–91 ("It is a certainty"), 292–93, citing *Time*, 1/28/66; Steinberg 10, 51, quoting Malhotra, *Indira Gandhi*, 84 ("the only man"), 53; Fallaci 158 ("flowery small talk"); Mansingh 34, quoting Oriana Fallaci, "Indira's Opposition: Moraji Desai," *New Republic* (Aug. 1975) ("She would ally"). Her early years as prime minister are documented at Fallaci 164–65 ("don't go to temples"), 171– 72 ("I think it's good"); James Warner Bjorkman, "Public Law 480 and the Policies of Self-Help and Short Tether," in Rudolph 386 ("India is a good"); Mansingh 23, 34, quoting Gandhi, interview, *Sunday Times*, 3/7/71 ("I am less"); Steinberg 32–34; Frank 293 ("Probably no woman"), 294 ("A woman ruler"), 295–300, 301 ("I am very fit," "I have always felt"), 303, quoting *Times of India*, 1/20/67 ("My family"), 304, 318, 326–27; Sisson and Rose 137–41. Crisis in East Pakistan and preparation for war are documented in Salman Rushdie, *Shame* (Knopf Canada 2010 ed), 186 ("two Wings"); Sam Manekshaw, interview, *The Quarterdeck* (1996), in Jacob 181 ("Look at this!" "Have you read the Bible?"); "A Life Lived Such – Field Marshal Sam Menakshaw"; Isaacson, *Kissinger*, 372–73; Panthaki 32–33, 91–92, 107–17; Fallaci 158 ("If what seems right," "If I'm happy"); "India, Backing Bengalis, Wary of Meddling Charge," *New York Times*, 4/9/71; Handi ("read the Bible"); "Dacca, City of the Dead," *Time*, 5/3/71; "Pakistani Refugees' Competition Angers Indian Poor," *New York Times*, 5/17/71; "Toll in West Bengal Said to Reach 8,000," *New York Times*, 6/6/71; Sisson and Rose, 141–45, 206–08, 212–13, 295 n. 21; Frank 329–31, 332, quoting P.N. Dhar, *Indira Gandhi, the Emergency and Indian Democracy*, 156 ("In our offices"), 333–34; Jayakar 165, 167, quoting Sam Manekshaw, interview ("Do you know," "If food," "If the Chinese"), 168, quoting Indira, speech, 5/24/71, 166, 170, 184–85; Mansingh 51–52; Sisson and Rose 146–47, 157, 172, 181–86, 199, 207–08, 216–17; Steinberg 35. Indira's diplomatic efforts are documented in Rajindar Sachar, "Indo-Pak War of 1971 – Some Not-So-Public-Facts," *Mainstream Weekly*, 12/27/11, at mainstreamweekly.net/article3227.html; Jayakur 169 ("You know"), 171; Mansingh 218, 221–22; "Notes on People," *New York Times*, 7/7/71; Sisson and Rose 151–53, 193, 200, 211; Steinberg 35; "U.S.-India Relations: A New Low," *New York Times*, 7/27/71; "Soviet and India Reach an Accord," *New York Times*, 8/9/71; "Bengal: Breaking Point is Near," *New York Times*, 10/10/71; Gandhi, BBC interview, at www .youtube.com/watch?v=nRAfs_LPFI4; "Warning by Mrs. Gandhi," *New York Times*, 10/19/71; "A Harder Line for India," *New York Times*, 11/2/71; Frank 333–35, quoting Kissinger, *The White House Years*, 848 ("not intended"); Nichter and Moss; Nixon and Kissinger, meeting transcript, 11/5/71, *Department of State Foreign Relations, 1969–1976, Volume E-7, Documents on South Asia*, 1969–1972, at http://2001-2009.state.gov/r/pa/ho/frus/nixon/e7txt/48557.htm; "Israel Helped India in 1971 War, Book Reveals," *Hindustan Times*, 11/1/13. The outbreak of war is found at Memorandum, Washington Special Action Group, 12/3/71, in Jacob 231–33; Jacob 101; Dixit 203 ("Black Dog"), 204–17; Fallaci 160, 162; Sisson and Rose 199, 213–15 (December 6 date), 217–20, 231–32, 262–64, 306 n. 23, 307 n.1; Frank 338–39; Jayakar 179; Gandhi, radio address, 12/3/71, reproduced at www.bharat-rakshak.com/1971/Dec03/ ("I speak to you");

Mansingh 222; Nichter and Moss, quoting Nixon to Vladimir Matsekevich, 12/9/71, *FRUS, XIV*, 770 ("If the USSR"); Maj. Gen. P.K. Chakravorty, "The Indo-Pak Bangladesh Liberation War," *India Strategic* (Dec. 2011); Isaacson, *Kissinger,* 375 ("screwed"), 377. The cease-fire at Dacca and peace negotiations come from Jacob 104, 147–48, 184–88, 201; Mansingh 191, 225; Jayakar 172–73, quoting Indira, interview, *Washington Post*, 1/31/80 ("What is"), 177, quoting Sam Manekshaw, interview ("Sam, you can't win"), 180–81, 184 ("The color red"); Frank 341–42, quoting Inder Malhotra, *Indira Gandhi*, 140 ("the right thing"); Sisson and Rose 225, 233–34, 262–64; "Statement of the Prime Minister of India," High Commission on India, hcidhaka.gov. in ("I have an announcement"); "Karan Singh Recalls Indira Gandhi's First Reaction to Indo-Pak 1971 Victory," *DNA*, 4/6/2010, at www.dnaindia.com/india/report-karan-singh-recalls-indira -gandhis-first-reaction-to-indo-pak-1971-victory-1367966 ("I was standing"); Interview, Lt. Gen. Jagjit Singh Aurura, 1984, accessed on youtube.com. Negotiating strategy was documented at Sisson and Rose 300 n.1; Jayakar 187–88; Mansingh 213 (total 10 million); Frank 344–46; Fallaci 190, 199 ("unbalanced," "a mediocre woman"); "Pakistan Reaches Accord with India on Major Issues," *New York Times,* 7/3/72; "The Untold Story of India's Decision to Release 93,000 Pakistani POWs," *TheWire.com*, 3/26/17. The political ramifications of the Indo-Pakistani War are discussed in Richard Nixon, conversation with John Chancellor, 12/24/71, accessed at https://video.scroll.in/316/listen-to-us-president-nixon-call-indira-gandhi-tougher-than-men -in-secret-white-house-tapes ("she's tough"); Frank 342–43; Jayakar 191; Steinberg 41–42. Ongoing Kashmiri conflict was documented in Mansingh 35; "War at the Top of the World," *Time*, 7/4/05. Operation BLUE STAR was documented at Steinberg 43–44; Jayakar 355, 358; Frank 480, 483; "Indira Gandhi Assassinated by Gunmen," *New York Times*, 10/31/84 ("I am not afraid"); "India Releases Stinging Report on Gandhi's Death," *New York Times*, 3/28/89. Her assassination and cremation were recounted in "Questions Still Surround Gandhi Assassination," *New Delhi Times Daily*, 11/24/84; Jayakar 372; Frank 492–93 ("I have done"), 499–501; "Gandhi, Slain, is Succeeded by Son," *New York Times*, 11/1/84; "Armed Indian Escorts Are Ordered for Trains," *New York Times*, 11/5/84; Chennai, India The Hindu, 1/7/08; "Sikhs Sought in Slaying," *New York Times*, 6/6/86; Steinberg 44–45. Her childhood admiration of Joan of Arc and her last comments were drawn from Steinberg 49, quoting Fallaci, *Interview with History*, 172–73 ("I don't remember"), and Mohan, *Indira Gandhi*, 187; Frank 487, quoting *Indira Gandhi, Remembered Moments*, 79 ("If I die").

Chapter Twelve: Golda

Golda's recurring dream was recounted in Klagsburn 525 and in Burkett 257–58, citing Amnon Barlizai, "Golda Meir's Nightmare," *Ha'aretz* (10/3/03) ("Suddenly"). Her childhood, emigration, and rise Zionist politics are documented in Fallaci 109–15; Steinberg 115–22, quoting Meir, *My Life*, 102 ("In Jerusalem"); and "Golda Meir," *Time*, 11/18/10 ("There is a type of woman"). Golda's role in Israel's War for Independence is drawn from Klagsbrun 299–332; Burkett 109, quoting Mapai, minutes, 3/27/44 ("We have"), 115, 117, quoting *The Pioneer Woman* (3/47) ("Kudos"); Klagsbrun 305 ("The Yishuv"); Fallaci 112 ("I've always found"); Klagsbrun 308 ("When history"), 233 ("Does putting an end"); Burkett 133, 148, quoting Golda Meir, *My Life*, 235 ("Make up your minds"). Her role in Israel's early government, including the 1956 Suez Crisis, comes from Klagsbrun 375–420, 456 ("no point"); Steinberg 128–29, 143, quoting Eban, *Personal Witness*, 554 ("Golda Meir had"), 153, quoting interview, Simcha Dinitz, 2/11/03 ("Golda entertained"); Avner 201–02; Burkett 174–75, 197, quoting Ester Herlitz, interview, 12/16/04 ("Many people"), 217; Fallaci 87; "Golda Meir," *Israel & Judaism Studies*, at www.ijs .org.au/Golda-Meir/default.aspx. The Six-Day War and Golda's role come from Klagsbrun

492–93 ("We don't want wars"), 596 ("If we have to have a choice"); Steinberg 133; Burkett 219–23, quoting David Kimche and Dan Bawley, *Sandstorm* (Stein and Day 1968) ("I understand"); Israel Ministry of Foreign Affairs, "The Six-Day War," at www.mfa.gov.il/mfa /aboutisrael/history/pages/the%20six-day%20war%20-%20june%201967.aspx; Kissinger, *Years of Upheaval*, 197. Her early years as prime minister come from Klagsbrun 514–51; Burkett 225– 26, quoting Abraham Harmon, interview, 1981, Golda Meir Library-Archives, University of Wisconsin-Milwaukee ("Golda knew"), 225, quoting *Newsweek*, 3/17/69 ("She comes clumping"), 232–33, quoting Rinna Samuel, interview, 12/18/04, 233–35, quoting Golda Meir, *My Life,* 379 ("I became"), 240–41; "Levi Eshkol, Israel's Third Prime Minister, Dead at 73," *Jewish Telegraphic Agency,* 2/27/69; Fallaci 120–21. Her views on war were described at Kissinger, *Years of Upheaval*, 220 ("Golda Meir was"); *Life*, 10/3/69 ("We have always said"); Fallaci 94–95 ("I've so often"), 96 ("We don't like"), 101 ("Are we"), 122 ("There's no difference"); *Vogue* (July 1969) ("We don't thrive"). The shift in Egyptian thinking and Israeli myopia from The Concept are found at "Golda: My Heart Was Drawn to a Preemptive Strike," *Times of Israel*, 9/12/13; "Three Years Too Late, Golda Meir Understood How War Could Have Been Avoided," *Times of Israel*, 9/12/13; Kissinger, *Years of Upheaval*, 197, 220–24; Rabinovich 8 ("that derives"), 11–13, 21–24, 38, 40, 47–53, 55; Burkett 267–269, quoting Meir, interview, 9/22/69 ("If the Arabs"), 312–15 ("eyes and ears"); Avner 222–24. Her decisions as war approached were documented at Klagsbrun 610–23; Rabinovich 17–18, 48, 54, 66; Avner 225; Burkett 326 ("There's a contradiction"), 317–18. Her decisions not to strike and to mobilize are found in "Golda: My Heart Was Drawn to a Preemptive Strike," *Times of Israel*, 9/12/13; "Three Years Too Late, Golda Meir Understood How War Could Have Been Avoided," *Times of Israel*, 9/12/13; Rabinovich 18–19, 83–84, 89–90, 94; Keating to Kissinger, 10/6/73, NARA, accessed at http://nsarchive. gwu.edu/NSAEBB/NSAEBB98/octwar-09.pdf; Klagsbrun 620–22 ("Land of Israel"); Burkett 319, quoting Meir, My Life, 426, and Rabinovich, *The Yom Kippur War*, 89–90 ("None of us"); "Who Killed the 20th Century's Greatest Spy?" *The Guardian*, 9/15/15; Steinberg 141, quoting Golda Meir, interview, 12/26/78, quoted in Safran, *Israel: The Embattled Ally*, 285–86 ("Look, this war"), Burkett 270, quoting Robert Slater, Golda (Jonathan David 1981) ("Do you think"), 319; Brent Scowcroft to Henry Kissinger, 10/5/73, NARA (accessed at http://nsarchive.gwu. edu/NSAEBB/NSAEBB98/octwar-07.pdf); Memorandum of Conversation, Dinetz and Kissinger, 10/7/73, NARA (accessed at http://nsarchive.gwu.edu/NSAEBB/NSAEBB98 /octwar-18.pdf); Keating to Kissinger, 10/6/73, NARA (accessed at http://nsarchive.gwu.edu /NSAEBB/NSAEBB98/octwar-09.pdf) ("I believe"); Richard Nixon, conversation with John Chancellor, 12/24/71, accessed at https://video.scroll.in/316/listen-to-us-president-nixon-cal l-indira-gandhi-tougher-than-men-in-secret-white-house-tapes ("look around the world"); Kissinger to Nixon, 10/6/73, NARA (accessed at Keating to Kissinger, 10/6/73, NARA, accessed at http://nsarchive.gwu.edu/NSAEBB/NSAEBB98/octwar-10.pdf); Memorandum of Conversation, Dinetz and Kissinger, 10/7/73, NARA (accessed at http://nsarchive.gwu.edu /NSAEBB/NSAEBB98/octwar-18.pdf). War's outbreak and early reverses are from Rabinovich 114–16, 171 ("We know how"), 175, 177–79; Burkett 321–23; Klagsbrun 624–26; "In 1973, Dayan Suggested Israel Prepare Nukes for Action," *Ha'aretz*, 10/3/13; Top Secret Memorandum, White House Map Room, 10/9/73, NARA (400 tanks and 49 warplanes). The nuclear options and further reverses come from Avner Cohen, "How Nuclear Was It?" ("There is no reason"); Arnan Azanyahu, interview, January 2008, Woodrow Wilson Institute, www.wilsoncenter.org /publication/avner-cohen-collection?utm_source=social&utm_medium=general&utm_campaign =social_media; Adam Raz, "The Significance of the Reputed Kippur War Nuclear Affair," *Strategic Assessment* (January 2014); Rabinovich 220 ("Get Simcha"), 230–31. Front stabilization was described at Rabinovich 232–52, 259 ("Holocaust Basement"), 260–68, 270, 303–04; Avner

249; Burkett 325 ("Today we hit"), 326–29; Zeev Schiff, *October Earthquake* (Tel Aviv: University Pub. Projects 1974) 148 ("It was strange"). American material intervention was documented at Klagsbrun 629 ("bloodied in the process," "We can't allow"); Kissinger, *Years of Upheaval*, 203–04 ("When all was"); Memorandum of Conversation, Dinetz and Kissinger, 10/7/73, NARA (accessed at http://nsarchive.gwu.edu/NSAEBB/NSAEBB98/octwar-18.pdf; Rabinovich 323–24, 491; Avner 246–48; Burkett 332. The war's final phase was documented at Avner 235–36 ("The stench"), 239–41 ("My father"); Rabinovich 358; Burkett 332, quoting Donald Neff, *Warriors Against Israel* (Amana Books 1988) ("We are back"); Rabinovich 348–66, 393, 412 ("You were there?"). Negotiations over the cease-fire come from Rabinovich 436, 442, 454, 465 ("How can"), 466, 477, 487; Steinberg 183; Memorandum of Conversation, 10/22/73, 1:35 p.m., NARA, accessed at nsarchive.gwu.edu/NSAEBB/NSAEBB98/#doc54; Memorandum of Conversation, 10/22/73, 4:15 p.m., National Archives and Records Administration, accessed at nsarchive.gwu.edu/NSAEBB/NSAEBB98/#doc54; UN Security Council Resolution 338, 10/22/73; Burkett 332, quoting Golda, interview, *CBS Face The Nation*, 10/28/73 ("For God's sake"); 334–35, quoting Isaacson, *Kissinger*, 528 ("In Vietnam"), 336, quoting Meir, *My Life*, 371–72 ("There is only one"), 343–44, quoting White House, memorandum of conversation, 11/1/73, NARA ("Madam Prime Minister"); Kissinger ("She felt herself"); Avner 249. Peace negotiations, the Camp David Accords, and Golda's death come from "Golda Meir: 'My Heart Was Drawn to a Pre-Emptive Strike,'" *Times of Israel*, 9/12/13; Burkett 346, quoting Meir, *My Life*, 448 ("For the first time"); Avner 250; Steinberg 143; *Hamilton* ("legacy").

Chapter Thirteen: Thatcher

The opening scene is documented by Thornton xviii; Thatcher, *Autobiography,* 343–44; Moore 665–66; and Campbell 180–82. Her youth, education, and climb to Conservative Party leader come from Thatcher, *Autobiography,* 1–25, 32–68; Berlinski 16–19, 21–45, 71–103; Aitken 27–28, 131–32; Charles C. Johnston, "Thatcher and the Jews," *Tablet*, 12/28/11; Campbell 29–31, 66, 191; Moore 101–02; Steinberg 213, 216, 243–44; "Why the Iron Lady Was the Ultimate Women's Libber," *The Daily Mail*, 2/3/12 ("Some of us"); "How Margaret Thatcher Built the Myth of the Iron Lady," *The Independent*, 4/9/13 ("Ditch the Bitch"); Shepherd 34, 160 ("Stalin's eyes"); "Sir Mick Jagger: 'Margaret Thatcher Didn't Change for Anyone,'" *The Telegraph*, 6/12/13; Ogden, *Maggie*, 112 ("I'll see them in hell"). Thatcher's image remake and 1979 campaign come from Steinberg 213; Campbell 66–68, 74, quoting *Daily Mirror*, 2/3/75 ("What people"); "How Maggie Thatcher Was Remade," *The Telegraph*, 1/8/12 ("Every politician"); Thatcher, *Autobiography*, 182-83; "The Margaret Thatcher Look," *The Guardian*, 4/8/13; Shepherd 22, 25, 226–28 ("ultimate power dresser"); "Margaret Thatcher," *Bio.com*, 4/19/13; Brian Monteith, in Dale 513 ("ideological steel"). Her early economic policies are from Steinberg 219, 221; Moore 660; Thornton 32–33 ("no alternative," "The lady's not"), 39–41; Berlinski 159; Campbell 185–86; Hastings 11. Her battle with the IRA is documented in Moore 608–09; Campbell 340–41, quoting MT, speech, 11/20/80 ("There can be"); Campbell 341, quoting MT, speech, 5/28/81 ("It would seem"); Campbell 190; Campbell 337–39, quoting MT, Airey Neave Memorial Lecture, 3/2/80 ("No democratic country"); Campbell 340–42. Her relationship with Reagan comes from Thornton 38–39; Campbell 217–19, quoting Thatcher, speech, 6/5/80 and 11/25/82 ("We should"); Campbell 260, quoting Geoffrey Smith, *Reagan and Thatcher*, 26 ("Isn't she"); Thornton 239 ("In a dangerous world"). Background for the Falklands War comes from Hastings 48–50; Moore 662–63; Thornton 94–95, 107. The initial invasion by Argentina is documented at Hastings 45–48, 50, 60–63, 66; Thornton 7, 43, 84, 114–15 (arguing *HMS Superb* had been dispatched on March 25); UKE to FCO, 3/20/82, FCO to Port Stanley

3/20/82, CINCFLEET to *HMS Endurance*, 3/20/82, MODUKNAVY to CINCFLEET, 3/23/82, MODUKNAVY to RBDWCR and NP 8901, 3/23/82, all in Thatcher Archives; Campbell 205, quoting Carol Thatcher, *Below the Parapet* (HarperCollins 1996), 201 ("miles and miles"); Armstrong to Thatcher, 3/31/82, Thatcher Archives; Thatcher to Carrington, 3/25/82, Thatcher Archives; Thatcher 341; MOD to Thatcher, 3/26/42, Thatcher Archives; Nott to Thatcher, 3/29/82, Thatcher Archives; CIA Directorate, Situation Report #2, 4/3/82, Thatcher Archives; FCO to UKE Buenos Aires, 3/27/82, Thatcher Archives; UKE Buenos Aires to FCO, 3/27/82, Thatcher Archives; UKE Buenos Aires to MODUK Navy, 3/30/82, Thatcher Archives; Berlinski 158–61, 179, quoting Thatcher, *The Downing Street Years*, 184 ("The Prime Minister"); Moore 656–57, 663–64, 673; Campbell 185–86. Thatcher's determination to fight is documented at Thatcher, *Downing Street Years*, 179 and Moore 665–66 ("The worst moment," "We can't"), 682 ("She wouldn't have done it"); Berlinski 161 ("If they are"); Hastings 66–69; Thatcher 344; "Bitter Royal Navy Battle With Sir Henry Leach Before Falklands," *Huffington Post*, 12/30/11; Engagement Diary, 3/31/82, Thatcher Archives; "Admiral of the Fleet Henry Leach," *The Telegraph*, 4/26/11 ("If we"); Undated memorandum on the history of the Prime Minister's room, PREM 19/866, at www.margaretthatcher.org ("Fait Bien"); Moore 667; Hastings 66–68; Thatcher 344 ("Now my"); Thatcher, interview for ITN, 4/5/82, Thatcher Archives, in Berlinski 167 ("I am not talking"); Moore 677; Campbell 188. The Falklands surrender is from Carrington to Haig, 3/28/82, Thatcher Archives; Thatcher to Reagan, 3/31/82, Thatcher Archives; Jim Rentschler, diary, 4/1/82, Thatcher Archives ("The Argentines"); Moore 668; Hastings 73 ("It looks"); Campbell 188–89; *HMS Endurance* to CINCFLEET, 4/2/82, Thatcher Archives ("This has been"); Moore 656; Thornton 112, 125, 129. Rallying the public comes from Thatcher, speech to House of Commons, 4/2/82 (audio recording), Thatcher Archives; Thatcher, notes for speech, 4/3/82, Thatcher Archives; Moore 672–73; Campbell 188; Berlinski 165–66; Thornton, citing Haig, *Caveat*, 284 for public opinion polls. Armada's preparation is from Moore 677; Thatcher 350 ("It was not"). Early US diplomacy comes from Campbell 342, quoting Renwick, *Fighting With Allies*, 342 ("That woman"); Thornton 62. Thatcher's war management comes from Campbell 189, quoting Peter Hennessy, *The Prime Minister* (Allen Lane 2000) 104 ("First"); "Sir Frank Cooper," *The Guardian*, 1/31/02; Moore 679, 681; Thatcher 349–50; Hastings 82–83; Moore 680; Armstrong, briefing for Thatcher, 4/6/82, Thatcher Archives; Moore 681, citing interviews, Sir John Coles and Sir David Omand; Thatcher 346 ("All these"), 359 ("The rules"). US wavering and decision to side with Britain come from Jim Rentschler, diary, 4/1/82, Thatcher Archives; Thatcher, notes of meeting with Alexander Haig, 4/14/82, Thatcher Archives; Campbell 194–95, citing Caspar Weinberger, *Fighting for Peace*, 149; Armstrong to Thatcher, 4/6/82, Thatcher Archives ("we have only to ask"), and 196, quoting Thatcher, speech, 5/6/82 ("We now"); Thatcher 346, 349; Moore 679, 683–84, quoting David Gompert, interview ("How can we"), 685, quoting Reagan, press conference, 4/5/82 ("It's a very") and quoting Jim Rentschler, interview ("The main thing"), 686–87, quoting Edward Streator, interview ("If you think"), and citing interview, Jim Rentschler, 688, quoting David Gompert, interview ("The Good Lord"), 690–94, 701, 709, quoting Reagan, press conference, 4/30/82 ("ice-cold bunch"), 710, quoting interview, Cecil Parkinson ("If the Argentinians"); Haig to Reagan, 4/9/82, at www.documentcloud .org/documents/329522-19820409-memo-to-the-president-discussions-in.html ("The prime minister"); Edward Streator, "Memorandum of Conversation: Secretary's Meeting with Prime Minister Thatcher on 8 April 1982," 4/10/82, at www.documentcloud.org/documents/329527 -19820410-secretarys-meeting-with-prime-minister.html; Berlinski 170, quoting James Rentschler, diary, 4/8/82, Thatcher Archives ("I beg you"); Hastings 102, 105–06, 169–70; Thatcher, telephone conversation with Haig, 4/14/82, Thatcher Archives ("Please don't"); Henry Kissinger, in Dale 495; Thornton 156–57, 168 ("conditional surrender"), 170–71, 212–13. The capture of South Georgia comes from Hastings 130; Moore 704; Berlinski 171, 173–74 ("Pleased to inform"); Thatcher, press announcement, 4/25/82 ("Rejoice!"); Thornton 171. The *Belgrano* and *Sheffield* attacks are recounted at Thatcher 368–69; Campbell 197, quoting Thatcher, 5/4/82 ("posed a very obvious"); Moore 711–13, 716, quoting Barry Strevens, interview ("Don't let"); CIA Directorate, memorandum, 4/2/82, Thatcher Archives; Thatcher conversation with Nott, Pym, and Lewin, 4/10/82, Thatcher Archives; Campbell 196; Moore 713; Hastings 151–54, 168; Thornton 207–09. Her anguish over war's cost comes from Jeremy Moore and John Woodward, "The Falklands Experience," *Royal United Services Institute for Defence Studies* (March 1983) 28; Moore 716, 728–31, 736, quoting Henderson, *Mandarin*, 465-66 ("Mrs T"); Andrew Roberts, lecture, New York Historical Society, 4/30/15 ("preemptive cringe"); Campbell 198, quoting Geoffrey Smith, *Reagan and Thatcher*, 83 ("He couldn't"); Berlinski 175; Thatcher, "Notes on Falklands War," ("Many of the public"); Thatcher 369, 372; Campbell 197–98; Berlinski 175; Hastings 168–71, 173; Campbell 200, citing Andrew Thompson, *Margaret Thatcher: The Woman Within* (Allen Lane 1989), 174–78; Shephard 38 ("not had such"). The invasion was documented at Thatcher 360, 373–75 ("How long"); Campbell 191–93, citing Ronald Millar, *A View From the Wings*, 298; Roberts, lecture, 4/30/15; Thornton 84, quoting Woodward, *One Hundred Days* (Naval Institute Press 1991) at 92 ("The land battle"), 106; Moore 734 ("Can we"), 735, quoting interview, Denis Thatcher ("Another ship!"); Thatcher, speech to Conservative Women Conference, 5/26/82, Thatcher Archives ("We must expect"); Hastings 89, 193, 205–07, 229; Hine 66–74; Campbell 198; Moore 676, 732–33 ("You couldn't find"), 742, 747–48. Thatcher's hard-line negotiations after the San Carlos landings are at Thatcher 376 ("snatch"); Moore 715, 735, 743 n.; Campbell 201 ("magnanimity"); "UN Defers Vote On Cease-Fire Resolution," *New York Times*, 6/4/82; "U.S. and the British Veto Resolution on Falklands," *New York Times*, 6/5/82 ("I am told"); Berlinski 176, quoting *Sunday Times*, 3/8/92 ("Just supposing"); Moore 734, 737–38, 740–41, 745–46. The final surrender comes from Thatcher 378–79 ("How bitterly," "Like everyone"), 380 ("As I went"); "Margaret Thatcher and the Falklands War," *The Telegraph*, 4/8/13 ("A feeling"); Moore 749-50, quoting Antony Acland, interview ("I don't think . . . Have a drink."). Political aftermath comes from Moore 750–51, quoting *House of Commons Debates*, 6/17/82 ("Is the right"); Hastings 313; Campbell 204; John Nott, in Dale 524 ("Above all").

Epilogue

Sources for the epilogue are Jansen 9–11, 20–21; George S. Patton, Jr., diary, 6/22/44, Library of Congress, Patton Papers (box 3) ("No general officer"); Harry Butcher, *My Three Years With Eisenhower* (Simon & Schuster 1946), 8; Jonathan W. Jordan, *Brothers Rivals Victors* (NAL 2011), 83–84 ("brickbats"); Rev. Jody Ray, sermon, 10/22/17 ("Almost").

INDEX

Pages followed by *m* indicate maps; pages followed by *n* indicate footnotes.

Abdul Hamid I (Ottoman sultan), 210, 218
Abdullah, Farooq, 253
Abu Bakr, Nusrat al-Din, 77, 79
Achaemenids, 7
Achillas, 25, 27–30
Acland, Antony, 318
Actium, Battle of, 43–47, 44*m*
Aegean Sea, 15, 207–8
Aeschylus, 15, 19, 20
Africa, 167–91
Agha Mohammad Khan (shah of Persia), 225
Agnew, Spiro, 280
Agranat, Shimon, 289*n*
Agrippa, Marcus, 41–43, 45
Ahenobarbus, Gnaeus Domitius, 42
Alexander Helios, 38, 41
Alexander the Great (king of Macedon), 23
Alexander VI (pope), 113–20, 125–28
Alexander VII (pope), 187
Alexandria, Egypt, 26–32, 46
Alexandrian War, 25–33
Allegre, Yves d', 124, 126, 127
Allon, Yigal, 277
Altan Tobchi, 90, 91, 94
Ambracia, Gulf of, 42
Amritsar, Battle of, 252–53
Andraste, 58

Andrew (duke of York), 313*n*
Anglo-Scots Wars, 137–39
Angola, 167–91
Anne (queen of Great Britain), 131
Antioch, 39
Antony, Marc, 32, 34, 36–49
Apollodorus, 29
Arab–Israeli War (1948), 259–61
Araxes River, 5*n,* 6, 8–10, 79
Ardabil, Emir of, 81
Ares, 13
Argentine Air Force, 317
Arsinoe, 29, 31, 33–35, 38
Arslan, Qutlu, 73, 74
Artemisia of Caria, 12–22
Ascension Island, 308
Asia, 86*m*
Assad, Hafez al-, 270, 274–76
Athens, 14–19
Atlee, Clement, 232
Augustus III (king of Poland), 203
Aurora, Jagit Singh, 245, 246, 249
Austria, 195, 200, 209, 223, 224
Austro-Hungarian Empire, 203
Awami League, 237, 238
Azerbaijan, 77–79
Azevedo, Paio de Araújuo, 179, 180

Babington, Anthony, 147, 148
Babone, Matteo, 111–12

Bagration, House of, 71, 72

Bangladesh, 231, 234, 238–40, 245–50

Bar-Lev, Chaim, 278, 284

Bar-Lev Line, 273, 275, 276

Basiani, Battle of, 79–81

Batu Mongke, 88, 89

Bayan Khan, 85–86

Bayan Mongke (Dayan Khan), 85–86

Bay of Bengal, 247, 249

Beg-Arslan (Turkic warlord), 85–87, 90, 92–94

Begin, Menachem, 258, 260–61, 289, 290

Bengalis, 237–39

Ben-Gurion, David, 258–60

Berenice IV (ruler of Egypt), 24

Bhindranwale, Jarnail Singh, 252

Bibikov, Alexander, 211, 212

Black September (Munich Olympics terror attack, 1972), 265, 269n

Blue Star, Operation, 252–53

Bogoliubski, Yuri Andreevich, 72–77

Boleyn, Anne, 135

Bolognesi, Bartolomeo, 121

Bona de Savoy (duchess of Milan), 98–99

Borges Madureira, Gaspar, 185–87

Borgia, Cesare, 117–27

Borgia, Lucrezia, 117

Borgia, Cardinal Roderigo, 100

Borijin, 86, 95

Botticelli, Sandro, 97, 100, 127

Boudica (Celtic queen), 50–63

Boudican revolt (62 A.D.), 54m, 54–60

Brezhnev, Leonid, 247, 255, 285–87

Burghley, Lord, 146, 148, 161, 162

Cadiz, 149, 150, 159, 162

Caesar, Julius, 25–34, 51

Caesarion, 34–35, 38, 41

Calabria, Duke of, 113

Camp David Accords, 290

Camulodunum, 52, 54–57

Capuchin missionaries, 189, 190

Cardoso, Bento Banha, 176–79, 181

Caria, 12–22

Cartagena, 146

Carter, Jimmy, 290, 309

Cassius, 35, 36

Castel Sant'Angelo, 101–4, 125–27

Caterina Sforza (countess of Forlì), ix, 96–128
    birth and childhood, 97
    death of, 128
    as prisoner of the Borgias, 124–27
    Battle of Ravaldino, 119–24
    in Rome, 99–100
    seizure of Castel Sant'Angelo, 101–4

Catherine of Aragon (queen consort of England), 135, 138n

Catherine the Great (empress of Russia), 119, 192–226
    coronation, 200
    Poland invasion, 223–24
    and Grigory Potemkin, 214–18
    and Pugachev's revolt, 210–14
    Russo–Swedish War, 219–21
    First Russo-Turkish War (1768-1774), 204–10
    Second Russo-Turkish War (1787-1792), 218–22
    war with Sweden, 219–21

Catholics and Catholicism
    in England, 143, 146, 148
    and Franco-Spanish détente, 161
    and Huguenots, 139–41
    Queen Mary and, 135
    and mixed-faith kingdoms, 136–37
    Queen Njinga and, 167, 173, 188–91

Cecil, Robert, 152

Celts, 51–52, 55–63

Cerialis, Petilius, 57

Cernunnos, 63

Cerretani, Bartolomeo, 96

Chamberlain, Neville, 309

Chancellor, John, 251

Charles (king of France), 114–15

Charles-Joseph Lamoral (7th prince de Ligne), 217

Charles XI (king of France), 140

Charmion, 49

Chenghua (Ming emperor), 87

Chengtian (Liao empress), 67

Chesme, Battle of, 208

China, 234, 240, 242, 250

Chinook helicopters, 315

Christianity, 169, 292

Churchill, Winston, 292, 294, 304, 305, 310n, 315

Cicero, 34

Claudius (Roman Emperor), 51, 52, 55, 56, 58

Cleopatra (queen of Egypt), 23–49
  Battle of Actium, 43–47
  Alexandrian War, 25–33
  Antony and, 36–40
  childhood, 23–25
  Republican War, 34–36

Cleopatra Selene, 38, 41

Cold War, 234, 247, 250, 281, 308

Congress (US), 236

Congress Party (India), 232, 235, 237, 251

Conservative Party (Tories), 293

Constantinople, 75, 77

Cooper, Sir Frank, 306

Corinth, Isthmus of, 15

Correia de Sousa, João, 171–76, 178–80

Coutinho, Manuel Pereira, 183

Cox, Archibald, 281

Crimea, 207–8, 215–18

Croesus (king of Lydia), 8–9

Cuba, 310

Cyrus the Great (king of Persia), 5–11

Dacca, Bangladesh, 245, 249

Damascus, Syria, 278–79

Damasithymos (king of Calynda), 20

Darius, 13

Dark Ages, 67

Davit Soslan (prince of Ossetia), 76, 78, 79, 81, 82

Davit V (king of Georgia), 71

Dayan, Moshe, 260–61
  at Golan Heights, 282
  offer of resignation, 276–77
  and prelude to Yom Kippur War, 268–70, 272
  and Six-Day War, 262
  and start of Yom Kippur War, 273, 276
  and Yom Kippur War, 278
  and Yom Kippur War Egyptian operations, 285, 287
  and Yom Kippur War strategy, 279

Dayan Khan, 89–91, 93–95

Decianus, Catus, 52, 53, 55–57

Denmark, 196

Denver, Colorado, 257

de Sousa, Ana, 173

de Sousa, Fernão, 174–76, 178, 179

Dhar, D. P., 246

Diderot, Denis, 192, 202

Dinitz, Simcha, 278, 280, 285

Dio, Cassius, 55–56, 58, 61

Dolabella, Publius Cornelius, 35

Donations of Alexandria, 41

Drake, Sir Francis, 141, 142, 145, 149–51, 153, 154, 157, 158

Dutch Republic, 183–88

Dutch West India Company, 184, 186, 187

East Anglia, 52

East Falkland Island, 302, 304, 312–15

East Pakistan. see Bangladesh

Egypt, 26m, 266–67
  Cleopatra, 23–49
  and prelude to Yom Kippur War, 268, 270
  Anwar Sadat's assumption of power, 266–67
  Six-Day War, 262, 263
  and start of Yom Kippur War, 275, 276
  Suez Crisis, 261–62
  Yom Kippur War, 270–72, 278, 279, 284–87
  Yom Kippur War cease-fire, 286, 289–90
  Yom Kippur War strategy, 279

Eisenhower, Dwight, 261

Elazar, David "Dado," 268, 270, 272–74, 276, 278, 279, 282, 283, 285, 287

Elizabeth (empress of Russia), 131, 193, 195

Elizabeth I (queen of England, Wales, and Ireland), ix, 133–66
  birth of, 135
  expulsion of French from Scotland, 137–39
  Huguenots, 139–41
  and Ireland, 162–66
  Pius V's heresy accusations, 143
  and privateering, 141–42
  and Royal Navy, 143–44
  speech to soldiers fighting the Spanish Armada, 155–56
  wars during time of, 134m

Elizabeth II (queen of the United Kingdom), 311

Erzurum, 76, 78

Erzurum, Sultan of, 76
Eshkol, Levi, 262, 264
Essex, Earl of (Robert Devereux), 158–65
Exocet missile, 311, 312, 317

Falklands War (1982), 291–92, 299*m*,
   300–318, 314*m*
Falmouth, England, 160
Feo, Giacomo, 113, 115
Ferdinand II (king of Aragon), 113
Finchley, England, 293
Flodden, Battle of, 138*n*
Florence, 99, 100, 105, 107, 114–18, 120,
   124–28
Foreign Office (Britain), 301, 312
Forli, 101–15
France, 114, 137–41, 158, 161, 223
Francis II (king of Austria), 223
Francis II (king of France), 137, 139, 140
Frederick II the Great (king of Prussia), 131,
   193, 195, 199, 203, 209
Frederick Wilhelm II (king of Prussia), 221–
   24
Freier, Shalhevet, 277
French Revolution, 222, 223
Freud, Clement, 294
Funji (sister of queen Njinga), 180, 186

Galeazzo Sforza (duke of Milan), 97–98
Galili, Israel, 269–70, 272, 277
Galtieri, Leopoldo, 300–302, 304, 306, 309,
   310, 313
Gandhi, Feroze, 232
Gandhi, Indira, ix, 231–55
   aftermath of Bangladesh war, 250–52
   assassination of, 254–55
   Operation Blue Star, 252–53
   childhood and education, 232
   election of 1980, 251
   Indo-Pakistani War of 1965, 234–35
   Operation Meghdoot, 252
   mindset during Bangladesh war, 248–49
   and outbreak of Bangladesh war, 246–48
   prelude to war in Bangladesh, 237–46
   rise to power, 235–36
   Margaret Thatcher and, 293
   victory speech after Bangladesh war, 249–50
Gandhi, Mahatma, 232, 238, 247
Gandhi, Rajiv, 232

Gandhi, Sanjay, 232
Genghis Khan, 84, 85, 87–89
George III (king of England), 222*n*
Georgia, Kingdom of, ix, 69–82, 70*m*, 225
Ghetti, Giovanni, 115–16
Giorgi III (king of Georgia), 71, 72
Giorgi IV (king of Georgia), 76, 78
Giorgi Lasha (king of Georgia), 82
Gnaeus, 26
Gobi Desert, 92
Golan Heights, 263, 267, 270, 272, 275, 276
Golitsyn, Alexander, 207
Goose Green, 316
Great Britain
   Falklands War (1982), 300–318
   and Indian independence, 232, 234
   and Israeli independence, 257–59
   Margaret Thatcher, 291–319
   US relations under Thatcher, 298, 300
Greece, Artemisia's invasion of, 14*m*, 14–22
Gregorian calendar, 152*n*
Gregory XIII (pope), 144, 145
Guise, House of, 137, 139, 140
Gustavus III (king of Sweden), 219–20, 222

Haig, Alexander, 304, 308–10, 312
Hari a Kiluanje (ngola of Ndongo), 175, 176,
   178, 183–85
Harrier fighter aircraft, 313, 316, 322
Harry VIII (king of England), 133
Hawkins, John, 141, 142
Hellespont, 13–14
Henri II (king of France), 137
Henri III (king of France), 157, 158
Henri IV (king of France), 158
Henry VII (king of England), 135, 137
Henry VIII (king of England), 133, 135, 138
Herod, 39
Herodotus, 6, 10, 13*n*, 14, 17*n*, 20
Hindus and Hinduism, 231, 234, 236, 248,
   254
Histadrut, 257
Hitler, Adolf, 257, 309
Hopkins, Harry, 298
House of Commons, 305, 310
Howard, Charles (duke of Effingham), 150–
   54, 157, 159, 160, 162
Huguenots, 139–41, 158
Hussein (king of Jordan), 262, 267, 269

Iceni uprising, 54*m*, 54–60
Imbangala, 171, 174, 179–84, 186–90
India, 231–55
Indian Air Force, 249, 252
Indo-Pakistani War (1971), 233*m*
Innocent VIII (pope), 104, 106, 109–10, 113
Invincible, HMS (carrier), 305–6, 310, 313, 313*n*, 315
Iras, 49
Ireland, 162–66
Irgun, 258
Irish Republican Army (IRA), 297–98
Isabella I (queen of Castile), 113, 131
Islam. *see* Muslims and Islam
Ismayil (*taishi* of the Oirats), 86, 87, 90, 94
Israel
    declaration of independence, 259–60
    elections of 1973, 268
    independence, 257–59
    Golda Meir and, 256–90
    Anwar Sadat and, 266–67
    Six-Day War, 262–63
    Suez Crisis, 261–62
    War of Independence, 259–61
    . see also Meir, Golda
Israeli Air Force (IAF), 268, 278–79
Israeli Defense Force (IDF), 262–63, 267, 269, 270, 272, 276, 284, 287–89

Jacobins, 222–24
Jagger, Mick, 292*n*
James I (king of England), 165*n*
James IV (king of Scotland), 138*n*
James VI (king of Scotland), 142, 144, 145, 148, 149, 165*n*
Jewish Agency, 258, 259
Joan of Arc, 254–55
João IV (king of Portugal), 184, 189
John Paul II (pope), 316
Johnson, Lyndon, 236
Jordan, 263, 269
Joseph II (Holy Roman emperor), 208–9, 217–18
Josephus, 36
Julian calendar, 152*n*
Justin, 10

Kalandula (Imbangala chief), 188

Kambu (sister of queen Njinga), 180, 186, 187, 189, 190
Kasa (Imbangala warlord), 174, 179
Kasanje (Imbangala chief), 180–81
Kashmir, 234, 247, 251–53
Kazan, Russia, 212, 213
Keating, Kenneth, 274
Khalsa, Bimal Kaur, 254*n*
Kindonga Islands, 176–77, 179, 181
Kipling, Rudyard, 1, 65, 129, 227
Kirkpatrick, Jeane, 308
Kissinger, Henry
    and Indira Gandhi, 242, 244–45, 247
    and Golda Meir, 265, 267, 274, 280–82, 285–88
Knesset, 285, 289
Kosciuszko, Thaddeus, 224
Kreisky, Bruno, 269*n*
Kronstadt, 198, 199
Kutaisi, 76

Labour Party, 293–94, 300
Lakshmibai, Rani, 229
Las Malvinas. *see* Falklands War
Leach, Sir Henry, 303
Leicester, Earl of, 151, 154–58
Leonardo da Vinci, 97, 105
Lewis, C. S., 292
Locke, John, 202
Lok Sabha, 237, 244, 249–51
Londinium, 55–58
Louis XII (king of France), 117, 124
Louis XIV (king of France), 320
Louis XV (king of France), 196
Louis XVI (king of France), 222
Luanda, 171–73, 183–84, 187
Ludovico Sforza (duke of Milan), 113–14, 117
Lygdamis (king of Halicarnassus), 12

Mabovich, Moshe, 256–57
Mabovich, Sheyna, 257
Machiavelli, Niccolò, 97, 109, 117, 124
Macmillan, Harold, 306
Malvinas. *see* Falklands War
Manduhai (queen of the Mongols), 83–95
Manduul Kahn, 85, 86
Manekshaw, Sam, 237, 239–46, 248, 249, 255
Mao Zedong, 240

Marathon, Battle of, 13

Mardonius, 15–16, 21

Maria Theresa (archduchess of Austria), 131, 195, 200, 203, 209

Marie Antoinette (queen of France), 222

Mary I (queen of England and Ireland) ("Bloody Mary"), 133, 135–39

Mary Stuart (queen of Scots), 137, 139, 142, 146–49

Massagetae, 5–11

Matamba, 169*m,* 170–71

Mawiyya (queen of Syria), 3

Mbande (king of Ndongo), 170–73

Mbundu people, 168–70, 175–76, 182–84, 187

Media, 39

Medici, Catherine de, 140

Medici, Cosimo de, 128

Medici, Giovanni di' (father), 116, 125

Medici, Giovanni di' (son), 116, 128

Medici, Lorenzo de, 100

Medicis, 99–100, 117, 126, 127

Medina Sidonia, duke of, 152–55

Meghdoot, Operation, 252

Meir, Golda, ix, 256–90

    appointment as Prime Minister, 264–65

    Arab–Israeli peace process, 267

    Camp David Accords, 290

    childhood, 256–57

    and Dayan's offer to resign, 276–77

    death of, 290

    elections of 1973, 268

    end of time as prime minister, 289–90

    at Golan Heights, 282–83

    and Israeli independence, 257–59

    leadership style, 265–66

    and military aid during Yom Kippur War, 282

    political style of, 263–64

    and prelude to Yom Kippur War, 269–70, 272–73

    and start of Yom Kippur War, 273–76

    Suez Crisis, 261–62

    War of Independence (1948), 259–61

    Yom Kippur War, 278, 284

    Yom Kippur War cease-fire, 285–89

    Yom Kippur War Egyptian operations, 285, 287–88

    Yom Kippur War strategy, 280

Mendoza, Don Bernardino, 147

Menendez, Mario, 318

Merhavia, 257

Meyerson, Morris, 257

Michelangelo, 97

Middle Ages, 67

Mikel IV (Orthodox patriarch), 72, 73

Milan, 97, 114

Ming dynasty, 87–88, 90, 92–94

Ministry of Defence (Britain), 301

Mithridates of Pergamon, 30–31

Mitla Pass, 284

Mitterrand, François, 294

Mona, Island of, 55

Mongol Empire, 83–95

Mossad, 265, 267, 273

Mountbatten, Lord Louis, 297

Mujib (Sheikh Mujibur Rahman), 237–39

Munich Olympics terror attack (1972), 265, 269*n*

Muslims and Islam, 77–78, 80, 81, 234, 238

Mustafa III (Ottoman emperor), 203, 204, 208–10

al-Nasir (caliph of Baghdad), 78

Nasser, Gamal, 261, 262, 266, 267

Ndongo Kingdom, 167–91, 169*m*

Nehru, Jawaharlal, 232, 234

Nero (Roman emperor), 52, 55, 63

Niazi, Amir Abdullah Khan, 249

Nickel Grass, Operation, 282

Nile River, 31

Ninth Legion, 50, 53, 56, 63

Nixon, Richard M.

    and Indira Gandhi, 240, 242, 244–45, 247, 251

    and Golda Meir, 267, 268, 274, 280–82

Njinga (queen of Ndongo–Matamba), ix, 167–91

Northern Ireland, 295, 297–98

Nott, 296

Nott, John, 296, 303, 310, 311, 319

nuclear weapons, 251, 277

Ochakov, 218, 219

Octavia, 39, 40

Octavian (Augustus), 34, 36, 38–49

Oirats, 84–87, 91, 92, 95–96
Olivier, Sir Laurence, 295
Ordelaffi family, 101, 105
Orlov, Alexi, 197, 199
Orlov, Grigory, 196, 197, 207
Orsi, Andrea, 109–12
Orsi, Checco, 105–9
Orsi, Ludovico, 105–9
Orthodox Church, 72, 75
Osmani, M. A. G., 246
Ostorius Scapula, Publius, 51–52
Ottoman Empire, 203–10

Pakistan, 234–52. see also Bangladesh
Pakistani Air Force, 246
Pakistani Army, 252
Palestine, 257
Palestine Liberation Organization (PLO), 269
Panin, Nikita, 196, 212
Panin, Peter, 198, 212, 213
Parliament, 293, 302
Parma, Duke of, 147, 149–52, 154, 155, 157, 158
Parthia, 38, 39
Patras, 41
Patton, George, 321
Paul (son of Catherine the Great), 194, 196, 225
Paulinus, Gaius Suetonius, 52
Peloponnese, 16
Pelusium, 28, 31, 47
Peres, Shimon, 260–61
Pérez de Guzmán, Alonso (duke of Medina Sidonia), 152
Persian Empire, 5–11, 7m
Peter III (emperor of Russia), 193–200
Pharsalus, Battle of, 27
Philip II (king of Spain), 135, 140, 143–47, 149, 157, 159, 160
Pius V (pope), 143
Plutarch, 23, 29
Poland, 202–5, 209, 222, 223, 298
Polyaenus, 12
Pompey the Great, 24–29
Poniatowski, Stanislaus, 194, 203
Pontus, 32
Port Stanley, Falkland Islands, 304–5, 317, 318
Portugal, 144, 167–68, 171–91

Poseidon, 13, 15
Postumus, Poenius, 59
Potemkin, Grigory, 198, 207, 213–21
Powell, Enoch, 302
Praga, Battle of, 224
Prasutagus (king of the Iceni), 51–53
Preobrazhensky Guards, 197, 198
Protestants/Protestantism, 136–43, 145, 146
Provisional Irish Republican Army, 297
Prussia, Kingdom of, 195, 203
Ptolemies, 23
Ptolemy Philadelphus (Egyptian pharaoh), 41
Ptolemy XII (Egyptian pharaoh), 23–31
Ptolemy XIV (Egyptian pharaoh), 34
Pugachev, Yemelyan, 210–14
Pym, Francis, 309–10

Qipchaks, 72
Quadra, Álvaro de la, 140

Rabin, Yitzak, 290
Rahman, Sheikh Mujibur. see Mujib
Raleigh, Sir Walter, 151, 159
Ravaldino, Battle of, 119–24
Razia al-Din (sultan of Delhi), 67
Reagan, Nancy, 298
Reagan, Ronald, and administration, 298, 304, 308–10, 316–17
Republican War, 34–36
Riario, Cesare, 115
Riario, Girolamo, 97, 98, 100–102, 104–7
Riario, Ottaviano, 100, 106, 109, 112, 113, 115–17, 126
Roman Republic, 23, 51–53
Rome/Roman Empire, 24m, 67
    Cleopatra and, 23–49
    Iceni and, 51, 54–60
Roosevelt, Franklin Delano, 310n
Rosario, Operation, 304. see also Falklands War (1982)
Rum, Sultan of, 69–70
Rumyantsev, Peter, 207, 210
Rushdie, Salman, 237
Russian Empire, 201m
Russian Orthodox Church, 193
Russo–Swedish War, 219–21
Russo-Turkish War (1768-1774), 204–10, 206m

Russo-Turkish War (1787-1792), 218–22

Rustaveli, Shota, 69, 71

Rusudan (princess of Georgia), 76

Rusudan (Tamar's aunt), 72, 73, 76

Sadat, Anwar al-, 266–67, 270, 276, 284, 286, 290

Salamis, Battle of, 17–22, 18*m*

Sands, Bobby, 297

Santo Domingo, 146

Schlessinger, James, 282

Schmidt, Helmut, 316

Scotland, Elizabeth's expulsion of French from, 137–39

Searchlight, Operation, 238–39

Selim III (Ottoman sultan), 221

Seljuks, 77, 80–82

Semenovsky Guards, 197

Seymour, Jane (queen consort of England), 135

Sforza, Caterina. *see* Caterina Sforza (countess of Forlì)

Sforza, Ludovico, 113–14

Sforza family, 126

Shamkor, Battle of, 77–79

Sharon, Ariel, 284

Shastri, Lal Bahadur, 234, 235

Sicinnus, 18

Sikh separatists, 252–53

Sinai Peninsula, 267, 278, 280, 284, 289

Singh, Beant, 254

Singh, Karan, 249

Singh, Satwant, 254

Singh, Zail, 253

Six-Day War (1967), 262

Sixtus IV (pope), 97–102

Skyhawk fighter aircraft, 268, 288, 314, 316

slave trade
    Netherlands and, 184–86
    Portugal and, 167–69, 171–76, 178, 183

Solidarity movement (Poland), 298

Sotomaior, Francisco de, 184–85

South Georgia Island, 301, 302, 311

Soviet Union
    and Bangladesh, 240, 247, 250
    and Kashmir, 234
    and Suez Crisis, 261
    and Yom Kippur War, 281, 285, 286
    . *see also* Cold War

Spanish Armada, 152–54, 157

Spargapises (Massagetaean prince), 9, 10

Stanisław II (king of Poland), 203–4, 217, 223

Suetonius, 52, 55–63

Suez Canal, 262, 270, 276, 284, 285

Suez Crisis, 261–62

Suleimanshah, Rukn ad-Din, II (sultan of Rum), 79, 80

Suvorov, Alexander, 210, 218, 219, 224

Sweden, 219–21

Syria, 263, 267, 270, 274, 275, 278–80

Tacitus, 59, 61–63

Tal, Israel, 279

Tamar (queen of Georgia), ix, 69–82

Tarsus, 37

Tembo a Ndumbo (Imbangala queen), 181, 182

Tevdore, 73

Thant, U, 262

Thatcher, Denis, 293, 294, 301, 315, 318

Thatcher, Margaret, 291–319
    and Argentine surrender in Falklands War, 318
    budget cuts, 296–97
    childhood, 292
    and decision to retake Falklands, 303–4
    early years in politics, 292
    election as prime minister, 296
    and Falklands victory, 318–19
    and Falklands War casualties, 315–16
    focus on Falklands victory, 316
    and military spending, 296–97
    and Northern Ireland, 297–98
    preparation for Falklands War, 304–8
    on recapture of South Georgia Island, 311
    and sinking of *General Belgrano,* 311–12
    softening of image to gain public support, 295–96
    and South Georgia, 301
    US relations, 298
    and war cabinet, 306–8

Themistocles, 17

Thermopylae, 15

Thompson, Julian, 316

Tobčhi, Altan, 83

Tomyris (queen of the Massagetae), 5–10

Trebizond, 79, 81
Trident nuclear missiles, 298
Trinovantes, 52, 54, 63
"Tsar Peter." *see* Pugachev, Yemelyan
Tudor, Edward, 135
Tyrone, Earl of (Hugh O'Neill), 163–65

Ukraine, 256–57
Une-Bolod, 86, 87, 89, 90
United Nations, 262, 267
United Nations Security Council, 247, 285, 286
United States
    and Bangladesh, 242, 247, 250–51
    and Falklands War, 308–10
    Gandhi–Nixon meeting prior to
        Bangladesh war, 244–45
    Indira Gandhi's first official trip to, 236
    Golda Meir's childhood in, 257
    Golda Meir's tours soliciting funds for
        Israel, 259, 263
    military aid to Israel, 282, 287–88
    Margaret Thatcher and, 298, 300
    and Yom Kippur War, 279–81, 285–88

Vatican, 99–100
Verulamium, 58
Victoria (queen of England), 229
Vietnam War, 236, 240

Walsingham, Sir Francis, 148, 153
Walters, Vernon, 306

Wang Yue, 93
War of Independence (Israel, 1948), 259–61
Wars of the Roses, 135
Watergate, 280–81
Weinberger, Caspar, 308
Wellington, Duke of, 309
West Africa, 167–91
West Falkland Island, 304
West Pakistan, 231, 234, 237, 250
Whitelaw, Willie, 318
Wilhelm II (king of Prussia), 221
Woodward, 315
Woodward, John "Sandy," 305, 311–13, 315
World War II, 309

Xerxes (king of Persia), 12–18, 20–22

Yaa Asantewaa (Ashanti queen), 229
Yahya Khan, Agha Muhammad, 238, 242, 244, 246
Yishuv, 257–59
Yom Kippur War (1973), 268–79, 271*m*, 285–88
Yuri Bogoliubski (Kievan warlord), 72–77

Zamir, Zvi, 270, 273
Zavkhan, 89–91
Zeira, Eli, 270, 272
Zenobia (queen of Syria), 3
Zionism, 257
Zuniga, Don Juan de, 146

ABOUT THE AUTHORS

Keith W. Dunn

JONATHAN W. JORDAN is the author of *New York Times* bestseller *Brothers Rivals Victors*, *American Warlords*, and the award-winning *Lone Star Navy*. He has written and lectured extensively on military history and wartime leadership.

Katherine D. Jordan

EMILY ANNE JORDAN is the creative force behind *The War Queens*. A researcher, freelance writer, and student at the University of Kentucky, this is her first book.